CONTEMPORARY SOCIETY - A GANDHIAN APPRAISAL

CONTEMPORARY SOCIETY
A Gandhian Appraisal

PROF. J.S. MATHUR

GYAN

Contemporary Society - A Gandhian Appraisal

Rs. 790

ISBN: 978-81-212-1030-0

Published in 2010 in India by
Gyan Publishing House
23, Main Ansari Road, Darya Ganj,
New Delhi-110002
Phones : 23282060, 23261060
Fax : 011-23285914
E-mail: books@gyanbooks.com
Website: www.gyanbooks.com

Lasser Type Setting by: Rudra Computer Graphics, Delhi
Printed at : GIAN RIDHI OFFSET PRINTERS

Dedication

To
My father, Late Shri Basant Bihari Lal Mathur
and
My Son, Late Shri Atul Kumar Mathur
and
All friends following in the foot - steps of Gandhiji

Contents

Preface

I inherited my interest in Gandhiji's thought from my father late Shri Basant Bihari Lal. He was a member of Mainpuri revolutionary group. He came under the influence of Gandhiji, worked as his loud speaker in the district of Mainpuri. He took a bow to use only his self-spun clothes and served the society as a leader and amateur homoeopath. Under his advice, I studied Gandhiji's thought, took to *Charkha* and resolved to wear *Khadi* only.

I presented my first paper in 1949, which was keenly debated and appreciated. Since then I have tried to interpret Gandhiji's thought in my own humble way and presented papers at National and International forums. I felt elated when Economist (UK.) commented on my first collection of Essays : "These essays will help to remove mystique about Gandhi, who is mystifying". My essay was published in World Encyclopaedia of Peace Pregamm Press and I received Peace Messenger Certificate from UN. for Institute of Gandhian Studies, University of Allahabad.

I am of the firm view that an objective understanding of Gandhiji's thought and techniques of social changes particularly amongst the youth, highest academic and administrative levels is required.

We are continuing paying a heavy price for neglecting Gandhiji's advice. It is not enough to observe 2nd October Gandhiji's birthday as Non - violence Day. We must have courage to implement his advice simply paying lip sympathy. I will feel amply rewarded if these essays arouse interest of every section of society, interested in a peaceful world order.

I had the privilege of receiving blessings from my D.Litt guide Late Prof. JK. Mehta, Acharaya JB. Kripalani who write Foreword for my book "*Economic Thought of Mahatma Gandhi*" and Shri Pyarelal Nayyar, Gandhiji's secretary and Late. Prof. J. Timbergen, Nobel Laureate Economist, who wrote Foreword for the second edition of "*Economic Thought of*

Mahatma Gandhi." I am thankful to Dr. Shiv Har Singh for his assistance towards the publication of "*Contemporary Society - A Gandhian Appraisal*".

I thank my publishers Gyan Publishing House for Publishing this book in record time. I dedicate this book to my father Late Shri Basant Bihari Lal, who initiated me to Gandhiji's Thought and to my Late son Atul Kumar, my right hand in my academic pursuits.

Matri - Anchal
3, Bank Road
Allahabad - 211002

1

Towards A Sane Society*

I do not consider myself suitable to deliver lecture in the memory of an eminent researcher and doctor Prof. Rajendra Prakash. Some outstanding personality from the field of medicine and health would have done justice. As I rise to deliver this lecture I remember saint poet Tulsidas who wrote, कवित विवेक एक नहीं मोरे, सत्य कहूँ लिखि कागज कोरे ।

As said earlier I cannot delve in the field of medicine and allied fields. But permit me to share my thoughts as a layman with this august audience.

May I, in all humility and with apologies, raise the question of exploitative nature of the present system of health care? I have a hunch that there is a league with evil design amongst pharmacists, medical men, and bureaucrats to make treatment costlier and costlier and thus not only deprive the poor of these benefits but also drain old retired people of their hard earned savings with adverse effects on the families. Several years back I read a report that dentists in U.S.A. were financing chocolate industries in their efforts to encourage, particularly children, to consume as much of these goods as possible.

In this connection I will like to draw your attention to the neglect of cheaper and indigenous system of medicine – *Ayurveda*, *Yunani*, Homeopathy, Nature cure and the like. I happened to read a book 'Home and Village Doctor'

---

* Lecture to be delivered in honour of late Prof. Rajendra Prakash, Prof. of Pathology, Maulana Azad Medical College, Delhi.

written by Dr. Satish Chandra Das Gupta under the advice and patronage of Mahatma Gandhi. The book had very-very cheap prescriptions for most of the ailments that people ordinarily suffer from. It is only when medicinal properties of *Tulsi*, *Neem*, *Haldi* etc. were discovered that some attention is being paid to these and similar remedies.

I have, because of my poor understanding, divided diseases into two broad categories – (1) disease of poverty and (2) disease of affluence. I need not elaborate what diseases of poverty are. These are well known. I read in a book "Geography of Hunger" that even birth rates will decline if nutritional levels are maintained and protein deficiency removed. Quite a number of diseases, even mental health cases and environmental problems, can be solved if poverty amongst the masses is removed.

However, I must now refer to what I have described as 'disease of affluence'. I learn that WHO has declared the year 2001 as the "Year of Mental Health". Mental health and allied problems of health are by and large diseases of affluence. We will discuss at some length the causes and remedies later on. International bodies and organizations like U.N., I.L.O., UNESCO, FAO, WHO pass pious resolutions – what else can they do. This is the easiest thing to do. They have neither the wish/will nor desire to see that these resolutions are implemented. This is because of the fact that they and each one of us are a part of a structure that is creating these problems and have no strength even to suggest a radical change in the structure. I am reminded of the saying "The road to hell is paved with good intentions". Yet there is another saying "If wishes were horses beggars will be riding".

Mental Health has wider connotation and need not be identified with lunacy, schizophrenia etc., depression, aggression, rape, murder, violence, frustration involving jealousy and resultant resort to smoking and drinking, all are mental health problems.

I have no love for statistics. I learnt as a student that there are three types of lies ; "Lies", "White lies" and "Statistics" and this is what I remember till today. Moreover, what is clear to objective observations and intuitive understanding needs no statistical support. That WHO has decided to observe 2001 year of mental health is conclusive proof that this problem has assumed serious proportions. Every country in the developed and under developed society in is facing these problems of mental health as is evident from rising crime rates as also cases of depression, frustration and suicides.

The latest reports of WHO, World Bank and Harvard University show a steep rise in heart diseases and depression says psychiatrist Dr. Harish

Shetty. Dr. Hemant Kumar Cardiologist in Lilavati Hospital, Mumbai observes "By the year 2010 forty per cent of the population will be victim of Coronary Artery Diseases....... Every third patient coming to me has high blood pressure and high blood sugar levels which is frightening scene" (Times of India, 18.6.2001). Rising incidents of violence, depression, and frustration amongst children indicates the seriousness of mental health problems.

Reports are now available that non-white race people were used for experimentation to test the tolerance limit of atomic radiation. Recent reports from Australia reveal that cremated bones of Australian people's dead bodies of a few weeks, five to nineteen years old and adults upto 39 years were shipped to U.S.A., UK from 1950 to 1970 to test for radioactive fall out from nuclear tests. Australia raised allegations that its troops were used as guinea pigs during British atom bomb tests. British media reported that bodies of still born children from Australia, Britain, Canada and Hong Kong were used in U.S. Nuclear experiments.

This reveals that problem of mental sickness is the attribute of the so-called rational, the intellectual and progressive elements of society which claim to be modern and progressive. Gandhiji described such a society as satanic.

An Analysis

Let us now pause a bit and try to find out the causes of such a sorry state of affairs. The cause is our socio-economic-political and cultural system that has given rise to mental health problems. In this age people are being exploited in the name of science and technology. Modern industrial societies are characterized by: (1) vastness i.e. giant sized units in comparison with which earlier units appear to be pygmies, (2) mechanization and automation; and you are out of date tomorrow, (3) specialization of an extreme degree; specialist is one who knows more and more about less and therefore cannot take a wholistic view. In passing may I refer to a book 'Brighter Than a Thousand Suns' detailing the manufacturing of the atom bomb? The Father of Atom Bomb Dr. Openheimer regretted and wrote in the last chapter that if he could understand the lethal consequences of atomic blast he would not have helped develop this energy, (4) standardization; even emotions are getting standardized, (5) Urbanisation; movement of people from rural to urban areas, (6) Money-commercial and impersonal relationships guided by profit motive, (7) Consumerism fanned by aggressive advertisement, (8) Divorce of labour, ownership and management.

All these factors lead to extreme degree of centralization and concentration of wealth and power. A steady trend towards increased human organizations is clearly noticeable in every institution from companies and corporations to colleges and universities, religious institutions, cities and governments. In practically all areas of human life we notice emergence of new levels of organization designed to coordinate, integrate, build and regulate men's action under the slogan of 'efficiency', security, stability, resource conservation and utilization, e.g., every drop of water should be used judiciously, every ounce of coal utilized properly and every moment of a man's time should be planned properly. These are symptoms of a desert civilization.

Insecurity and Insignificance

Such a situation has led to several contributing factors towards ill mental health. One among these is the feeling of insecurity among people viz., of unemployment, i.e., of losing jobs and incomes. The modern economists hold the view that unemployment should be recognized fact as a of the changing scenario and is the price for progress and modernization. Coupled with unemployment is social, cultural and political insecurity. One must remember that constant change is constant instability.

The other fallout which leads to mental problem is the feeling of insignificance, isolation amongst people, dehumanisation and lack of significant social purpose. The individual feels completely alone and isolated. This leads to mental disintegration, nervous disorders, psychological disbalance, physical ailments like hypertension, family disorders, neglect of children and the like. One scholar made the following observation:

"A child born today in United Kingdom stands ten times greater chance of being admitted to a mental hospital than to University; this can be taken as an indication that we are driving our children mad more effectively than we are genuinely educating them. Perhaps it is our way of educating them that is driving them mad"

(Prof. R.D. Laing, quoted G.F. Capren in 'The Turning Point')

A growing feeling of powerlessness and insignificance overtakes the individual. He gets used to some addiction or the other; smoking, alcohol or some other subtle forms like gambling, working obsessively, watching television constantly, useless travelling etc.

Violence

Yet another problem that causes fear and depression is the creation of psychology of violence in general and amongst children in particular. Violence is to be interpreted in larger context.

This attitude is reflected by the reaction of a child on the death of grandmother. The child remarked how could she die? There are no marks of a knife or a bullet. Children are fast developing a psychology that violence is essential, inevitable and that they should be prepared for more and more sophisticated forms of violence.

Modern games depict varieties of violence and military oriented games; guns, gunboats, pistols, anti-aircraft guns, inculcate violence right from childhood. To cap all of these are video games, which develop incredible hand-eye brain coordination. According to President Reagan these kids will be outstanding pilots should they fly jets.

Late General of the *Army Omur Bradely* said :

"We have grasped the mystery of the atom and rejected the Sermon on the Mount. Ours is a world of nuclear giants and ethical infants. We know more about the war than we do about peace. We know more about killing than we do about living".[2]

The same author quotes Nikita Khrushchev as saying "the living will envy the dead. The life for survivors everywhere ..... will not be worth living."

Helplessness and Hopelessness

Technological and scientific advancement has created a feeling of helplessness and hopelessness even amongst top thinkers. A few quotations will not be out of place:

Winston Churchill remarked:

1. The dark ages may return, the Stone Age may return on the gleaming wings of science".[3]

   Russell observed:

2. "We are perhaps living in the last age of man, and if so, it is science, that he will owe his extinction:[4]

   He continued.

3. "I do not know what horrors may be in store for us, no one can doubt that unless something very radical is done, scientific man is a doomed species. In the world in which we are living there is an active and dominant will towards death, which has so far at every crisis got the better of sanity. If we are to survive, this state of affairs must not continue"[5]

Albert Schweitzer observes in 'Decay and Restoration of Society' that "it is clear now to every one that the suicide of civilization is in progress"[6]

If eminent social scientists suffer from a feeling of despair and despondency one can imagine the lot of the individual and small groups. They are bound to feel crazy and mentally and emotionally sick. I cannot resist the temptation of quoting Gandhiji who said:

"*........If modern civilization stands for all this and I have understood to do so, I call in Satanic ...... I would destroy the system today if I had the power. I would use the most deadly weapons, if I believed that they would destroy it. I refrain only because the use of such weapons would only perpetuate the system though it may destroy its present administration*".[7]

Technology Beyond Human Control

A system obsessed with growth and expansion has relied solely upon excessive technological changes for increasing productivity at any cost, expansion and growth. An environment has been created in which life has become physically and mentally unhealthy. Polluted air, irritating noise, traffic congestion, chemical contamination, radiation hazards, physical and psychological stress have become everyday life. Technology is severely damaging and disrupting the ecological processes that sustain environment and are the very basis of our existence.

In this connection the growing emphasis on nuclear power is alarming. Experts view with concern the problem of disposal of radioactive waste and by-products, which may remain dangerous for millions of years. What moral right we have to leave such a deadly legacy to thousands and thousands of generations.

It is estimated that at least 500,000 (five lakhs) fatal lung cancers per year for at least about 50 years will occur as a result of this waste. Ernest Stevigless Prof. Emeritus of Radiology of University of Rittsburg estimates that 50-million cancer death will take place if Cassini explodes in atmosphere. It is also noted that there are at least 200 million environmental refugees.

It may be worth noting that most of the research in science and technology is for military use and to subjugate the individual. Human beings are being used as guinea pigs. Science and technology are the instruments that deaden the inner being in mankind. We must realize that if we have too many clever machines we will have too many stupid people.

Harris Brown in his book 'The Challenge of Man's Future' warns that: "*Where in the previous times the lives of individual nations and culture was at stake, today at stake is the destiny of mankind.*"[8]

Centralisation and State

An offshoot of technological development has been highly centralized institutions; highest concentration of political and economic power in the hands of a small elite group. In modern technological society the road towards totalitarianism is unidirectional. Modern technology has conferred unprecedented power on the state. Successful revolt against despotism becomes more or less impossible. Gasset said:

"In our days the State has come to be a formidable machine which works in marvelous fashion by reason of the quantity and precision of its means. Once it is set up in the midst of society it is enough to touch a bottom for its enormous levers to start working and exercise their overwhelming power on any part on whatever of the social framework …… spontaneous social action will be fructified. Society will have to live for the State, man for Governmental machinery".[9]

Exploitative System

We have a structure and system that results in a violent and exploitative socio-economic system. Exploitation has wider connotation; exploitation by rich industrialized countries of the South, by metropolitan towns of smaller towns, by urban areas of rural areas, by present generation of future generations as reflected by pollution etc. and exhaustion of resources.

Severe competitive spirit for acquisition of material goods and the desire for material wealth can hardly be satisfied; and ever increasing inequalities create frustration, depression and despondency. Lack of satisfying jobs and unemployment are demoralizing. Unemployment insurance is public charity and is demoralizing and dehumanizing. With ever changing technology feeling of obsolescence and insecurity rises. All this leads to tremendous strain and causes tensions for individuals, small groups leading to conflict, nervous breakdowns, emotional and psychological imbalances and mental disorders. The ever-increasing number of psychiatrists is proof enough of this sorry state of affairs.

Towards a Sane Society

If we desire to have a sane society; peace for the individuals and within social groups all that goes in industrial society should be radically changed. Mahatma Gandhi was one such person who suggested an alternate system.

In the words of Lord Altrincham:

"Gandhi, like Christ lit beacons on distant hills towards which posterity must grope its way in darkness".

Yet another tribute by Martin Luther King:

"Gandhi was the only morally and practically sound method open to oppressed people in their struggle for freedom".

World View

Gandhiji had a world view and he was working towards a new peaceful, non-exploitative international world order. A few quotations from his writings will not be out of place.

> "Through the deliverance of India I seek to deliver the so-called weaker races of the earth from the crushing heels of Western exploitation".[10]
>
> "Let us hope that India will rise to the occasion not only for its own sake, but for the sake of the world .... It is my faith and hope that independent India will set up an object lesson to the world in the way of people, non-violence and brotherhood".[11]
>
> "The freedom of my dreams means the kingdom of God within us and its establishment through us on earth"[12]

Iyer has given the following quotations:

> "I am fully aware that my mission cannot be fulfilled in India alone" (p. 56).
>
> "If I can say without arrogance and with due humility my message and methods are indeed essential for the whole world". (p. 53)
>
> "I do not want to think in terms of whole world. My patriotism includes the good of mankind in general. Therefore my service of India includes the service of humanity". (p. 52).

These quotations will prove that Gandhi was experimenting for a new international order. It was an accident of history that he was born in India. He titled his auto-biography as 'The Story of My Experiments with Truth'. Let us hope that these experiments will continue so that a sane society emerges.

A lot has been written about Gandhiji's fight against colonialism and racism. In my view these were only marginal issues. As mentioned earlier, his mission was a radical complete overhauling of the existing socio-economic structure.

Gandhiji's Revolutions

Gandhiji in his lifetime sowed seeds of several revolutions, which will sooner, rather later fructify in full blossoming trees. These revolutions can be stated as follows:

1. Revolution against consumerism and unbridled materialism

2. Revolution against technology beyond human control.
3. Revolution for human motivations.
4. Revolution for decentralization of the socio-economic and cultural system.
5. Revolution to rehabilitate the individual.
6. Revolution for full and gainful employment.
7. Revolution for non-violent and peaceful methods of change
8. Revolution for ecological balance and pollution free society.
9. Revolution against monoculture i.e. preservation of cultural identity of nations and small communities.

It will not be possible for me to discuss all these revolutions initiated by Gandhiji in detail. I will refer to these briefly.

Revolution against Consumerism and Unbridled Materialism

Let me, at the outset point out that Gandhiji was dead against poverty. In his own words:

"To a people famishing and idle the only acceptable form in which God can dare appear is work and promise of food as wages"[13]

He wrote to Gurudev Tagore

"I have found it impossible to soothe suffering patients from a song of Kabir. The hungry millions ask for one poem; invigorating food. They cannot be given it. They must earn it. And they can earn only by the sweat of their brow".[14]

While he was vehemently opposed to poverty he was equally opposed to affluence. Affluence, which is relative term, is possible only for the few. Affluence breeds competition, inequalities, violence and decapitated individuals and small groups for social service and non-violent action. Gandhi observed:

Civilization in the real sense of the term consists not in the multiplication but in the deliberate and voluntary reduction of wants: This alone promotes real happiness and contentment and increases the capacity to service."[15]

Gandhiji's ideas are now being echoed by thinkers, and scholars from the affluent West. Maurice Strong remarks:

"....economic growth in countries like physical growth in people is natural and healthy upto a certain point. After that it can become cancerous or as self-indulgent as an expanding waistband. From that stage we should regard real growth as intellectual, moral and social".[16]

Gunnar Myrdal, the Nobel Laureate disapproves expansive conspicuous public consumption such as moon flights and too heavy military expenditure and quotes Mangholt when he says that "if our purpose is to reach a non-polluting system of production and creation of recycled economy, one must foresee considerable reduction in the consumption of material goods per inhabitant to be compensated by the extension of less tangible goods".[17]

Yet another thinker remarks:

"Materialism should not be the common philosophy but the common enemy".[18]

Revolution Against Technology Beyond Human Control

At the outset it need be clarified that Gandhiji has quite been misunderstood and dubbed as anti-science anti-machine. Gandhi observed:

"To say that is to caricature my views. I am not against machinery as such, but I am totally opposed to it when it masters us".[19]

On another occasion to a question:

"Are you against all machinery", his answer was ... emphatically No. But I am against its indiscriminate multiplication .... But simple tools and instruments and such machinery as saves individual labour and lightens the burden of the millions of cottages I should welcome."[20]

Let us distinguish between tools and implements and large-scale machine, between technology that increases productivity of individuals and small groups and technology that leads to concentration of power, between technology that is dependent upon renewable sources of energy and one that leads to exhaustion of non-renewable sources of energy. The one leads to peace, cooperation, fellow feeling and universal brotherhood and the other leads to violence, concentration of power in the hands of few persons, indispensed irresponsibility and utter hopelessness and helplessness, aggression and exploitation. Committed to the ways of Truth and Non-violence Gandhiji desired to give new direction to technological development.

Gandhiji would welcome every improvement in the cottage machinery and even a few large ones as an exception working under ideal conditions. These exceptions will end:

"Just where they cease to help the individual and encroach upon his individuality. The machine should not be allowed to cripple the limbs of man".[21]

Willemsen made the following observations:

"The control of technology means a severe limitation demanding almost savage asceticism on the part of an age drunk, not merely with

synthetic emotions and pleasures manufactured by entertainment factories but, dreams of power and of the conquest of the outer space".[22]

Revolution for New Concept of Growth and Human Motivations:

There is nothing sacrosanct about the present economic system with its exclusive emphasis on 'standard of living' which is measured in terms of annual consumption of material goods which should keep on increasing along with a system of production that supports this constant increase in materialist consumption. Under different dispension this may turn to be false. Thus for example, if we come under the influence of Naga sadhus we will be the first to throw away our clothes. Economics is a derived virtue and depends upon our approach to individuals and society.

Gandhiji, therefore, advocated a different concept of growth. To quote him:

"..... whereas religion to be worth anything must also be capable of being reduced to terms of economics, economics to be worth anything must be capable of being reduced to terms of religion or spirituality...... "[23]

On another occasion he observed-

"I must confess I do not draw sharp or any distinction between economics and ethics. Economics that hurts the moral well-being of an individual or a nation are immoral and therefore sinful".[24]

In planning for economic development undue emphasis has been placed on the acquisitive instinct of man. Rational use of resources for irrational wants cannot be said to be true economics. Economising of resources from the long-range viewpoint in the interest of humanity will require 'newer set' of motivations.

The Cocoyoc Declaration mentions that our "first concern is to redefine the whole purpose of development. This should not be to develop things but to develop man. Any process of development that does not lead to their basic needs fulfillment or even worse, disrupts it is a travesty of the idea of development".[25]

Late Prof. J. Tinbergen, Nobel Laureate advocated the concept of Gross National Happiness. Maurice Strong observes:

"It will take a moral and spiritual revolution which goes far enough to alter our life styles and penetrate our political and industrial system".[26]

Revolution for Decentralisation

Gandhiji was opposed to system and methods that result in centralisation and concentration of power and authority. He had realized that effective decentralisation in social and political spheres depend upon decentralisation of the economic structure.

Gandhiji's concept of decentralisation is radically different from decentralisation and delegation concept that is being currently advocated. Under the modern concept power remains with the centralised authority. Decentralisation permits, if at all, insignificant freedom to the people. Like in doll show the real power rests with those who command from behind and pull the strings. Without involvement of people in decision-making there shall be no economic, social and political stability. Decentralisation should not be confused with dispersal of industrial units and production of different parts in distant places at the behest of a central authority. Decentralisation as conceived by Gandhiji has the basic philosophy of giving strength to small groups to be able to resist exploitation. In the words of Gandhiji:

"My idea of village (small communities) is that it is complete republic independent of its neighbourers for its own vital wants, and yet interdependent for many other things in which dependence is necessity".[27]

Decentralisation should mean small local macro-economies, self-sufficient in essentials of life, which will provide the base for that kind of development. It will provide for distributive justice and not disturb ecological balance. Local face-to-face communities are truly the nurseries of the people. They can obviously function as the basic units of participating democracy and development. Centralised units are too large for people's participation, initiative and sharing. They only serve the needs, aspirations, conspicuous consumption and luxurious and extravagant life styles of microscopic cross-section of societies. Centralisation attributes bigness to things of niggardly low utility in relation to the needs of entire population. Even the WCED Commission regards: "Community participation and local initiatives are the key to sustainable development".

Rehabilitation of the Individual

The Bible mentions: "What shall it avail a man if he gains the whole world and loses his soul".

Gandhiji explained the above sermon:

"In modern terms it is beneath human dignity to lose one's individuality and become mere cog in the machine. I want every individual to become a full blooded fully developed member of the society".[28]

The individual is the corner-stone of a democratic society. All philosophies and 'issues' that loses right of the individual are fascist and totalitarian.

Democracy should not be simply right to vote periodically but it should extend to all spheres of life – economic in particular. It should become a way of life.

Gandhiji's, as has been elaborated in earlier pages; decentralised system of production, control over technology and campaign against materialism worked for political, social, religious and economic equality and simplicity of life. The objective was to free individual from external authority so that he may lose himself in finding out his true self in the service of humanity.

To quote Gandhiji once again:

".... Through Khadi we are struggling to establish the supremacy of man in the place of supremacy of power driven machinery over him. Through Khadi we are striving for equality of men and women in the place of gross inequality to be witnessed today. We are striving to attain subservience of capital under labour in the place of insolent triumph of capital over labour."[29]

Revolution for full and gainful employment

Unemployment is one of the greatest curses that an individual can face. It is in a way economic capital punishment. Lord Beveridge while preparing his scheme of social security listed unemployment as one of the five major giants, which have to be fought.

Employment is the method of relating oneself to society. It makes one feel significant. An unemployed person loses his social relatedness and simultaneously self-esteem. It is demoralising. Unemployment insurance; system of organised charity; is no remedy for unemployment.

Gandhiji gave high priority to provision of employment for all able bodied persons. Unemployment and idleness of millions must lead to anti-social values and even a bloody strife. This is what we are witnessing these days. He observed:

"I should never be satisfied until all men had plenty of work, say eight hours a day .... Because I know that millions will not employ themselves on work for the sake of it. If they did not need to work for their bread they would lack the incentive".[30]

"Leisure is good and necessary upto a point only. God created man to eat his bread in the sweat of his brow and I dread the prospect of our food stuffs out of a conjurer's hat"[31]

His plea for decentralised system of production through cottage and village industries has been with the objective of providing full 'gainful and satisfying employment'. Work has a social and cultural aspect. Work should provide normal satisfaction of work, pleasure of physical activity, opportunity for personality development through work, self-esteem and self-respect from useful work, well done and social esteem won by recognition from others of the importance of one's work. These satisfactions are not provided by industrial work.

Ecology and Environment

It is only recently that thinkers all over the world are worried about ecology, pollution, exhaustion of resources, green-house effect, ozone layer etc. Gandhiji had foreseen these problems in the beginning of the 20th Century. He observed:

"It is not possible to conceive of Gods inhabiting a land which is made hideous by the smoke and the din of mill chimneys and factories whose roadways are traversed by rushing engines dragging numerous cars crowded with men who know not for the most what they are after.."[32]

Since Gandhi made the above observation conditions have deteriorated speedily.

It can be asserted that in a world devoid of other living creatures, man himself would die. All living things, even the tinniest insects – are inter-related. Civilisation got extinct because of destruction of living environment by man.

Artificial processes and science and technology is incapable of providing for continuity of human life by substituting its methods for those of nature. We must be aware of shallow environmentalists who want to give more power by advocating more efficient control and management of natural environment.

Efforts to solve specific problems like cleaning up of Ganga is like treating symptoms of a disease. Exclusive reliance on technological solutions and development of more and more sophisticated technology will only sow seeds of second and third generation problems, which will be more difficult and more widespread.

The solution lies in what Gandhiji suggested; change in life styles, reversal in sense of values which encourage conspicuous and wasteful expenditure, small-scale, self-sufficient decentralised communities and a technology that assists and helps the individual, to live in harmony with nature. We can destroy nature but cannot create nature.

Revolution Against Mono-Culture

Dominance of westernized industrial civilization has resulted in the subordination of individual's small communities – countries to western culture.

This can be observed in every day life in our dress, games, language and forms of salutations etc. in different countries. Western dress style can be noticed not only in international conferences but in every day lives of people. Traditional national dresses are being abandoned.

Similarly indigenous forms of connoting different relationships e.g. (1) ma, amma, being replaced by mom/mummy, (2) babaji by daddy-papa, chachu-chachi-bua-phuphuji to uncle and aunty. Similarly Jairamji-namaskar are outmoded and have been replaced by good morning, good night and bye.

Extinguishing lamps (Diya) was considered inauspicious in our country. Extinguishing candles and lamps is the hallmark of modernization and progress.

The joint-family system is giving place to nuclear families creating several social problems. While in some western countries experiments are being made in community living, we in India are abandoning joint family.

Every region in our vast country had its own customs and traditions and culture. Folk culture songs, art and music are now to be seen in T.V. programmes or exhibitions.

Even our Gods have been mis-spelled. Thus Ram is Rama, Krishan is Krishna, Shiv is Shiva, Yog as yoga.

Pilgrimage; resulting in national and cultural integration; has been replaced by tourism; faith and reverence giving place to commercial culture damaging our eco-system and environment.

Gandhiji by insisting upon decentralisation of the socio-economic system planned to preserve this diversity. He had emphasized time and again that villages will not be able to maintain their independence under a centralised system.

He did not want a closed society. He was for accepting the good from every source. At the same time he desired to preserve cultural identity of people. He once observed:

"I do not want my house to be walled on all sides and my windows to be stuffed. I want the culture of all lands to be blown about my house as freely as possible. But I refuse to be blown of my feet by any".[33]

Non-violent System

Initiating a radical new thinking as discussed above, Gandhiji worked for a peaceful non-exploitative social system which will permit a fuller and richer life to every one in all spheres of life and would be conducive to peaceful cooperation amongst individuals, small groups and nations and the world community at large. In the words of Gandhiji:

"Man's triumph will consist in substituting the struggle for existence by the struggle for mutual service. The law of the brute will be replaced by the law of man"[34]

Describing his concept of a non-violent system he observed:

"... the society must naturally be based on non-violence ... in this structure composed of innumerable villages there will be ever widening, never ascending circles. Life will not be a pyramid with the apex sustained by the bottom. But it will be an oceanic circle whose center will be the individual always ready to perish for the village, the latter ready to perish for the circle of villages, till at least the whole becomes one life composed of individuals, never aggressive in their arrogance but ever humble, sharing the majesty of the oceanic circle of which they are integral units. Therefore, the outer circle will not wield power to crush the inner circle but will strengthen all within and derive its own strength from it.[35]

The Change Agents

A question that will legitimately arise is how a change is to be brought about. Gandhiji has a two-fold strategy viz., the individual as a change agent and secondly structural change that his technique will bring about. Gore, the atheist follower of Gandhiji said:

"Gandhiji's contribution to modern civilization is the method of releasing man from the feeling of insignificance and of oppression by political and economic institutions and of enabling him to realize the power of the individual through a call to bold and abiding action and through adoption of Satyagraha".

Gandhiji's ashrams were laboratories to train people to play their role in the creation of a new social order. He prescri-bed eleven vows for inmates of his ashrams viz., (1) Non-violence, (2) Truth, (3) Non-stealing, (4) Brahmacharaya, (5) Non-possession, (6) Bread labour, (7) Non-palate, (8) Fearlessness, (9) Equal respect for all religions, (10) Swadeshi and (11) Removal of untouchability.

These vows are interdependent; the observance of one necessitates the observance of the other. Thus the individual will be able to play an effective role in the restructuring of the society. To quote Gandhiji once again:

"....begin with the first convert. If there is one such, you can add zeros to the one and the first zero will count for ten times the previous number. If, however, the beginner is zero, in other words no one makes the beginning, multiplicity of zeros will also produce zero value"[36]

Another scholar observes:

"From the beginning of time people have heard the still small voice of obligation and brotherhood. When they have listened society has worked. When they have refused to listen society has broken up."[37]

Structural Change

This aspect has been discussed in some detail in the earlier pages. What is being emphasized is that Gandhiji did not approve cosmetic social changes. He was essentially a revolutionary and worked for fundamental structural change. He was for empowering the people. His ideal in his own words:

"Our capacity to Swaraj depends upon our capacity for solving without reference to Government all the varied and complex problems that must arise in the affairs of one of the biggest and the most ancient nation like ours."[38]

Methodology of Change

Non-violent Action on Satyagraha. Unadulterated non-violence and the technique of satyagraha was Gandhiji's technique. He observed:

"The existing structure of economic society will not last for twenty four hours if my weapon of Satyagraha can be gripped by the people."[39]

On another occasion he remarked:

"I would advise the adoption of non-violence to the utmost extent possible and that will be India's great contribution to the peace of world and the establishment of a new world order."[40]

Trusteeship

This was the doctrine advocated by Gandhiji. Trusteeship combines the benefits of public ownership of communism and of individualism and ensures economic equality which is life nerve of any progressive and radical system.

Trusteeship is not for maintaining status-quo but for a radical change in the system. This is a method of giving chance to the privileged to voluntarily abdicate power and pelf that they enjoy and share them with the poor. The power behind trusteeship is the principle of Satyagraha. To quote Gandhiji:

"Exploitation of the poor can be extinguished not by affecting the destruction of a few millionaires but by removing the ignorance of the poor and teaching them non-cooperation with their exploiters. This will convert the exploiters also."[41]

Concluding Observations

The day humanity ceases to believe in ideals it will descend to level of beasts. We may feel that all that Gandhiji advocated is utopia. Gandhiji refuted this charge in the following words:

"I may be taunted with the retort that this is all utopian and therefore, not worth a single thought. If Euclid's point, though incapable of being drawn by human agency, has an imperishable value, my picture has its own for mankind to live.... We must have a proper picture of what we want, before we can have something approaching it ...."[42]

But we must not lose hope for the survival of humanity, Gandhiji is the only option for a violence -troubled world. Today the future of humanity is at stake.

Gandhiji wrote in Harijan of January 1937 that 'a thousand Gandhis will arise out of my ashes'. Here lies the hope. Each one of us can make our humble contribution for a new world order. Our age of anxiety is in a great part due to trying to do today's job with yesterday's tools and concepts. A beginning is to be made. Every day begins with a dawn. The longest journey begins with the first step. One Gandhiji giving all his time to peace made news all over the world. Many people giving some time for new world order can make history. The idealist of yester years has become the only realist of today.

Louis Fisher observed:

"If man is to survive, if civilization is to survive and flower in freedom truth and decency what lies beyond twentieth century must belong to Mahatma Gandhi."

As a child I read a poem of Longfellow:

"Our doubts are traitors
And make us loose the good
Which we oft might attain
By fearing to attempt"

An Australian poet expressed these sentiments in the following words:

"One brick in the wall
you may be
One voice in the crowd
But without you
we are weaker
And our song may
not be heard

One drop in the ocean
And each drop
will swell the tide
So be you one brick
in the wall
Be one voice
in the crowd"

Let the spirit of Gandhiji guide us to do our duty towards humanity. Let us with the poetess late Sarojini Naidu invoke his spirit:

"May the soul of my master, my leader, my father rest not in peace. Donot rest Keep us to our pledge. Give us the strength to fulfill our promise, your heirs, your descendants, your students, guardians of your dreams".

References

1. Prof. R.D. Laing: quoted in F. Capra in 'The Turning Point' p. 420.
2. Caldicoth Helen: Missile Envy, p. 126
3. Winston Churchil: quoted in Tribute, p. 16.
4. B. Russel: Impact of Science in Society, p. 27.
5. B. Russel: Has Man a Future, pp. 36-37.
6. Decay and Restoration of Civilisation, p. 16.
7. Mahatma Gandhi: Economic Thought of Mahatma Gandhi (ETMG) p. 81.
8. The Challenge of Man's Future, p. 266.
9. Ortege Y. Gassett: Revolt of the Masses, pp. 87-88.
10. M.G., ETMG.
11. Pyarelal: Last Phase Vol. II.
12. Pyarelal: ETMG.
13. *Ibid*, p. 529.
14. *Ibid*, p. 531.
15. *Ibid*, p. 471.
16. Maurice Strong: quoted by Geoffrey Lean in Rich World: Poor World, p. 321.
17. Gunnar Myrdal: Against the Stream – Critical Essays on Economics, p. 226.
18. Rich World: Poor World, p. 319.
19. M.G. ETMG, p. 501.
20. *Ibid*, p. 647.
21. *Ibid*, p. 476.
22. Willemsen: Failure of Technology, p. VI.
23. M.G. ETMG, p. 86.

24. *Ibid*, p. 529.
25. Rich World: Poor World, p. 321.
26. *Ibid*, p. 320.
27. M.G. ETMG, p. 323.
28. *Ibid*, p. 570.
29. *Ibid*, p. 267-68.
30. *Ibid*, p. 500.
31. *Ibid*, p. 502.
32. *Ibid*, p. 523.
33. *Ibid*.
34. *Ibid*, p. 510.
35. *Ibid*, p. 623.
36. *Ibid*, p. 632.
37. Barbare Ward TOI – 10.8.90.
38. M.G. ETMG, p. 277.
39. UNESCO Symposium – Truth and Non-Violence, p. 173.
40. M.G. Harijan 21.6.1942.
41. M.G. ETMG, p. 605.
42. *Ibid*, p. 623.
43. Rajendra Prasad: Legacy of Gandhi, p. 99.

2

Industrial Relations: Gandhian Approach

Industrial relations environment in the country has deteriorated considerably during the post-independence period. Number of industrial disputes in 1974 were roughly three times more than what they were in 1951. Number of workers involved had in the meantime gone up by more than four times, while there was more than ten-fold increase in the number of man days loss. The worsening of the industrial relations atmosphere is also indicated by the fact that percentage of disputes that lasted more than twenty days in the meantime have gone up from about 10.7 per cent in 1951 to about 29.6 per cent in 1974. Increasing recourse to violence, coercion, intimidation, hunger strike, gherao and similar other methods indicates progressive deterioration and strain in the relationship of workers and the employers. This wave of discontentment is not confined to private sector or industrial workers but has spread far and wide and now extends not only to employees in the public sector but to all sections of society. Even those groups of society where recourse to direct action was unimaginable have taken to this method of ventilating their grievances. Thus teachers, doctors, nurses, engineers, government employees and even gazetted officers have joined this list. In a recent conference of surgeons the president advocated the use of 'trade union' methods for protection of legitimate interest of the surgeons. The entire atmosphere appears to be surcharged and this just cannot be explained by the thesis of letting off steam after the lifting of emergency.

While it is not the purpose of this chapter to analyse the causes of the present state of affairs, it needs to be pointed out that diverse causes have resulted in this unhappy situation. The socio-economic environment is one of expectations explosion in the wake of tall claims and false promises. One witnesses complete lack of faith and confidence in leadership. The good is at a heavy discount while the evil is at a premium. Economic situation has worsened considerably with increasing poverty of the masses, more or less static real wage level, rising unemployment, worsening working and service conditions, housing and social security benefits. Inequalities, in the meanwhile, have gone up and the entire system is giving fillip to the luxuries of the few creating some sort of a dual economy. The working of political democracy has only added fuel to this fire of discontentment. Employers' attitudes have not undergone any significant change and existence of black money, which is sometimes estimated as much as Rs. 40,000/- crores is a testimony to the policies that are being pursued. Multiplicity of trade unions and rivalry amongst various trade union centres, small sized trade unions progressively becoming smaller and smaller, domination of trade unions by outside leadership which is quite often interested in using trade union strength for narrow personal and political ends has made confusion worse confounded. State policy has not given any lead in the whole matter. The whole policy has been one of drift and adhocism dominated by an inefficient bureaucracy. The policies that have been pursued thus far have not helped matters or laid down guidelines for action to lay the foundation of a new industrial relation order.

It is in this background that we have to analyse Gandhiji's approach to industrial relations. We must realize that "peace in industry is not merely a negative concept, the reconcilement of hostile forces, so as to avoid destructive action, but a positive policy of cooperation promoting mutual gain and evoking mutual goodwill, that is both cause and effect of fruitful cooperation".[1] "In every day life good human relations imply mutual respect, mutual respect born of a tradition of fair play on either side, and a mutual capacity for understanding, which means that both parties make an effort to reduce friction surrounding issues........"[2]

In the ultimate analysis "the problem of industrial dis-content is inherent in and arises from the structure of society, from its social organizations and political forms: from its religious and ethical norms and the attitude to property and work which these inculcate and which are given expression in its laws. In fact, it is time to say that in the last analysis the problem of industrial discontent is rooted in fundamentals of our way of living which are so much a part of ourselves that we seldom stop to question them. Consequently we may fail to realize that these fundamentals are neither universal nor immutable, and that in other times and places and in other forms of society they may be quite different".[3]

Gandhiji's approach to a solution of the problem of removal of discontent and its replacement by happy human relations in all walks of life, including those in the production processes, is a comprehensive and integrated one. We propose to analyse this approach as under:

1. Attitudinal change.
2. Institutional change.
3. Role of the State.
4. Right to strike and organise.

Attitudinal Changes

For happy relations amongst individuals and groups Gandhiji advocated a radical change in the attitudes that are prevalent today. He remarked as early as December 8, 1921 ".... The so called laws laid down in books on economics are not immutable ... nor are they universal".[4] He was making efforts through his activities "to substitute false and non-human economics by true and human. Not killing competition, but life giving cooperation is the law of the human being".[5]

He, therefore, advised a revolutionary change in our way of life, thinking and motivations. He prescribed eleven vows for his Ashram inmates, his training ground for future leadership. These vows are (1) *Ahimsa* (Non-Violence), (2) *Satya* (Truth), (3) *Brahamcharya* (Abstinence), (4) *Asavad* (Non-taste), (5) *Asteya* (Non-stealing), (6) *Aparigraha* (Non-possession), (7) *Abhaya* (Fearlessness), (8) Removal of Untouchability, (9) Physical (Bread) Labour, (10) Equal respect for all religions, and (11) *Swadeshi.*

If the leadership accepts these vows, even haltingly and imperfectly, we will bring about far-reaching and fundamental changes in our attitudes towards fellow workers. He was emphatic that the initiative in this respect has to be taken by those who are entrenched in positions of power and authority. "It is the so-called superior that has to descend from his heights, if the reform is to be peaceful. Those who for ages have been trained to consider themselves as the lowest in the social scale cannot suddenly have the equipment of the so-called higher classes. They can therefore rise to power only by bloodshed, in other words by destroying society itself".[6]

These vows are inter-dependent and acceptance of one leads automatically to the acceptance of others. Gandhiji questioned the very basis of undiluted materialism. "I do not believe that multiplication of wants and machinery contrived to supply them is taking the world a single step nearer its goal.... I whole-heartedly detest this mad desire to destroy distance and time, to increase animal appetites and to go to the ends of the earth in search for their satisfaction. If modern civilization stands for all this, and I have understood it to do so, I call it Satanic".[7] The desire to amass wealth was considered as 'highway robbery' by him. He considered that society as "highly cultured in which every man and woman knows what he or she wants and what is more, knows that no one should want anything that others cannot have with equal labour".[8] This is how one should interpret the law of non-stealing and non-possession. And it is only when one accepts these principles he can be truthful, non-violent and fearless in the real sense.

We laid particular stress on his doctrine of "Bread Labour", —viz., that every one was bound to labour with his body for bread, and that most of the grinding misery in the world was due to the fact that men failed to discharge their duty in this respect ......"[9] He regarded "all schemes to ameliorate the poverty of the masses by the philanthropy of the rich while they themselves shirked body labour and continued to live in luxury and ease as hypocrisy and a sham and suggested that if only men get off the backs of the poor much of the so-called philanthropy would be rendered unnecessary".[10]

Bread-labour will be an effective method for bridging the gulf between manual and non-manual work and solve the problem of isolation and alienation of the workers from the socio-economic system.

Similarly, he advocated a changed attitude towards work and leisure. In the present set-up since labour is considered as a source of discomfort and pain and not as a source of pleasure every one is hankering after leisure. "Leisure is good and necessary upto a point only. God created man to eat his bread in the sweat of his brow, and I dread the prospect of our being able to produce all that we want, including our food stuffs, out of a conjurer's hat".[11] He explained his position as "Mere mental that is intellectual labour is for the soul and is its own satisfaction. It should never demand payment. In the ideal state doctors, lawyers and the like will solely work for the benefit of the society, not for self. Obedience to the law of bread labour will bring about a silent revolution in the structure of society. Man's triumph will consist in substituting the struggle for existence by the struggle for mutual service. The law of the brute will be replaced by the law of man".[12]

He wanted to restore dignity of labour and even suggested "the qualification for franchise should be neither property nor position but manual work, such for example as suggested for Congress franchise ...... By Swaraj I mean the Government of India by the consent of the people ascertained by the vote of the largest number of adult population .... Who have contributed by manual labour to the service of the State......"[13]

Institutional Changes

While advocating changes in the attitude of people and suggesting social incentives for work Gandhiji tried to introduce far-reaching changes in the institutional set-up as well. He pleaded and made experiments for a decentralised set-up. Centralisation must lead to concentration of power, exploitation, struggle and strife and is inconsistent with non-violent structure of society. Decentralisation of production processes will remove most of the evils, which are associated with the present day industrial society based on machine culture with its emphasis on 'consumption society'. Decentralisation of production of at least vital necessities will simultaneously assist the organization of society on non-violent lines with capacity to resist authority when abused. "When production and consumption both become localized the temptation to speed up production, indefinitely and at any price disappears. All the endless difficulties and problems that our present day economic system presents, too, would come to an end"[14].

A decentralised order would permit larger participation of the workers in production and management decisions and obliterate the distinction of high and low, the manager and the managed to a considerable degree. There shall be no divorce between ownership, control, worker, the manager and the consumer.

Decentralisation does not mean static economy or good-bye to science or technological improvements. Gandhiji dis-approved machines that led to concentration and consequent exploitation. He was in favour of every machine that improved the efficiency and productivity and lightened the burden of the artisan and the cottage worker. "My machinery must be of the most elementary type which I can put in the homes of the millions"[15].

Even under this decentralised system there will be need for some large scale industries. To quote him, "...I am socialist enough to say that such factories should be nationalized, or state-controlled. They ought only to be working under the most attractive and ideal conditions, not for profit, but for the benefit of humanity, love taking the place of greed as motive. It is an alteration in the conditions of labour that I want. This mad rush for wealth must cease, and the labourer must be assured, not only a living wage, but a daily task that is not a mere drudgery".[16]

The Role of the State vs. Trusteeship

Attitudinal changes along with decentralised socio-economic policy will obviate state action and confine it to very narrow field of providing ideal working and service conditions in those factories which have to be centralised and state-controlled. As a general rule Gandhiji was opposed to increasing power getting concentrated in the hands of the bureaucracy, which will get stronger and stronger under state dominance. "I look upon an increase of the power of the state with the greatest fear", observed Gandhiji, "because although while apparently doing good by minimizing exploitation, it does the greatest harm to mankind by destroying individuality, which lies at the root of all progress".[17] On another occasion he remarked "The state represents violence, in a concentrated and organised form".[18] He was doubtful, "whether Government institutions can be depended upon to remain loyal to the interest of the people .... If they are not controlled by and not run in the interest of the people".[19]

He, therefore, introduced the concept of trusteeship for property and class relationships. He wanted to abolish 'capitalism' and the 'capitalist' through his non-violent technique. Moneyed men or the capitalist, you will never succeed. What you must do is to demonstrate to the capitalist the power of labour and they will consent to be trustees of those who toil for them.......".[20]

Gandhiji's concept of trusteeship is not a plea for status quo or exploitation but for a new motivation and relationship to be enforced through the power of Satyagraha.

Right to Organise and Strike

Gandhiji held the view "that strikes are an inherent right of the working men for the purpose of securing justice".[21] A similar view was propounded by G.D.H. Cole "Organised labour must at all costs preserve its right for strike; and nobody can compensate for the loss of that supreme and final defence against intolerable oppression. The strike is labour's expression of free-will, surrender that, and the worker becomes the merest wage slave".

While advocating 'that strikes are an inherent right of the working men for the purpose of security justice' Gandhiji hedged this right with several conditions.

The first of these conditions was organization of workers on right lines. "In my humble opinion labour can always vindicate itself if labour is sufficiently united and self-sacrificing..... If labour could only understand and recognize that capital is perfectly helpless without labour, labour will immediately come to its own".[22] On another occasion he observed "The labourer has but to realize that labour is also capital. As soon as laboures are properly educated and organised and they realize their strength, no amount of capital can subdue them. Organised and enlightened labour can dictate its own terms".[23]

Organisation of labour is essential and is independent of labour policies that might be pursued by the employer — whether private or public. In the absence of organization amongst workers, a large number of their grievances cannot be attended to. Labour policy of the employers, howsoever progressive and enlightened, will primarily take into consideration the good of the unit. However much that the company may do by way of welfare work, it would do so only from its point of view.

While commending formation of trade unions and organization of workers Gandhiji warned the countrymen and the workers that unless the trade unions are run on right lines they can become a source of irresponsible social behaviour. "In the struggle between capital and labour, it may generally be said that more often than not the capitalists are in the wrong box. But when labour comes fully to realize its strength, I know it can become more tyrannical than capital".[24]

Shortly after having organised the Ahmedabad Mill workers he gave vent to his opinions: "Let me briefly tell you what in my opinion you should do to come to your own. Combination among yourselves in the form of the unions is undoubtedly the first. But I can tell you from experience that your every union can become one of the causes of your bondage if you do not comply with other conditions which I shall presently mention to you".[25]

These conditions were elaborated.

(1) Each member must behave in a socially responsible manner. "Each one of you should consider himself to be a trustee for the welfare of the rest of his fellow labourers and not be self-seeking".[26]

(2) In a state of social and economic backwardness in which the average worker finds himself his advise to the workers was "to use your union as much for internal reformation as for defence against assaults from without and remember that while it is quite proper to insist upon your rights and privileges, it is imperative that you should recognize the obligation that every right carries with it".[27]

(3) That the workers and the unions should think of the consequences of their actions on the society, "the more unfortunate millions in India.....to establish a living bond between them and yourselves, especially if you......consider that India is the mother state......".[28]

(4) That organised labour must not take recourse to violence. "Without that necessary discipline in non-violence" observed Gandhiji, "they would have internecine strife and would never be able to develop the strength that is needed to enable them to realize the power that they possess.....But after that realization has come, and they have come to their own, non-violence does not become superfluous. If they were to bid goodbye to it, they would be as bad as capitalists and turn exploiters themselves".[29] On another occasion he remarked, "It would be suicidal if the labourers rely upon their numbers or brute force, i.e., violence. By so doing they will do harm to industries in the country".[30] He observed that workmen would be committing suicide and India would have to suffer indescri-bable misery if working men were to vent their anger by criminal disobedience of law of the land.

(5) Labour unions in order to increase their strength and also to bring about greater involvement of the workers with union activities must train their "members to a supplementary occupation in addition to their principal occupation in the mills so that in the event of a lockout, strike or loss of employment otherwise, they would always have something to fall back upon instead of being faced with the prospect of starvation".[31] Mill workers cannot save for the rainy day out of the meager wages that they get to maintain bare subsistence level. Enforced idleness and living on public charity is highly demoralising and undermines self-respect. "The working class will never feel secure or develop a sense of self-assurance and strength unless its members are armed with an unfailing subsidiary means of subsistence to serve as a second string to their bow in a crisis".[32] Gandhiji laid emphasis on this aspect of the organization of the workers and held "that working knowledge of a variety of occupations is to the working class what metal is to the capitalist"[33] This will also provide relief from the cramping influence of soulless, mechanical occupations which leave little scope for the development of the intellect. To quote him once again, "Let him only be organised along right lines and have his intelligence quickened, let him learn a variety of occupations, and he will be able to go about with his head erect and never be afraid of being without means of sustenance".[34]

As has been mentioned earlier that Gandhiji considered the right to strike as an inherent right of the working class, ".... There is bound to be non-cooperation, wherever there is evil, oppression and injustice, whether anybody wishes it or not..... Non-cooperation is the quicker method of creating public opinion.....a change of manners or.....of heart".[35] Discussing the relationship between capital and labour he stated his views as follows:

"There is in English a very potent word.....it is 'No' and the secret that we have hit upon is that when capital wants labour to say 'Yes' labour roars out 'No' if it means 'No'. And immediately labour comes to recognize that it has got the choice before it of saying 'Yes' when it wants to say 'Yes' and 'No', when it of saying 'Yes' when it wants to say 'Yes' and 'No', when it wants to say 'No'. Labour is free of capital and capital has to woo labour. And it would not matter in the slightest degree that capital has guns and even poison gas at its disposal. Capital would still be perfectly helpless if labour would assert its dignity by making good its 'No'.[36]

While conceding the right to strike Gandhiji disapproved use of this weapon without thorough preparation and in an irresponsible manner for narrow, personal or group interest. In a well ordered society there should be no occasion for strikes to be declared. "Strikes ought to be impossible when there is perfect understanding between capital and labour, mutual respect and recognition of equality".[37]

To reach this state of understanding each one of us have to make efforts. In the meanwhile, there may be occasions when workers may be forced to strike. Here also Gandhiji laid down certain principles:

(1) "There are certain matters in which strikes would be wrong. Sweepers' grievances come in this category".[38] He also disapproved strikes by police and remarked that "the police like the scavengers, should never go on strike. Theirs was an essential service and they should render their service irrespective of pay".[39] Gandhiji did not favour strikes even during the transitory period in essential services. It will be travesty of argument if we include amongst essential services an industry or service, which is really not essential. It need not be argued that Gandhiji advocated that working and service conditions for workers in these industries should remain static or low. While discussing 'Pen Down' strike of A.G. Office employees Calcutta in 1947 he remarked — "Why should the Director get Rs. 2000/- a month and *chaprasi* Rs. 20/- a month? It certainly sounded odd. He for one, believed that under ideal conditions the barrister and the *bhangi* should both get the same

payment. But he knew, as everybody else did, that society all the world over was far from ideal...... Society needed patient and sustained education to bring it to the same level of earning. It required much advanced training to reach that state of equality. Mean-while every effort must be made to bridge gulf between the payments of the higher and the lower ranks".[40]

(2) Strikes, for economic betterment, should not be declared with any ulterior political purpose. Backwardness, poverty and ignorance of workers is likely to be exploited by unscrupulous labour leaders. Those who are living under extensive poverty cannot think of other interests except their own. Political action by such groups cannot be sustained. Strikes if they fail are likely to demoralize workers and may lead to violence. His advice therefore was: "The secret of success lies in a refusal to exploit workers for political purposes outside their own personal and felt grievances. Organisation round a specific wrong they would understand".[41] "In my opinion, it will be a most serious mistake to make use of labour strikes for such a purpose. I do not deny that such strikes can serve political ends. But they do not fall within the plan of non-violent non-cooperation. It does not require much effort of the intellect to perceive that it is a most dangerous thing to make political condition of the country and are prepared to work for the common good. This is hardly to be expected of them all of a sudden and until they have bettered their own conditions so as to enable them to keep body and soul together in a decent manner. The greatest political contribution, therefore, that labourers can make is to improve their own condition, to become better informed, to insist on their rights and even to demand proper use by their employers of the manufacturers in which they have such an important hand....Strikes, therefore, for the present should only take place for the direct betterment of labourers' lot, and when they have acquired the spirit of patriotism for the regulation of prices of their manufacturers".[42] In 1946 when the country witnessed a spate of strikes he cautioned "strikes for economic betterment should never have a political end as an ulterior motive. Such a mixture never advances the political end and generally brings trouble upon strikers.....Political strikes must be treated on their own merits and must never be mixed with or related to economic strikes".[43]

Political strikes are not completely ruled out. But this is an extreme step, which should not be taken lightly. It requires a strong, stable united and socially conscious trade union movement, which has a clear philosophy of a new socio-economic order. "Political strikes have a definite place in non-violent action. They are never taken up haphazard. They must be open and never led by goondaism. They are calculated never to lead to violence".[44]

On similar grounds Gandhiji disfavoured sympathetic strikes. Misuse of such strikes is a common feature. Unless merits of a dispute have been examined, such an action is premature and causes public inconvenience. His advise therefore, was "sympathetic strikes must be a taboo until it is conclusively proved that the affected men have exhausted all the legitimate means at their disposal and until the Congress has been proved to have betrayed or neglected their interest or until the Congress has called for sympathetic strikes, in order to secure justice from obdurate and unsympathetic authorities".[45]

(3) Strikes must be declared after full preparations and a careful and judicious examination of the demands of the workers. Organised workers must shun irresponsible demands. "Obviously there should be no strike which is not justifiable on merits. No unjust strike should succeed".[46]

Gandhiji was in favour of declaration of strikes only when the same were likely to succeed. He, therefore, suggested 'conditions of a successful' strike......and held the view that 'when they are fulfilled, a strike need never fail'. These conditions were: (1) the cause of the strike must be just (2) there should be practical unanimity among the strikers (3) there should be no violence used against non-strikers, (4) strikers must be able to maintain themselves during the strike period without falling back upon union funds and should, therefore, occupy themselves in some useful and productive temporary occupation, (5) a strike is no remedy when there is enough labour to replace strikers"[47], (6) strikes must fix an unalterable minimum demand, and declare it before embarking upon strike "A strike should be spontaneous and not manipulated. If it is organised without any compulsion there would be no chance for goondaism and looting. Such a strike would be characterized by perfect cooperation amongst the strikers. It should be peaceful and there should be no show of force. The striker should take up some work either singly or in cooperation with each other, in order to earn their bread. The nature of such work should have been thought out beforehand. It goes without saying that in a peaceful, effective and firm strike of this character there will be no room for rowdyism or looting...... I have not presented a Utopian picture"[48].

Negotiations and Voluntary Arbitration

Gandhiji laid great stress on negotiations prior to the declaration of a strike. If negotiations fail, be advocated recourse to voluntary arbitration. "Strikes should not be risked without previous negotiations with the mill owners. If the mill owners resort to arbitration, the principle of Panchayat should be accepted. And once the panch are appointed the decision must be accepted by both the parties alike, whether they like it or not".[49]

The principle of arbitration is based upon the assumption of acceptance of social responsibility by workers, employers and their organization and placing social good and welfare higher than sectional or group interests. It is expected that the leadership of the workers and the employers, realizes the socio-economic implications of their direct action methods and do not want to put the public to avoidable hardship and inconvenience. They voluntarily agree to restrict their right to strike or to lockout, the same is not surrendered at the behest of any external agency or the State.

Even when we assume considerable sense of responsibility on the part of workers, they may be imperceptibly influenced by class consideration and bias. Those who are directly involved cannot consider the issue involved with complete detachment or objectivity. It is, therefore, desirable that they should agree to an examination of their point of view by experts of their own choosing. "The public has no means of judging the merits of a strike, unless it is backed by impartial persons enjoying public confidence. Interested men cannot judge the merits of their own case. Hence there must be an arbitration accepted by the parties or judicial adjudication"[50].

Conditions for the success of voluntary arbitration are also crystal clear. The success of voluntary arbitration depends upon assurance of reasonable and fair working and service conditions. These should provide for:

1. the hours of labour must leave the workmen some hours of rest.
2. they must get facilities for their education.
3. provision should be made for an adequate supply of milk, clothing and necessary education for their children;
4. there should be sanitary dwellings for the workmen;
5. they should be in a position to save enough to maintain themselves during their old age.[51]

These conditions are only illustrative. Gandhiji laid emphasis on giving the workers what is their due: "not what capitalists consider as due but what labour itself would so consider and enlightened public opinion acclaim as just"[52].

Employers' Attitude

Gandhiji emphasized that there is need for a radical change in the attitude of the employers — whether they are in the private or public sector. He advocated a conscious effort to reduce inequalities and warned the countrymen: 'A non-violent system of Government is clearly an impossibility as long as the gulf between the rich and the hungry millions persists. A violent and bloody revolution is a certainty one day unless there is a voluntary abdication of riches and the power that riches give and sharing them for the common good"[53]. G.D.H. Cole also expressed similar views: "As long as social inequality persists, industrial disputes will go along with it: when inequality has been swept away we may begin penal legislation in favour of industrial peace, if we need to do so. Strikes happen because of inequality and injustice and until the people realize the depth of that inequality and that injustice it will be useless for it to apply the miserable standards of social justice in the hope of securing social peace. Social peace is an ideal and the two shall come together, if they come at all."

Gandhiji's advise to the capitalists was, "If I was a capitalist, I should not continue my business for a single day, if my men felt that they were being exploited and they had not their minimum wants and comforts satisfied".[54]

On another occasion he remarked, "I do not think there need be any clash between capital and labour. Each is dependent on the other. What is essential today is that the capitalists should not lord it over the labourer. In my opinion the mill hands are as much the proprietors of their mills as the shareholders, and when the mill owners realize that mill hands are as much mill owners as they, there will be no quarrel between them".[55]

To the question, 'How should capital behave when labour strikes'? Gandhiji disapproved of the method of supperssion. "The other way, right and honourable", said Gandhiji, "consists in considering every strike on its merits and giving labour its due — not what capital considers as due what labour itself would so consider and enlightened public opinion acclaim as just"[56].

In the light of the discussion that we had in the preceding paragraphs we can appreciate Gandhiji's advocacy of trusteeship — his attitude towards property and his concept of relationship amongst individuals, smaller groups and sections within a nation and amongst nations in the world. Every effort to bring about institutional and attitudinal change as suggested by Gandhiji will take us nearer the goal of happier socio-economic order devoid of any form of exploitation. Organisation of workers along right lines with 'the inherent right to strike' and 'non-cooperation' is the surest guarantee against misuse of authority and exploitation. It is not charity that Gandhiji desires but equity and justice as a matter of course and right. Gandhiji was experimenting and in his words "India is trying to evolve true democracy, i.e., without violence. Our weapons are those of *Satyagraha* expressed through *Charkha*, the village industries, primary education through handicrafts ...... prohibition and non-violent, organisation of labour".[57] Through the structural and attitudinal changes that he envisaged and with the organisation of labour and other groups on proper lines he thought that we can have a society based on truth and non-violence. "In this structure composed of innumerable villages, there will be ever widening, never ascending circles. Life will not be a pyramid with the apex sustained by the bottom. But it will be an oceanic circle whose centre will be the individual always ready to perish for the village, the latter ready to perish for the circle of village till, at last, the whole becomes one life composed of individuals, never aggressive in their arrogance but ever humble, sharing the majesty of the oceanic circle of which they are integral parts".[58]

References

1. Hobson: The Conditions of Industrial Peace, p. 22.
2. International Labour Review, September-Oct. 1954.
3. Hare, A.E.C.: The First Principles of Industrial Relations, p. 4.
4. J.S. Mathur & A.S. Mathur (Ed): Economic Thought of Mahatma Gandhi, p. 36.
5. *Ibid*, p. 391.
6. *Ibid*, p. 542.
7. *Ibid*, p. 80-81.
8. *Ibid*, p. 623.
9. *Ibid*, p. 549.
10. *Ibid*, p. 530.
11. *Ibid*, p. 502.
12. *Ibid*, p. 574.
13. *Ibid*, p. 533-34.
14. *Ibid*, p. 491.
15. *Ibid*, p. 493.
16. *Ibid*, p. 475.
17. *Ibid*, p. 579.
18. *Ibid*, p. 578.
19. *Ibid*, p. 537.

20. *Ibid*, p. 385.
21. *Ibid*, p. 357.
22. *Ibid*, p. 385.
23. *Ibid*, p. 389.
24. *Ibid*, p. 361.
25. *Ibid*, p. 372.
26. *Ibid*, p. 372.
27. *Ibid*, p. 372.
28. *Ibid*, p. 373.
29. *Ibid*, p. 404.
30. Young India, p. 7, 16.2.20.
31. Economic Thought of Mahatma Gandhi, p. 401.
32. *Ibid*, p. 401.
33. *Ibid*, p. 402.
34. *Ibid*, p. 402.
35. *Ibid*, p. 366.
36. *Ibid*, p. 385.
37. *Ibid*, p. 412.
38. *Ibid*, p. 423.
39. *Ibid*, p. 419.
40. *Ibid*, p. 420.
41. *Ibid*, p. 409.
42. *Ibid*, p. 359-60.
43. *Ibid*, p. 417.
44. *Ibid*, p. 417.
45. *Ibid*, p. 417.
46. *Ibid*, p. 416.
47. *Ibid*, p. 36.
48. *Ibid*, p. 41.
49. *Ibid*, p. 362.
50. *Ibid*, p. 416.
51. *Ibid*, p. 361.
52. *Ibid*, p. 412.
53. *Ibid*, p. 610-611.
54. *Ibid*, p. 573.
55. *Ibid*, p. 374.
56. *Ibid*, p. 412.
57. *Ibid*, p. 603.
58. *Ibid*, p. 623.

3

A New Strategy for Rural Development

We have been talking a lot about rural development for several decades. Recently it appears that this problem has assumed renewed significance. This, I presume is mainly due to the following reasons:

Changes in the political scene and the formation of Janta Party Governments. It is significant that the Janta Party Members of Parliament took oath at the Samadhi of Mahatma Gandhi and pledged and re-dedicated themselves to usher in a socio-economic order based upon Gandhiji's concept. It may however be pointed out that every one who comes to power swears by Gandhiji. Dr. Rajendra Prasad wrote: "Jesus Christ once said to a disciple of his 'before the cock crows twice, thou, will deny me thrice'. It strikes to me that we are doing the same thing to Gandhiji:"[1].

Our experience of growth and development during the independence period has been most disheartening. The strategy adopted has not only not solved the pressing problems of poverty and unemployment but worsened them leading to tremendous frustration.

Every one concerned recognizes the urgency of finding a solution to these problems. We cannot, and should not adopt an ostrich like policy of pleading our inability to solve these problems because of their vastness or of their historicity. Prof. Gunnar Myrdal had an occasion to remark that if solutions to pressing problems are not found urgently "people and sometimes whole nations come to lose their confidence in peaceful change through democratic and non-violent means and so become desperate and opt to resort to force".[2]

We must also understand the term 'exploitation' in its true perspective. We generally use this term in a very narrow sense of misuse of power and authority by 'multinationals', foreign powers, and vested foreign interests. Exploitation remains exploitation when Delhi exploits Lucknow, Lucknow exploits smaller towns and they in their turn exploit the rural areas surrounding them. It will be no exaggeration that science and technology has given enormous power to the present generation to exploit the coming generations. Ecological imbalances, exhaustion of resources, environment pollutions are some of the after effects of this exploitation.

In the light of preliminary remarks made above I may point out that the sixth plan strategy should plan for rural development and not simply agricultural development. In my opinion this distinction should be clarified. Agricultural development can co-exist with or without rural development. Thus far agricultural development minus rural development has taken place. Figures can be compiled of output of food grains, non-food crops, production and consumption of fertilizers, increase in irrigation facilities, rural electrification, green resolutions, etc. to prove that agricultural development has taken place consistent with rural backwardness. Agriculture is being commercialized without in any way leading to a balanced development of rural areas.

Our country cannot grow unless we change the face of the five lakh and odd villages of our country in such a manner that the process of economic development subserves the accepted ideas of reducing inequalities not only in the economic, but in the non-economic spheres as well. Conditions should be created which enable the fullest possible development of an individual's personality. At the same time it should be ensured that this process of development of individuals does not take place at the expense of weaker sections of the society — nay the smallest and the weakest individual. To quote Gandhiji "My socialism means even unto the last. I do not want to rise on the ashes of the blind, the deaf and the dumb".[3]

Essential conditions for rural development can be studied under the following heads:

1. A rational priority schedule to tackle the various problems of rural society

This implies not only realizing the most pressing problems that masses face but also trying to find a solution that can give quick results. If we just make masses conscious of their problems we are likely to generate mass frustration and discontentment. To quote Gandhiji — "To awaken among them a feeling of discontentment with their lot without providing them means of removing the cause therefore is to court certain destruction, anarchy, outrage and plunder in which they themselves will be the chief victims".[4]

The basic problem of the rural areas is poverty because of non-availability of employment opportunities as also backward agriculture.

Swaraj has no meaning for the millions if they do not know how to employ their enforced idleness. "To a people famishing and idle, the only acceptable form in which God can dare appear is work and promise of food as wages. God created men to work for his food, and said that those who are without work were thieves. Eighty per cent of India are compulsorily thieves half the year".[5] He continued — "I have found it impossible to soothe suffering patients with a song from Kabir. The hungry millions ask for one poem — invigorating food. They cannot be given it. They must earn it. And they can earn only by the sweat of their brow".[6]

Gandhiji explained this problem vividly in the following words — "Imagine therefore what a calamity it must be to have 300 million unemployed, several millions becoming degraded every day for want of employment, devoid of self-respect, devoid of faith in God. I dare not take them the message of God (to economists it signifies slogans like socialist pattern of society, national development, economic growth, etc.). I can take before them a message of God only by taking the message of sacred work before them. It is good enough to talk of God whilst we are sitting here after a nice breakfast and looking forward to a nice luncheon, but how am I to talk of God to the millions who have to go without two meals a day. To them God can appear only as bread and butter".[7] He therefore advocated that "no industry, indigenous or foreign, can be allowed to increase unemployment and thus harm the true interest of the commu-nity as a whole".[8] He was clear and knew that "unemployment and idleness of millions must lead to bloody strife". On another occasion he remarked, "The problem with us is not how to find leisure for the teeming millions inhabiting our villages. The problem is how to utilize their idle hours, which are equal to the working days of six months in the year.[9]

2. A sense of participation and identification of the masses and the classes

The strategy of growth need give a sense of participation to those who are to be benefited by the process of development. Not only the masses should get a sense of participation, but they should also feel that the leadership is making common cause with them and actually participating with them shoulder to shoulder in this process of development. It was for this reason that Gandhiji defined swadeshi as "that spirit which required us to serve our immediate neighbours before others and to use things produced in our neighbourhood in preference to those more remote".[10] Sacrificial spinning by leaders was one such visible symbol of the identification of the leaders with the masses. Gandhiji "presented the spinning wheel as a symbol of their identification with the poorest of the soil. Mere lip profession was not enough. Even a genuine sensation of pity was not enough...... The only effective way of inducing the millions to exchange a listless inane life of beggary for that of dignified and easy labour was for us to invite them to take up the spinning wheel by turning it ourselves".[11] Yet on another occasion he remarked that *Khaddar* is "calculated also to make the poorest of India, whether men or women, conscious of their strength and make them partakers in the struggle for India's freedom".[12] "The spinning wheel means national consciousness and contribution by every individual to a definite constructive national work".[13] *Khaddar* alone leads to mass demonstration and mass effort. It is the platform on which all can work hand in hand".[14] For Gandhiji the test of swadeshi was the universability of participation in the production or manufacture of articles of universal use.

Gandhiji therefore recommended that "*Khadi* must be taken with all its implications. It means a wholesale swadeshi mentality, a determination to find all the necessaries of life in India and that through the labour and intellect of the villagers".[15] Such an attitude will make every "single Indian feel aglow with the possession of a power than has lain hidden within himself, and makes him proud of his identity with every drop of the ocean of Indian humanity".[16] *Khadi* and village industries occupied an important place in his constructive programme because "millions of people can take their share in this work".[17] Gandhiji could carry the masses because of such programmes. He claimed that without the constructive activity of which *Khadi* or the *Charkha* was the centre, the awakening of the villages would not have been possible".[18]

3. Local availability of resources — men and material

Plans for rural development should utilize locally available resources by and large and should not depend for their success upon imported skill and material from the towns. "The ill-clad or the naked millions of India need not charity but work that they can easily do in their cottages. Have not the poor any feeling of self-respect or partiorism"?[19] Gandhiji remarked, "For them (masses) liberty, God, and all such words are merely letters put together with the slightest meaning. They jar upon them. They will extend a welcome to any person who comes to them with a morsel of food. And if we want to give these people a sense of freedom we shall have to provide them with work which they can easily do in their desolate homes and which would give them at least the barest living".[20] It was for this reason that Gandhiji suggested that "*Khadi* is the only true economic proposition in terms of the millions of villagers until such time, if ever, when a better system of supplying work and adequate wages for every able-bodied person above the age of sixteen, male or female, is found for his field, cottage or even factory in every one of the villages of India, or till sufficient cities are built up to displace the villages so as to give the villagers the necessary comforts and amenities that well regulated life demands and is entitled to".[21] He, therefore, advocated that village uplift is possible through the revival of village industries and handicrafts. "You cannot reconstruct them (villages) unless you revive village life with its defunct handicrafts ..... The peasant in his cottage home can be revived only when he gets back his craft and depends for his necessaries on the village and not the cities as he is compelled to do today".[22] He advocated that mass production as far as vital necessities are concerned, should disappear. In respect of these requirements consumption and production should become localized, Village uplift is impossible unless the pressing economic problems are solved. He considered any scheme that will utilize the idle hours of the villagers as a solid rural uplift work.

4. Equality

Working towards equality should be the essential feature of the process of economic development. Growth and develop-ment of rural areas must lead to an equalitarian sharing of benefits. This process should be inherent and built in the development process. The humblest, the poorest must feel the change to the largest extent. Gandhiji remarked that "If India was not to perish, we had to begin with the lowest rung of the ladder. If that was rotten, all work done at the top or at the intermediate rungs was bound ultimately to fall".[23] Economic equality was an important item of Gandhiji's constructive programme. He amplified his point when he wrote — "a non-violent system of Government is clearly an impossibility so long as the wide gulf between the rich and the hungry millions persists. A violent and bloody revolution is a certainty one day unless there is a voluntary abdication of riches and the power that riches give and sharing them for the common good."[24]

He, therefore, pleaded for the necessary courage to set aside fashion, which can only be sustained at the expense of our starving millions. He remarked, "By all means let moneyed people have tasteful ornamentation, whether in dress or office surroundings, but I do plead for an observance, as between themselves and their starving brethren, of a due sense of proportion such as is always observed in well ordered society... let not those, who would raise the minimum and multiply India's wants achieve the end by first multiplying their own wants at the expense of the poor, and without in the same proportion enabling and inducing the latter to raise their standard of living."[25]

His constructive programme was a practical proposition for the attainment of this ideal. "The *Charkha* and the allied industries practically abolish all inequalities, both social and economic. The rising consciousness of the strength which non-violence gives to the people, and their intelligent refusal to co-operate in their slavery must bring about equality".[26]

5. A sense of urgency

Our technique and methods must manifest a sense of urgency in tackling the problems — economic and otherwise, that rural society is facing. Gandhiji could not wait or postpone efforts in that direction. He said, "we must refuse to wait for generations to furnish us with a patent solution of a problem which is ever-growing in seriousness. Nature knows no mercy in dealing stern justice. If we do not wake up before long, we shall be wiped out of existence".[27] In 1931 Lord Irwin, the then Viceroy of India, suggested to Gandhiji to give up boycott of liquor and foreign cloth for three months as a gesture and then resume the same. Gandhiji's characteristic reply was, "I could not give it up for minutes". In all movements of national importance he imparted this sense of urgency. Let us remember his slogan "swaraj in one year". His Salt Satyagraha and the famous Dandi March and his resolve not to return to the Ashram before independence was achieved, are instances where he was able to impart the sense of urgency and a revolutionary fervour to his followers and the masses.

These cardinal principle of uplifting the rural masses by attending to their strongly felt vital needs through efforts and processes which will give them not only a sense of belonging and participation but also lead to closer identification of the leadership and the masses; processes which will subserve to the ideal of a classless and casteless society, approach have been forsaken in post-independence period. The result is deepening frustration and loss of confidence in our capacity to solve problems with popular support. We may be able to solve various problems by other methods. But in such a process the masses are likely to lose and continue to be exploited. Gandhiji emphasized "Give up *Khaddar* and you will find it impossible to lift the masses from economic and moral degradation...... I gladly concede that you can easily fight the government with arms — and without the spinning wheel. The result will be not *Swaraj*; but plunderer giving place to his superior and between the two a greater grinding of the masses".[28]

6. Undervaluing cities

Gandhiji, therefore, advocated revival of cottage and village industries. Cottage and village industries of Gandhiji's definition will not be prototypes of the western variety catering for markets far and wide, but those that will be meeting the felt needs of the village inhabitants. "The revival of the village is possible only when it is no more exploited. Industrialisation on a mass scale will necessarily lead to passive or active exploitation of the villagers as the problems of competition and marketing come in. Therefore we have to concentrate on the village being self-contained, manufacturing mainly for use".[29]

This necessitates a different set of values and different definition of the concept of development. We have to give up our desire to urbanise rural India. "We are inheritors of a rural civilization. The vastness of our country, the vastness of the population, the situation and climate of the country have destined it for a rural civilization. To uproot it and substitute for it an urban civilization seems to be an impossibility unless we are prepared by some drastic measure to reduce the population from three hundred million to three or say even thirty".[30]

On another occasion he remarked "urbanisation in India is slow but sure death for her villages and villagers...... urbanisation can never support ninety per cent of India's population which is living in her villages".[31] Urbanization of values has resulted in brain drain from the villages. Those with slightest initiative, education and enterprise, those who can provide leadership to the rural areas are migrating from the villages in large numbers. This process must be reversed. It will mean that we must abandon our efforts of wholesale commercialization of agriculture and agree with Gandhiji that "without a cottage industry the Indian peasant is doomed. He cannot maintain himself from the produce of the land. He needs a supplementary industry".[32]

Gandhiji, therefore, advocated revival of *Khaddar* and other village industries. He compared *Khadi* as the sun and other village industries as planets of the village solar system. "*Khadi* is the sun of the village solar system. The planets are the various village industries which can support *Khadi*, in return for the heat and sustenance they derive from it..... without the revival of other industries, *Khadi* could not make further progress. For villages to be able to occupy their spare time profitably, the village life must be touched at all points".[33]

The critics may point out that this emphasis on cottage and village industries is against modernization and scientific development and that this reflects an irrational opposition to the machine method. To those who think on these lines it may be submitted that a blind imitation of western economic system has landed this country in the situation in which we find ourselves today. Gandhiji did not oppose modernization or even machinery if it helped in the solution of our problems. He would favour the use of the most elaborate machinery if thereby India's pauperism and resulting idleness could be avoided. He explained that, "mechanization is good when, the hands are too few for the work intended to be accomplished. It is an evil when there are more hands than required for the work as is the case in India".[34] He emphasized that he would welcome every improvement in the cottage machine. He would have the machine upto the point "just where they cease to help the individual and encroach upon his individuality. The machine should not be allowed to cripple the limbs of man".[35] He may have a few centralised industries for public utility which cannot be undertaken by human labour. But he was "socialist enough to say that such factories should be nationalised or state controlled. They ought to be working under the most attractive and ideal conditions not for profit but for the benefit of humanity, love taking the place of greed as motive".[36] Centralised industries will only subserve village industries.

If we act upto these principles we can fulfill the ideal which Gandhiji described towards the end of his life in the following words:

"In this structure composed of innumerable villages, there will be ever widening, never ascending circles. Life will not be a pyramid with the apex sustained by the bottom. But it will be an oceanic circle whose centre will be the individual always ready to perish for the village, the latter ready to perish for the circle of villages, till at last the whole becomes one life composed of individuals, never aggressive in their arrogance but ever humble, sharing the majesty of the oceanic circle of which they are integral units".[37]

In this short chapter it is not possible to elaborate Gandhiji's ideas about a new socio-economic order in greater detail. What he prescribed for India holds good for a new world economic order. I conclude by quoting from an article "The New International Order and Gandhian Thought" of Prof. J. Timbergen, Noble Laureate economist, "........several aspects of the idea on the desirable new order show intimate relationship with some of the fundamental thoughts of Mahatma Gandhi. This constitutes, on the one hand, a tribute to the Great Master and on the other hand a proof that closer study and elaboration of Gandhian Thought can be of eminent relevance for the attainment of a better world. To put it bluntly, Gandhiji's ideas are by no means outmoded, as some believe, and, on the contrary might well be applied more often in today's world".

References

1. Rajendra Prasad: Legacy of Gandhi, p. 99.
2. Gunnar Myrdal: Against the Stream — Critical Essays, p. 288.
3. Mathur, J.S. & A.S.: Economic Thought of Mahatma Gandhi, p. 625.
4. *Ibid.*, p. 34.
5. *Ibid.*, p. 529.
6. Economic Thought of Mahatma Gandhi, p. 531.
7. *Ibid.*, p. 143.
8. *Ibid.*, p. 197.
9. *Ibid.*, p. 297.
10. *Ibid.*, p. 59.
11. *Ibid.*, p. 57.
12. *Ibid.*, p. 54.
13. *Ibid.*, p. 53.
14. *Ibid.*, p. 59.
15. *Ibid.*, p. 211.
16. *Ibid.*, p. 211-12.
17. *Ibid.*
18. *Ibid.*
19. *Ibid.*, p. 31.
20. *Ibid.*, p. 319.
21. *Ibid.*, p. 313.
22. *Ibid.*, p. 611.
23. *Ibid.*, p. 85.

24. *Ibid.*, p. 615.
25. *Ibid.*, p. 24.
26. *Ibid.*, ppp. 40-41.
27. *Ibid.*, p. 502-503.
28. *Ibid.*, p. 280-81.
29. *Ibid.*, p. 296.
30. *Ibid.*, p. 8.
31. *Ibid.*, p. 298.
32. *Ibid.*, p. 297.
33. *Ibid.*, p. 476.
34. *Ibid.*, p. 475.
35. *Ibid.*, p. 621.
36. *Ibid.*, p. 475.
37. *Ibid.*, p. 623.

4

The Gandhian Content in Economic Planning in India

Before we analyse the impact of Gandhi's ideas on economic planning we must understand the basic economic philosophy that Gandhiji prescribed for the country. Gandhiji's ideas can be better summarized in his own words: "Economics to be worth anything must be capable of being reduced to terms of religion or spirituality".[1]

We must not confuse the words 'religion, or 'spirituality' with any creed, dogma, rituals or efforts to individual salvation or the like. Religion or spirituality in Gandhian approach have social connotation. After having attained independence, Gandhiji was advised to retire to Kashi or Himalyas. His characteristic reply was: "I laugh and tell them that the Himalyas of my penance are where there is misery to be alleviated, oppression to be relieved".[2] For Gandhiji a system that tolerated poverty and exploitation amidst millions was devoid of religion and spirituality. He was quite emphatic that poverty leads to all round degradation — physical, intellectual and moral. He therefore emphasized that the evil of poverty should be fought in the shortest possible period. "We must refuse to wait for generations to furnish us with a patent solution of a problem which is ever-growing in seriousness. Nature knows no mercy in dealing stern justice. If we do not wake up before long, we shall be wiped out of existence".[3]

While Gandhiji made efforts to fight poverty in the shortest period, he was practical enough to realize that removing poverty does not mean aspiring for affluence in the context of the eco-nomic situation that prevailed in the country.

His opposition to affluence was based on account of his fundamental belief that multiplication of wants does not permit fullest development of human personality. It makes a man socially irresponsible also. He had also realized that planning for affluence will mean increasing inequalities and sharing of gains of increased production by the elite at the top and perpetuation of poverty of the masses. In his scheme of things removal of the poverty of the masses was to be one supreme consideration. It was for this reason he once advised Pt. Nehru that the suitability of any scheme and its success should be judged by the sole criterion of its capacity to remove poverty of the lowliest in the shortest possible period.

He had realized that unemployment amongst the masses was the greatest evil from which the economy of the country was suffering. In a healthy society concentration of riches in a few people and unemployment among millions is a great social crime or disease, which needs to be remedied. His plan for economic regeneration of the country was employment oriented and not surplus oriented. "The so called economical character of factory production as compared to handicrafts production today is not an inherent quality, but only a conferred attribute depending on the standard of values which society has adopted or considers desirable to adopt. The only unalterable and rock bottom test of whether an occupation or method of production is economic or otherwise, is how far it answers life's vital needs, what the making of it means to the producer".[4]

In view of the large number of people inhabiting the country and the more or less impossible task of transferring these to urban areas in the foreseeable future Gandhiji advocated revival of village and cottage industries. These industries were to produce for the felt needs of the people rather than catering for outside markets or trying to multiply wants ad-infinitum. He remarked, "Unemployment and idleness of millions must lead to bloody strife. Khadi is the only alternative to this and not the so-called socialism, which presupposes industrialism. The socialist that India can assimilate is the socialism of the spinning wheel".[5]

Gandhiji was opposed to inequalities and an economic order that enables the few to ride on the backs of the many. He had warned his countrymen that 'a violent and bloody revolution is a certainty one day unless there is voluntary abdication of riches and the power that riches give and sharing them for the common good".[6] He was further of the view that planning for equality must begin at once and that the socio-economic order should not first create inequalities in the garb of planning for affluence and abundance.

"If ever we are to achieve equality the foundation has to be laid now. Those who think that major reforms will come after the advent of Swaraj (in the distant future) are deceiving themselves as to the elementary working of non-violent Swaraj. It will not drop from heaven all of a sudden one fine morning. But it has to be built up brick by brick by corporate self-effort".[7]

Since majority of the people in our country live in villages the unit of development in Gandhian technique was the village itself. We should very clearly realize the impracticability of urbanizing our country. It has taken nearly a century for the urban population to increase by 10 per cent. If we want to have an urban population of 80 per cent or so on the pattern of western industrial societies it may take us another 50-80 years to urbanise this land of ours. Gandhiji therefore did not plan this impossible task and wanted to develop rural India. He was interested in developing the villages and not in urbanizing the village life. Let not the sceptic claim that Gandhi wanted a static standard of living or poverty for the people of the country.

The strategy that Gandhiji advocated was that greater reliance he put on development of village and cottage industries. Even here the emphasis should be on production for use and not production for the market or commercial purposes. This does not mean that he was totally opposed to large scale industries. These were only to supplement and not supplant village and cottage industries. Similarly, it is wrong to suppose that Gandhiji was opposed to technological improvements. He was all for improving the productivity of the village artisan, but he was not in favour of technology that will further concentrate economic power or reduce employment. "In this there is no room for machines that would displace human labour and that would concentrate power in few hands. Labour has a unique place in a cultured human family. Every machine that helps every individual has a place"[8]

What Gandhiji advocated has been accepted by those who are at the helm of affairs in the country in principle, "The constitution of India has guaranteed certain fundamental rights to the citizens of India and enunciated certain Directive Principles of State Policy, in particular, that the State shall strive to promote the welfare of the people by securing and protecting as effectively as it may a social order in which justice, social, economic and political, shall inform all institutions of the national life and shall direct its policy toward securing among other things (a) that the citizens, men and women equally, have the right to an adequate means of livelihood (b) that the ownership and control of the material resources of the community are so distributed as best to subserve the common good; and (c) that the operation of the economic system does not result in the concentration of wealth and means of production to the common detriment".

Similar sentiments can be traced in the various plan documents. It is not the purpose of the present chapter to quote extensively from various plans to prove that Gandhiji's ideas had profound impact on the formulation of plan documents and laying down of policies. But one is reminded of the old saying, 'If wishes were horses beggars will be riding'; what we missed in our planning was a concrete plan of action on the lines suggested by Gandhiji. The strategy of growth and development was influenced by ideas of western thinkers and concepts of growth and development that were adopted by western industrially advanced countries. We put our faith on centralised, large scale capital intensive industries in the fond hope that the industries, as they grow, will be able to generate more employment and lead to a progressive improvement in the standards of living of the teeming millions — many of them living at the margins of starvation.

The consequence of abandoning Gandhiji's ideas in the early phase of planning has been disastrous for our country. It has resulted in widening of economic inequalities. The rich have become richer and poor poorer during these years. In the rural areas it is estimated that as on June 30, 1971 the top one per cent of the population possessed 14.3 per cent of the total assets of rural households. This percentage improved to 35.27 per cent for the top five per cent; to 50.56 per cent for the top 10 per cent; to 74.70 per cent for the top 25 per cent and 91.89 per cent for the top 50 per cent. There has been slight increase in inequalities in rural areas since 1962 as the percentage for the top five per cent was 37.0 per cent, for the top 25 per cent it was 74 per cent and 91.3 per cent for the top fifty per cent in 1962. It is significant that as on June 30, 1971, about 20 per cent of the rural households in India had either no assets or very nominal assets not worth mentioning. Their share in overall assets was not even one per cent of the total.[9] We must bear in mind that collection of data in our country has severe limitations and that it might be quite possible that the collecting machinery is biased in favour of proving that disparities have gone down.

Similarly poverty of the masses remains undisturbed. It is being officially accepted that 40 per cent of the people remained below poverty line in spite of effort to raise their living standards during the post independence period. We get the following figures about average per capita consumer expenditure in rural and urban areas from NSS 18th round survey.

Average per capita consumer expenditure is Rs. Per 30 days. (All India Averages)*

Quintile group	*Rural*	*Urban*
0-2	9.92	12.69
20-40	14.58	18.82
40-60	18.64	24.85
60-80	24.42	34.71
80-100	44.02	74.92
General population	22.32	33.92

* Economic and Political Weekly – April 10, 1976, G.S. Chatterjee, Disparity in Per capita Household Consumption in India.

Per capita income in real terms (60-61 base) keeps on fluctuating and was Rs. 347.2 in 1973-74 and declined to Rs. 341.4 in 1974-75. As according to a study published in the Reserve Bank of India Bulletin, Sept. 1976 issue per capita national income at constant prices (60-61) has risen at an annual rate of 1.3 per cent only for the period 1960-71 to 1974-75. These are revealing statistics when one knows that a large part of expenditure, which is included under calculations for GNP, NNP, does not favourably affect the real standards of living of the masses.

The problem in respect of unemployment is getting worse so much so that now no efforts are being made even to have a rough estimate of the persons unemployed and under-employed. Each successive plan resulted in the number of the unemployed increasing. The figures that are published by Employment Exchanges, even though they suffer from severe limitations, are sufficient guide to the worsening situation on the front of employment generation.

Problems referred to above have compelled serious rethinking on our part to chalk out a strategy of development on Gandhian lines. We have been now talking of labour intensive technology and evolution of appropriate technology in suit the requirements of our country. It may mean abandoning or at least severely limiting the western type of industrialisation "My views on national planning differ from the prevailing ones. I do not want it along industrial lines. I want to prevent our villages from catching the infection of industrialisation"[10]. He elaborated his views on another occasion in the following words in reply to question from Dr. Lohia:

"If I can convert the country to my point of view, the social order of the future will be based predominantly on the *charkha* and all it implies. It will include everything that promotes the well-being of the villagers. It will not exclude the industries mentioned by my correspondents so long as they do not smother the villages and the village life. I do visualize electricity, shipbuilding, iron works, machine making and the like existing side by side with the village handicrafts. But the order of the dependence will be reversed. Hitherto, industrialisation has been so planned as to destroy the villages and village crafts. In the state of the future it will subserve the villages and their crafts. I do not share the socialist belief that centralisation of the necessaries of life will conduce to the common welfare when the centralised industries are planned and owned by the state".

We must distinguish between rural industrialisation as advocated in India and rural development as visualized by Gandhiji. Our efforts have been to commercialize production of rural industries; cottage and village industries. These industries cannot be developed if the products of these industries are to be sold in competition with the products of organised large-scale industries. Gandhiji's advice was clear and unequivocal "The revival of the village is possible only when it is no more exploited. Industrialisation on a mass-scale will necessarily lead to passive or active exploitation of the villagers as the problems of competition and marketing come in. Therefore, we have to concentrate on the village being self-contained manufacturing mainly for use. Provided this character of the village industry is maintained, there would be no objection to villagers using even the modern machines and tools that they can make and afford to use. Only they should not be used as a means of exploitation of others".[12]

This implies that we have to believe and realize that the socio-economic factors of India have destined it to be a rural civilization. "We are inheritors of a rural civilization ..... To uproot it and substitute for it an urban civilization seems to me an impossibility unless we are prepared by some measures to reduce the population from three hundred millions to three or say even to thirty. I can therefore suggest remedies on the assumption that we must perpetuate the present rural civilization and endeavour to rid it of its acknowledged defects".[13] These words were spoken in 1929. Since then our population has gone to 650 million and is according to expert opinion likely to rise to 1000 millions by the end of the century.

Gandhiji's strategy, in the context of our country was that planning should not lead to further impoverishment of the rural areas. Industrialisation was bound to accentuate this tendency. "The half a dozen modern cities are an excrescence and serve at the present moment the evil purpose of drawing the life blood of the villages. Khaddar is an attempt to revive and reverse this process and establish a better relationship between the cities and the villages. The cities with their insolent torts are a constant menace to the life and liberty of the villages".[14] On another occasion he remarked that "urbanisation in India is slow but sure death of her villages and villagers. Urbanisation can never support ninety per cent of India's population which is living in her villages".[15]

Our efforts thus far have been to urbanise rural India and make relationships economic and commercial. In our desire to remove poverty we have tried to create desires and wants which we know full well cannot be satisfied and thus have increased frustration and have created a system which is leading to additional and increased unemployment of the rural people. Gandhiji held the view, "Swaraj for them can only be an ability to support themselves without begging. To awaken among them a feeling of discontent with their lot without providing them means of removing the cause thereof is to court certain destruction, anarchy, outrage and plunder in which they them-selves will be chief victims".[16]

It was for these reasons he pleaded for the revival of cottage and rural industry. "Give up *Khaddar* and you will find it impossible to lift the masses from economic and moral degradation...... I gladly concede that you can easily fight the government with arms and without unity, without the spinning wheel. The result will not be *Swaraj* but one plunderer giving place to his superior and between the two a great grinding of the masses".[17]

Gandhiji therefore, advocated technologies known by the people. This could also enable mobilization of support of the common man for a common purpose of improving the standard of life of the common man. "Swadeshi means even distribution of wealth from an occupation, next in importance to agriculture. It supplements agriculture and therefore automatically assists materially to solve the problem of our growing poverty. Thus *Swadeshi* is our veritable *kamdhenu*, supplying our wants and solving many of our difficult problem".[18]

In our plans thus far no effort was seriously made to adopt Gandhiji's techniques of development. State policy did make some apologetic steps to revive rural and cottage industries. The faith was however, in large-scale industrialisation of a western model. It is because we have not planned to develop the village as a whole that piece-meal efforts in the shape of various measures of land reforms; isolated measure of agricultural improvements—better seeds, fertilizers, provision of irrigation facilities, etc., and even rural electrification, and new technology have left the weaker sections in the country largely untouched. It will be no exaggeration that measures like the ones mentioned above have created circumstances in which the powerful sections and groups have become still more powerful.

We must radically change our concept of planning and development. We must abandon planning for affluence. Instead we must plan to fight poverty in the shortest possible period. This will require drawing inspiration from what Gandhiji said and worked for. In his opinion "khadi is the only true economic proposition in terms of millions of villagers until such time, if ever, when a better system of supplying work and adequate wages for every able bodied person above the age of sixteen, male or female is found for his field, cottage or even factory in every one of the villages of India, or till sufficient cities are built up to displace the village so as to give the villagers the necessary comforts and amenities that a well-regulated life demands and is entitled to".[19]

References

1. Economic Thought of Mahatma Gandhi, p. 86.
2. Pyarelal: The Last Phase, p. 211.
3. J.S. Mathur & A.S. Mathur: Economic Thought of Mahatma Gandhi, p. 24.
4. *Ibid.*, p. 605.
5. *Ibid.*, p. 291.
6. *Ibid.*, p. 610-611.
7. *Ibid.*, p. 611.
8. *Ibid.*, p. 624.
9. Sreelakha Basu: Economic & Political Weekly, July 10, 1971.
10. Economic Thought of Mahatma Gandhi, p. 513.
11. *Ibid.*, p. 598.
12. *Ibid.*, p. 503.
13. *Ibid.*, p. 280-81.
14. *Ibid.*, p. 82.
15. *Ibid.*, p. 296.
16. *Ibid.*, p. 34.
17. *Ibid.*, p. 40-41.
18. *Ibid.*, p. 9.
19. *Ibid.*, p. 170.

5

Prospects for Change on Gandhian Lines

Every political party, every leader of some eminence, every thinker cries hoarse about his allegiance to the principles and socio-economic order suggested by Gandhiji. Yet, what we witness today is a complete denial, nay negation of every principle laid down by the Mahatma.

Why has this happened? Is it because people had no clear concept of what Gandhiji was aiming at; what we had experimented with was beyond our capacity; what he had visualized was utopian and not practical? Or is it because of our incompetence; lack of proper understanding of the problems that humanity is facing at large and more so in countries like ours which have recently acquired independence and are struggling to solve the problems that the masses face in the third world countries? Is it because of the strong hold of vested interests and ideas—our efforts to solve today's problems with ideas, instruments and techniques of yesterday? A humble effort is being made to analyse these issues and to assess the practicability of Gandhiji's ideas for regeneration of the people, the society, the nation and the world order towards a peaceful socio-economic system.

One can firmly believe that each one of those who mattered in the shaping of the destiny of this country in the post-independence period, whether in Government or outside had a fairly clear concept of Gandhiji's view of new socio-economic order—free from violence (which includes all forms of subtle, overt and covert exploitation) and an order which will provide for peaceful resolution of conflicts and a steady growth for fuller development of human personality, small groups and communities, nation states and the world community at large.

The question that is uppermost in our mind is as to why persons trained under Gandhiji failed to live up to his cherished ideals upon which he was experimenting all through his life.

One can begin answering this question by pointing out the removal of Gandhiji from our midst so suddenly that it appeared that our society has become rudderless; the guiding light is gone and there is all darkness. Pt. Nehru remarked "The light has gone out of our lives and there is darkness every where ..... we will not run to him for advice and seek solace from him...."

These might have been the expression of sentiments but for the millions of this country—nay the down-trodden humanity in the world at large—these experiments for a new socio-economic order received a severe jolt. Gandhiji on the eve of India's independence had started realizing that the political leadership that came to power has no use for his ideas and techniques of social change. He compared himself to a spent bullet and yet did not give up his efforts to fight for the cause dear to him. When he was advised to retire he remarked that he would continue to struggle for the removal of all forms of exploitation and for the upliftment of the down trodden.

He prepared a scheme to change the Congress and have a new body of devoted workers. At one stage he requested Pt. Nehru to clarify his ideas of the new India after independence. He even suggested that the measuring rod of the correctness or otherwise of any scheme or step should be in terms of the poorest among the poor and the immediacy with which his problems can be solved. There are reasons to believe that if he was amidst us he would have even offered *Satyagraha* against policies that were pursued—and the history of the progress of his country might have shaped differently. But Providence willed otherwise. Gandhiji was disowned in his own country by those for whom he was 'Father of the Nation'.

Several reasons can be assigned for this dethronement of Gandhiji's ideas and techniques of change. The greatest and the most important reason has been the stronghold of western economists, social scientists and western ideas for the solution of problems that beset India and other developing countries. Gandhiji had observed in his Indian Home Rule, "India's salvation consists in unlearning what she has learnt during the past fifty years or so".[2] In his foreword for the subsequent edition of this booklet he wrote "The booklet is a severe condemnation of 'modern civilisation'. It was written in

1908. My conviction is deeper today than ever. I feel that if India will discard 'modern civilisation' she can only gain by doing so".

This does not mean that Gandhiji wanted to pursue a close door policy or was thinking that Indians can live in isolation uninfluenced by developments that are taking place in the field of science, technology, social science etc. He fore-warned us of the dangers that stare us in the face and that pose a severe threat to the human race. He repeatedly and periodically drew our attention to these grave perils. His message was, therefore, for the whole mankind, "........the message of the spinning wheel is much wider than its circumference. Its message is one of simplicity, service of mankind, living so as not to hurt others, creating an indissoluble bond between the rich and the poor, capital and labour, the prince and the peasant. That larger message is naturally for all".[3] "I have not the slightest doubt that the saving of India and of the world lies in the wheel. If India becomes the slave of the machine, I say, heaven save the world".[4]

Gandhiji had world view of life and society. He made experiments in India. We did not lay emphasis on this world view of Gandhiji. Gandhiji's relevance for India cannot be advocated unless we can prove that Gandhiji is relevant for the world—nations that are tying to grapple with their problems of backwardness, mass poverty and exploitation (developing nations) and nations that are industrialized to the teeth and are dangers to a peaceful world order because of their armaments race and exploitative 'economies'. India took a back seat at international forums. We were even apologetic in recognizing the relevance of Gandhiji for our own country. Gandhi became irrelevant in his own country because his followers and disciples failed to explain this world view and were submerged and over-awed by western thought and could not give up their dependency on western experts.

Gandhi was also let down by his disciples and followers. They used Gandhiji to pursue their own selfish ends. Everyone wanted to stick to power somehow or other. Gandhiji's samadhi became a pilgrimage for laying of wreaths and garlands by visiting dignitaries and rituals by us on his birth and martyrdom days. This desire to stick to power resulted in widespread corruption and a collusion between vested interest, the political leadership, bureaucracy and the rising industrial and business class. Gandhiji was and is being quoted by these vested interests to make their designs.

Increasing reliance on state power and machinery to solve problems that we face is partly because of these developments. While Gandhiji warned us against concentration of power and more particularly in the state the leadership planned for the opposite. Decentralisation, if it is to be effective, has to be in all walks of life. Decentralisation in the political field is not possible and practicable without economic decentralisation. But, as has been mentioned earlier, we were dominated by state welfarism. Instead of trying to strengthen masses and mass action and movements through constructive programmes (by which I mean programmes that will involve masses and grow out of their felt needs) we took recourse to legislation and solution of problems through state machinery. The result has been corruption, demoralization and frustration.

The fast developing large scale industrial sector – both in the public and private sector with state patronage is proving to be another serious obstacle in the way of implementation of Gandhiji's concept. Since the leaders in power could not completely disown Gandhiji they paid left handed compliments by laying down a policy on paper for development of cottage and village industries; while at the same time permitting these industries to languish and die in the face of competition from organised sector. Gandhiji used the term 'peaceful penetration' for this subtle form of exploitation.

Thinking on these lines has encouraged consumer culture. In order to protect the way of life to which urban people have got used to under western influence, efforts are being made to make these a criterion for growth and progress. Synthetic desires are being encouraged and in this whole process the average man and the downtrodden is suffering and is being made to pay the price to maintain urban standards and way of life. The whole might of the highly industrialized units of the west is also supporting these developments.

However, prospects to adopt Gandhiji's ideas and techniques have improved recently. The reasons for this slow change are several.

One of the reasons is the realization of relevance of Gandhiji's ideas in western countries. Scholars in the industrially advanced countries are getting fully aware of the basic weaknesses of an industrial society. The problems that the western nations face and pose for the survival of the human race need not be recounted. Books like 'Failure of Technology', 'Small is Beautiful', 'Challenge of Man's Future' have discovered the message of Gandhiji. Seminars and discussions are being organised to discuss Gandhiji's idea that in the world 'there is enough for everybody's needs but not for everybody's greed'. Those who mattered at power centres in our country have learnt from these developments. This is how Gandhiji is to be rediscovered and is being rediscovered in our own country. Professor Toyanbee observed, "In this hurricane of annihilating material power mankind will not be able to save itself from self destruction unless we, all of us, manage to practise non-violence in our relations with our fellow-men". He charged us with the responsibility to discover Gandhiji and observed, "You have incurred a rather formidable obligation towards both the Gandhiji and history".

Coupled with this development in thinking outside India the worsening of the social and economic situation in our own country leading to frustration and demoralization has also forced us to think of Gandhiji and his ideas. With each successive plan unemployment has been rising, the number of people living under poverty line has been on the increase and inequalities have become far greater. These problems of poverty and unemployment, the demoralization that poverty leads to and the inadequacy of the accepted techniques of growth and development to solve these problems have compelled people to think in terms of Gandhiji's approach which was essentially based on the promises that process of growth and development should enable the lowliest and the humblest to feel the glow, to get deeply involved in this process and prevent misuse of the process of growth and development for sectional and group interest. Since circumstances and conditions under which Gandhiji formulated his concrete scheme of production of wealth through decentralisation of industries have not been even slightly changed, they remain valid and meaningful. People are fast getting disillusioned. Under these circumstances people and sometimes whole nations come to lose their confidence in peaceful change through democratic and non-violent means and so become desperate and opt to resort to force.

The country had, during recent years, witnessed, several mass movements. The movement under the leadership of Jai Prakash Narain did awaken the masses to realize that if their interests are to be guarded and the country's march towards progress has to be in terms of relief to the downtrodden, state authority should be kept in proper check. Several such move-ments have been organised on different scales to deal with problems—movements like 'Chipko Andolan', 'Mitti Bachao Andolan' etc. It is true that these movements are more of an indication of the resentment of the people rather than signals for the creation of a new socio-economic order. Nevertheless this only indicates that the potentialities of awakening of the masses is still existent. This potential could not be mobilized or made more effective because the leadership that organised these movements did not build up cadre on the basis of constructive programmes as Gandhiji did during his life time and could not give a clear image of the new order. While replying to Dr. Lohia, Gandhiji observed, "Agitation against every form of injustice is the breath of political life. My contention is that, divorced from the constructive programme it is bound to have the tinge of violence".[4]

Those in authority are conscious of the strength of these developments and have started talking in terms of decentralisation, area planning, labour intensive technique and appropriate technology, *Antyodaya* and the like. The next step should be to redefine these concepts in Gandhiji's terms and ideology so that we can build a new socio-economic order which eschews violence and exploitation, encourages cooperation among individuals, groups and nations, brings about greater equality and enables socio-economic changes through the initiative of the people through non-violent means with rapidity. Shorn of Gandhiji's ideas these moves may become means for perpetuating status quo and exploitation.

References

1. P.D. Tandon: Humanities Tribute to Gandhiji, p. 17.
2. J.S. Mathur, A.S. Mathur (Ed) Economic Thought of Mahatma Gandhi, p. 461.
3. *Ibid.*, p. 477.
4. *Ibid.*, p. 598-99.

6

Economics of Sarvodaya

This is an age of planning. In our country also plans are being formulated to usher in an era of rapid economic development. Several such plans have already been implemented and we will have more of five-year-plans. In the planning that we have, the role of the State, as it is being termed, is becoming a 'welfare state', i.e., the enormous responsibility of looking after the welfare of individual citizens is to be increasingly shouldered by the State. The objectives in a modern plan are generally an increase in the national income through industrialisation (relying mostly on heavy and key industries) and an equitable distribution of the increased wealth so that while the standard of living of the common man increases, it also leads to a socialistic pattern of society.

The outstanding features of the planning that we have are several. In the first place our planning concentrates mainly on economic planning. We plan to increase the national income very quickly; we plan for an equitable distribution of the increased national income mostly through fiscal measures. In brief, we plan to improve the standard of living of the people. We however, do not plan the non-economic life. We do not consciously plan that citizens will become more law-abiding, more truthful, more cooperative, more democratic, etc. It is not being suggested that such a development will not take place. It may happen that after the success of a plan people will, in general, develop what we may call certain non-economic qualities. So also if the plan does not get success, or for that matter if the formulation or implementation of the plan is defective, the opposite tendencies may get manifested. During and after the plan frustration may increase and dishonesty, corruption, intolerance, etc. may be at a premium. Suffice it to say that our plans concentrate on the economic side exclusively. That certain non-economic virtues will develop is a by-product of general economic development. There is no plan for what we may term as the non-economic or ethical side of the people.

Even in the sphere of economic planning we plan primarily for a quick increase in the national income of a country. In India plans are being formulated to double the national income within a period of 25 years. Other questions are of subsidiary importance. The question of equitable distribution is to be talked more as a slogan, an eye-wash for the common folk. So also the means for economic development are not very relevant. We have to adopt those means that will permit a very rapid increase in national income. In other words, the means to be adopted are rapid industrialisation and vast technological developments. We are not concerned with the social repercussions of these changes.

In the formulation and implementation of these plans we rely more and more on central authority. In every country there is a central planning authority, which formulates the plan, lays down targets and agencies for its implementation. An average citizen is only remotely and most indirectly associated with the formulation or implementation of the plan. As a matter of fact, an attitude is developing in which we look for our welfare to the State; for all our ills we tend to look to the State for relief. It may not be an exaggeration if we term this arrangement as "State-welfare" rather than "welfare state". A decision even in respect of the desirability or otherwise of certain measures has to be decided by experts and specialists. They have command over the vast propaganda machinery to force the people to swallow their prescriptions and remedies. Very soon it is the expert whose will prevails. Even in respect of extremely personal affairs like food, education of children, hobbies, dress, etc., the expert has to be consulted.

For the common man what do our plans offer? The slogan is an improvement in the standard of living (and not standard of life). What does an improvement in standard of living precisely imply? It means that every individual will have more to feed, more to clothe, better house to live, more of comforts and later on more of luxuries. In other words, an increase in the standard of living means that people desire more of material goods and that this increased desire should be satisfied. It is considered good to desire more and try to work for the satisfaction of these increased wants. Rather it is a criterion to have more and soon to judge the people not with what they are but with what they have. A high salary, a car, a television, etc., determine the social status and the place that an individual should occupy. As far as individual action is concerned, the motivating force is multiplication of wants and efforts to satisfy wants, which will ever remain insatiable.

"This kind of planning has an irresistible fascination for the town-bred intellectuals. It enables privilege to the equated with patriotism and progress with the satisfaction of urban values and the sophisticated way of life in which they have grown up and which in consequence have grown upon them. The rural masses (in Indian conditions particularly) will have ample opportunities to jack themselves up to the urban level of culture and civilization, by providing voluntary labour. In brief, it means political and social domination of the town, and power and much-coveted perquisites for the elite, who constitute the ruling class".[1]

The concept of *Sarvodaya* differs fundamentally from these basic tenets of what we term as 'welfare state'. A welfare state is inherent in a *Sarvodaya* social order. It may not be true vice versa. In a *Sarvodaya* social order we desire to bring about a socio-economic set up in which there will be welfare of every individual. It is not the greatest good of the greatest number that we aspire for. We desire that in the good of the society should be reflected the good of all. The maxim 'greatest good of the greatest number' indirectly permits exploitation of those who are lesser in number or those who have not been vocal enough to carry large sections of people with them.

The basic postulates of a *Sarvodaya* social order, as said above, are different from a 'welfare state'. Here efforts are to be made for the development of the integrated whole. "Our planning has therefore, to be for total and integrated life, both of the individuals and of the human society of which we are but parts. Planning may and should begin with economics, since that is the base on which man stands and lives and breathes and moves. But the body is but an instrument and a house, a tabernacle of the spirit. We are not mere bodies ensouled, we are rather souls embodied. We have to take note of this important fact. Man can be said to live a full life and be a perfect being only when his body and his life of the senses lead him to the higher and nobler spheres of consciousness. Man's life can be said to be perfect and integrated only when his body is healthy and shining, his mind is clear and penetrating; his emotions are pure and rich with truth, love, goodness and beauty; his ethical being is sensitive and responsive to the claims and needs of others; and his personality is ever widening and broadening till it reaches the very confines of universality.

This is the attainment of *Sarvodaya*, total progress by the individual. Similarly, when everyone in society attains this development, that state of things may be termed *Sarvodaya* of the whole society. The social system and structure, in which this kind of harmonious individual and social development is planned and made possible may be said to be a *Sarvodaya* social order—a system of total and integrated progress of all".[2] We may then suggest that the objective is advancement of human welfare under conditions of truth and prosperity for everybody.

The aim is not simply an economic ideal. Standard of living should increase but so also must be standard of life. Economic development and growth, if it does not improve the non-economic or ethical aspect of a nation and an individual's life should be viewed with suspicion. It may not always be desirable and good. Gandhiji had realized that "it was impossible and unwise to keep these cognate sciences (ethics, politics and economics) relating to man in his every day affairs of life and rules of conduct, strictly apart".[3] He would not and could not consent to such an absolute divorce between Ethics and Economics, as the successors of Adam Smith and Ricardo had insisted upon. The critics rightly dubbed it the 'Dismal Science' not only because of its tendency to consider all human values in terms of money only, but also because they seemed to ignore all other wants, all other joys, all other forms of human happiness except those that could be satisfied with material goods or measured in money. Gandhiji did not make any distinction between economics and ethics. "I must confess", he wrote, "that I do not draw a sharp or any distinction between economics and ethics. Economics that hurts the moral well-being of an individual or a nation is immoral and therefore sinful".[4] "If socialism ever comes", writes Bertrand Russel, "it is only likely to prove beneficial if non-economic goods are valued and consciously pursued".

It should not be inferred that in a *Sarvodaya* social order poverty will be at a premium. Like our ancient seers Gandhiji did not rely exclusively on material welfare. "It was not because he did not realize the importance of the material requirements of existence, or neglected their bearing on the welfare of men. In fact, amongst the four *Purusharth* as, our ancient law-givers and treatise writers insisted upon *Artha* or material gain proper, not only as important as any of these three—*Dharma* (duty), *Kama* (love or desire) and *Moksha* (final emancipation from *Karma* or the toils of life}".[5] Material needs and requirements are considered to be the essence or root, the prime mover so to say, of all other activities. Paradoxical as it may seem, removal of the poverty of people is one of the active programmes that Gandhiji pursued. He was materialist enough to believe that our thinking is conditioned by what we do with our hands, particularly the activities related to the satisfaction of our primary needs, more than what we are taught or told. It was, therefore, nearly always that whenever any mass movement was to be launched or whenever masses were to be approached Gandhiji had some economic base for the movement. The salt satyagrah is a glaring example of this realization. No one can go on preaching sermons to the poor folk for long. It is only when we can talk to the masses in terms of their daily wants and show them how they can realize their freedom through their own voluntary and cooperative effort that we can carry them with us. Gandhiji's emphasis on economics was only subsidiary. He wanted to dethrone economics from the exclusive pedestal that it has been occupying in the present-day thinking. Material prosperity is a means to an end. "For a country, a nation or state economic prosperity means the stable, peaceful maintenance of the social structure, of the organisation and institution of community which are designed to provide means and opportunities for every individual to secure a decent existence, to ensure an adequate self-fulfillment, self realization and to achieve thereby his own release from the bondage of the earthly existence".[6]

The *Sarvodaya* concept goes a step further when it strikes at the very foundation of modern economic thinking, viz., a rise in the standard of living beyond a certain limit is always conducive to human welfare. The idea that a progressive rise in the standard of living of people must invariably lead to a better, contented and happier life is of doubtful value. Mahatma Gandhiji was "never enamoured of an undefined, indefinite, unlimited rise in the standard of our living as dependent upon external things. While he wanted that we should have our essentials of life, that no one should be troubled by want of these essentials, he also felt that no one was entitled or at any rate no one should desire to have more than the essentials. These essentials were not to be determined by the individual himself, but by the other considerations".[7] Not the multiplication of wants but their curtailment consistent with honest, dignified living and efficient working should be the criterion. "We are not always aware of our real needs, and most of us improperly multiply our wants, and thus unconsciously make thieves of ourselves. If we devote some thought to the subject we shall find that we can get rid of quite a number of our wants. One who follows the observance of non-stealing will bring about a progressive reduction of his own wants. Much of the distressing poverty in this world has arisen out of breaches of the principle of non-stealing".[8]

A ready-made criterion is being suggested whether wants of an individual are consistent with the *Sarvodaya* concept or not. The measuring rod is the requirements of others. Is the want in question essential for others also? Can it be shared with all? Is the want in question being satisfied by depriving others of their essentials or more pressing wants? In other words, not individual whims but public requirements, public consideration should determine to what extent wants might be permitted to increase and standard of living to improve. Individual standard of living should not be permitted to rise by depressing the standard of living of the masses. "Everyone must have a balanced diet, a decent house to live in, facilities for the education of one's children and adequate medical relief".[9] That constituted his (Gandhiji's) picture of economic equality. He did not want to taboo everything above and beyond the bare necessaries but they must come after the essential needs of the poor are satisfied. First things must come first. We must, on the one hand, try to raise the standard of life of those who are poor and on the other hand lower the standard of those who are extremely rich. The process must start on both ends. In the words of Gandhiji, "It means the leveling down of the few rich in whose hands is concentrated the bulk of the nation's wealth on the one hand and a leveling up of the semi-starved naked millions on the other. A non-violent system of government is clearly an impossibility so long as the wide gulf between the rich and the hungry millions persists".[10]

It is also being clearly recognized that an exclusive emphasis on improving one's standard of living creates in the socio-economic life certain wrong values, which undermine social and collective good. Mutually contradictory tendencies are being encouraged. As individuals we are being asked to try to increase our standard of living—we should have more, acquire more and constantly aspire for more. The means that we adopt to acquire this wealth are not very relevant. We are asked to believe individually in the 'economy of acquisition', which had been practised only by rare and fabulous persons in the past. It is surprising that the planners in our country think of ushering in an era of socialism or socialistic pattern on the foundation of this 'economy of acquisition' to be practised and worshipped by individual citizens. "Not individual wealth but the individualistic propensity towards the acquisition of wealth is the central devil. Not the physical elimination of commodities but the suppression of the crime towards the avaricious accumulation and monopolistic possession of things, that may be and are needed by others would bring the millennium".[11]

In his characteristic manner Gandhiji suggested non-possession or poverty. "Our ignorance or negligence of the Divine Law, which gives to man from day to day his daily bread and no more, has given rise to inequalities with all the miseries attendant from them. The rich have a superfluous store of things, which they do not need and which are therefore neglected and wasted, while millions are starved to death for want of sustenance. If each retained possession only of what he needed, no one would be in want and all would live in contentment. As it is, the rich are discontented no less than the poor. The poor man would then become a millionaire and the millionaire a multi-millionaire. The rich should take the initiative in dispossession with a view to universal diffusion of the spirit of contentment. If only they keep their own property within moderate limits, the starving will be easily fed, and will learn the lesson of contentment along with the rich".[12] Such an ideal can be practised in society only when it is realized that the modern economic notion of indefinite multiplicity of wants is not a socially desirable objective. Unless the concept of standard of living is subordinated to standard of life, the society cannot expect good out of it. "Civilization, in the real sense of the term, consists not in the multiplication, but in the deliberate and voluntary reduction of wants. This alone promotes real happiness and contentment, and increases capacity for service".[13]

It may, however, also be pointed out that this emphasis on the multiplication of wants leads to a large number of social and psychic evils. Individuals are always hankering after more and more and aspire for higher and still higher standards of material comforts. In other words, we bring about a social set up which is highly competitive and in which each individual envies the gains of another. This creates mass frustration resulting in a large number of suicides, mental derangements, crimes, neurosis etc. That such a socio-economic order is intensely undesirable need not be questioned. "We are unhappy, we degenerate morally and mentally. The groups and nations in which industrial civilisation has attained its highest development are precisely those which are becoming weaker and whose return to barbarism is the most rapid. But they do not realize it. They are without protection against the hostile surroundings that science has built about them. In truth our civilisation has created certain conditions of existence which, for reasons still obscure, renders life itself impossible. The anxieties and the woes of the inhabitants of the modern city arise from their political, economic and social institutions, but above all from their own weakness. We are the victims of the backwardness of the sciences of life over those of matter".[14] Where will this acquisitive spirit lead us to? What will be the socio-economic order in which wants keep on multiplying? Under conditions of industrial progress, when we are continually manufacturing new and previously unwanted sources of pleasure, so that the old luxuries become new necessities alike for those who can afford and for those who cannot, we will require a continually increasing amount of income in order to produce the same degree of material welfare. This must obviously lead to industrialisation, growth of large factories, mechanization and rationalization. Under such an arrangement the classes will ride on the back of the masses. Individual freedom will be demanded and guaranteed by the state. But "What is claimed as individual freedom is, more often than not, a sanction for social or economic injustice, or for a life of exploitation".[15] This will obviously mean more and more centralisation. Centralised big industries organised on a capitalist basis, produces injustice, exploitation, imperialism and war. In this process true democracy is destroyed and international peace endangered. To prevent exploitation and injustices the State must interfere. State intervention must keep on increasing progressively till we reach the ideal of industries being organised and owned by the state. Centralised big industries communistically organised leads in effect to state capitalism, which cannot function without the expert, the bureaucrat and ultimately the dictator. This tendency is noti-ceable in every country be it a communistic country like former Russia or a democratic country like U.S.A. The difference is only one of degree, which too is being diminished as mechanization is becoming intense and widespread. Every technological deve-lopment encourages concentration of economic power and financial control over the production and distribution of goods and services.

The first casuality in such an atmosphere is individual liberty and democratic principles. Democracy does not mean simply political democracy or adult franchise. "It is a mistake to think of democracy in this way and to speak as though there were two forms of 'democracy'. 'Economic democracy' means economic equality—or at least equality of economic opportunity. 'Political democracy' merely signifies the machinery or constitutional forms through which democracy may be put into effect within the political sphere. But democracy as an ideal is a form of society, an association of free men in which the free development of each is the condition of free development of all. So far all that can be said to have been achieved in the 'Western democracy' is the political machinery of democracy. To regard democracy as nothing more than a 'political form of government' is to miss what matters most".[16]

Similarly a democratic set up should not be confused with material welfare. Material welfare, if it leads to deterioration of non-economic qualities of man, will be positively undemocratic. "Democracy is a vision of good living, it is not an easy ideal; it requires sacrifice to achieve and to maintain it. It would not be worth attaining unless it meant not only material welfare but also the developing of the characteristics of the human spirit".[17] It means that a democratic form of society can subsist and progress only when qualities like self-restraint, cooperative spirit, tolerance, consideration for others, and the like are nurtured and encouraged. Unless this is done a democratic society cannot last. "The democratic ideal does not confine a man within the limits of his own narrowly conceived self-interest; it widens his interest to include all men, so far as this is possible to the limited intellectuals group and groping imagination of a finite human being".[18] Gandhiji defined democracy as "the art and science of mobilizing the entire physical, economic and spiritual resources of all the various sections of the people in the service of the common good of all".[19]

Therefore, unless we can shorten the size of the world to be intelligible to a common man we will certainly be encouraging undemocratic developments. It appears that science and technology has widened the world for an average man without at the same time trying to increase his understanding and correct comprehension. "Human beings have not grown so rapidly as the institutions spring from their brains. It is chiefly the intellectual and moral deficiencies of the political leaders and their ignorance which endanger modern nations".[19]

Such a socio-economic order must necessarily be based on exploitation and violence. The term violence is of far-reaching connotation and does not imply simply physical violence. It means all efforts and endeavours on the part of a few which prevent fullest possible development of other fellow beings. Democracy and violence go ill together. The remedy lies in basing society on non-violence. Units of administration should be shortened and active cooperation of every individual should be sought and encouraged. The machinery must be such "as will enable every man to have his needs considered and to contribute to the working of this machinery according to his ability. No one must be slave neither to another nor subject to the arbitrary will of any of his fellow—whether he leads or be led. We must create such an economic order as to allow to every man the satisfaction of his primary needs and to permit the development of himself as an individual".

If such be the ideal, it should be seriously considered whether it is not desirable to bring in Gandhiji's idea of society in which needs would be limited. Without this limitation exploitation cannot be ended. If exploitation cannot be ended, it means violence cannot be ended. Therefore, we should aspire for the creation of society in which the principal factor would not be the multiplication of wants or the means of supplying these wants in the quicker manner possible but a society which would ensure to all which is necessary and at the same time not create conditions which cannot but end in competition, and ultimately in violence. Because if wants are simplified and machines are made available to all with a view to lighten their burden we can create a socio-economic order in which we can show to the people how they can realize their freedom through their own effort and by dint of cooperation amongst themselves. Thus we can create a basis for discipline and organisation that rests not upon force but upon its opposite. It will give the masses a sense of cohesion and enable them to resist aggression and exploitation by the power of non-violence.

It may then be argued that if we adopt this approach (of limitation of wants) we will be turning back the wheel of progress. Should we abandon the fruits of scientific knowledge and advancement which has enabled us to control nature and go back to ancient society in which life will become static? We should not readily accept all such notions without deeper thought. "In every age the men who want us under their thumb, if they have any sense, will put forward the particular pretension which the hopes and fears of the age render most potent. They 'cash in'. It has been magic; it has been Christianity. Now it will certainly be science".[20] To argue that the abandonment of material welfare must necessarily lead to stagnation or static society like the one that existed in ancient times need not necessarily be correct. "In this age of vast material progress, too many of us are prone to limit our definition of civilization by the very prejudices born of our own particular type of culture... to regard civilization in terms of our mechanistic achievements, and to look down pityingly from the altitude of our progress to the backwardness of other times and people".[21] Opinions as to what is static or dynamic may be considerably divergent. As regards life in ancient India, Professor K.T. Shah observes: "Another similar misapprehension about life in ancient India is the general belief that society here was and has remained perhaps static, and not dynamic as modern Western communities are claimed to be. In other words, while India has been standstill, Western countries, their economy and culture have been progressive. This involves, in the first place, a question as to what is meant by the two contrasted terms? How is progress or dynamism to be measured? Our ideas on the subject cannot be, and have not remained, stationary. Nor have the norms, the indices by which such phenomena could be measured, remained unchanged. What therefore could be justly taken as index and a measure of change, growth and development or progress in one country, or in one age cannot be accepted and adopted in another". Further, he remarks: "Progress cannot be measured always by mundane or material standards; and the contrast therefore, between a static and a dynamic socio-economic system must not be judged by the outward symbols most commonly in use in the industrialized communities of today".[22]

A welfare state cannot step in to check the present day tendencies effectively. Any increase in the power of the state will worsen matters. Individual freedom is likely to be devoured. The universal experience is that where there is increasing dependence on the state, its inevitable result is that "the people become a herd of sheep, always relying on a shepherd to drive them on to good pastures; the shepherd's staff soon becomes a rod of iron, and the shepherds turn into wolves". To quote Gandhiji, "I look upon an increase of the power of the state with the greatest fear, because although apparently doing good by minimizing exploitation it does the greatest harm to mankind by destroying individuality which lies at the root of all progress".[23] Gandhiji assessed progress "not in terms of kilowatts of power or millions of tons of steel or even millions of bushels of wheat, but in terms of self-confidence and habits of industry, self-help and spontaneous cooperation that people developed and which constitute the foundation of the democracy".[24] The people should be shown 'how to face the handicaps of life through their own collective effort instead of its being effortlessly helped to live any how". The modern welfare state does not believe in it. "The modern state exists not to protect our rights but to do us good or make us good anyway, to do something to us or to make us something.......We are less their subjects than their wards, pupils or domestic animals. There is nothing left of which we can say to them 'mind your own business'. Our whole lives are their business".[25] This will make those who run the governments to become more powerful. Actual government is and always must be oligarchical. "All that can really happen is that some men will take charge of the destiny of others. They will be simply men; none perfect; some greedy, cruel and dishonest. The most completely we are planned, the more powerful they will be. Have we discovered some reason why this time, power should not corrupt as it has done before?"[26]

Gandhiji desired and worked to rehabilitate the individual. Man should be measure of all. On the contrary he is a stranger in the world that he has created. "By moralizing politics and group life on the basis of truth, non-violence and scrupulous regard for means, by adopting *Satyagraha* as the method of settling disputes, by his constructive programme based on regional economy and the decentralised industry free from exploitation, by a healthy and vigorous local self-government through village panchayats and above all by an integrated life of the individual and the community engaged in fruitful work Gandhiji proposed to co-ordinate and synthesise moral, social, economic and political life, establish effective democracy and work for world peace. To sum up then, Gandhiji wants to solve the problems of political conflict and economic inequality and over-centralisation in industry and administration and establish his social order where personal liberty and initiative will be made consistent with authority and the general good, by a strict adherence in collective and group life, as in individual life, to the basic principles of society, truth and non-violence and the purity of means".[27]

This is the time when our plans are going wrong that we should seriously think about the very basis of our planning. There is awful lack of public cooperation and enthusiasm. We owe it to the people, to the masses and under-privileged to be very frank and sincere in our outlook and approach. This is the time when we must gird up our loins. In the words of Jai Prakash Narain, "the auspice time is being lost. Tomorrow it may be too late".

References

1. Pyare Lal: The Last Phase, Vol. II, p. 644.
2. R.R. Diwakar: Gandhi Marg, May-April 1958.
3. K.T. Shah: Ancient Foundations of Economics in India, p. 29.
4. Mathurs, J.S., A.S. (Ed.) Economic Thought of Mahatma Gandhi, pp. 529-3.
5. K.T. Shah: Ancient Foundations of Economics in India, p. 3.
6. *Ibid.*
7. Gandhian Outlook and Technique, p. 333.
8. From Yarvada Mandir
9. Harijan, 1946, p. 63.
10. Constructive Programme, p. 18.
11. V.P. Verma, Gandhi Marg, July 1958, p. 234.
12. From Yarvada Mandir.
13. *Ibid.*
14. Alexis Carrel: Man: The Unknown, p. 33.
15. Gandhian Outlook and Technique, p. 371.
16. Susan Stebbing: Ideals and Illusions, pp. 153-54.
17. *Ibid.*, p. 129.

18. Pyare Lal: The Last Phase, vol. II, p. 657.
19. Man, the Unknown, p. 33.
20. C.W. Lewis: "Is Progress Possible?" The Hindustan Times, Aug. 3, 1958.
21. Quoted by Ethel Monism in "What is Civilization", Gandhi Marg, October 1958, p. 359.
22. Ancient Foundations of Economics in India, p. 464.
23. Young India, 1924.
24. Pyare Lal, "Gandhiji and Planning", The Hindustan Times, October 31, 1958.
25. C.W. Lewis: 'Is Progress Possible?', The Hindustan Times, August 2, 1958.
26. *Ibid*
27. Kripalani in Gandhian Outlook and Technique, p. 364.

7

Some Aspects of Gandhian Economic Order

India is on the threshhold of great economic development; but before deciding the economic order that must prevail in this country we should be quite clear about the end in view and herein we should keep in mind the special cultural and socio-logical factors prevailing in this land of ours. We must keep in mind that economic values can no longer be divorced from human and cultural values of life. In the traditional archives of knowledge, religion, sociology and economics have all been reserved their separate and exclusive spheres. Man has been divided into several watertight compartments. The left hand is not to know what the right does. But nature does not recognize such divisions. She deals with life as a whole. And any economic order must take man, as he is, a complex being actuated by hopes, ideals and aspirations and not merely dominated by economic motives. Any economic order, which aims to be adequate, permanent and abiding must secure above all human well-being and not cheapness or mere abundance of material goods. However, it must also be borne in mind that the economic order does not bring about excessive regimentation of the masses by divesting them of their legitimate liberty in social, economic and political life. We must plan for democracy and not for totalitarianism—not for increasing the coercive power of the authority. Besides, our economic order must also guarantee to every citizen the right to earn his livelihood and not mere doles and unemployment reliefs. Everyone must have a right to gainful employment and then alone we can truly enjoy freedom and democracy. "Real democracy and real enjoyment of reasonable amount of freedom", writes Professor Cole, "are impracticable without the removal of insecurity by the achievement of conditions of full employment". These then must be the objectives before us.

Simplification of wants: One of the fundamentals of Gandhian economics is simplification of wants and way of living. It does not, however, mean that Gandhiji is in any way advocating that the material wants be unnecessarily reduced. His conception is that material wants should not become an end in themselves. They are good as long as they can, in any way, help in increasing human welfare; but they are to be discarded if they in any way add unnecessarily to the drudgery of human life. He was perfectly aware that the complexities created by the use of money and machine may contain more dangers for the poor and uneducated masses of mankind than for those who are more privileged and it is about these millions that he was most concerned. "I do not believe", he observed, "that multiplication of wants and machinery contributed to supply them is taking the world a single step nearer its goal". If by a higher standard of living is meant increasing the multiplicity of wants, has this, as is often claimed, brought about happiness or freedom from drudgery to the masses? On the other hand, for them the drudgery of life has considerably increased. Maximisation of satisfaction can be brought about only by limitation of wants. The lesser the number of unsatisfied wants the lesser pain we have and the maximum of happiness as a result thereof. This aspect is only of academic interest for us, for whatever the approach of modern economists may be on this problem, we cannot afford to have a complex standard of living for millions of people of this country. We will be forced, if not by will then by force of circumstances, to have a simple standard of living at least for decades to come.

Human Values : The modern economist may not agree with all this for he has forgotten the end in view; but is sticking only to the means as end in itself. Money which began simply as a medium of exchange has now itself become the most coveted commodity and the world groans under its tyrannical reign. Generally economics has been considered too mundane to have any moral values. Scholars have attempted to deal with it in an abstract scientific way with the result that economic theory has gone to seed in mathematical formula, rather than being presented as a fascinating psychological study of human nature. But for Gandhiji this is a false conception of economics. "I must confess", he writes, "that I do not draw a sharp or any distinction between economics and ethics. Economics that hurts the moral well being of an individual or a nation is immoral and therefore sinful". It is no use saying that under socialism this will not happen, as then we will have to keep non-economic ends in view. "If socialism ever comes", writes Bertrand Russel, "it is only likely to prove beneficial if non-economic goods are valued and consciously pursued". For Gandhiji too progress is not identified with increased complexity of material wants. To him a progressive economic system should lead to greater simplicity through fuller life.

Non-violent and Democratic Society : The creation of a non-violent and democratic society is another foundation on which will be built the structure of Gandhian economic order. There will be no room for exploitation in any form. We may be inclined to mock away this idea as mere sentimentalism, but Prof. Laski and others too support the idea of a non-violent society. Even the Atlantic Charter is forced to concede that "all the nations of the world, for realistic as well as spiritual reasons, must come to the abandonment of the use of force". Gandhiji's non-violent and democratic society cannot be dismissed as a futile sentiment.

Dignity of Labour : Dignity of labour is very fundamental to Gandhiji's economic order. Like Prince Kropotkin, Gandhiji also thinks that 'with us work is hobby, and idleness an artificial growth' and he therefore regards the cry for more leisure as dangerous and unnatural. Leisure is good and necessary upto a point only. "Under my system", he once wrote, "it is labour which is the current coin, not metal. Any person who can use his labour has that coin, has wealth". Even the most die hard follower of Marx will not go to this extent of making labour the measure of value.

Thus on the corner-stone of simplicity, non-violence, dignity and sanctity of labour and human values, he builds his ideal economy.

Growth of a controlling oligarchy : Gandhiji was quite alive to the problems that the centralised form of production may create for the masses who may simply become slaves of those who guide and control. "These villages cannot retain the freedom that they have enjoyed from times immemorial if they do not control production of prime necessaries of life" was his firm opinion. Dr. Gyan Chand is also aware of this inherent weakness in centralised from of production. He writes, "The dangers of economic and political despotism inherent in a system of centralised control of the entire system of production have to be admitted. It is bad enough to have to be subservient to an employer for one's living but subservience imposed by the state which controls every avenue of employment in infinitely worse". "Any centralised form of Government", writes Prof. Ginsberg, "is bound to be oligarchical in tendency. We are told that the State will wither away....But in that case there is certain to arise a new dominant minority". Any policy of reconstruction that is to be of real value must aim at decentralisation; socialization or socialism is no solution of the problem. "The vast concentrations of economic power are political menace, however efficient they may be in their economic conduct". "Organisation is a position to wield such power, whatever their present motives or the current ideals of those responsible for their policy, present democracy with its greatest problem". Even in Russia, the concentration of all economic and political power is in the hands of a well-knit compact oligarchy.

Degeneration of masses : All centralised forms of production will in time lead to the degeneration of the producing masses as no initiative is left with them, their function being one of merely carrying out higher orders. The work requires little intelligence in the worker. It by itself is incapable of educating him. Education and knowledge have to be superimposed on him as something external. This in itself is an admission that work under large-scale production is incapable of developing the intelligence of the worker. There is no joy in modern labour and hence this clamour for seeking leisure and outward pleasure. But millions cannot keep themselves fit by games and athletics. They are all right today for a change and recreation. They will jar upon us when they become a necessary occupation in order that we may have the appetite for eating food in the production of which we had no hand or part. In all centralised systems of production the worker becomes a mere hand where the faculties of head and heart are hardly exercised. In such economic organisations culture has to be acquired from outside work—psychologically an altogether artificial way of introducing culture into those who have been deprived of it through natural channel of works.

Absence of Human values : Both under capitalism and communism human values are not fully taken into account, man being looked as gun fodder under capitalism and a cogwheel under communism. Both have failed to deliver the goods as they were taken to extremes. We are to have a mixture of both. For the advance of each individual it is necessary to allow a certain amount of self-interest; and decentralised system of production ensures it without in any way harming the social good. While group activity has a contribution to make within a limited community, it is open to serious doubt whether such activity is possible on a national scale for any length of time.

If the above defects are to be rectified and work be made a means of developing one's personality in all its three aspects of intelligence, character and artistic sense, then it is obvious that work cannot be planned and dictated from the centre but must be decentralised. We have to discontinue the use of such aid to production that leads to concentration of power and substitutes these by such tools as will loosen drudgery without concentrating power. "If we would save men from being degraded into a beast or an automation we have to face this situation where work will cease to be a means of concentrating wealth and power but will become a means of distributing these".

Problems of Distribution : Centralised methods of production have given rise to the varied problems because of the round-about way of distributing income through a host of middlemen who should be and who can be easily dispensed with to promote healthy cooperation between consumption and production. Today the producer is so far away from the consumer that there are inevitable periods of glut or scarcity and price variations. The object being the ultimate consumer, it has been suggested that instead of discarding centralised production could be equalized, would not mass production be freed of its evils? But Gandhiji's reply is that the evil is inherent in the system. "Distribution can be equalized only when production is equalized, in other words when distribution is simultaneous with production. Distribution will never be equal as long as you want to tap distant markets to dispose of your goods". Most of the present day economic evils will go 'if production and consumption become localized as the temptation to speed up production at any price disappears'. Mass production cannot raise the standard of living of the masses as is being claimed. "I do not believe in it at all", said he; "Without simultaneous distribution on an equally mass scale the production can result only in a great world tragedy". "You cannot distribute wealth" observed C. Rajgopalachari, "after producing it you won't succeed in getting men to agree to it. But you can so produce wealth as to secure equitable distribution before producing it". This then is the *Khadi* and village industries movement.

Subjection to a dominant minority : Centralised systems of mass production have not been able to free masses from the oppressive subjection to a dominant minority, even though the system be wholly run on socialistic lines. Even in Russia, a complete socialist state, with all its professions of human welfare, and advancement of the individual, the masses were not free to control and regulate the system of production. With increasing technological development—and it is bound to come in a system of production, which cares more for price and material needs than for ultimate consumption and development of human personality—the vast majority of workers have become unskilled and incapable of running industries requiring specialized skill. These causes were responsible for not bringing about a socialist state in Russia.

Mere abolition of property rights cannot bring about a classless society. Production is a social process and not that of an individual and in all complex societies there is a particular and relatively small group of men that controls the chief instruments of production. "Within the process of production, the gap estimated both in the amount of skill and training and of difference in types of function, between the average worker and those who are incharge on the technical side of the process of production, is far greater today than in the past" and this enables this minority to dominate and deprive the masses of the 'surplus value' the thing most disliked by Marx.

Unemployment : And again, centralised system of production have not been able to solve the problem of unemployment. The number of unemployed persons has been increasing even in highly industrialized countries of the West. The problem before Marx was of greater production and he therefore blessed the centralised methods of production. But today the problem is of giving employment. It is said that persons thrown out of employment by mass production can find alternative employment in the long run—a time, which we never hope to see. In an organised country where there are only fixed and limited avenues of employment, where the worker has become highly skilled in the use of one particular kind of machinery, this is hardly possible. This has made labour immobile for the short period—a period that alone counts much for the masses. America, Britain and other industrially advanced countries of the world have not been able to solve this problem. Even the socialist state of Russia has not been able to absorb her annual growing population in industries and they are being forced on the land. Unemployment insurance and other measures are only a means of bypassing their fundamental defect and not a remedy for the same.

Decentralisation : Gandhiji was far-sighted enough to visulise the gravity of all these problems and raised his voice against centralisation and for decentralisation. He alone is not for complete decentralisation. Henry Ford, the great American industrialist, also favours this idea. He said, "To carry a product 500 miles to the consumer if that product can be found within 2 miles is a crime". Wherever it is possible, a policy of decentralisation ought to be adopted. Wherever it is possible the section that produces the raw material ought to produce also the finished product. Our communities ought to be more complete in themselves. They ought not to be unnecessarily dependent on railway transport. Out of what they produce they should supply their own needs ship the surplus. And how can they do this, unless they have the means of taking their raw materials and changing them into finished products. If private enterprise cannot do this a group of farmers can do so. The chief injustice sustained by the farmer today is that being the greatest producer, he is prevented from being also the greatest merchandiser, because he is compelled to sell to those who put his products into merchantable form. If he could change his raw material into finished product, not only he would receive fuller benefits of his product, but he would render his nearby communities more independent of railway exigencies (or central authority). The thing is not only reasonable, and practicable but it is becoming absolutely necessary. "It will be an essential part of planning for full employment", observes Professor Cole, "to diversify industries in each area so as to provide a wide range of alternative jobs".

If it can be true of America, it is hundred times more so for India where about 80% of her population resides in villages scattered throughout the length and breadth of the country. Gandhiji's decentralisation takes the form of village communism because of the peculiar features prevailing here. Not only he but eminent economists like Prof. Colia Clark, Prof. Cole and others support this view. "The villages", writes Cole, "with its super abundant supply of labour and its very low level of productivity, needs a more balanced economy, such as it can get only by developing industrial production in the village itself and not far away in mills of Bombay and Calcutta". Gandhiji too is of this opinion. He writes, "This cry of 'back to the villages' some critics say is putting back the hands of clock of progress. But is it really so? Is it going back to the villages or rendering back to it what really belongs to it? Is there any single raw material that the city dwellers can obtain except from the villager? If they cannot why not teach him to work on it himself, as he used to do before and as he would do now but for our explicating inroads".

"I do not know if a vast country like India with her millions of people having four months of forced idleness on their hand can afford to have large-scale industries, and yet live a life of tolerable comfort. Large-scale centralised industries in India, except such industries as cannot be possibly carried on in villages, must mean stagnation of millions, unless honourable employment is found for displaced millions". His economic order envisages some industries to be run on centralised large-scale basis. He is not after wholesale revival of all cottage industries. "I should examine each one of them, find out their place in the economy of village life and if I see that they must be encouraged because of inherent merit, I should do so". Large-scale, high speed machinery is adapted to and can be efficient and profitable only with a large and therefore distant market; divorcing the consumer from the producer, inevitably results in high costs of production, mutual ignorance, unbalance gluts, unemployment and often uneconomic and political mistakes of a serious nature. Village production and distribution automatically correlates the amount and kind of production to consumption and keeps them in balance, and for small decentralised markets hand-operated machines may be just as efficient by both engineering and price criteria. "And when broader social and psychological factors are considered the slower implements are probably better and more conductive to a sound and permanent civilization".

"Any increase in large-scale production is not likely to absorb even the annual increase in the working population by the growth of numbers. The balance cannot be restored except by developing a large number of small-scale and medium scale industries. Such economic reconstruction cannot mean a mere copy of Western industrialisation. It means the installation of a new economic order in which we have variegated production through units considered perhaps too small in the industrially advanced countries, but which will be nearer optimum size in our country in view of the relative abundance of labour and scarcity of capital. Moreover, such a reconstruction would involve a planning of the geographical distribution of industries so that they go to the village and small town rather than get concentrated in few cities".

Decentralised system of production, besides providing gainful employment to those who are unemployed, solving the problem of distribution and consumption by correlating all the three, also increases the mobility of labour. The training and education needed to learn simple arts and crafts is not so specialized as to take too much time of an individual. He can learn new crafts within months, if not weeks, and this considerably increases not only the mobility of labour but also its bargaining capacity. Besides, decentralised small-scale methods of production are also socially and psychologically justifiable and good. Such work not only removes economic distress but is also of such a nature as to relieve the adverse mental and moral effects of unemployment. The usual arguments advanced against a decentralised form of production is that it will unnecessarily raise the prices of many products as cottage industries cannot fully utilize the byproducts. This can be done in decentralised units as well, as is being done at Nalwadi at the tannery of Shri Satish Chandra Das Gupta. The remedy lies not in abandoning cottage units but in bringing light of science to cottage workers. This is where we have failed and we need scientists to adapt their knowledge to the simplicity of cottage resources. Difference in price of khaddar and mill cloth would be found illusory if full account were given to the national costs of unemployment, disruption of normal village life and impairment of the former sound balance between manufacture and agriculture. The individual purchaser of cloth does not feel these intangible costs, but they, nevertheless, oppress him. Many of the costs of Western industrialism are disguised, but show up partly in the high cost of living and high taxes. And, again, whether high prices are good or not will depend on the cost constituents that make up the price. If the price is made up largely of costs of materials, low prices are good; but if such prices are made up of human labour represented by wages, then high prices will represent a better tendency to distribute wealth. Therefore, under an economy of cottage units, where labour largely enters into composition of price, high prices are good.

Decentralised methods are also opposed on the grounds that they will considerably weaken the defence position of the country. Nothing is far from the truth than this statement. Today centralised forms of production are more amenable to air raids, which are likely to shatter the whole economy. Disruption from inside by enemy agents is also possible if production is centralised. Decentralised methods remove both these fears and will considerably increase the defence potentialities of the country. Besides, we can have centralised methods of production for goods that cannot be conveniently produced on a small scale.

Decentralisation, as has already been mentioned, takes the form of village communism in the form of development of self-sufficient village communities. "Under this scheme the unit for which production will be restricted will be a village or group of villages which will be a corporate whole and aim to be self-sufficient for its primary requirements". We shall have to see that the villagers become first of all self-contained and then cater for the needs of the city dwellers. In regard to certain articles the unit of self-sufficiency will vary and may be as large an area as a district or province or even a country. There will be no rigidity. As far as possible, whatever is needed in the village will be produced there and especially those commodities the demand for which is highly inelastic. This will also help us in doing away with exploitation, which can be done in the supply of these commodities.

Yet there is another aspect of this policy of decentralisation and I cannot help quoting extensively Dr. Gregg who writes, "The control of large machines gives great power—physical, economic, social and political. Those who advocate rapid industrialisation of India are in effect advising Indians to adopt machinery first and take the chance that the control of it will not slip into the hands of those who are eager to exploit them and use the power for selfish ends. Mr. Gandhi proposed rather to secure a measure of economic independence for each peasant, largely autonomous control of the economic life of each village and the control of industry as well as of politics by the masses through the disciplined use of organised mass non-violent resistance. After such controls are firmly established, well practised and fully understood by all groups in the nation India can then perhaps safely consider the question of extending her use of selected big machinery owned and operated by the village, municipality, provincial and central government. If India wants more machinery and modern industry it will bring greater complexity in her life. If nevertheless she chooses that way she will be wise first to develop popular control of economic resources and processes through disciplined mass Satyagraha. Mr. Gandhi certainly prefers economic simplicity, but his full programme also offers the surest and wisest preparation for complexity, if India prefers that. Until the control which he advocates has been secured, the limitations of machinery seems to be a reasonable plan whose wisdom is as probable as that of any other plan. Economic self-support and self-reliance must go along with moral and political self-support and self-reliance. Soviet Russia established her control before she began to expand her mechanization of production. Although the form and method of industrial and political control by the people as proposed by Mr. Gandhi is different from that of Russia, nevertheless India will be wise enough not only to emphasise the prior importance of establishing control by masses, but also to establish suitable limitations or principles that quantitative relationship (of science, mechanization or money) shall not grow so powerful as to starve the qualitative aspects and relationships of civilization. The establishment of such limitations would put India in a sounder position than that of Russia, U.S.A. or other industrialized countries. The realization of the superior importance of qualitative relationships must find concrete expression in methods of work and the organisation of daily economic life of the people. And that is one of the values of Khaddar programme."

Place of machinery : One of the charges levied against Gandhiji is that he is opposed to all modern machinery and that he gives no place to machinery as such. This is wrong—machinery has a place in his economic order. He is not opposed to machinery for the sake of opposition. "I have no partiality for return to the primitive methods of production. I suggest that return, because there is no other way of giving employment to the millions of villagers who are living in idleness". What he objected to was the craze of machinery, not machinery as such. "The craze is for what they call labour-saving machinery.

Men go on 'saving labour' till thousands are without work and thrown on the open streets to die of starvation. I want to save time and labour not for a fraction of mankind, but for all. I want the concentration of wealth not in the hands of the few, but in the hands of all". Today machinery merely helps a few to ride on the backs of the millions. The impetus behind this all is not philanthropy but greed. Gandhiji's opposition to machinery is because it leads to centralisation and its attendant evils. The problem with us is not how to find leisure for the teeming millions inhabiting our villages. The problem is how to utilize their idle hours, which equal to the working days of six months in a year. Strange as it may appear, every mill generally is a menance to the villagers. "I have not quite worked out the figures" explains Gandhiji, "but I am quite safe in saying that every mill hand does the work of at least ten labourers doing the same work in their villages at the expense of the fellow villagers. It is no answer to say that they turn out cheaper better cloth, if they do so at all. For if they have displaced thousands of workers, the cheapest mill-cloth is dearer than the dearest Khadi woven in the villages". "I hold that machinery method is harmful when the same thing can be done easily by millions of hands not otherwise occupied". The individual must be the one supreme consideration and the object of machinery should be the saving of labour of individual "and for that matter any machinery which does not deprive masses or men of the opportunity to labour, but which helps the individual and adds to his efficiency and which a man can handle without being its slave," should be encouraged. "My machinery must be of the most elementary type which I can put in the homes of the millions". He can have no consideration for machinery which is meant either to enrich the few at the expense of the many or without cause to displace the useful labour of many. In his system mass production of vital necessities will disappear and along with it exploitation to a very great extent. "The movement of the spinning wheel is an organised attempt to displace machinery from that state of exclusiveness and exploitation and to place it in its proper state". Labour should be the means of distributing wealth and therefore there should be as large number of producers as possible and the means of production should be within easy reach of all. We, therefore, need not have large machines of the western type but simple machines, which may increase efficiency of the individual and remove his drudgery.

Place of centralised and heavy industries : Not only this but in the village movement there is definite place for centralised industries; not for their own sake but as adjuncts and subsidiaries to decentralised units of key industries, whereby is meant those industries which provide the machinery, fuel and raw materials for small industries (dewing machine and plant to manufacture it), public utility industries (railways, telephone) which require centralised manufacturing and control will be carried on a large scale. "The heavy machinery for work of public utility which cannot be undertaken by human labour has its inevitable place; but all that would be owned by the State and used entirely for the benefit of the people" was his considered opinion. We can better appreciate this view when he says, "If we could have electricity in every village home, I should not mind villagers plying their implements and tools with the help of electricity. But then the village communities or State should own power houses". Many such industries will have to be run on a centralised basis. But he is socialist enough to say that such factories should be nationalized or State controlled. "They ought only to be working under the most attractive and ideal conditions, not for profit but for benefit of humanity, love taking the place of greed as motive. This mad rush for wealth must cease and the labourer must be assured not only a living wage, but a daily task that is not a mere drudgery".

Trade and Isolation : This process of decentralisation need not mean economic or other kinds of isolation or barriers. Rather, by lessening exploitation, it will tend to promote mutual trust and respect. There can be no truly sound economic interna-tionalism until there is mutual economic respect between the nations founded on economic strength and a certain economic self-reliance in each nation and a full recognition thereof by other nations. For any one to fear that economic self-reliance in the prime essentials of life will result in isolation seems to be based on a assumption that there is only limited amount of materials, products, ideas and ideals which can be shared. This is not true of either individuals or nations. If international trade in bare necessities is reduced to the minimum, most of our international economic problems will go. When we speak of decentralizing production we do not imply that all relations with the outside world will be broken.

The Ideal of Swadeshi : The duty to purchase goods produced by one's immediate neighbours, does not imply that there will be no trade. Village or groups of villages will be free to exchange goods and products that are surplus in one area with the surplus of that of another area. Trade in respect of prime necessities will be avoided as far as possible. Similarly, international trade should only be confined to such articles as cannot be consumed in a country. "I have never been an advocate of prohibition of all things because they are foreign. My economic creed is a complete taboo in respect of all foreign commodities whose importation is likely to prove harmful to our indigenous interests. This means that we may not, in any circumstances, import a commodity that can be adequately supplied from our own country". When markets are wide it is not possible to ensure free and adequate return to the producers. As long as the producer has no hold in international market and is not well enough to understand their working, it will be suicidal to go beyond our land.

Place of Money : Money occupies a very inferior position partly because trade is limited to few surplus articles of one area and partly because of human standards attached to every transaction. The ultimate object of all economic activity is the actual completed supply of food, clothing and other needs of mankind to the ultimate consumers. In estimating the relative efficiency of two different forms of production our units of measurement must be somehow correlated or corrected by considerations of ultimate object. Otherwise our results will not be valid in the realm of economics though perhaps quite satisfactory otherwise and therefore money values should go. Money symbols are useless as money fluctuates so often. They are harmful because people take to them as being the important thing and forget the reality behind. Money is subject to so much manipulation and control that it is an insufficient gauge of economic activities. In a society where the standard of living of people is near the subsistence level and their purchasing power spent mostly on food and other necessaries, the introduction of money will divert the purchasing power into luxuries to some extent and thus lower the true wealth computed in terms of human values.

To avoid pitfalls we have to correlate the perishability of consumable goods with the medium of exchange if we are to place both consumers and producers on equal footing and encourage consumption. Therefore under Gandhiji's economic system, 'it is labour which is current coin and not metal. Any person who can use his labour has that coin, has wealth'. He converts it in what he needs. If he wants something which he cannot produce, he uses the surplus product of his labour for exchange. "It is exchange of labour on free, fair and equal terms and hence it is no robbery. You may object it as reversion of the primitive system of barter. But is not all international trade based on the barter system"? No socialist has gone to this extent. Money economy has widened the gulf between the producer and consumer. The basic principle of barter is to reduce the chain of exchange and we can effectively reduce this chain by supporting local industries. Money economy has carried us beyond our depths and extended the market beyond our control. Barter provides a ready means of restraining any tendency to run amuck.

The individual and the economic order : All the philosophies and "isms" that lose sight of the individual are fundamentally fascist and totalitarian. Any creed that tends to obscure the individual is an enemy of democracy and as such inescapably fascist in effect. The individual must be freed from the mass, must be salvaged from the mass, must be protected and nursed as such. The individual is the foundational unit of social democracy and so his needs and his position must form the inspiration of legislation, the basis of social policy. It is not a question of deification of the individual as opposed to deification of the mass but placing of the individual where he belongs, in his rightful niche as the corner-stone of democracy.

Keeping this in view we must seek to formulate the principles on which we may build our economic order. What-ever this order may or may not secure for us, it must not be said of it that it cannot lead to human well-being or the development of even the humblest. At the same time that it leads to the development of an individual, it must lead also to the development of his neighbours. The individual losing himself for the good of the group to discover that thus he has found himself and the group seeking the good of even the least of its members and only in this finding is the justification of its existence.

Conclusion : If we want to preserve individual liberty as something sacred, it would appear, then, that the only way is to decentralise production and let each man stand on his own legs so far as that is possible. Democracy and government by the people to be genuine requires to have its roots in the economic order; you cannot have a centralised economic order, where naturally power and control are vested in the centre and not in the people, and try to get over its evil effects by superimposing on it the outward forms of democracy. Genuine rule by the people can take place only when the economic order is such that, as far as possible, each man is master of his own enterprise, for then he will be his own ruler at least for most things. Unless the economic order is such as to make self-governing individuals a possibility, self-government will be but an empty show. If men cannot be trusted with freedom and self government in their daily work, all talk of conferring freedom and self-government on them in large spheres of the nation is nothing but moonshine.

If this is also the ideal of the socialists then decentralised economic order, which in India means growth of village commu-nities, is nothing but socialism — socialism decentralised and freed from violence — for only thus it would seem the socialist ideal of each for all and all for each can really be attained and made realizable through decentralisation and non-violence. And then alone we can make democracy a reality — an order where government is not only of the people, for the people but also by the people.

8

Cottage Industries: Need for Clear Perspective

The question of place of cottage industries in our economic set up has been debated since long. Gandhiji gave this problem a new dimension and sense of urgency which was not associated with the discussion of this problem earlier.

Planners' Support

Today no one in our country denies the role of cottage industries. Even the industrialists, while they formulated their plan for economic development of India, remarked, "It is an essential part of our plan for the organisation of industries that adequate scope should be provided for small-scale and other industries. This is important not only as a means of providing employment but also of reducing the need for capital, particularly of external capital in the early stages of the plan. It is difficult to define the considerations on which the choice between large and small-scale and cottage industries should be determined. The factors involved in the choice are numerous and often conflicting. But generally it may be stated that while in basic industries there is little scope for small industrial units, they have an important and useful place in consumption goods industries where their function is in many cases complementary to that of large units". The Planning Commission has also expressed similar opinion: "Village industries have a central place in rural development programmes. The scope for such industries depends in part, on their relation to the corresponding large-scale industry; in part, on the development of agriculture and the growth of rural amenities" (First Plan). Similar sentiments were expressed in subsequent plans.

Accordingly Government policy was to support the development of these industries. With this objective, state policy provided for greater financial help and assistance, setting up a number of All India Boards or Commissions to deal with the problems of different cottage and small industries: acceptance of a stores purchase policy which enjoined that certain classes of stores should be reserved exclusively for purchase from small and village industries and that price differentials should be allowed, and, enforcing a policy of common production programme. Such common production programme visualized: (i) reservation of spheres for large scale and small and village industries, (ii) non-expansion of the capacity of large-scale industries, (iii) imposition of a cess on the products of large industries, (iv) arrangement for the supply of raw material to small and village industries and (v) coordination of research.

Efforts were also to be made to deal with the problems that such industries faced. "If village industries are to be developed, it is necessary to deal with the deficiencies which have led to their decline. These relate to (1) Organisation, (2) State Policy, (3) Finance, (4) Raw Materials, (5) Research, (6) Technical Guidance, (7) Supply of equipment and (8) Marketing" (First Plan).

We are supposed to believe that with the state in the vanguard of the movement of reviving these industries the country has made sufficient progress in this direction. "Village and small industries have made a significant contribution in the First and Second Plans in realizing the objectives of expanded employment, large production and more equitable distribution. With the large dimensions of the tasks to be accomplished in the Third Plan, their role will be even more important" (Third Plan, p. 421).

Decline in Employment and Income

Objective study, however, will not be able to agree with these sentiments. Dr. K. Prasad, in his thesis "Technological Choice of Under Developmental Planning" has given the table concerning employment in organised industries.

The number employed in household industry according to 1961 census is about 11 million. These figures reveal that both in absolute numbers and more so in relative terms the importance of small and village industries is declining.

Similarly, in an agro-industrial study of Sirur Taluka conducted by Samaj Prabodhan Sanstha, Poona, it was discovered that the number of persons engaged in crafts had declined from 13.7 per cent in 1911 to 4.6 per cent in 1961; and those engaged in other non-agricultural occupations accounted for only 6.6 per cent as against 14.3 per cent in 1911. The number of oil presses had declined to 29 in 1961 as against 55 in 1911. There was none to ply the 35 woolen and 110 cotton looms in 1961. The contribution of small enterprises to national income has declined from 10.1 per cent in 1948-49 to 6.5 per cent in 1964-65. There are reasons to believe that employment situation in small and village industries and their relative position in national economy is steadily declining.

The reasons for this sorry state of affairs are to be found in our ignoring the advice of Mahatma Gandhi whose contribution towards the revival of these industries no one can surpass. He had visualized an altogether different role for these industries. This calls for an altogether different approach to the economic and social planning of our country.

No Impact on Economy

This may be no exaggeration to state that the policy of the Planning Commission has been to regard these industries as appendages of largescale industries. "They—the sector of village and small industries—are not to be viewed as a static part of the economy, but rather as a progressive and efficient decentralised sector which is closely integrated on the one hand with agriculture and on the other with large-scale industry" (Second Plan p. 429).

Comparison Between Industry Sectors

(In millions)

Year of census	*Total self-supporting people occupied in industries*	*Total number of workers employed in factories.*	*Difference between 2 and 3 approximately engaged in unorganized industries*
1911	17.5	1.5	16.0
1921	15.7	1.0	14.7
1931	15.3	1.1	14.2
1951	14.4	2.9	11.5

The Village and Small-Scale Industries Committee (Karve Committee) had suggested one of the three principle aims for developing these industries is "to avoid as far as possible, during the period of the Second Plan further technological unemployment such as occurs specially in the traditional village industries" (Second Plan p. 432). The Third Plan, while discussing the role of village and small industries remarks that "the pace of technical change will have to be so regulated that large scale technological unemployment with consequent hardship and misery to millions of people is avoided" (Third Plan p. 426).

These industries have, consequently, failed to have any deep economic and social impact on rural India. It appears that like the traditional puppet shows these industries are supposed to behave at the dictates of large-scale units and the Government as a stop-gap arrangement and as an apology for reducing unemployment. Whatever progress these industries have made or are making is illusory. State support appears to be like an oxygen cylinder for artificial respiration for a patient to enable him to survive a little longer.

Khadi: Decentralisation

Gandhiji defined Swadeshi as "that spirit in us which required us to serve our immediate neighbours before others and to use things produced in our neighbourhood in preference to those more remote. So doing we served humanity to the best of our capacity. We could not serve humanity by neglecting our neighbours. Similarly, with our wants, we were bound to supply them through the agency of our neighbours and therefore, prefer their labour and wares to those of others".[1] His concept of Swadeshi was an industry in which the masses can participate and make their contribution. "The test of Swadeshi is not the universality of the use of an article, which goes under the name of Swadeshi, but the universality of participation in the production or manufacture of such article".[2] This was the basic consideration of Gandhiji's economic ideas. He, therefore, had a different approach to the decentralised economic order. He says, "The science of Khadi requires decentralisation of production and consumption. Consumption should take place as nearly as possible where khadi is produced. We may produce for the demands of the cities, but should never depend upon them as we would depend on the local market. We must first study the local market and supply its wants".[3] Khadi must be taken in its true perspective and we must realize the full implication of this approach. It means a wholesale Swadeshi mentality, a determination to find all the necessaries of life in India and that through the labour and intellect of the villages. That means a reversal of the existing process. That is to say that instead of half a dozen cities, living on the exploitation and ruin of the 7,00,000 villages of India, the latter will be largely self contained and will voluntarily serve the cities of India and even the outside world so far as it benefits both the parties". Thus khadi mentality means decentralisation of the production and distribution of necessaries of life.

Village vs. Cities

It must, however, be mentioned that when we use the term khadi or khadi mentality we include other village industries as well. To quote Gandhiji, "I have often said that khadi is the centre, sun, round which the other village industries revolve like so many planets. They have no independent existence. Nor will khadi exist without other industries. They are absolutely interdependent". While this was the objective for the immediate present Gandhiji had selected two things of the most vital importance—articles of diet and articles of dress and he wanted that villages should become independent of cities in respect of these basic human requirements. "My ideal of village swaraj is that it is a complete republic independent of its neighbours for its own vital wants, and yet interdependent for many others in which dependence is a necessity".[4]

This demands an altogether different approach to the revival of cottage and village industries. "The revival of the village is possible only when it is no more exploited. Industria-lisation on a mass scale will necessarily lead to passive or active exploitation of the villagers as the problems of competition and marketing come in. Therefore, we have to concentrate on the village being self-contained manufacturing mainly for use".[5]

He warned his countrymen that "urbanisation in India is slow but sure death for her villages and villagers, urbanisation can never support ninety per cent of India's population which is living in her villages. And when the village handicrafts disappear, the villagers working only with their cattle on the field, with idleness for six or four months in a year, must be reduced to the level of the beast and be without proper nourishment, either of the mind or the body, and, therefore, without joy and without hope".[6]

Restriction on Centralised Industries

Therefore, he was of the opinion that for the development of cottage and village industries state must prevent the growth of centralised industries. After independence, the question of granting licences for the setting up of new textile mills in Madras came up. He analysed the problem in the following words, "The question has arisen as to whether the Government can admit new mills, and at the same time promote hand spinning on a national scale. My answer is emphatically in the negative, if the encouragements of hand spinning is meant to be sincere".[7] As late as 1946 he observed, "I would not shed a single tear if all the mills, were to close. If mills flourish khadi must die". A few months later, he remarked that if he was the Prime Minister and had to select the members of his Government, the latter would stop all new mills and would expect those already established to sell all their manufactures at controlled rates outside India. He was clear that no industry indigenous or foreign, can be allowed to increase unemployment and thus harm the true interest of the community as whole.

Swaraj Not Without Khadi

He had warned the countrymen that simply to make the masses conscious of their poverty and low standard of living will lead them to demoralization and frustration. "Swaraj for them can only mean ability to support themselves without begging. To awaken in them a feeling of discontent with their lot without providing them means of removing thereof is to court certain destruction, anarchy and outrage in which they themselves will be the chief victims".[8] On another occasion, he remarked, "Give up khaddar and you will find it impossible to lift the masses from economic and moral degradation. The re-enthronement of the spinning wheel in India's sixty million homes gives you the requisite strength to fight the Government, if you are non-violent. I gladly concede that you can fight the government with arms without unity and without the spinning wheel. The result will not be Swaraj; but one plunder giving place to his superior and between the two a greater grinding of the masses".

Unfortunately these warnings were not heeded by those in power in free India. They remained content by simply paying lip tributes to the idea of revival of cottage and village industries. Spinning demonstrations on ceremonial occasion of Gandhiji's birthday while having faith, rather absolute reliance, on large scale industries to solve major economic problems that the masses face cannot lead to proper development of cottage and village industries. All these years we have made efforts to commercialise khadi and other village industries and compete with mill-made goods. In this effort we are not likely to succeed. The so-called development is only window dressing. "In the open market, a more organised industry will always be able to drive out a less organised one, much more so when the former assisted by bounties and can command unlimited capital and can therefore afford to sell its manufactures at a temporary loss. Gandhiji described this inroad by mill sector on the village industries as 'peaceful penetration'. The result would be the same as between hand-made goods and those made by power driven machinery. We are seeing this process going on before our eyes. This displacement of village labour is impoverishing the villagers and enriching the moneyed men. If the process continues sufficiently long, the villages will be destroyed without any further effort. No Chengiz Khan could devise a more ingenious or more profitable method of destroying these villages".[9]

Spirit Behind Rural Industries

Gandhiji therefore wanted to reverse this process. He wanted to downgrade cities and urban way of life. Thus exploitation of the villages could be avoided. The fact is that we have to make a choice between India of the villages that are as ancient as herself and India of the cities which are a creation of foreign domination. Today the cities dominate and drain the villages so that they are crumbling to ruin. My khadi mentality tells me that cities must subserve villages, when that domination goes. Exploitation of villages is itself organised violence. If we want Swaraj to be built on non-violence we will have to give the villages their proper place. He warned his countrymen that "you must realize that it is not cities that make India, but villages and that you cannot reconstruct them unless you revive the village life with their defunct handicrafts. Industrialisation cannot bring life to moribund villages. The peasant in his cottage home can be revived only when he gets back his craft and depends for his necessaries on the village and not on the cities as he is compelled today".

We have an opportunity to implement the vision of Gandhiji in the gramdan villages. Those who believe in the revival of cottage and village industries need make a firm resolve that in these villages they will not permit the import of any product that can be taken up by the villages with a little organisation. Nothing should be allowed to be produced by the cities, which can be equally well produced by the villages with a little support, care and organisation. Social and constructive workers may have to oppose Government policy. When it was pointed out to Gandhiji, that after India attains freedom and gets political power, mill-owners can be a graver danger to villages; he reacted strongly and replied, "If I am still alive then, and if such a catastrophe happens I make bold to say that the mills will be destroyed in the process".

This is the spirit of dedication that is needed to revive cottage and village industries.

It was our misfortune that we lost the Father of Nation when he was needed most. But we, who swear by his name day and night, must keep before us his ideal that "real *Swaraj* depends upon our capacity for solving without reference to, or intervention of, the Government. All the varied and complex problem that must arise in the affairs of one of the biggest and the most ancient nation like ours".

References

1. Mathur J.S. & A.S. (Ed.): Economic Thought of Mahatma Gandhi, p. 5.
2. *Ibid.*, p. 167.
3. *Ibid.*, p. 68.
4. *Ibid.*, p. 323.
5. *Ibid.*, pp. 502-603.
6. *Ibid.*, p. 296.
7. *Ibid.*, p. 248.
8. *Ibid.*, p. 34.
9. *Ibid.*, pp. 169-70.

9

Evolution of Gandian Economic Concepts

"Just as the spirit of Jesus shines all the more against the background of the Treachery of Judas, so the spirit of Mahatma Gandhi shines all the more against the background of the betrayal of his spirit, often by those who named his name", wrote Rev. Stanley Jones, a Christian Missionary. It is a pity that many of us have not clearly understood the philosophy of Mahatma Gandhi while others have paid only a lip service to the ideals for the realization of which he had devoted his entire time and energy. In this brief chapter it is proposed to study the economic ideas of Gandhiji.

Though the object of this brief study is to find out Gandhiji's economic ideals, however, it must be emphasised at the very outset that Gandhiji did not recognize compartmentalisation of human personality. He believed that life was an indivisible whole. The subject of his study was normal man moved by desires, anger and emotion. His economic ideas should, therefore, be studied in the background of his conception of man and society. His economic ideas changed constantly with changes inside the country. And, therefore, a little reflection on the conditions prevailing in the country, when Gandhiji came on the scene, would not be out of place.

The foremost problem before Gandhiji was the revival of national self-confidence. People had lost confidence in themselves and always looked up to others for help. Gandhiji wanted the nation to believe and feel that it could reach its political salvation by its own strength. For the revival of national self-confidence people had to be strengthened economically. Hence, while trying to revive national self-confidence, Gandhiji had to strengthen the people economically and to show them the inter-relationship between political and economic independence. That a nation cannot work out its own salvation unless it is free, was held to be a mischievious notion by Mahatma Gandhi.

When Gandhiji entered the Indian scene, conditions were altogether hopeless. The British had to be got rid of before any improvements could be brought about. To achieve that end the means that he preferred to employ were non-traditional in nature. His were non-violent and pure methods. He did not believe that ends justify the means. For him ends and means were convertible terms. He believed that good ends could not be realized through bad means. So many wars have been fought to end war and yet we are nowhere near peace. Wars and violence have been the prime causes of war and violence.

Gandhiji also believed that no sudden and drastic reforms could be enforced on a society. Any such enforcement would deliver men from one set of evils only to plunge them into another. Human nature is conservative and it is essential therefore that social reformers should abstain from introducing drastic changes.

Another ideal that Gandhiji placed before us was the development of the individual. The individual should be granted facilities for an all-round development of his self. Any order that does not provide for the fullest development of human personality was to be discarded. Society is important but only in as much as it facilitates the development of human personality. No reform which leaves the mass of the people wallowing in the slothful irresponsibility of passive disobedience to authority is a genuine change for the better. The initiative must rest with the individual. Every thinker, every philosopher, thinks in terms of the development of human personality. Even communism believes in the development of the individual as it aims at the ultimate abolition of the State. But it appears statesmen have taken the view that men are made for democracy and not democracy for men.

Thus on these basic assumptions of the development of human personality by a slow and gradual process of change (which for Gandhiji meant the adoption of non-violent and truthful means) Gandhiji worked towards the attainment of freedom and democracy for India. His emphasis on non-violent and truthful means was exclusive. His definitions of non-violence and truth were wide enough to exclude the minutest form of exploitation. We may be inclined to mock at this idea as mere sentimentalism but Prof. Laski and others also support the idea of a non-violent society. Even the Atlantic Charter is forced to concede that "all the nations of the world, for realistic as well as spiritual reasons, must come to the abandonment of the use of force". Gandhiji's non-violent and democratic society cannot be dismissed as a mere sentiment.

And if it is agreed that society should be organised on a non-violent basis economics should also be directed towards that end. Generally, economics has been considered to be too mundane to have any moral values. But for Gandhiji this is a false conception of economics. "I must confess", he writes, "that I do not draw a sharp or any distinction between economics and ethics. Economics that hurts the moral well-being of an individual or a nation is immoral and therefore sinful". This fact has been recognized even by Western thinkers and philosophers. "If Socialism ever comes", writes Bertrand Russel, "it is only likely to prove beneficial if non-economic goods are valued and consciously pursued........Ideals of social justice and public morality do enter into what people find to be best and that ethical aspects of an economic system cannot be regarded as irrational or even as non-economic considerations".

Thus because of these considerations and his emphasis on non-violent and truthful means Gandhiji had to seek the cooperation of people. Violent revolutions do not require mass support. But non-violent revolutions cannot succeed without active mass support. A revival of confidence was therefore absolutely necessary. The importance of economic matters in this revival was well recognized by him. When he pleaded for hand-spinning, he realized that "Paupers cannot become willing sufferers. They have never known the pain of plenty to appreciate the happiness of voluntary suffering, hunger or other bodily discomfort. Swaraj for them can only mean ability to support themselves without begging. To awaken among a feeling of discontent with their lot without providing them means of removing the cause thereof is to court certain destruction anarchy, outrage and plunder in which they themselves will be the chief victims. Hand spinning alone can possibly supply them with supplementary and additional earnings......Therefore those who offer civil disobedience for the sake of *Swaraj* must know hand-spinning".[1]

The country needed a powerful organisation. People who had lost confidence and initiative were to be relieved from the life of passive submission. Gandhiji sincerely felt that the only means of organizing the people and creating enthusiasm in them was simply through the spinning wheel. He wrote, "He will find it in Swadeshi, in the spinning wheel. India will be permanently organised to the extent that hand spinning is organised.....It gives the country an incentive to industrial effort and renders cooperation on a national scale absolutely necessary for success. The *Khadi* movement is revolutionizing the village life and putting hope into millions of human breasts".[2] He again wrote, "Give up *Khaddar* and you will find it impossible to lift the masses from economic and moral degradation". "..... In that way not only could the power of initiative among the village masses be restored or be given further opportunities for growth, but the Congress *Swaraj* propaganda would also be on the way to secure strong foothold among the masses throughout the vast continent. And then every other item of Congress programme could be easily made to take root".[3] He wrote again in 1924 about the spinning wheel; "It is the most efficient aid to mass discipline without which mass civil disobedience is impossible". Spinning wheel was thus to bring about a powerful organisation in the country. Not only this, the spinning wheel was expected to bring about communal harmony and an improvement in the status of women.

As has already been pointed out, Gandhiji's methods were non-violent and truthful methods. For the success of a non-violent revolution close and active cooperation of the masses is absolutely essential. A violent revolution can succeed without active mass support. In a violent revolution a dominant minority forces its will on the majority who have to be mere passive followers. But a non-violent revolution rests on the willing cooperation of the masses. This cooperation of the masses could not be secured unless the leadership identified itself with the masses; it must live and feel like the masses. Any distance between the leaders and the masses would have resulted in the failure of non-violent revolution and the principle which was so dear to Gandhiji. It is therefore that Gandhiji presented the spinning wheel to the leaders and the country. "I then presented the spinning wheel as a symbol of their identification with the poorest of the soil. Mere lip profession was not enough. Even a genuine sensation of pity was not enough. We wanted the poor to feel that, if they toiled for us, we spin for their sake. The half-fed millions were in a state of blank despair. They had lost faith in themselves and in us. They had resigned themselves to death by slow and painful starvation. They had become so accustomed to charity doles that they almost refused to work. They had become less than animals; they were living sepulchers. If we wanted these million to earn a few pieces by doing honest and honourable toil, the only possible instrument to them was the gentle and graceful spinning wheel, which could be turned even by the most delicate. The only effective way of inducing the millions to exchange a listless, insane life of beggary for that of a dignified and easy labour was for us to invite them to take up the spinning wheel by turning it ourselves. In the words of Sita what great ones did the simple folk copied".[4] "That the spinning wheel was not the only means of this identification of leaders with the masses was recognized but it appeared to be the only visible link that indissolubly binds us to the lowest in the land and thus gives a hope". In Young India of September 1924 he wrote, "I suggest to all that they should give their mental cooperation and that they should mentally identify themselves with the masses, and as a visible and tangible token thereof they should earnestly spin for at least 30 minutes per day in their name and for their sake".

The spinning wheel also symbolized the economic basis of his struggle. Gandhiji had realized that it was very difficult, if not impossible, to organise people without some economic base. His salt satyagraha was a clear demonstration of this fact. Gandhiji did not believe that economic motives are or should be the most important considerations for action. But at the same time he was practical enough to realize the power of economic considerations. In a country like ours where the vast masses are forced to live under conditions of abject poverty, in a country of half-clad and half-fed millions it would have been impossible to organise these masses into active workers without an economic foundation. To talk of democracy, truth and honesty, freedom of spirit, etc. would have been futile before people who could not even satisfy their bare minimum requirements. The requirements of flesh are to be looked after first and foremost. The demands of the spirit can wait. The spinning wheel, which was associated with the masses since times immemorial, appeared to be the best means of organizing people and was accordingly presented by Gandhiji to us.

Gandhiji's intense dislike for machinery was also responsible for his emphasis on the spinning wheel and all that it represented. In the beginning machinery was a great sin for him. Later, however, his views about machinery underwent considerable change. In his early life, he associated machinery with satanic civilization, which resulted in the downfall and degeneration of the human race. He writes, "Machinery is the chief symbol of modern civilisation; it represents a great sin" (Hind Swaraj). He continues: "I cannot recall a single good point in connection with machinery. Books can be written to demonstrate its evils". "Do not therefore, forget the main thing. It is necessary to realize that machinery is bad. We shall then be able gradually to do away with it. Nature has not provided any way whereby we may reach a desired goal all of a sudden. If, instead of welcoming machinery as a boon, we should look upon it as an evil it would ultimately go". In the beginning he was an uncompromising critic of machinery and therefore he advocated spinning wheel as a means of attaining Swaraj. His belief in hand spinning and all it represented was supreme and unshakeable. He could not even think of India gaining her independence without the spinning wheel.

While fighting the British for freedom and independence of the country Gandhiji wanted that the real power must rest with the masses. He did not want merely a change in the rulers at the top. He was not prepared for a change of white bureaucracy for a black one. He wanted that real power must remain in the hands of millions of people who should not remain simply passive followers of the rulers at the top. The masses could not retain power and control without economic freedom and hence he wanted to decentralise economic power. Political freedom; freedom of franchise; this sounds all very fine But freedom for whom? Franchise for whom? Do we expect men suffering pangs of hunger, men who for the very means of keeping their body and soul together are dependent on others, to exercise their freedom of franchise? As well throw a man into the sea tied hand and foot and tell him he is free to swim. Gandhiji felt that Swaraj that did not set the masses economically on their feet would be a boon only to the capitalist class. We should not be proud of such a *Swaraj*. "If the same process of capitalist exploitation of the Indian masses is to continue under Indian *Swaraj* as under any other system, there is no virtue in *Swaraj* as against foreign rule, so far as at any rate masses are concerned. For the economic industrial exploitation of the Indian millions may, without let or hindrance, proceed equally under an Indian *Swaraj*, if from the very start it is not made clear that *Swaraj* for India means above all things a free economic life for the Indian masses. Hence the need for the universal adoption of hand-spun and hand-woven *Khadi*. Thus *Khadi* and a true *Swaraj* are vitally and indissolubly linked".[5] Those who believe in *Swaraj* as essentially a problem of acquiring the power of self-help in national life would be easily persuaded to value the universal adoption in India of hand spinning and hand weaving as the second of the three great pillars on which must be built up the giant fabric of *Swaraj* in India......Self help in economics means the capacity of the people or the masses to resist commercial exploitation, whether of outsiders or of our own countrymen by all economic means open to them.......The free nation must, in the second place, be as far possible economically free. In respect of her essential economic wants, namely in the matter of food and clothing, every free nation must make all possible efforts to be self-dependent or to approach as far as possible the conditions of self-dependence, or the chances of a free national life would be precarious or at best contingent. Those, therefore, who cannot understand how *Khaddar* will lead to *Swaraj* would do well to ponder over this second aspect of *Swaraj* life for every aspiring people".[6] He wrote again "In India where millions of people scarcely enjoy one full meal per day, let us see what the masses would be gaining after they have made all the sacrifices that we call upon them to attain 'political freedom'. Unless we want to identify India's freedom with exercise of political power by a narrow governing group, unless we want our masses to find at the end of their efforts that their troubles have just begun, that they have begun just like a traveler who travels farther only to fare worse, we should clarify our ideas about 'political freedom' a little and understand that whatever the case with other countries *Swadeshi* must constitute the very warp and woof of India's *Swaraj*".[7] Similar views were expressed when he wrote that "the spinning wheel is the only means by which the Indian people can maintain their self-respect and individual freedom by providing them with independent means of subsistence. It is the surest guarantee against the tyranny of centralised democracy or the power passing into the hands of a narrow oligarchy kept in power by the support of vested interests and is hence heedless of the masses, because it represents political consciousness even among the poorest. Not mere declaration of policy can insure equality of distribution of wealth, but the cause of the masses shall be safe in the hands of Congress so long as Swadeshi in the sense of hand-spinning and hand-weaving is its creed".[8]

In a non-violent revolution the constructive side of the revolution is of as great, if not of greater, importance as its destructive aspect. Both construction and destruction have to proceed side by side. There are periods when active struggle has to be given up for some time when the leaders may have to undertake self-introspection. But the zeal of the masses must be directed to some useful and healthy activities, otherwise the resulting frustration would be disastrous. *Khadi* and the spinning wheel were expected to serve both these objects at the same time. The *Khadi* movement had two aspects — political and constructive. "The work before us", wrote Gandhiji, "is of a two-fold nature. We have in the first instance to carry on a vigorous propaganda to make the people realize to the fullest possible extent the political significance of *Khadi* work by showing on the one hand how *Khadi* alone can help to bring about a speedy and effective boycott of foreign piece-goods resulting in the economic freedom of this country, and on the other hand, how it can help us to build up a network of organi-sation throughout the length and breath of this country enabling us to offer concerted and disciplined *Satyagrah* for the attainment of our goal".[9] He wrote again, "Í believe in *Khaddar*, I believe in the spinning wheel. It has two aspects; terrible and benign. In its terrible aspect, it ís calculated to bring about the only boycott we need for independent national existence, viz., that of foreign cloth. It alone can kill the demoralising British self-interest. Then and then only, when that interest is killed, shall we be in a position to talk to British statesmen on equal terms..... In its benign aspect it gives a new life and hope to the villager.....It is life-giving".[10]

And thus evolved what we now term as economic concepts of Gandhiji. It is not possible to trace the growth of Gandhiji's economic thought in such a brief chapter. Gandhiji's views underwent considerable changes during all those years when he was leading the nation towards the cherished goal of independence. The ideal of the spinning wheel, which was adopted because of economic expediency, was reflected in the develop-ment of all village industries. The spinning wheel became the sun around which moved all other village industries getting life and light from it. The development of small-scale industries was to bring about decentralisation of economic power and the development of autonomous villages, self-sufficient, as far as possible, in respect of their basic minimum requirements. Trade was to be limited to few surplus commodities which were to be exchanged on the basis of barter between these largely autonomous self-sufficient village communities. Class barriers were to be removed and a classless society formed through non-violent means. His scheme of voluntary trusteeship where the maximum income was to bear a definite relationship with the minimum in the same community and his basic education scheme were contemplated to bring about a classless society without the necessity of shedding a drop of blood. In the society which he wanted to bring about "it is the labour which is the current coin and not metal. Any person who can use his labour has the coin, has wealth".

His views about machinery also changed considerably. In the early years he could not find even a single good point in favour of machinery. Later on he explained that he was not against all machinery. "How can I be", he observed, "What I object to is the craze for machinery as such". He wanted machinery which could lighten the burden of the individual and not enable the few to ride over the backs of the millions, "....... and for that matter machinery which does not deprive masses or men of the opportunity to labour but which helps the individual and adds to his efficiency and which a man can handle without being its slave". He also conceded that highly mechanized and centralised industries have come to stay. He simply wanted to narrow down their sphere to the utmost. These have a definite place not for their own sake but as adjuncts and subsidiaries to decentralised units. "The heavy machinery for work of public utility which cannot be undertaken by human labour had its inevitable place; but all that would be owned by the state and used entirely for the benefit of the people". He clarifies his stand when he observed "If we could have electricity in every village home, I would not mind villagers plying their implements and tools with the help of electricity. But I am socialist enough to say that such factories should be owned by the nation or state-controlled. They ought only to be working under the most attractive and ideal condition, not for profit but for benefit of humanity, love taking the place of greed as motive. This mad rush for wealth must cease and the labourer must be assured not only a living wage but a daily task that is not mere drudgery".

In their organizational aspect *Khadi, Charka* and all that they represented were expected to enable the country to establish the desired adjustment between modern civilization and Indian culture and tradition. "If India takes to *Khaddar* and all that it means, I do not lose the hope of India taking only as much as of the modern machinery system as may be considered necessary for the amenities of life and for life saving purposes". He proposed to secure a measure of economic independence for each peasant, largely autonomous control of the economic life of each village and the control of industry as well as of politics by the masses through the disciplined use of mass non-violent resistance. After such control has been firmly established, well practised and fully understood by all groups in the nation, India can safely consider the question of extending her use of this machinery and modern industry. She would be wise first to develop popular control of economic resources and processes through disciplined mass satyagraha. "Although the form and method of industrial and political control by the people as proposed by Mr. Gandhi is different from that of Western nations, nevertheless India will be wise enough not only to emphasise the prior importance of establishing control by masses but also to establish suitable limitations or principles that quantitative relationships shall not grow so powerful as to starve the qualitative aspects and relationship of civilization".[11]

Gandhiji never forgot to stress the importance of the individual. Man should be the measure of all; on the contrary he is a stranger in the world that he has created. The individual must be freed from the mass, must be salvaged from the mass, must be protected and nursed as such. The individual is the foundation unit of social democracy and so his needs and his position must form the inspiration and basis of social policy. It is not the deification of the individual as opposed to deification of the masses but placing of the individual where he belongs, in his rightful niche as the corner stone of democracy. The modern civilization, although constructed by our own efforts, is not adjusted to our own selves. Gandhiji wanted to remove this drawback. It is a pity to find that even close followers of Gandhiji have shown woeful ignorance of the principles and ideals for which Gandhiji laid down his life. The hopes kindled by him are in danger. Our freedom is in danger and we must gird up our loins to defend the same. "For freedom we know is a thing that we have to conquer afresh for ourselves every day, and we are losing freedom because after each victory we think we can now settle down and enjoy it without further struggle......The battle of freedom is never done and the field never quiet". Let us hope the masses of our country will not forget the principles and ideals of Gandhiji and will rise to defend and die for the same.

References

1. Young India, November, 1921.
2. *Ibid.*, January 1922.
3. *Ibid.*, May 1922.
4. *Ibid.*, September 1924.
5. *Ibid.*, May 1922.
6. *Ibid.*
7. *Ibid.*, September 1922.
8. *Ibid.*, November 1922.
9. *Ibid.*, February 1924.
10. *Ibid.*, June 1924.
11. Gregg, Economics of Khaddar.

10

Gandhian Non-Violence and Contemporary World

Before Gandhi non-violence was an individual virtue and individuals used non-violent methods to fight against injustices to which they were subjected to.[1] Such instances can be found in the history of religions of nearly all countries. Since I know my own country I can give two examples—one of Prahlad son of a king, who fought his father and won though he was subjected to tortures. Another example has been of Anguliwal, who was a fierce and dreaded robber. His life style was changed as he came in contact with Lord Buddha.

Gandhiji used his non-violent technique not only for the redress of individual injustices but for solving social, political and even economic problems that the society faced. He used his non-violent direct action (*Satyagraha*) for fighting British colonialism (political purpose) for fighting the problem of untouchability (social purpose) and for the redress of the problems of excessively high rents and exploitation of the rural people at Bardoli and Champaran (economic purpose) and again to fight communal problems—more specifically on the eve of Independence of the country (socio-religious and political purpose) Gandhiji's experiments during his life time were very successful.

Why did Gandhiji succeed? The answer to this question is that he practiced what he preached ("My life is my message", said Gandhiji) and was able to train leadership of the country through strict observance of rules (vows) that he had prescribed for his close followers. Under Indian conditions there were eleven (vows) items of the code of conduct, which were to be enforced strictly. Thus his insistence on Non-violence and Truth meant that the leaders would eschew all manifestations of violence and untruth (exploitation, unfair practices, misuse of authority) and will not surrender to and compromise with untruth and violence, rather actively oppose every form of injustice through non-violent means.

The leaders can acquire this spirit only when they control their baser instincts and desires which can be satisfied only by depriving others what is legitimately their due. (In Gandhiji's terminology, this means *Brahmacharya*, non-palate, non-stealing and non-possession).

This discipline also meant that these leaders will not suffer from a feeling of high and low and will rise above the feeling of caste, racial superiority and religious intolerance.

Through the strict enforcement of these (vows) codes of conduct Gandhiji was able to build up a leadership which could mobilize the masses to great heights through their personal examples.

Besides training the leaders, Gandhiji had a plan for the involvement of the masses in the struggle of not only their political emancipation but also of their release from social and economic bondage. He prescribed eighteen items of his constructive programme. Each one of these items had the result of forging an indissoluble link between the leaders and the masses, create conditions for the emergence of new leaders and at the same time revive the confidence of the masses in their capacity to solve their problems without recourse to violence or help from an external authority.

Gandhiji however felt that if a non-violent order is to be ushered in permanently then foundations of a new social order should be raised. He therefore prescribed the basic postulates of new social order based on principles of non-violence which will necessitate control of materialism, technology, decentralisation of the economic and social order and new motivations.

In the post-Gandhian era several successful efforts were made in the use of his technique of Satyagraha-non-violence, non-cooperation. The Bhoodan Movement (and gifts movement) of Acharya Vinoba Bhave, a very close associate of Gandhiji, is one example. Through this movement those having more land were persuaded to part with their land so that the same could be distributed amongst those who were at the lower level.

The Chipko Andolan to save forest wealth is another example from India. Inspired by one of the followers of Gandhian technique, common people hugged the trees, held the trees by their hands and stuck to them to prevent their felling by the contractors. They challenged that these trees can be cut over their bodies. They were subjected to torture but ultimately this movement succeeded.

Another example of such mass action had been the protest of the people against wine and liquor in the areas of Uttar Pradesh. The ladies took the initiative and drove liquor contractors through their non-violent action.

In the world also Gandhiji's technique has been successfully tried. Martin Luther King, used this method of non-violence to fight the problem of discrimination on the basis of colour and race.

The South African Government's policy of discrimination on the basis of colour stands condemned in the eyes of the world.

All over the world there have been mass demonstrations against nuclear armaments and arms race. The UNO has resolved to observe 18th September of every year as Peace Day. Universities and institutes for peace studies and research have been set up in different countries of the world. The film on Gandhi produced by Lord Attenborough is having tremendous impact on people. People everywhere have been talking of new life styles. "The new generations of the world need not only economic solutions, they need new ideas to inspire them, hopes to encourage them and first steps to implement them. They need a belief in man, in human dignity, in basic human rights, a belief in the value of justice, freedom, peace, mutual love, respect and generosity, in reason rather than force" (Willy Brandt). A question does arise. Simultaneously with peace talks and efforts violence and tensions both at the international and national levels are mounting. To quote Gandhiji "Peace cannot be established through mere conference. Peace is being broken, as we all see, even while conferences are being held".

The main reason to my mind is the insincerity of all of us who talk about peace without making serious efforts to change the socio-economic structure that breeds violence. A vested interest in violence and tension seems to have emerged. Peace will adversely affect those who enjoy power and privilege today. Nations who talk of peace must have non-exploitative social economic structures within their national boundaries — reduction of inequality and control of technology that has become beyond human control. We are not prepared to change our life styles. Nations whose social and economic system is not conducive to peace cannot usher in a peaceful world order.

Yet another reason has been that while putting faith in a peaceful world order and non-violent methods of social change serious efforts have not been made to train leaders and involve masses in this effort. "You cannot take up non-violence in the same way as you take to throwing of stones. It is insane to ask a nation or nations or group to answer an invasion with non-violence if that nation or group does not have leaders who believe in non-violence before. There must be cultivation of the basic attitudes of non-violence before the question becomes meaningful".[1]

Gandhiji, in his long efforts of about fifty years, trained people and built up leadership for non-violent action. Exploitation of the poor can be extinguished not by affecting the destruction of a few millionaires but by removing the ignorance of the poor and teaching them to non-cooperate with the exploiters. That will convert the exploiters also".[2]

Gandhiji had full confidence that non-violent action for change can be taken by all. "Non-violence however is not a cloistered virtue confined to the hermit and the case dweller. Being soul force, it is capable of being practiced equally by all children, young men and women, by grown up people by individuals as well as by groups. Even the masses can well practise non-violence".

What is needed is people and leadership who have faith in unadulterated non-violence, who have abounding confidence and capacity to sacrifice. To quote Gandhiji "Ahimsa is one of the world's great principles which no earth can wipe out. Thousands like myself may die to vindicate the ideal but ahimsa will never die. And the gospel of Ahimsa can be spread only through those who die for the cause".[3]

Gandhiji made experiments in non-violent methods. These experiments have to continue so that the world is saved from catastrophe. It is the young in all countries that have to carry Gandhian experiments forward.

Q. What was the meaning of Gandhi's Spinning Wheel Movement to India and the rest of the world? Although it is favourable for the economic development to spin cotton effectively by building cotton mill or making use of the electricity, Gandhiji was against the introduction of (large scale) machinery. Why?

A. The Spinning Wheel Movement had two meanings. First it was the symbol of plural approaches on Gandhi's view of economic and social motivations. Second, it had immediate relevance to the Indian situation in those days. A new factor was absolutely necessary to drive away the British rule, to do away with the vested interests, and to bring about the non-violent techniques of change.

For Indian development, the regeneration of rural areas is essential. It could be attained by providing the rural people with employment. People in the rural areas in India are out of work for about six months a year. Gandhiji thought that people could find a job and meet the basic needs of a minimum amount of clothes by the spinning wheel movement. And that in this process, people could get organized, get initiated, and then come to fight against any exploitation to which they were subject.

Gandhiji meant that the machine should be under people's control. According to him, the machinery produces the slavery of modern civilization and this is what the industrial societies are. It is not the technological advances in the industrial countries that bring peace. It is questionable how much of modern civilization will be left when perfect disarmament is realized.

The message of the Spinning Wheel Movement for the world is that you can live in peace only when you do not exploit others. It is true that India did not follow Gandhiji's advice. And it might also be true that if India as well as other developing and developed countries had stayed on Gandhiji's lines, the present world situation, especially the economic production system, would have been on completely different lines.

Q. What is the influence of Gandhi's thought on India today?

A. Pt. Jawahar Lal Nehru, the ex-prime minister of India observed towards the end of his life that the country suffered because of not following Gandhi's prescriptions. But now, the Iindian government has realized that the generation of employment can be brought only by having a decentralized economic system. That is one step of Gandhi's ideas. The next step may be towards the non-commercial production of the basic necessities of life, which means production basically for local consumption. That will be fully satisfied if every village has a spinning mill, a sugar mill, a paper mill and so on.

Q. You talked about the problem of satyagraha before development. In the face of development, we may use the means of non-violence and non-cooperation. However, we may add also the problem of training in this regard. Could you please explain a little about the meaning of training people in the face of the development problem?

A. Training can be of two types: (1) leadership—which is strict training; (2) training the people. Non-violent methods cannot be used without the cooperation of the people.

Violent methods that have been tried have not resulted in the transference of power to the people or even the solution of their everyday problems.

The masses must believe that a simpler life is possible. They must also believe that problems can be solved by negotiation and peaceful methods and recourse to violence even in solving minor problems is not desirable.

The leadership must involve the common man in larger social issues (ex.: observing fast; Gandhi's opposition to salt tax).

Q. I was also very impressed by seeing Attenborough's picture on Gandhi, so I understand very well that, for the problem of social injustice, people should be mobilized by non-violent action. However, at the individual level, if some individual faces immediate danger (i.e., pistol), if this person holds a non-violent belief, how far can he hold this belief?

A. Gandhiji said, "If there is a choice between cowardice and violence, I would prefer violence". Please do not carry the impression that Gandhiji advocated violence. Non-violence should not be correlated with cowardice.

Non-violence can be tried at all levels....say, at the family level. If the child does not take food he is offering, at his own level, non-violent resistance to what he is being subjected to.

Even if you think in terms of solving problems with violence, it is not the just who will win, it is the more violent who will win. The problem remains unsolved. If there is competition in violence, there is no end to it. And, therefore, the individual and the society as a whole must keep to non-violent methods of resolving differences.

Some may lose their lives, Gandhi himself lost his life, but this is all I can suggest at the moment.

Q. If I understand well, the non-violence movement must be very difficult because it adopts first praying or a non-cooperation. This all means that you will sacrifice yourself. In today's India, how far is this non-violent movement penetrating? For example I was told that there was a violent communal opposition between Sikhs and Hindus and so how far are people in touch with this non-violent movement?

A. History should be re-interpreted. In the life of a nation, these violent eruptions are only very, very microscopic and they get attention out of all proportion. Something, which is abnormal, is a news item and something, which is normal, is not a news item. The normal social life is non-violent. Therefore, it does not get prominence as such.

It has taken several thousand years for violence to grow in the shape of the weapons of mass destruction that we are seeing. Experiments in non-violent movement date back only to 1905 or so when Gandhi was the man to attack African racialism. It will take some time for non-violent techniques to be made perfect.

If non-violent methods are to succeed, the whole social, economic, political systems have to be restructured.

Q. If one nation receives some aggression from outside, how does non-violent action reply?

A. If the nation's social and economic system is basically non-violent, the need for aggression from outside will not arise.

If the country is organized non-violently, it will be largely self-sufficient and therefore, either aggression will not take place, and if aggression takes place the population can non-cooperate with the invading army.

Q. You told us there is difference between non-violence and (*ahimsa*) positive love so I was very much impressed by the profound ideology, philosophy inherent in India's cultural tradition. However, in today's India, I was told that the Indian government is developing nuclear weapons and shows a very chauvinistic attitude and so how do you explain today's Indian Government's attitude?

A. I am not here to criticize or defend the Government of India. The mistake that our country is committing, and I think I am also responsible for it to some extent, is that we did not project Gandhian technology and methodology on a wider scale. To my knowledge, no non-peaceful use of nuclear energy is proposed.

Q. I saw the film on Gandhi and also I knew that, at the time of the salt march, many people were beaten. Seeing that, I felt that it is very hard to be beaten. I don't like to die for the state's cause—for this kind of abstract purpose, I don't like to die. Also if it is non-violence or social justice, I wouldn't accept to be beaten without saying anything. May be my attitude might be selfish, however, may be my attitude might be natural. How do you reply?

A. Nation is a purely abstract concept. We have been so trained about the concept of nation that we are prepared to do what is asked of us. Even in violent methods, when war takes place, millions die. But they die, without leaving a social impact. So, for a cause, people have to die. People have to die. How can the cause advance unless the people are prepared to make sacrifice? At this point in time, it appears that it is difficult to die. But when people are imbued with the non-violent spirit, it may not be difficult for them to die.

References

1. (Arne Naess; UNESCO Symposium on Gandhi, p. 123).
2. Mathurs, J.S. & A.S.: Economic Thought of Mahatma Gandhi, p. 605.
3. Harijan, May 19, 1946.

11

Nation and Nationality in Gandhian Philosophy

Gandhiji had a world view of a socio-economic system based on non-violence and non-exploitative structure. Nations and ideas related to this concept were of use to him only to the extent they helped individuals, small groups and nations to strive towards this ideal. His field of action was India where he had his experiments. It is significant that he titled his auto-biography as "The Story of My Experiments with Truth". Through India he was giving his message, "I would not like to live in this world if it is not to be one world. I would certainly like to see the dream realized in my life time" observed Gandhiji while addressing the Inter-Asian Relations Conference in Delhi.

Gandhiji did not contemplate India isolated and cut off from the rest of the world. He used to remark that he wants the windows of his room kept wide open so that fresh ideas could come but he did not want to be swept off the ground. His internationalism was inherent in his nationalism. "India he once remarked, "has a far nobler mission viz., to establish friendship and peace in the world. Peace cannot be established through mere conferences. Peace is being broken, as we all see, even while conferences are being held".

Thus it will be clear that Gandhiji's concept of nation was not one of self-centred regional entity unmindful of its action on the world at large—nay quite often trying to benefit at the cost of other nations and people. In fact, he had realized that wrong emphasis and interpretation of national interest has mortgaged that future of human race. This is the reason that all nations—big and small, industrially advanced or otherwise, are arming themselves to the teeth and have scarified the real interest of the people of their countries. They have planned for concentration of power and national interest have been wrongly defined and have been co-related with the so-called interests of the upper class.

Gandhiji described his concept of nation and society by taking example of oceanic circles—each circle dying for the sake of the bigger circle ultimately the whole becoming one. It is not to be a reverse vertical structure, the base being sustained by the top. In fact he was of the view that in the structure that he had visualized the individual will willingly agree to die for the small groups, the small group for the larger group, i.e., nation and the nation for the world community. "I am like a drop of ocean, which seeking to find its fellow drop loses itself in the wide ocean".

But this should come as a voluntary sacrifice and not forced from an external authority. This will be possible if there can be sacrifice of narrow self interests and involvement in social and community life. It was for this reason that he wanted to build up a strong nation of India. He wanted people to rise above narrow sectarian interests. His constructive programme containing eighteen items was his technique of action to forge the national spirit in the people. These items contained the essential of forging national unity—communal unity, removal of untouchability, prohibition, khadi and village industries, basic and adult education, rural health and sanitation, improvement in the status of women, development of regional languages and national language, economic equality, organisation of peasants, and workers on non-violent lines, involvement of students for social and national causes, cow-protection and leprosy service and eradication.

We must realize that each of these items can be realized only through identification of the leadership with the people, involvement of the people in the solution of the problems that affected them deeply and directly. This process will build con-fidence in the people give them initiative and leadership and thus lay the foundation of a nation in which "from each according to his capacity and to each according to his needs" principle will operate. Gandhiji used to say that in this world there is enough for every body's needs but not for every body's greed.

Gandhiji's struggle for India's political independence and his efforts to have a strong nation did not mean a militarized India. It signified India where every individual, small group (village) and every state is so developed that no harm is caused to others. Divisive forces will progressively get weakened.

These principles and practices of Gandhiji have not attracted that much importance that they deserve. We have paid a heavy price for this neglect. It is time we become aware. It is never too late to begin. Every day begins with a dawn.

Total Revolution

GURUDEV Tagore has beautifully described the ideal for which every nation, and at least our country, should strive for:

"Where the mind is without fear and the head is held high;

Where knowledge is free;

Where the world has not been broken up into fragments by narrow domestic walls;

Where words come out from the depth of truth;

Where, tireless striving stretches arms towards perfection?

Where the clear stream of reason has not lost its way into the dreary desert sand of dead habit;

Where the mind is led forward by Thee into ever widening thought and action;

Into that heaven of freedom, my Father, let my country awake.

The above is a pen picture of total revolution, of a concept that has become popular once again ever since Sri Jai Prakash Narain used these words. In our country Mahatma Gandhi devoted his whole life to usher in a society based upon justice in all walks of life. "That Swaraj is the poor man's Swaraj or Ram Rajya, Ram symbolized justice and equity, Rama symbolized truth and charity".[1] Gandhiji's slogan was even, 'unto the last'. The constitution of our country has enshrined sum of these ideas in its preamble.

How short is public memory that we have forgotten the Father of the Nation, who fought all his life to change the basic structure of socio-economic order. Independence was only a means for the attainment of total revolution;— "I am not interested in freeing India from merely the English yoke, I am bent upon freeing India from any yoke whatsoever. I have no desire to exchange 'King log for king stork".[2]

What we should study is as to how and why we failed to lay the foundation of total revolution, a just socio-economic order, after we attained independence. In my humble opinion the reason is that we disowned Gandhiji, his ideas, his concepts of *Swarajya* and his techniques of bringing about socio-economic changes, so much so that *Satyagraha* degenerated into *duragraha* which is worse kind of violence.

Who is to be blamed? I think the blame rests squarely on the leaders whether they were in the Government or outside. Each one of them is to be blamed. Gandhiji has such a hold on Indian leadership that every one swears by his name, but denies him in practice. Dr. Rajendra Prasad our first President and a close associate of Gandhiji lamented, 'Jesus Christ once said to a disciple of his; before the cock crows twice though will deny me thrice". It strikes me that we are doing the same thing to Gandhiji.'[3]

Rev. Stanely Jones observed "Just as the spirit of Jesus shines all the more against the background of the treachery of Judas so the spirit of Mahatma Gandhi shines all the more against the background of the betrayal of his spirit often by those who named his name".

This betrayal was reflected in the adoption of pattern of economic development on the part of those in authority and in Government based upon Western economic concepts. We tried to imitate the western nations and are consequently torn by contradiction. We put faith in undiluted industrialism of western model and ignored repeated warnings of Gandhiji that "Industrialism is, I am afraid, going to be a curse for mankind. Industrialism depends entirely on your capacity to exploit."[4] When it was pointed out to Gandhiji that mechanization will take hold of the country. Gandhiji reacted, "Then there is no escape from violence. Complete mechanization is impossible in India without its resulting in violence in some shape or other."[5] On another occasion he observed, "My views on national planning differ from the prevailing ones. I do not want it along industrial lines. I want to prevent our villages from catching the infection of industrialisation. American exploitation has added neither to the moral height of the exploited countries nor of the exploiting countries."[6]

These ideas of Gandhiji were rejected by the leadership of Free India. The planning that we adopted has left the legacy of centralisation, worsening mass poverty, demoralization, frustration, corruption and recurrence of social evils.

Those who were outside the Government have to share the blame, if not to a larger extent, equally and squarely. They lost faith in Gandhiji's programme, through trained leadership. Gandhiji was emphatic that if tried in right earnest and with sincerity his techniques can be not only effective but speedy as well. "The existing structure of economic society will not last for twenty-four hours if my weapon of satyagraha can be gripped by the people."[7]

They believed that in free India there is no, or atleast very limited scope, for Satyagraha and mass action. They did not oppose, even passively, Government policies leading to centralisation and gradual but certain withdrawal of initiative from the masses. They had scant regard for constructive programme advocated by Gandhiji which they felt was suited to pre-independence period.

Gandhiji's technique of total revolution had two facets — one of evolving various items of constructive programme which could involve large masses in nation building work and at the same time strike at the very roots of some deep social or economic malaise. His eighteen items of constructive programme gave an opportunity to each and every one to be in the main stream of national life and to make his contribution to the restructuring of society. Who can assert that working out of these eighteen items would not have resulted in total revolution? When a nation marches it marches on all fronts.

When we became free we bade good-bye to constructive programme and consequently lost faith in mass non-violent action. Initiative slipped from our hands and got concentrated in bureaucratic machinery. We became increasingly incapacitated to organise satyagraha. "Civil disobedience, without the backing of the constructive programme is criminal and waste of efforts."[8] In 1942 Gandhi remarked, "He who has no belief in the constructive programme has no concrete feeling for the starved millions. He who is devoid of that feeling cannot fight non-violently."[9]

Various item of constructive programme were instruments of forging a link between the leaders and the masses. Through the successful implementation of various items of constructive programme Gandhiji wanted to identify the leadership with the masses, create conditions for the emergence of new leaders and revive the confidence of the masses in their capacity to solve their problems without recourse to violence or extreme dependence on external agencies.

Gandhiji trained leadership in his Ashrams—his laboratories in social experiments. The leaders were expected to subject themselves to strict discipline and make radical and revolutionary changes in their lives. One can refer to eleven Ashram vows in this regard.

For third years the followers of Gandhiji played a second fiddle to government in the hope that total revolution will come through state initiative and action. We have paid a heavy price for neglecting Gandhiji's techniques. It is time we realize the mistake and pledge ourselves to bring about total revolution which is possible only through non-violent methods and technique.

We must remember freedom, we know is a thing that we have to conquer afresh for ourselves everyday, and we are losing freedom because after every victory we think we can settle down and enjoy it without further struggle. The battle of freedom is never done and the field never quiet.

References

1. Mathur (Ed.): Economic Thought of Mahatma Gandhi, p. 559.
2. *Ibid.*, p. 533.
3. Rajendra Prasad: Legacy of Gandhi, p. 99.
4. Economic Thought of Mahatma Gandhi, op. cit. p. 489.
5. *Ibid.*, pp. 495-96.
6. *Ibid.*, p. 573.
7. *Sri G.* Ram Chandra quoted: "Truth and Non-violence", p. 173.
8. *G.*N. Dhawan: Political Philosophy of Mahatma Gandhi, p. 191.
9. *Ibid.*

12

The Gandhian Concept of *Ahimsa* and his Socio- Economic Ideas

There is considerable interest all over the world in Gandhiji's method of social change. Gandhiji's non-violence should not be compared with non-activity or submission to injustice or inequality. His *Ahimsa* is positive and an active method to bring about fundamental change in the existing socio-economic structure. Gandhi's technique holds good for the whole mankind.

What is Gandhiji's *Ahimsa*? I am not competent to give its philosophical interpretation. While every individual is free to work for his salvation, which according to Gandhiji will be possible only when the individual adheres to principles of non-violence in his individual life. Gandhiji' *Ahimsa* is a powerful social force to bring about changes in the society and lead it towards a peaceful non-exploitative socio-economic order. Gandhiji once asserted "The existing structure of economic society will not last for twenty four hours if my weapon of *Satyagraha* can be gripped by the people". Thus Gandhiji's *Ahimsa* is a method of social change, a method which can be used by every individual. It is not a cloistered virtue confined to the hermit and the cave dweller. Being soul force it is capable of being practiced equally by all, children, young men and women and grown up people, by individuals as well as groups.

Love is the other side of non-violence. One cannot love unless he believes in non-violence. This will develop only when there is realization of the essential fact that there is a fundamental basic unity that exists between us all. We are the members of the same universe. This universe consists not only of human beings but all living animate and inanimate objects. This unity must be realized and life style so formed that they do not unnecessarily disturb the eco-system.

Training in the practice of non-violence and love requires training of selected individuals in the theory and practice of non-violent methods. They in their turn will be able to mobilize the masses to take recourse to non-violent technique to take society towards the goal of a non-violent peaceful socio-economic order. Thus Gandhiji prescribed several *Ashrama* vows like Truth, Non-violence, Brahmacharya, Non-possession, Non-stealing, control of palate etc. to his close associates, who were to lead the society towards his cherished goal of a peaceful sound economic order. His approach was to begin with the first convert and if you add zeros this will lead to a ten fold increase in the power and add efficacy to non-violence.

At the same time in order to involve the masses and develop their potential for *Ahimsa*, he gave various items of his constructive programme. Non-violence means not only resistance to violence in non-violent ways, but a positive, constructive and global strategy for socio-economic change. Gandhiji's different items of constructive programme are variety of sub-strategies to involve people to deal with problems of their every day life in a peaceful manner but also lay foundation for a peaceful socio-economic order. Thus he laid emphasis on several burning problems that resulted in a violent socio-economic order. I refer particularly to the injustices that existed for women, untouchables, addiction to liquor and drugs. He also advocated development of feelings of brotherhood towards members of other religious, ethnic-cultural groups. He also advised that people and groups get involved in one particular and concrete economic activity that helps bring about grater sanity and fairness in the relationship between the rich and the poor. This was the reason that Gandhiji advocated the use of the spinning wheel and advocated the doctrine of trusteeship.

In this background let us examine Gandhiji's concept of a new socio-economic order. The basic principles are non-violent order, revolution against unbridled consumption, movement against technology beyond human control and a revolution to provide human motivation in our dealing with fellow men and eco-sphere and real and effective decentralisation. Let us devote some attention to these.

Non-violent order as visualized by Gandhiji will be peaceful, non-exploitative socio-economic system. Such a system would permit a fuller and richer life to individuals, establish rapport between the individual and social order, enable individuals to earn their livelihood with ease and comfort, reduce drudgery associated with work and labour, make work pleasurable, extinguish possibilities of exploitation of individuals by individuals, of one group by another, of villages by cities, of cities by metropolitan towns, of weaker nations by stronger nations and by the present generation of future generations. It would provide for conservation of natural resources and do away with problems of exhaustion of resources, pollution, ecological imbalance and the like and enable peaceful socio-economic changes consistent with changing times and aspirations of the people and permit individuals and small groups and communities to retain initiative and leadership with them.

Revolution against unbridled consumerism is another fundamental concept of Gandhiji's socio-economic system. Gandhiji was against poverty and had once remarked "to a people famishing and idle, the only acceptable form in which God can dare appear is work and promise of food as wages". At the same time he warned us that an exclusive emphasis on materialism and rush for material comforts will spell ruin for mankind. Increase of material comforts, it may generally be stated is not in any way conducive to moral growth whatsoever. While he was against poverty he was equally opposed to affluence. Affluence breeds competition, inequalities and violence and incapacitates individuals and groups for social service and non-violent actions. What is true of individuals is true of groups and nations. Geoffrey Lean observes in Rich World: Poor World: "Materialism should not be the common philosophy but the common enemy" "Economic growth in countries like physical growth in people is natural and healthy upto a certain point. After that it can become cancerous, or as self-indulgent as an expanding waist band. From that stage we should regard real growth as intellectual, moral and social".

Technology beyond human control is one of the gravest dangers before mankind. The need for having a fresh look on technology is imperative. If there are too many clever machines we will have too many stupid people. We must distinguish between technology that increases productivity of individuals and small groups and gives them strength and technology that leads to concentration of power; between technology that is dependent upon renewable sources of energy and technology that leads to exhaustion of non-renewable sources of energy, ecological imbalance, pollution etc. The one leads to peace, cooperation, fellow-feeling and universal brotherhood, the other leads to violence, concentration of power in the hands of fewer and fewer persons, indispensed irresponsibility by these and utter helplessness and hopelessness, aggression and exploitation. Committed to the ways of truth and non-violence Gandhiji desired to give new direction to technological developments. To quote Gandhiji "What I object to is the craze for machinery, not machinery as such. The craze is what they call labour saving machinery. Men go on saving labour till thousands are without work and thrown in the open streets to die of starvation. I want to save time and labour not for a fraction of mankind but for all. I want the concentration of wealth, not in the hands of a few but in the hands of all. Today machinery merely helps a few to ride on the back of millions. The impetus behind all is not philanthropy to save labour but greed. It is against this constitution of things that I am fighting with all my might".

We also need newer motivations, new values to guide our relationships. These have to be moral and ethical. The three aspects of the individuals: the mind, the heart and the skill to use ones hands need be developed. The competitiveness that pervades most Western and Asians schools is excessive. Reacting against this Gandhiji said that unless and until we learn to get away from that spirit of competition and create a dynamic and cooperative spirit, we are not educating ourselves in the best sense of the term. Gandhiji tried to develop an educational system, which provides newer motivation and prepares the individual to fit into a non-exploitative social structure. We have placed undue emphasis on the acquisitive instinct. The view that man can be motivated only by consideration of profit and self-aggrandisment should be abandoned. By proper planning, training and education individuals and groups can be motivated by altruistic motive. To quote Gandhiji "Whereas religion to be worth anything must also be capable of being reduced to terms of economics, economics to be worth anything must also be capable of being reduced to terms of religion or spirituality therefore in this religion cum economics there is no room for exploitation........ there is no room in true economics for the owning of slaves whether they are human being, cattle or machinery."

Decentralisation of the socio-economic system was another basic concept of Gandhiji's *Ahimsa.* Gandhiji's concept of decentralisation is radically different from the concept of decentralisation and delegation as they are regarded in modern times under which power remains with the centralised authority and permits, if at all, insignificant freedom to the people. Decentralisation as conceived by Gandhiji has the basic philosophy of giving strength to groups to resist exploitation and unfairness. Local face-to-face primary communities are truly nurseries for the people and can function as the basic units of participatory democracy and development. Prevalent centralised units are too large for the people participation, initiative and sharing. They only serve the needs, aspirations, conspicuous consumption and extravagant life styles of the microscopic cross-section of the societies in a comparison to the whole population. Gandhiji therefore, laid emphasis on evolution of independence and development from the grass-roots level upwards. To quote Gandhiji "Independence must begin at the bottom. Thus every village will be a republic or panchayat having full powers. It follows, therefore that every village has to be self-sustained and capable of managing its affairs even to the extent of defending itself against the whole world. It will be trained and prepared to perish in the attempt to defend itself against any onslaught from without." This can happen only when decentralised units (villages in India) become independent of its neighbours for its vital wants and inter-dependent for many other things in which dependence is a necessity. Khadi mentality really means decentralisation of the production and distribution of the necessaries of life."

As mentioned earlier a peaceful socio-economic order will be possible only when masses gain the strength to resist injustice and exploitation. This strength will come through decentralisation, new motivations, newer life-style and right type of dedicated leadership. "Nonviolence with its technique of Satyagraha and non-cooperation will be the sanction of the village community", observed Gandhiji. He had no faith in the increasing power of the state, which in his own words 'represents violence in a concentrated and organised form'. Therefore he laid down the maxim that 'our capacity for Swaraj depends upon capacity for solving without reference to or intervention of the Government, all the varied and complex problems that must arise in the affairs of one of the biggest and the most ancient nations like ours'.

In one of his letters to Pt. Nehru Gandhiji wrote "I am convinced that if India is to attain true freedom and through India the world also, then sooner or later the fact must be recognized that people will have to live in villages, not in towns, in huts not in palaces........I hold that without truth and non-violence, there can be nothing but destruction for humanity.... I must not fear if the world is going the wrong way. It may be that India too will go that way and like the proverbial moth burn itself eventually in the flame around which it dances more and more fiercely. But it is my bounden duty upto my last breath to try to protect India and through India the entire world from such a doom."

We may be tempted to dismiss these ideas as utopians. Gandhiji faced similar criticism during his life. To this he reacted "I may be taunted with the report that this is utopian and, therefore, not worth a single thought. If Elucid's point, though incapable of being drawn by human agency has an imperishable value, my picture has its own for mankind to live.....We must have a proper picture of what we want, before we can have something approaching it".

The Gandhian concept and strategy is a challenge to us. If we want a world that is secure and human, we have respon-sibility to change our lives. We have a responsibility to make changes around us that will improve the lives of others. The new age demands higher values. Those who spoke of peace and a new socio-economic order based thereon were once called idealists, but in this nuclear age the idealists have become the only realists.

13

Sarvodaya Concepts and Industrialised Societies

In recent years the attention of great scholars has been increasingly drawn towards the dangers that mankind faces in the wake of astounding advance of science and technology. Gulf between the rich and the poor nations is widening. Several commissions and conferences to bring about a peaceful order are witnesses to worsening international climate and acceleration of tensions and conflicts. Poverty and hunger still prevail while resources are being misutilised for production of all types of arms and armaments and the spread of the war psychosis in different countries. Political leadership in different countries is sticking to power by playing upon this sentiment of national security rather than trying to find ways and means to solve the problems of hunger and want and work towards the creation of a new world order which eschews violence and exploitation, encourages cooperation amongst individuals, groups and nations, brings about greater equality and enables rapid structural changes with active participation of the people.

It is in this background we may examine the idea of Sarvodaya — a concept mooted by Gandhiji and examine the relevance of this concept for the world community. Prof. J. Tinbergen observes, "With this state of affairs the work of Mahatma Gandhi has in a few years come back to our minds. Almost suddenly we now become aware of the possibility that in many respects he may have had messages also for the world of today. In the new light of what we were almost unaware of ten to fifteen years ago we shall receive inspiration from that India's great spiritual leader already several decades ago was teaching".[1]

A new world order implies radical changes both in attitudes and structures. Thus far we have been trying with the idea that a new world order can evolve while keeping the present socio-economic order more or less intact, the industrially advanced countries in their own interests advocating that they should become a bit more generous, and supportive of efforts of the developing countries to imitate their economies, values and patterns of growth.

Mahatma Gandhi gave a glimpse of a new world order. His field of action was India. He addressed Indian masses and therefore used symbols and words to be able to communicate effectively with his countrymen whose social and cultural background was different from that of industrialised countries. He did visualize a new international order. To quote him:-

"The message of the spinning wheel is much wider than its circumference. Its message is one of simplicity, service of mankind, living so as not to hurt others, creating indissoluble bond between the rich and the poor, capital and labour, prince and the peasant. The larger message is naturally for all....... "[2]

Gandhiji had warned us against several drawbacks of the modern mad rush for material comforts. He quoted the Biblical saying 'it is easier for a camel to pass through the eye of a needle than for a rich man to enter the kingdom of heaven'. The following quotations will elaborate his viewpoint:-

"Civilisation, in the real sense of the term consists not in the multiplication, but in the deliberate and voluntary reduction of wants. This alone promotes real happiness and contentment and increases the capacity for service".[3]

"Our civilisation, our culture, our Swaraj (freedom) depends not upon multiplying our wants — self-indulgence, but upon restricting our wants — self denial".[4]

"A certain degree of physical harmony and comfort is necessary, but above a certain level it becomes a hindrance rather than help. Therefore, the ideal of creating an unlimited number of wants and satisfying them seems to be a delusion and a snare. The satisfaction of one's physical needs, even the intellectual needs of one's narrow self, must meet at a certain point a dead stop, before it degenerates into physical and intellectual voluptuousness. A man must arrange his physical and cultural circumstances so that they do not hinder him in his service of humanity on which all his energies should be concentrated."[5]

Let one remain under no mis-conception that Gandhiji advocated poverty. To quote him:

"To a people famishing and idle the only acceptable form in which God can dare appear is work and promise of food as wages".[6]

"I have found it impossible to soothe suffering patients with a song of Kabir (religious poet). The hungry millions ask for one poem — invigorating food. They cannot be given it. They must earn it. And they can earn only by the sweat of their brow".[7]

"........For them liberty, God and all such words are merely letters put together without the slightest meaning They jar upon them (the hungry millions).[8]

Thinkers in the industrially advanced countries too are slowly realizing that materialism should be severely controlled. 'Materialism should not be the common philosophy, but the common enemy'[9] remarks Geoffrey Lean.

The author quotes Maurice Strong "economic growth in countries, like physical growth in people, is natural and healthy upto a certain point. After that it can become cancerous, or as self-indulgent as an expanding waistband. From that stage we should regard real growth as intellectual, moral and social".[1]

And in this sphere also Gandhiji had given us firm opinion that moral, ethical and spiritual values should be dominant. To quote Gandhiji once again:-

"Economics to be worth anything must be capable of being reduced to terms of religion and spirituality".[11]

"I do not draw a sharp or any distinction between economics and ethics. Economics that hurts the moral being of an individual or a nation are immoral and therefore sinful".[12]

"That economics is untrue which ignores or disregards moral values. The extension of the law of non-violence in the domain of economics means nothing less than the introduction of moral values as a factor to be considered in regulating international commerce".[13]

It is only recently that eminent scholars have recognized the truth of the damage that has been done by a blind devotion to a limitless material progress. It may not be out of place to quote Maurice Strong's view: "It will take a moral and spiritual revolution which goes far enough to alter our life styles and penetrate our political and industrial systems".[14] Changing the style means a fundamental change in our ways of living and as also a change in collective life and thought. Similar sentiments were expressed by E.F. Schumacher in his 'Small is Beautiful'. Eminent economists have been talking of Gross National Happiness.

These ideas should prompt us to rethink about technology. Technology beyond human control is one of the gravest dangers before mankind. Gandhiji during the course of his attempts to restructure Indian economy pointed out to the inherent dangers that a machine civilisation poses. The following abstracts from his writings are noteworthy:-

"God forbid that India should ever take to industrialisation after the manner of the west. The economic exploitation of a single tiny island kingdom, England is today keeping the worldin chains. If an entire nation of 30 millions (now more than 60) took to similar exploitation, it would strip the world bare like locusts".[15]

"I do not believe that industrialisation is necessary in any case for any country. It is much less for India. Indeed I believe that Independent India can only discharge her duties towards a groaning world by adopting a simple life by developing her thousands of cottage and living at peace with the world........".[16]

"The critics say that water, air, soil and electricity should be fully utilized as they are being utilized in the go-ahead west. They say that control over these hidden powers of nature enables every American to have 33 slaves. Repeat the process in India, and I dare say that it will thirty times enslave every inhabitant of this land, instead of giving every one thirty three slaves."[17]

"The movement of the spinning wheel is an organised attempt to displace machinery from that state of exclusiveness and place it in its proper state".[18]

After Gandhiji similar sentiments were expressed by people in the west. "The control of technology means a severe limitation of its hitherto unchecked growth, a limitation demanding almost savage asceticism on the part of an age drunk, not merely with synthetic emotions and pleasures manufactured by the entertainment factories, but with dreams of power and of the conquest of the outer space".[19]

The responsibility of the industrially advanced countries towards the creation of a new world order is considerable. "And since all the material means of effective navigation — research, trained manpower, capital resources, commercial experience— lie in overwhelming superiority on the side of the wealthy, it is to them that the plea is chiefly addressed. They must let their moral energy equal their material resources".[20]

This implies, amongst others a conscious effort on the part of these nations to restructure their economics and decentralise the productive process.

To quote Gandhiji, "You cannot build non-violence on a factory civilisation, but it can be built on self-contained villages.......Rural economy, as I have conceived it, eschews exploitation altogether, and exploitation is the essence of violence".[21]

To have international peace the economy of the partici-pating units must be free from exploitation of the poor by the rich, of the masses by the classes, of the villages by the towns and of the weaker or so-called under-developed races by the stronger and more advanced ones. In a large measure international tensions are because of socio-economic tensions within the nations. To quote Gandhiji:

"Peace is unattainable by part performance of conditions ....If the recognized leaders of the mankind who have control over engines of destruction were wholly to renounce their use with full knowledge of its implications permanent peace can be obtained. This is clearly impossible without the great powers of earth renouncing their imperialistic designs. This again seems impossible without great nations ceasing to believe in self-destroying competition and to multiply wants and thereby increase their material possessions".[22]

Only after this firm resolve to abandon materialism and have new concepts of growth that the industrially advanced countries can look at international problems of peace and war, poverty and alarming inequalities between the conditions under which the rich and the poor live in the right perspective. "A non-violent system of government is clearly an impossibility as long as the wide gulf between the rich and the hungry millions persists......A violent and bloody revolution is a certainty unless there is a voluntary abdication of riches and the power that riches give and sharing them for the common good"[23] warned the Mahatma about half a century earlier.

It is only then that the rich countries will not think in terms of transplanting their economics and growth concepts to the poorer nations of the world. Export of sophisticated technologies has done considerable harm to these countries and has resulted in distortions of consumption patterns, widening inequalities and creation of pockets of affluence amidst widespread poverty and unemployment. This has also resulted in uprooting of people from their cultural backgrounds. The economies in nearly all the countries have become increasingly exploitative giving birth to tension and violence. This is the anti-thesis of Sarvodaya Concept.

One can argue that these are good sentiments but at the same time are not practicable in countries, which have tasted fruits of materialistic growth. This will be mere defeatism and postponement of decisions, which should be taken at the present juncture. The answer is straight and simple. If plain life is worth living, then the attempt is worth making even if only an individual or a group makes the effort. Gandhiji was making such experiments in India and wanted his country to demonstrate the practicability of these ideas and concepts. The remedy lies that the masses should be aroused to think of the inherent dangers of the present styles of living. Their involvement towards the evolution of a new order should be invoked. "The new generations of the world need not economic solutions, they need ideas to inspire them, hopes to encourage them, and first steps to implement them. They need a belief in man, in human dignity, in basic human rights, a belief in the values of justice, freedom peace, mutual respect, in love and generosity, in reason rather than force".[24]

Gandhiji was not confident of a complete restructuring of the society through mass action and cooperation of the people that he once observed: "The existing structure of economic society will not last for twenty four hours if any weapon of satyagraha can be gripped by the people".[25]

Gandhi demonstrated in his life-time that the might of the mightiest authority can be challenged through non-violent methods and mass movements. You cannot have such vast changes merely for the asking. People have to be trained through the leadership of those who are dedicated and committed to bring about a new system.

The success of such mass movements largely depends upon the leadership who have to make revolutionary changes in their life-styles and in the capacity of the leadership to evolve a strategy of identification with the common man. Various items of constructive programme that Gandhi prescribed under Indian conditions was such an example. If the leadership is intelligent and honest and lives upto its belief the masses, even though their belief may be unintelligent, can contribute their might towards this end.

The time for action has arrived. Gandhiji's advice was: "We must refuse to wait for generations to furnish us with a patent solution of a problem which is ever growing in seriousness. Nature knows no mercy in dealing stern justice. If we do not wake up before long, we shall be wiped out of existence".[26] It is never too late to retrace our steps and start afresh from the point where we took the wrong turning. One day dawns from the moment we are awake.

References

1. Foreword to Economic Thought of Mahatma Gandhi.
2. Mathurs J.S. and A.S. (Ed.) Economic Thought of Mahatma Gandhi, p. 477.

3. *Ibid.*, p. 612.
4. *Ibid.*, p. 527.
5. *Ibid.*, p. 583.
6. *Ibid.*, p. 529.
7. *Ibid.*, p. 531.
8. *Ibid.*, p. 59.
9. Rich World, Poor World, p. 319.
10. Economic Thought of Mahatma Gandhi, p. 321.
11. *Ibid.*, p. 421.
12. *Ibid.*, p. 530.
13. *Ibid.*, p. 533.
14. Quoted in Rich World Poor World, p. 324.
15. *Ibid.*, p. 486.
16. Economic Thought of Mahatma Gandhi, op.cit., p. 517.
17. *Ibid.*, p. 297.
18. *Ibid.*, p. 47.
19. Wilhelmsen, Introduction to Rich World, Poor World.
20. Barbara Ward's Foreword to Rich World, Poor World.
21. Economic Thought of Mahatma Gandhi, p. 319.
22. *Ibid.*
23. *Ibid.*, p. 610-11.
24. Willy Brandt: Introduction to North-South: A programme for Survival.
25. Truth and Non-violence UNESCO Symposium p. 173.
26. *Ibid.*, p. 24.

14

Gandhian Approach to Work Culture

Gandhiji was greatly influenced by the ideas of Leo Tolstoy and Ruskin. Tolstoy's emphasis on "Bread Labour" had a tremendous impact on his approach to work culture. Ruskin's book "Unto This Last" prompted Gandhiji to change his lifestyle. Under the caption 'Magic Spell of a Book' Gandhiji tells us how he read this book on the twenty hours journey from Johannesburg to Durban. He summarized the message of the book as follows:

1. The good of the individual is contained in the good of all.
2. Lawyer's 'work' has the same value as barber's, as all have the same right to earn their livelihood from their work.
3. A life of labour, i.e., the life of the tiller of the soil and the handicraftsman, is a life worth-living.

Gandhiji's views on work were strengthened by the cultural traditions of India and he tried to influence people's approach to work and leisure.

The need for having a Gandhian look at 'work culture' can be appreciated better in the background of the work ethics of present-day society. This society is beset with many problems.

Without going into details one can safely assert that the present-day work culture represents the following:

(i) Labour and work are associated with pain and consequently everyone avoids work. The general notion is that the more distant you are from work, the more leisure you have, the more civilized you are. Work is not considered a source of satisfaction. "The normal satisfaction of work, the pleasure of physical activity, the opportunity of self-expression and the development of personality through work, the self-esteem and self-respect derived from useful work well-done, and the social esteem won by recognition from others of the importance of one's work are none of them, properly realizable under industrial conditions".[1]

(ii) The other major characteristic of work is that profit motive is all dominating. By profit motive we mean the desire to benefit oneself unmindful of its effects on others and the society at large. "The motive of personal gain thus tends to become the dominating motive of the worker, for there remains little of nothing in work to make it worthwhile except the money that can be got out of it." This is the dominating motive, not only for the workers but also for every member of society.

This is not the place to analyse in detail the causes for such an attitude towards work and labour. Increasing mechanisation and the sophistication of the machine method cause an extreme division of labour, specialization had a control over every aspect of worker's life. These lead to a feeling of insecurity, frustration and alienation and a lack of socially responsible behaviour.

"In the field of economic activity the profit-oriented attitude manifests itself in a widespread discontent which leads quite often to outbursts of strikes, demonstrations in other forms of industrial discontent, social frustration and lack of involvement.

The general lack of interest in work that causes carelessness and waste, that saps energy and initiative and produces unwillingness and indiscipline, is a far more formidable problem fraught with much greater consequences for human well being than the dramatic outburst of industrial strife which attracts attention...... All these are symptoms of a general underlying human unhappiness in relation to work."[3]

In this context let us look at Gandhiji's approach to work and leisure. It must however be emphasised that Gandhiji's was not only a struggle for India's political freedom but essentially an effort and experiment to restructure human society which has lost its moorings. He was, through his methods, laying the foundation of a truly non-violent and non-exploitative system permitting the fullest development of human personality.

Under Gandhiji's scheme work is a means of associating and involving people and the masses with society. "Non-violence on a mass scale can only be observed by the masses being usefully and knowingly occupied for the sake of the country."[4]

Gandhiji's advocacy of sacrificial spinning by leaders had the twin objectives of identifying them with the masses and getting their cooperation as also bridging the gulf between these two and enshrining the principle of body labour and dignity of labour.

Gandhiji advocated physical labour. His principle of bread labour required everyone, irrespective of his place, to undertake physical work. A visitor expressed his doubts about Gandhiji's insistence on physical labour by eminent scholars like Rabindra Nath or Raman and termed it a sheer wastage, when he suggested that brain workers be considered on a par with manual workers for both of them perform useful social work, Gandhiji's reply was:

"Intellectual work is important and has an undoubtful place in the scheme of life. But what I insist on is the necessity of physical labour. No man, I claim, ought to be free from that obligation. It will serve to improve the quality of his intellectual output."[5]

Gandhiji's insistence was on physical labour. To quote: "I will never be satisfied until all men had plenty of productive work, say eight hours a day…… I know millions will not employ themselves in work for the sake of it. If they did not need to work for their bread (basic needs) they would lack the incentive."[6]

His opposition to avoidance of physical labour was because he felt that the fundamental law of our human society should be that we must work for our bread and that we eat our bread by the sweat of our brow. He observed: "God created man to eat his bread by the sweat of his brow and I dread the prospect of our being able to produce all that we want, including our food stuffs, out of a conjurer's hat."[7]

Gandhiji was of the strong opinion that body labour should be one of the main sources for the restructuring of the society. He was so emphatic on this source that he observed:

"By Swaraj I mean the government of India by the consent of the people ascertained by the vote of the largest numbers of adult population ……. who have contributed by manual labour to the service of the state and who have taken the trouble of having their names registered as voters."[8]

His scheme of basic education of *Nai Talim* laid emphasis on inculcating in children the need, desire and capacity for physical labour. That is why he insisted upon training and education through craft. As these children grow and become citizens they will appreciate the need for physical labour and understand the dignity of labour. They can thus become the pillars of a new non-exploitative social order. Gandhiji's diagnosis of the evils of the society was lack of real education or rather, mis-education of the people. The only cure that he knew was a gigantic effort in right education on a mass-scale. And that could be done best through the propagation of simple handicrafts and industries on a cooperative basis. It would help to drive away unemployment, poverty and ignorance and inculcate in poor a sense of interdependence and community of interest.

"Physical labour is essential for the observance of Non-stealing and Non-possession. Man can be saved from injuring society as well as himself only if he sustains his physical existence by physical labour."[9]

This emphasis on labour was because Gandhiji had realized that the masses cannot involve themselves in what is considered intellectual work. He was opposed to a machine culture that deprives people of opportunities for physical labour. He once remarked: "The machine should not tend to make atrophied the limbs of man."[10]

He explained his position in the words: "If the craze for machinery method continues, it is highly likely that a time will come when we shall be so incapacitated and weak that we shall begin to curse ourselves for having forgotten the use of living machines given to us by God. Millions cannot keep themselves fit by games and athletics. And why should they exchange the useful, productive hardy occupations for the useless, unproductive and expensive games and exercises."[11]

It will be wrong to think that Gandhiji did not visualize a place for what is commonly known as intellectual labour. But he did not approve of mere mental or intellectual jugglery. "The satisfaction of one's physical needs, even the intellectual needs of one's narrow self, must meet at a certain point a dead stop, before it degenerates into physical and intellectual volumptuousness."[12]

Mere mental that is intellectual labour is for the soul and its own satisfaction. It should never demand payment. "In the ideal state doctor, lawyer and the like will work solely for the benefit of society, not for self. Obedience to the law of bread labour will bring about a silent revolution in the structure of society. Man's triumph will consist in substituting the struggle for existence by the struggle for mutual service. The law of the brute will be replaced by the law of man."[13]

Thus work in Gandhiji's thought is a method of identification of the people with society. It is to be performed with the fullest sense of social responsibility. That is why Gandhiji advocated the principle of Trusteeship. Trusteeship is not only of property or material possessions. Trusteeship is also of one's talents and capacity. Labour has its unique place in a cultured human society.

Speaking of social responsibility due emphasis must be placed on the fact that in Gandhiji's work-scheme work does not lead to inequalities or concentration of riches and power. This he ensures by having a decentralised system of production through cottage and village industries and appropriate technology on the one hand and trusteeship on the other. Work in Gandhiji's ethics will be a source of satisfaction, joy and enjoyment and not the opposite of it as at present. The conditions of industrial work have disintegrated the unity of satisfaction of the craftsman. Extreme division of labour and specialization have alienated the worker not only from his work but society as well. They distort the motivation pattern as well, and create a tremendous feeling of insecurity.

"Man has to belong to something real, purposeful, useful, creative; he must belong to his job and to his industry, or it must belong to him. What gnaws at the psychological and moral roots of the contemporary world is that most urban people, workers belong to nothing real, nothing greater than their own impersonal pecuniary interest. The escape from this profound tragedy of our industrial society is the great issue of our time, for a world in which neither the owner nor the worker is morally identified with his source of income has not the principle of continuity. No institution can survive a moral vacuum."[14]

Gandhiji through his emphasis on decentralisation and cottage and village industries was laying the foundation of a new social order. "India is trying to evolve true democracy, i.e., without violence. Our weapons are those of Satyagraha expressed through Charkha, the village industries, primary education, through handicrafts........ prohibition and non-violent organisation of labour."[15] This will lay the foundation of a new work culture which in turn will lead to a society of Gandhiji's dreams — a casteless and classless society, in which there are no vertical divisions but only horizontal ones, no high or low, all service has equal status and equal wages; those who have more use their advantage will not be for themselves but as a trust to serve others who have less; the motivating factor in the choice of vocation is not personal gain but self-expression and self-realisation through the service of society.

References

1. A.E.C. Hare: First Principles of Industrial Relations, p. 59.
2. *Ibid.*
3. *Ibid.* p. 2.
4. Mathurs J.S. and A.S.: Economic Thought of Mahatma Gandhi, p. 197.
5. *Ibid.* p. 629.
6. *Ibid.* p. 488.

7. *Ibid.* p. 502.
8. *Ibid.* p. 534.
9. *Ibid.* p. 548.
10. *Ibid.* p. 475.
11. *Ibid.* p. 488.
12. *Ibid.* p. 226.
13. *Ibid.* p. 574.
14. Tannbaun: The Philosophy of Labour, p. 106.
15. Mathurs J.S. and A.S.: Economic Thought of Mahatma Gandhi, p. 197.

15

Peace — Need for Clear Concepts

The UN declared 1986 as Year of Peace. The 'First Earth Run'—a global relay of torch bearing runners carrying the message of peace for children all over the world in which leading world athletes took part was used to symbolise this desire for Peace. Torch was received and in turn handed over by top political heads in various states. The media, and more particularly the T.V. gave wide publicity to such marches.

Pious resolutions at big conferences and Peace marches in big metropolitan cities guided by those who themselves are responsible for violence and tensions may just dramatize this issue. Peace has been broken even while such conferences were being held and resolutions drafted. Masses have remained untouched. Peace must come from the people.

The UN Secretary General's statement for the International Day of Peace, i.e., 16 September 1986, made the following observations: "The Year was inaugurated with a clear articulation of the elements of danger and promise in the present international situations. Although it was not realistic to expect quick, miraculous solutions to the complex problems facing mankind, yet it was only natural to hope that a credible beginning would be made towards a healthier and safer course of international affairs...... The hope still remains unfulfilled. Tensions persist in many regions of the world. No significant progress has been made in curbing the arms race. The danger of nuclear catastrophe continues to cast a grim shadow over human existence......"

Our concepts should be clear. Peace should not be judged by negative yardsticks of absence of hot war, explicit violence, control over armaments and banning of all nuclear arms or having satisfaction that a World War has not taken place even though several cases of limited war are on record. The concept of peace should be defined more positively. A peaceful world should provide and create conditions where individuals can lead fuller and richer lives i.e., a balanced development of human personality in its social, cultural, political and economic aspects. Predominance of one aspect (economic as at present) would not be conducive for peace amongst individuals, small groups, nations, states and the world community at large. It should provide for rapport between the individual and the social order and permit peaceful socio-economic changes consistent with changing times and aspirations of the people. Initiative and leadership should remain with individuals and small groups. In such an order conflicts at individuals and small groups, national and international levels will be reduced to insignificant dimensions. In those rare cases where conflicts may still arise these can be resolved speedily by peaceful methods.

This will require a fundamental restructuring of the existing socio-economic order. I draw attention to three major revolutions that we need today:- (1) revolution against un-bridled consumerism, (2) revolution against technology beyond human control and (3) revolution to provide human motivations in our dealing with fellow-men. Mahatma Gandhi had pointedly and repeatedly referred to these revolutions. If India and the developing countries had heeded his advice the world commu-nity would have been several steps closer to a peaceful world order.

We must recognize that international relations are to a very large extent reflections of the internal situations that prevail in different countries. Violence and tension abroad and in our dealings with others are largely because of the tensions and frustrations that is the lot of individuals and groups in a society.

Gandhiji had warned us against unbridled consumerism. The following quotations are worth mentioning:

"Civilisation, in the real sense of the term consists not in the multiplication but in the deliberate and voluntary reduction of wants. This alone promotes real happiness and contentment and increases the capacity to service."[1]

"A certain degree of physical harmony and comfort is necessary but above a certain level it becomes a hindrance rather than help......... The satisfaction of one's physical needs, even the intellectual needs of man's

narrow self, must meet at a certain point a deed stop before it degenerates into physical and intellectual voluptuousness........"[2]

It will be travesty of truth to suggest that Gandhiji advo-cated poverty. "To a people famishing and idle the only acceptable form in which God can dare appear is work and promise of food as wages"[3], was his observation.

This view is now being advocated by scholars even in industrially advanced countries. "Materialism should not be the common philosophy but the common enemy"[4], remarks Geoffrey Lean. Maurice Strong observes that "Economic growth (consumerism; my interpretation) in countries like physical growth in people, is natural and healthy upto a certain point. After that it can become cancerous, or as self-indulgent as an expanding waist band. From that stage we should regard real growth as intellectual, moral and social."[5]

Technology beyond human control is one of the gravest dangers before mankind. The need for having a fresh look on technology is imperative. If there are too many clever machines we will have too many stupid people. We must distinguish between technology that increases productivity of individuals and small groups and gives them strength and technology that leads to concentration of power; between technology that is dependent upon renewable sources of energy and technology that leads to the exhaustion of non renewable sources of energy, ecological imbalances, pollution etc. The one leads to peace, cooperation, fellow-feeling and universal brotherhood; the other leads to violence, concentration of power in the hands of fewer and fewer persons, indispensed irresponsibility by these and utter hopelessness and helplessness, aggression and exploitation. Committed to the ways of Truth and Non-violence Gandhiji desired to give new direction to technological developments. "What I object to is the craze for machinery, not machinery as such. The craze is for what they call labour saving machinery. Men go on 'saving labour till thousands are without work and thrown in the open streets to die of starvation. I want to save time and labour, not for a fraction of mankind but for all. I want the concentration of wealth, not in the hands of a few but in the hands of all. Today machinery merely helps a few to ride on the back of millions. The impetus behind it all is not philanthropy to save labour but greed. It is against this constitution of things that I am fighting with all my might."[6]

To a suggestion by one of the visitors that mechanisation will take hold of the country, Gandhiji's reaction was: "Then there is no escape from violence. I saw it as long ago as 1908, and ever since I have shaped all my activities in terms of non-violence. Complete mechanisation is impossible in

India without its resulting in violence in some shape or the other."[7] "The movement of the spinning wheel is an organised attempt to displace machinery from that state of exclusiveness and place it in its proper place"[8], was Gandhiji's considered view.

"Wilhelwism', in his Introduction to 'Junegers' 'Failure of Technology' observed: "The control of technology, means a severe limitation, demanding almost savage asceticism on the part of an age drunk, not merely with synthetic emotions and pleasures manufactured by entertainment factories but with dreams of power and of the conquest of outer space."

Why hate and aggression would often have the better of love and cooperation is because enough thought, effort and courage have not gone into the building up of the forces of love and altruism. It goes without saying that peace technology lags far behind war technology.

We also need newer motivations, new values to guide our relationships. These have to be moral and ethical. Gandhiji remarked, "Whereas religion to be worth anything must also be capable of being reduced to terms of economics, economics to be worth anything must be capable of being reduced to terms of religion or spirituality. Therefore, in this religion-cum-economics there is no room for exploitation......there is no room in true economics which is convertible with religion for the owning of slaves, whether they are human beings, cattle or machinery. There is no room for slavery in economics."[9]

In the planning of our development undue emphasis has been placed on the acquisitive instinct. The view that man can be motivated only by considerations of profit and self-aggrandi-sement should be abandoned. By proper planning, training and education individuals and groups can be motivated by altruistic motives. After all what happens in war? Are not people motivated and mobilized for reasons which do not lead to any personal gain or advantage? People can rise to unthinkable heights only if they are guided by and led by people who are motivated for this purpose. Gandhiji, in his life, not only demonstrated but proved effectively of such a possibility.

In his Introduction to the Report of the Independent Commission on International Development Issues, Dr. Willy Brandt emphasised that ideologies of growth in the North have had too little concern for the quality of life and that there is need for industrialised countries not to stick to a guiding philosophy which is predominantly materialistic and based on a belief in the automatic growth of the gross national product and of what they regard as living standards. It is only when this basic attitude is changed that we can think of a peaceful world order.

Gandhiji's experiments in this direction with three basic elements need serious consideration.

1. Creation of human society involving non-violent methods of resisting exploitation.
2. Educating the oppressed to take positive and constructive steps to resist exploitation.
3. Ushering in of non-exploitative decentralised economic and political institutions.

This will involve (i) equality and independence of all nations big and small, (ii) simultaneous disarmament and renunciation of force by all powers, (iii) removal of the causes of internal tensions of which international tensions are very often projections, (iv) a relentless struggle against the passion of selfishness, lust and greed within us of which violence is the culmination and inculcating these values in the people at large.

This will imply:

1. Adoption of a decentralised economy in the true sense of the term and a system of full regional autonomy on the widest scale.
2. Attainment of self-sufficiency in respect of all vital needs.
3. Eradication of exploitation or domination in any form of the poor by the rich, of the masses by the classes of the villages by the towns, of the weaker and less developed nations by the stronger and more developed ones and of the future generations by the present as manifested in exhaustion of resources, ecological imbalances and environmental pollution.
4. Adoption of a new way of life and culture based on the principles of self-discipline and self-restraint as opposed to the doctrine of self-indulgence and numberless wants and of a socio-economic system conducive and contributory to it.

Peace necessitates non-exploitative decentralised economic and political institutions. Systems and methods that result in centralisation and concentration of power and authority should be abandoned. Decentralisation in social and political spheres depends upon the decentralisation of the economic structure. Decentralisation for peace should be radically different from "decentralisation and delegation as is being talked about these days". Under the modern concept power remains with centralised authority. Decentralisation permits, if at all, insignificant freedom to the people. As in the traditional doll shows the decentralised units retain only that much of power that is permitted by the controlling hand. Decentralisation for peace has the basic philosophy of giving strength to small groups to be able to resist exploitation and unfairness.

Local face-to-face primary communities are, truly, the nurseries for the people. They can obviously function as the basic units of participatory democracy and development. Prevalent centralised units are too large for people's participation, initiative and sharing. They only serve the needs, aspiration, conspicuous consumption and luxurious and extravagant life-styles of the microscopic cross-sections of the societies in comparison to the whole population. Centralisation attributes bigness to things of niggardly low utility in relation to the needs of the entire population.

To quote Gandhiji: "I regard the growth of cities as an evil thing, unfortunate for mankind and for the world, unfortunate for England and certainly unfortunate for India........The blood of the villages is the cement with which the edifices of the cities are built. I want the blood that is today inflating the arteries of the cities to run once again in the blood vessels of the villages."[10]

This in turn will require decentralisation of several items of production and attainment of self sufficiency in respect of all vital needs. "My idea of village is that it is a complete republic independent of its neighbours for its own vital wants, and yet interdependent for many other things in which dependence is a necessity."[11] He elaborated his concepts, ".......Khadi mentality means decentralisation of the production and distribution of the necessaries of life......."[12] Thus for a peaceful social order these should not become items of commercial or market economy.

Eradication of exploitation will be possible only when masses gain the strength to resist injustice and exploitation. This strength will come, as mentioned earlier, through decent-ralisation and new motivations and also through right type of dedicated leadership. "Non-violence with its technique of Satyagraha and non-cooperation will be the sanction of the village community."[13] Concentration of power in the hands of the State does not provide lasting solution to the problem of exploitation and unfairness. "The State" observed Gandhiji, "represents violence in a concentrated and organised form...... I look upon an increase of the power of the State with the greatest fear, because although while apparently doing good by minimizing exploitation, it does the greatest harm to mankind by destroying individuality, which lies at the root of all progress".[14] Therefore he laid down the maxim. "Our capacity for Swaraj depends upon our capacity for solving without reference to, or intervention of the Government, all the varied and complex problems that must arise in the affairs of one of the biggest and the most ancient nations like ours."[15] Yet on another occasion he observed: "I have always held that social justice even into the least and the lowliest is impossible by attainment of force... At times non-cooperation becomes as much a duty as cooperation. No one is bound to cooperate in ones undoing or slavery."[16]

The need for a newer life-style and newer motivations has already been discussed. Gandhiji demonstrated in his life time that self-discipline and self-restraint is possible. This needs evolution of a two-fold strategy — training of individuals and a radical restructuring of the socio-economic system. The inmates of Gandhiji's Ashrams had to undertake several vows e.g., Truth, Non-violence, Non-possession, Bread Labour etc. He wanted to train a few to work for a non-violent peaceful order in thought, words and deeds so that they could guide and inspire the masses.

We may be tempted to dismiss these concepts as Utopian. It may be argued that most men and women are not fit to act upto this ideal. They are too selfish and irresponsible. "If that be so, and if these qualities are too deep rooted for anything to be done about them, all I can say that the outlook for humanity is poor indeed."[17] Our Age of Anxiety is, in greater part a result of trying to do today's job with yesterday's tools — with yesterday's concepts.

References

1. Economic Thought of Mahatma Gandhi (Ed.) J.S. Mathur, A.S. Mathur, p. 612.
2. *Ibid.* p. 535.
3. *Ibid.*, p. 529
4. Rich World: Poor World, p. 319.
5. Quoted in Rich World: Poor World, p. 321.
6. Economic Thought of Mahatma Gandhi (Ed.) J.S. Mathur, A.S. Mathur, p. 475.
7. *Ibid.*, p. 496.
8. *Ibid.*, p. 477.
9. *Ibid.*, pp. 86-87.
10. Quoted by Geoffey Lean in Rich World: Poor World, p. 105.
11. Economic Thought of Mahatma Gandhi (Ed.) J.S. Mathur, A.S. Mathur, p. 323.
12. *Ibid.*, p. 212.
13. *Ibid.*, p. 323.
14. *Ibid.*, pp. 578-579.

15. *Ibid.*, p. 277.
16. *Ibid.*, p. 601.
17. G.D.H. Cole: The Case for Industrial Partnership, p. 117.

16

Non-Violence and Rapidity of Change – Gandhiji's Experiments

Humanity is faced with baffling problems. Even the industrially advanced affluent nations of the world have problems, which defy solutions. The problems of isolation, lack of purpose, alienation, a sense of insecurity and fear has gripped masses. Mad race for armament and command over means of mass destruction have brought humanity on the brink of complete annihilation. This is broadly the picture of affluent societies. The less developed nations on the other hand, have their share of poverty, unemployment, rigid institutional and social structure, rising mass expectations coupled with mass frustration because of progress at a snail's pace towards the solution of problems which face large majority of citizens of the less developed world.

It is in this context that we have to examine the efficacy of non-violent techniques. We may accept the ultimate ideal of society based on non-violence and the resolving of group and social problems by this technique, yet we may be tempted to ignore this methodology of change if we are not convinced that non-violent technique can bring about rapid social, economic and consequential institutional changes. For many of us violent techniques stand on their own right and claim sort of self-justification to bring about rapid changes. It is generally believed that quick change cannot be brought about without the use of violence. Therefore, in the common mind revolutionary movements are generally associated with bloodshed. Violent methods have an appeal because of their so-called dramatic manifestation. Secrecy associated with violent movements keep them mystic.

But in spite of the supposed efficacy of violent methods one can point out several instances of the failure of such move-ments in the attainment of objectives that the leaders of these revolutionary movements had kept before them. The French Revolution raised the slogans of Liberty, Fraternity and Equality. But violence and bloodshed has not brought France nearer these goals. The goal of the Russian Revolution was the withering away of the State. The Russian society is far away from this ideal. It may not be an exaggeration to state that just the reverse of the ideal is clearly visible and the state is becoming omnipotent and omnipresent in that great country.

It is not being suggested that these revolutions did not bring about fundamental changes in those countries. It is true that old social order was uprooted and shaken from its founda-tion. But the desired goal, the objective for which the revolution was made, has generally become a casualty.

On the contrary, several instances can be given of rapid changes because of non-violent acts. Indian religious scriptures are full of instances of rapid, rather immediate, conversion of individuals to new values and new modes, which revolutionized their lives. We learn that Valmiki, the renowned poet was a confirmed dacoit and maintained himself and his family by looting others. But once he realized the sin of earning his livelihood in this manner, he not only gave up this mode but undertook great penance and became a disciple of God. Similarly, we read about the conversion of Angulimal, a noted criminal, when he came in contact with the Buddha. Such instances from religious scriptures of different religions can be multiplied. No one will be foolhardy to deny the possibility of such conversions.

The critics are sceptic about non-violent techniques succeeding in dealing with group and social problems with such rapidity. The success that was attained by various movements led by Gandhiji disproves this thesis completely. Several satyagrahas were organised during his lifetime with remarkable success.

Gandhiji began his experiments in South Africa. With unlettered coolies, indentured labourers who had become slave labour, as his soldiers he demonstrated to the world that non-violence has capacity to test the might of the mightiest power and that a small unlettered, poverty stricken minority could defy the might of a great State armed to the teeth. And this campaign of Gandhiji resulted in the rapid change in the values of mankind. To quote Philip Noel-Baker: "when he (Gandhiji) started his campaign in 1893, apartheid was accepted by the world at large, not a voice was raised against it. Today ninety-nine out of every hundred human beings reject apartheid."[1]

Thereafter when he came to India he tried this technique for the redress of social and political problems with commendable success. It is doubtful whether violent methods would have succeeded with the same rapidity. The Champaran Satyagraha that he organised produced remarkable results with lightning speed. The indigo farmers were subjected to all sorts of indignities by the planters. There appeared to be no way out. Gandhiji organised the farmers. The unbearable hardships and oppressive exactions which the farmers were subjected to by indigo planters was the issue at stake. These grievances were not even looked into by the authorities for several decades. In the wake of mass awakening and their readiness to suffer for their just cause the Government was forced to yield and remove the grievances.

Similar was the experience of Bardoli Satyagraha which was organised against the arbitrary enhancement of land revenue and for the holding of an impartial enquiry into the same. The Government unleashed severe repression. Forfeiture notices for land seizure, attachment of movable property, police violence, mis-representation of facts by the vast propaganda machinery of the Government, use of minority groups by the authorities to wreck the campaign and wide-scale arrests of all authentic leadership from amongst 88,000 peasants could not break the resolve of the population. When every leader and worker was in prison the women of Bardoli came to the forefront. Some 380 women challenged the might of the British Government and took the pledge of independence. "Not one of the women stood up, not one retreated and not one cried out, although more than half of them had their sarees drenched in blood. But they would not budge; the police had to drag them into waiting lorries and taken them away to prison."[2] "The Government with all its mighty resources and in spite of a frightful reign of terror failed to crush the no-tax campaign and had to yield to practically all the demands of the satyagrahis. The Government had also to restore the forfeited lands of the satyagrahis which had been sold out and to reinstate the village officials who had resigned in protest."[3]

This method was tried for the solution of the dispute between the workers and mill magnates at Ahmedabad in 1918. It must be remembered that there did not exist any trade union organisation to protect the interest of the workers. The dispute was ultimately settled to the satisfaction of all. A new principle of voluntary arbitration was initiated for the settlement of labour problems. The satyagrah resulted in the organisation of the Ahmedabad

Textile Labour Association, one of the most powerful workers' organisation not only in our country but a model of its own for the world, and a changed outlook on the part of the workers and the employers.

Gandhiji gave a death blow to the system of untouchability and the system of caste as was practised in our country. His Ashrams had people from all castes. His efforts to remove these barriers have undermined the hold of caste. In this connection it may be worthwhile to recollect that with Gandhi's blessings, but not directly under his leadership, the "Vykom Temple Road Satyagraha" was organised in the former princely state of Travancore from spring of 1924 to autumn of 1925. This was a fight against deeply entrenched social evil of untouchability. As generally happens, the satyagrahis were subjected to violent retaliation, imprisonment and other hardships. But ultimately they won and the immediate objective of the opening of road to all users was fully achieved (formerly the road passing the temple could not be used by untouchables). This satyagraha had far-reaching consequences. Areas and temples in other parts of the country were opened for the untouchables; their conditions improved and this campaign constituted a major turning point in the fight against untouchability.

Similarly, Gandhi's fast against separate election for the scheduled caste brought about lightning effect. The conscience of the whole country was aroused and a settlement was brought about. It is no exaggeration to suggest that Gandhiji's fight against this age-old evil created an altogether different environment. Dr. Ambedkar, one of the founders of our Constitution, Shri Jagjivan Ram and a host of other important leaders belonged to the depressed classes. But for Gandhiji's methodology it is doubtful whether a socio-political environment would have been created for such leadership to evolve and rise to the top.

Gandhiji's non-violent struggle against the Rowlett Bill and his Salt Satyagraha need special mention. These were countrywide campaigns and led to mass awakening on an unprecedented scale. Satyagraha against Rowlett Bills was organised in March-April 1919. Under Gandhiji's leadership millions of people participated in all parts of the country. Even women and children participated. The official British report mentioned the "unprecedented fraternization" between Hindus and Muslims, even those of the lower classes. The campaign was suspended by Gandhiji because of outbreak of violence. He undertook a penitential fast for three days. This Satyagraha could not take its full course. But even then it can be opined that it was successful. Pandit Motilal Nlehru described the change brought about because of this satyagraha as "A new force was suddenly introduced into our politics, a force with the most tremendous potentialities. India's masses were suddenly awakened and the message of satyagraha entered the humblest home." Gandhji's 'Himalayan miscalculation' in his words enabled him to realize the shortfalls in the organisation and method of such a nationwide campaign for future guidance.

The Salt Satyagraha was another instance when the whole nation was infused with new courage and hope like a flash. Gandhiji had announced well in advance that he intended to break the salt laws. On 12th March 1930 he set out for his historic Dandi March. The whole nation watched and when Gandhiji broke the law the whole nation rose. Pt. Nehru wrote: "It seemed as though a spring had been suddenly released." Everywhere people began to make salt. They collected "pots and pans and ultimately succeeded in producing some unwholesome stuff, which we waved in triumph, and often auctioned for fancy prices." The main thing, Pt. Nehru continued, "was to commit a breach of the 'obnoxious salt law"........As we saw the abounding enthusiasm of the people and the way salt-making was spreading like a prairie fire, we felt a little abashed and ashamed for having questioned the efficacy of this method when it was first proposed by Gandhiji. And we marveled at the amazing knack of the man to impress the multitude and make it act in an organised way."

The rapidity with which non-violent techniques succeeded is amply demonstrated by sheer personal deeds of Gandhiji during the period of communal disturbances that took place in the country during 1946 and 1947. On the eve of independence the country faced communal carnage. But Gandhiji was able to stop this communal carnage from engulfing the whole sub-continent. At Calcutta he fasted and the result was peace. The same results followed his last fast at Delhi. What the military failed to achieve was realized by Gandhiji. Lord Moutbatten described him as 'one man force'. One can venture to suggest that the efforts of Gandhiji, which even resulted in his assassination, saved the country from communal trouble for a number of years after 1948. That this monster is raising its head once again is largely because we have abandoned the path shown by the Father of the Nation.

It may not be out of place to mention that the Pathans under the able guidance of their leader Khan Abdul Gaffar Khan were able to imbibe the spirit of non-violence. The Khudai Khidmatgar Movement had tremendous effect on the Pathan society. The movement not only introduced women into political action — a far cry from the seclusion of purdah — but it posed a challenge to other social and economic institution".[4]

Examples of effectiveness of non-violent techniques can be had from countries other than India. The Norwegians organised an effective non-violent resistance against authorities during German occupations in the Second World War. In recent times the Czechs organised a protest against Russian army for a couple of days. These movements were not so effective as the movements and campaigns organised by Gandhiji in India. There were certain basic shortcomings in these limited campaigns. Yet the possibility of mass and rapid action was clearly demonstrated even by these experiments.

The examples of Martin Luther King and other Negro leaders in their struggle for civil rights has once again demons-trated the effectiveness of non-violent techniques in the solution of social problems. In 1941, threatened with a mass march of some 10,000 Negroes, President Roosevelt issued his famous executive order establishing a war time Fair Employment Practice Committee giving the Negro Federal protection, aboli-shing discrimination in all Government departments and jobs connected with defence industries. The famous Montgomery struggle against colour discrimination in public transport and subsequently non-violent protest by young college students against discrimination on the basis of colour in public restaurants have brought about demonstrable change in public facilities. Besides, these movements have highlighted some basic problems and forced the leaders to think about constructive solutions.

These instances clearly reveal that if tried in right earnest and with sincerity non-violent techniques can be more effective and speedier than violent methods. Gandhiji asserted "The existing structure of economic society will not last for twenty four hours if my weapon of satyagraha can be gripped by the people".[5]

Success depends upon several factors. One essential condition is a faith that non-violence can be organised on a mass scale effectively. "Non-violence, however, is not a cloistered virtue confined to the hermit and the cave dweller. Being soul- force, it is capable of being practised equally by all, children, young men and women, and grown-up people, by individuals as well as groups. Even the masses can practise non-violence." Gandhiji who claimed to be a practical idealist demonstrated that given proper guidance "it is possible to run a Satyagraha campaign with people who have no faith in non-violence as a creed provided they sincerely and implicitly follow the rules as a discipline and work under the leadership of unadulterated non-violence".[6]

The leader of non-violent action must also have confidence and faith in the ultimate conversion of the opponent. It is true that non-violence works in a subtle, non-dramatic but sure manner. "In violence there is nothing invisible. Non-violence, on the other hand, is three-fourth invisible, and so the effect is in the inverse ratio to its invisibility. Thus, non-violence when it becomes active, travels with extraordinary velocity, and then it becomes a miracle".[7] On another occasion Gandhiji explained, "Passive resistance is a misnomer for non-violent resistance. It is much more active than violent resistance. It is direct, ceaseless, but three-fourths invisible and only one-fourth visible...... In its invisibility it appears ineffective but it is really intensely active and most effective in ultimate result..... Non-violence is an intensely active force when properly understood and used. A violent man's activity is most visible while it lasts. But it is always transistory".[8]

It may be argued that Gandhiji's methods succeeded because the adversary were more civilized and democratic traditions and public opinion could influence the British Government's policy. Conversion of a die-hard fascist may not be so easy. "A man who could make the unlettered coolies of South Africa challenge the brutal power of the South African Government would have found a non-violent remedy under Hitler. That he happened to be in particular circumstances of history was not his choice. It was one of the great accidents of history that he found himself in a certain situation and in that situation he found the remedy. To say that in other circum-stances he would not have succeeded is to talk historical nonsense."

"After Gandhiji discovered the weapon of Satyagraha the old imperative of history disappeared altogether. It is no longer imperative in this world for the weak to surrender or to perish. It is now open to the weakest in the world to assume a weapon in which they can fight the strongest, with a sporting chance of success".[9]

It is no use discussing this aspect any further. No general or leader will choose to fight with a weapon and strategy in which he himself does not have confidence. Even the general of a militant group must have faith in the efficacy of the violent methods that he tries. Without this faith demoralization will set in. What is expected of non-violent general is nothing more than a faith in the efficacy of his non-violent technique.

It must, however, be emphasised that non-violence should not become a cloak for cowardice or non-activity. Gandhiji repeatedly emphasised the need for constant action and activity. On a number of occasions he told us that if there was ever a choice between cowardice and violence, he will prefer violence. This does not mean that he considered violence to be more efficacious. In fact Gandhiji considered, as has already been pointed out, non-violence for more powerful and courageous. Gandhiji was man of action. "The first imperative of Gandhiji was to act — here, now, in the living present against injustice and evil. In doing so his inevitable corollary was that action to be truly effective must be non-violent." So when he said, "where there is only a choice between cowardice and violence, I would advise violence", he was expressing his passionate conviction that there must be action, not words, not thought in the face of contingency — this was his way of clearing non-violence from the odium that it is inaction, cowardice and running away.[10]

The success of non-violent technique largely depends upon the leadership. The leaders have to make revolutionary changes in their own lives. Gandhiji prescribed a number of vows for his Ashram inmates. Thus those who wanted to be true satyagrahis were to take vows of brahmacharya, satya and ahimsa, aparigraha, asteya, swadeshi, bread labour, fearless-ness and courage, and a few others which were significant in the context of our country like equality of all religions and removal of untouchability. This is the ethical discipline that a satyagrahi must undergo. "The discipline involves the control and sublimation of divisive appetites and emotions, particularly those of sex, acquisitiveness, pugnacity, fear and hatred. The discipline is, in the words of Mr. Andrews, "a singular blending of different inward acts of conscience which issue in outward acts of observance".[11]

Doubts may be expressed that such a discipline is impossible for the masses. But this strict discipline is not prescribed for the masses. Gandhiji felt that though every one has within him the divine spark and the potentiality to acquire this discipline but such discipline is essential for the leaders only who seek to evolve truth by their own effort. It may be pertinent to remember that Gandhi did not permit the use of 'fast' by anyone except his ownself. The followers of the leaders, are only expected to accept the advise like disciplined militia of the non-violent army. When the question was posed before Gandhi ji that can masses practise non-violence, when we know that they are all prone to anger, hate, ill-will and fight for the most trivial things, his reply was, "They are, and yet I think, they can practise non-violence for the common good. Do you think the thousands of women that collected contraband salt had ill-will against anyone? They knew that the Congress or Gandhi had asked them to do certain things, and they did those things in faith and hope. To my mind, the most perfect demonstration of non-violence was in Champaran. Did the thousands of ryots who rose up in revolt against the agrarian evils harboured the least ill-will against the Government or the planters? Their belief in non-violence was unintelligent, even as the belief in the earth being round is unintelligent. But their belief in their leader was genuine and that was enough. With those who lead it is another matter. Their belief has to be intelligent, and they have to live up to all the implications of the belief".[12]

But such belief and faith in the leadership will come simply by the example of personal lives of the individual leaders. These vows will train the leaders to be non-violent in thought, words and deeds. But they must identify themselves with the common man, the downtrodden and must be able to give vent to their aspirations in a non-violent manner. The problems that they face, the hardships which is their lot and the exploitation and injustices that they face, be constantly attacked by the leader. He must evolve a strategy of action in which those who are affected can participate. Through this mass-action the situation must be changed for a better socio-economic order. The leader must feel one with the masses. It was for this reason that Gandhiji insisted upon his constructive programme. Through the successful implementation of various items of constructive programme, Gandhiji wanted to identify the leadership with the masses, create conditions for the coming up of new leaders and revive the confidence of the masses in their capacity to solve their problems without recourse to violence or help from an external authority. At the same time he felt that foundation of a really socio-economic non-violent order could be laid through such actions. To Gandhiji, "constructive work, therefore, is for a non-violent army what drilling is for any army designed for bloody warfare. Individual civil disobedience among an unprepared people and leaders not known to or trusted by them is of no avail, and mass civil disobedience is an impossibility".[13] On another occasion he remarked, "unaccompanied by the spirit of service, courting imprisonment and inviting beating and lathi charges, becomes a species of violence".[14] "Civil disobedience, without the backing of the constructive programme, is criminal and waste of effort".[15] In 1942 he wrote, "He who has no belief in the constructive programme has no concrete feeling for the starved millions. He who is devoid of that feeling cannot fight non-violently".[16]

If one analyses various items of constructive programme, he is bound to be impressed by the fact that nearly all of these items can be worked only with the cooperation of the masses. The initiative will pass on to them and thus the foundation of a truly non-violent socio-economic order be laid. Let us not remain under any misconception that Gandhiji was for 'status quo'. On the contrary he was ceaselessly working through his non-violent technique to bring about revolutionary changes in the shortest period of time. One who refused to sooth suffering patients with a song of Kabir, one who said that "to a people famishing and idle, the only acceptable form in which God can dare appear is work and promise of food as wages"[17] and who had realized that "a non-violent system of government is clearly an impossibility so long as the wide gulf between the rich and the hungry millions persists. A violent and bloody revolution is a certainty unless there is voluntary abdication of riches and the power that riches give and sharing them for the common good"[18], is a true revolutionary. He was so impatient that when Lord Irwin asked him to wait for three months, he refused to wait even for minutes. In history Gandhi ji stands out as the one single individual who tried his utmost to bring immediate relief to millions of hungry people. His advice was, "We must refuse to wait for generations to furnish us with a patent solution of a problem which is ever growing in seriousness. Nature knows no mercy in dealing stern justice. If we do not wake up before long we shall be wiped out of existence".[19]

The eighteen items of constructive programme that were suggested by Gandhiji are only illustrative. The details of the constructive programme may differ from country to country, but the main principles are not local or temporary in character. The main is the regeneration of society by ridding it of violence, and this requires a decentralised economic structure; social equality and right type of education.

We must also not forget that what Gandhiji did was an experiment in the use of non-violence. Never before in history this method was tried to solve problems of society. Gandhiji was trying to evolve new methodology. His Ashrams were laboratories in the use of Ahimsa of the brave. He might not have succeeded fully "had he been to select the crusaders and to train them for their respective roles in the satyagraha operation, the movements might have been ever more dramatic. Even so, the degree of success with which they met is specially striking when one considers that they worked on an ad hoc basis, and that they dealt with a mass populace which had no prior understanding of the techniques involved and very few of whom had any consistent discipline in the application of these techniques".[20]

Experience of India in the post-independence period appears quite disappointing. If Gandhiji had lived he would have made new experiments. He longed to live for 125 years. His real work was to begin after we attained independence. Had he been spared he would have guided us for another 50 years towards the evolution of non-violent techniques. But providence willed otherwise.

We who are to carry forward the task that he had left behind must take up the work in right earnest. "You cannot take up non-violence in the same way as you take a throwing stone. It is insane to ask a nation or group to answer an invasion with non-violence if that nation or group does not have leaders who believe in non-violence. There must be the cultivation of the basic attitudes of non-violence before the question becomes meaningful".[21]

It must be clearly realized that in the wake of powerful states and governments non-violence is the only technique that is practicable. "In our days the State has become a formidable machine which works in marvellous fashion, of wonderful efficiency by reason of the quality and precision of its means. Once it is set up in the midst of society, it is enough to touch a button for its enormous levers to start working and exercise their overwhelming power on any portion whatever of social framework".[22] Gandhiji observed, "I look upon an increase in the power of the State with the greatest fears, because although apparently doing good by minimizing exploitation, it does the greatest harm to mankind by destroying individuality which is at the root of all progress".[23]

Humanity is steadily marching towards acceptance of non-violent techniques for the speedy attainment of socio-economic system based on justice and fair-play. Who could have ever imagined that some eighteen per cent of U.S.A. citizens, 'a very small affair' according to White House spokesman, but about 38 million people would go out into the streets to demonstrate for peace? "The presence of Gandhi in our contemporary world was a kind of providential retort to the unheard of upheaval of violence in the human race. Violence came to be considered by some important thinkers as a privileged tool in the progress of human race........or such was their theory. Gandhi denounced this tremendous error of our time........Gandhi is the living retort to this exceedingly grave development in the history of mankind".[24] Satyagraha may, i.e. non-violent action in fact, be the only means available to an oppressed people in this age of highly technical means of oppression. The chances of success are certainly as great as are the chances of violent revolutions under the modern police-state system.

That Gandhiji did not succeed as fully as he wanted to or that complete theory and line of action in varied circumstances are not available does not disprove the efficacy of the non-violent methods. Gandhiji's experiments have not yet been completed.

In the end, I can only quote Gandhiji "Ahimsa is one of the world's great principles which no power on earth can wipe out. Thousands like myself may die to vindicate the ideal but Ahimsa will never die. And the gospel of Ahimsa can be spread only through believers dying for the cause".[25] "Let those who believe in non-violence as the only method of achieving real freedom, keep the lamp of non-violence burning bright in the midst of the present impenetrable gloom. The truth of the few will count; the untruth of millions will vanish like chaff before a whiff of wind".[26]

References

1. Truth and Non-violence: UNESCO Symposium on Gandhi, p. 221.
2. G. Ramchandran: Truth and Non-Violence – UNESCO Symposium on Gandhi, p. 100.
3. Dhawan, G.: Political Philosophy of Mahatma Gandhi, p. 252.
4. Bondurant Joan, V. : Conquest of Violence, p. 143.
5. G. Ramchandran: Truth and Non-violence – UNESCO Symposium on Gandhi, p. 173.
6. Pyarelal: Quoted by Bondurant Joan, V. in Conquest of Violence, pp. 103-04.
7. Non-Violence in Peace and War, Vol. I, p. 130.
8. Harijan: March 20, 1937.
9. G. Ramchandran: Truth and Non-violence – UNESCO Symposium on Gandhi, pp. 303-04.
10. G. Ramchandran: Truth and Non-violence – UNESCO Symposium on Gandhi, p. 131.
11. Dhawan, G. : Political Philosophy of Mahatma Gandhi, pp. 101-02.
12. Harijan: November 4, 1939.
13. Young India: January 9, 1930.
14. Harijan: March 25, 1939.
15. Dhawan, G. : Political Philosophy of Mahatma Gandhi, p. 191.
16. *Ibid.*, p. 191.
17. Mathurs (Ed.): Economic Thought of Mahatma Gandhi, p. 529.
18. *Ibid.*, pp. 610-611.
19. *Ibid.*, p. 24.
20. Bondurant, Joan, V.: Conquest of Violence, p. 41.
21. Arne Naess: UNESCO Symposium on Gandhi, p. 123.
22. Ortega Y. Gasset: The Revolt of the Masses, p. 85.
23. Mathurs (Ed.): Economic Thought of Mahatma Gandhi.
24. Oliver Lacombe: Truth and Non-violence – UNESCO Symposium on Gandhi, p. 307.

25. Harijan: May 19, 1946.
26. Quoted by Gopi Nath Dhawan in Political Philosophy of Mahatma Gandhi, p. 345.

17

A Peaceful World Order —Gandhiji's Concepts and Contributions

A. Introduction

I have chosen this subject because I firmly believe that in the present world situation catastrophe can be avoided and a new peaceful world order ushered in only when we faithfully follow the path laid down by Mahatma Gandhi. His personality has been aptly described by Sarojini Naidu in the following words: "Great soldier of liberty, great seer of human destiny, martyr of the world's sorrow, prophet of the world hope, what visions of the future are enshrined in the mystic temper of your eyes? What deep secrets of spiritual experience and fulfilment are guarded by those closed compressed lips that have uttered words of wisdom and beauty and power. Serene in the midst of world tumults, oft defeated but always invincible in faith, old in years yet ageless in spirit, you have been to myriads of humanity the living symbol of surpassing love and Truth that conquers Death."

Seldom has a man's death evoked such wide spread grief, sorrow and sense of personal loss among all classes of people as Gandhiji. A remarkable feature of the world reaction to Gandhiji's death was the sense of bereavement it brought to people who had never met or even seen him. "I never saw Gandhi, I do not know his language, I never set foot in his country" observed a French citizen, "and yet I feel the same sorrow as if I had lost some one near and dear. The whole world has been plunged into mourning by the death of this extra-ordinary man".

Gandhiji in his own person and in his thoughts represented the lowliest and the humblest, his problems and aspirations and provided a method and technique to these to solve their problems and in the process gain courage and strength not only to solve these problems but simultaneously lay the foundation of a new peaceful socio-economic-politic and cultural order. "He stopped at the thousands of huts of the thousands of dispossessed, dressed like one of their own. He spoke to them in their own language; (of love, humanity – words are mine) here was only living truth at last and not only quotations from books........In direct contact with truth, the crushed forces of the soul rise again".[1]

B. Gandhiji and his World View

Gandhiji, it appears, was engrossed in solving the vast and deep-seated problems that beset Indian sub-continent. These problems were social, cultural, political and economic. But it will be a travesty of right thinking if we confine Gandhiji's ideas only to Indian conditions. What he prescribed holds good not only for all developing countries but to the whole world. It was an accident of history that Gandhiji was born in India. He, therefore, made experiments in India (He titled his Autobiography – 'The Story of My Experiments with Truth') and used language and symbols so that he may be able to communicate effectively and speedily with the vast illiterate teeming millions with a rich cultural heritage of religion (not confined to any sect, creed or religious practices), ethics and morality and whose socio-cultural background was different from that of industrialized countries. He did not contemplate that India will be isolated and cut off from developments in the world. He observed that he wanted to keep the windows of his rooms open to let in fresh ideas, but he did not want to be swept off the ground. His internationalism was inherent in his nationalism. "India" he once remarked, "has a far nobler mission viz., to establish friendship and peace in the world. Peace cannot be established through mere conferences. Peace is being broken, as we all see, even while conferences are being held".[2]

Addressing himself "To American Friends' he observed: "The message of the spinning wheel is much wider than its circumference. Its message is one of simplicity, service of mankind, living as not to hurt others, creating an indissoluble bond between the rich and the poor, capital and labour, the princes and the peasants. *The larger message is naturally for all*".[3]

Addressing the Inter-Asian Relations Conference in March 1947, Gandhiji told the representatives of the Asian nations gathered in New Delhi:

"I would not like to live in this world if it is not to be one world. I would certainly like to see that dream realized in my life time".[4] In one of his letters to Pt. Nehru he wrote, "I am convinced that if India is to attain true freedom and through India the world also (emphasis mine), then sooner or later the fact must be recognized that people will have to live in villages, not in towns, in huts, not in palaces..... I hold that without truth and non-violence there can be nothing but destruction for humanity.........I must not fear if the world today is going the wrong way. It may be that India too will go that way and like the proverbial moth burn itself eventually in the flame around which it dances more and more fiercely. But it is my bounden duty upto my last breath to try *to protect India and through India the entire world from such a doom.*[5]

Gandhiji had a world view. He did not contemplate India isolated from the world community, but India contributing her whole might for the emergence of a non-violent, non-exploitative world order. This idea can be epitomized in the following verse of Gurudev Tagore whom Gandhiji revered and whose thoughts and ideas made significant contribution in the evolution of Gandhiji's ideas.

"Where the mind is without fear
and the head is held high;
Where knowledge is free;
Where the world has not been broken
up into fragment by narrow domestic walls;
Where words come out from the
depth of truth;
Where tireless striving stretches
the arms towards perfection;
Where the clear stream of rason
has not lost its way into the
dreary desert and of dead habit;
Where the mind is led forward
by Thee into ever widening
thought and action;
Into that heaven of freedom
My Father, let my country awake."

C. The Present Day World Order

The present day situation is fraught with danger. In the wake of astounding advance of science and technology the problems that the human race faces not only remain unresolved but newer and newer problems beset mankind. While planning for peace we have created a world of violence, acceleration of tensions and conflicts. Poverty and hunger still prevail while resources are being increasingly mis-utilized for production of arms and armaments. War psychosis has been created and vested interests in promoting dis-stability have grown. Problems of hunger, poverty, unemployment, inequalities and exploitation defy solution. The world is faced with a situation of energy shortages, ecological imbalances, exhaustion of non-renewable resources, environmental pollution and highly sophisticated technology that is fast becoming beyond control and a technology that is ignoring and undermining human values. The worst has been ever increasing feeling of helplessness, drift, isolation, alienation and lack of significant social purpose in individuals, small groups nay even amongst nations in the face of the impending catastrophe. The following quotations from some of the eminent thinkers in the West are representative of this feeling:

"We are perhaps living in the last age of man, and, if so, it is to science that he will owe his extinction".[6]

Several more quotations can be given from the works of Mumford, Schumachar and several others. Gandhiji called this civilisation Satanic. To quote him: "........If modern civilisation stands for all this and I have understood it does so, I call it Satanic..........I would destroy that system today if I had the power. I would use the most deadly weapons, if I believed that they would destroy it. I refrain only because the use of such weapons would only perpetuate the system though it may destroy its present administrators".[7]

D. Basic Postulates

(i) *Non-violent World Order*

Gandhiji had visualized a peaceful, non-exploitative social system. The essential features of such a system can be enumerated as under:

(1) The system should permit a fuller and richer life to individuals (a balanced development of human personality in its economic, social, cultural, political aspects. Predominance of one aspect (economic as at present) would not be conducive for peace amongst individuals, small groups, nations, states and the world community at large).

(2) Establishment of rapport between the individual and the social order.

(3) Enable individuals to earn their livelihood with ease and comfort.

(4) Reduce drudgery associated with work and labour and make work pleasurable.

(5) Reduce possibilities of exploitation of individuals by individuals, of one group by another; of villages by cities, of cities by metropolitan areas and of weaker nations by stronger nations and of the future generations by the present generation.

(6) Provide for conservation of natural resources and do away with the problems of exhaustion of resources, pollution, ecological imbalances and the like.

(7) And enable peaceful socio-economic changes consistent with changing times and aspiration of the people. In other words, individuals and small groups and communities be able to retain initiative and leadership with them.

To the criticism that it is an utopian concept he remarked, "I may be taunted with the retort that this is an utopian and therefore not worth a single thought. Elucid's point, though incapable of being drawn by human agency, has an imperishable value, my picture has its own for mankind to live...... We must have a proper picture of what we want, before we can have something approaching it".[8]

Willy Brandt expressed his views as: "The new generations of the world need not only economic solutions, they need new ideas to inspire them, hopes to encourage them and first steps to implement them. They need a belief in man, in human dignity, in basic human rights, a belief in the values of justice, freedom, peace, mutual respect, in love and generosity, in reason rather than force".[9]

(ii) *Planning for Consumption*

Gandhiji, as early as 1908, when he wrote Hind Swaraj or Indian Home Rule had realized the fundamental weakness of the world socio-economic system. "Increase of material comforts, it may generally be laid down, does not in any whatsoever conduce to moral growth".[10] "Millions will always remain poor. Observing all this our ancestors dissuaded us from luxuries and pleasures".

Gandhiji had warned us that an exclusive emphasis on materialism and rush for material comforts will spell ruin for mankind. He was against poverty, but he was equally opposed to affluence. Affluence, which is a relative term, is not possible for every one, but only for the few. Millions will always remain non-affluent. Moreover, planning for affluence breeds compe-tition, inequalities and violence and decapacitates individuals and small groups for social service and non-violent actions. What is true for individuals is true for groups and nations. To quote Gandhiji: "Civilization in the real sense of the term consists not in the multiplication, but in the deliberate and voluntary reduction of wants. This alone promotes real happiness and contentment and increases the capacity to service".[11]

It will be a travesty of truth to suggest that Gandhiji advocated poverty. He held the view that: "To a people famishing and idle the only acceptable form in which God can dare appear is work and promises of food as wages".[12]

Scholars and thinkers in industrially advanced countries too are slowly realizing that consumptions should be severely regulated. "Materialism should not be the common philosophy but the common enemy.[13]

It is pertinent to point out that voluntary poverty was one of the vows in Gandhiji's Ashram where he was trying to build up leadership for the future.

(iii) Control of Technology

Gandhiji's views on technology have been much mis-understood and mis-interpreted. He has been accused of being reactionary and anti-growth and modernization. This is rather unfair to a person who devoted his whole life to lay foundations of a non-violent system.

Technology beyond human control is one of the gravest dangers before mankind. In restructuring the world order the need for having a fresh look on technology is imperative. If there are too many clever machines we will have too many stupid people. "If the craze for the machinery method continues, it is highly likely that a time may come when we shall be so incapacitated and weak that we shall begin to curse ourselves for having forgotten the use of living machines given to us by God. Millions cannot keep themselves fit by games and athletics. And why should they exchange the useful, productive, hardy occupations for the useless, unproductive and expensive games and exercise".[14]

Gandhiji distinguished between tools and implements and large-scale machine; between technology that increases productivity of individuals and small groups and technology that leads to exhaustion of non-renewable sources of energy. The one leads to peace, cooperation, fellow-feeling and universal brotherhood and the other leads to violence, concentration of power in the hands of few persons, irresponsibility and utter hopelessness and helplessness aggression and exploitation. Committed to the ways of Truth and Non-violence Gandhiji desired to give new direction to technological developments. To a suggestion of one of the visitors that after political freedom mechanisation will take hold of the country, Gandhiji reacted, "Then there is no escape from violence. I saw it as long ago as 1908, and ever since I have shaped all my activities in terms of non-violence. Complete mechanisation is impossible in India without its resulting in violence in some shape or the other".[15]

Addressing his message 'To American Friends' on a query about the message of the spinning wheel and its spiritualizing effect he said, "Yet it is not an attempt to spiritualise machinery because that seems to me an impossible task, but to introduce, if it is at all possible, a human or the humane spirit among men behind the machinery. Organising of machinery for the purpose of concentrating wealth and power in the hands of a few and for the exploitation of many I hold to be altogether wrong. Much of the organization of machinery of the present age is of that type. The movement of the spinning wheel is an organised attempt to displace machinery from that state of exclusiveness and place it in its proper state".[16]

Thus far the whole philosophy of growth and development has been to exploit nature for narrow selfish ends of material comforts. The race has to be abandoned and a severe restraint put on technological changes. "The control of technology means a severe limitation demanding almost savage asceticism on the part of an age drunk, not merely with synthetic emotions and pleasures manufactured by entertainment factories, but with dreams of power and of the conquest of the outer space".[17]

Explaining his position Gandhiji explained" "What I object to is the craze for machinery, not machinery as such. The craze is for what they call labour-saving machinery. Men go on 'saving labour' till thousands are without work and thrown on the open streets to die of starvation. I want to save time and labour, not for a fraction of mankind, but for all. I want the concentration of wealth, not in the hands of a few but in the hands of all. Today machinery merely helps a few to ride on the backs of millions. The impetus behind it all is not philanthropy to save labour but greed. It is against this consti-tution of things that I am fighting with all my might".[18]

(iv) Decentralization

Gandhi was opposed to systems and methods that result in centralisation and concentration of power and authority. He had realized that effective decentralisation in social and political spheres depends upon decentralisation of the economic structure. Gandhiji's concept of decentralisation is radically different from decentralisation and delegation as is being talked about these days. Under the modern concept power remains with the centralised authority. Decentralisation permits, if at all, insignificant freedom to the people. Like doll show the real power rests with those who command from behind and control the strings. The dolls retain only that much freedom that is permitted by the controlling hand. Decentralisation should not be confused with dispersal of industrial units and production of different parts in distant places at the behest of a central authority. Gandhiji's views are entirely different from this concept. Decentralisation as conceived by Gandhiji has the basic philosophy of giving strength to small groups to be able to resist exploitation and unfairness. "My idea of village (small communities) is that it is a complete republic independent of its neighbours for its own vital wants, and yet inter-dependent for many other things in which dependence is a necessity".[19] He observed: "But; the Khadi mentality means decentralization of the production and distribution of the necessaries of life. Therefore, the formula so far evolved is, every village to produce and use all its necessaries and, in addition, produce a certain percentage as its contribution to the requirement of the cities. Heavy industries will necessarily be centralised and nationalized. But they will occupy the least part of the vast national acltivity".[20]

On another occasion he remarked: "You cannot build non-violence on a factory civilisation, but it can be built on self-contained villages......Rural economy as I have conceived it eschews exploitation altogether, and exploitation is the essence of violence. You have therefore to be rural minded before you can be non-violent, and to be rural minded you have to have faith in the spinning wheel".[21]

Gandhiji maintained that local face-to-face primary communities are, truly, the nurseries for the people. They can obviously function as the basic units of participatory democracy and development. Prevalent centralised units are too large for the people participation, initiative and sharing. They only serve the needs, aspiration, conspicuous consumption and luxurious and extravagant life styles of the microscopic cross-section of the societies in comparison to the whole population. Centralisation attributes bigness to things of niggardly low utility in relation to the needs of the entire population. Gandhiji therefore, laid emphasis on evolution of independence and development from the grass-root level upward. He put forth, "Independence must begin at the bottom. Thus every village will be a republic or panchayat having full powers. It follows therefore that every village has to be self-sustained and capable of managing its affairs even to the extent of defending itself against the whole world. It will be trained and prepared to perish in the attempt to defend itself against any onslaught from without. Thus ultimately, it is the individual who is the unit. This does not exclude dependence in and willing help from neighbours or from the world. It will be free and voluntary play of mutual forces. Such a society is necessarily highly cultured in which every man and woman knows what he or she wants and what is more, knows that no one should want anything that others cannot have with equal labour".[22]

Gandhiji's philosophy of decentralized economy has for its goal not the greatest good of the largest number but the good of all — even unto this last. It does not shy away from our numbers but aims at developing their full potential so that instead of being a source of weakness they shall be our strength — indeed, our most valuable asset.

To sum up, the salient features of Gandhiji's system of decentralized economy are: (i) intensive, small-scale, individual, diversified farming supported by cooperative effort as opposed to mechanized, large-scale or collective mono-culture; (ii) development of cottage crafts as ancillary to agriculture; (iii) a predominantly cattle based economy with strict enforcement of the "law of return", viz., to return to the soil in organized form what is taken out of the soil, calculated to provide full employ-ment to our human and cattle population; (iv) a proper ecological balance between both human and animal, and plant life, united in a symbiotic relationship, i.e., relationship of mutually beneficial association; and (v) voluntary protection of both human and animal power against the competition of machinery as the price of social insurance.

In addition, (1) it aims at conversion of work directly into the values of life by preserving the primary producer's inward linkage with the soil and with the goods that pass through his hands, instead of turning it first into commodities that have only an indirect bearing on his life's upkeep, (2) It aims at resolving the conflict between work and recreation, production and consumption, occupation and leisure, (3) It does not regard toil as the "Curse of Adam", or a symbol of man's slavery but as a necessary condition of his emancipation and the source of life and health, (4) It has for its goal, not the maximum good of the greatest number but the largest good of all, "even unto this last" — the man at the bottom rung of the ladder, (5) It does not necessarily mean a lowering of "standard of living" but gives first place in the order of priorities to "standard of comfort", i.e., the primary well-being of the common man, (6) While it lays the greatest emphasis on economic progress, it regards economic progress as a means of realizing the highest realizable in life which on the secular plane, is summed up in the three-fold ideal of equality, fraternity and individual freedom.

(v) New Concepts of Growth and Motivations

Gandhiji's approach to these can be summarized in his own words: "......whereas religion to be worth anything must also be capable of being reduced to terms of economics, economics to be worth anything must be capable of being reduced to terms of religion or spirituality. Therefore, in this scheme of religion-cum-economics there is no room for exploitation......... there is no room in true economics which is convertible with religion for the owning of slaves whether they are human beings, cattle or machinery. There is no room for slavery in economics".[23]

On another occasion he remarked: "I must confess I do not draw a sharp or any distinction between economics and ethics. Economics that hurts the moral well-being of an indivi-dual or a nation are immoral and therefore sinful".[24]

Gandhiji was of the firm view that in the planning of economic development undue emphasis has been placed on the acquisitive instinct of man. The view that man can be motivated only by consideration of profit and self-aggrandisement never appealed to Gandhiji. He felt that by proper training and education persons and groups can be motivated by altruistic motive. Gandhiji felt that man can rise to heights unknown only if they are guided and led by people who are socially oriented.

Maurice Strong observes: "that economic growth in countries like physical growth in people, is natural and healthy up to a certain point. After that it can become cancerous, or as self-indulgent as an expanding waistband. From that stage we should record real growth as intellectual, moral and social".[25]

Gandhiji, therefore, wanted that there should be a radical change in our concepts of growth and development. As has been mentioned earlier, Gandhiji was opposed to poverty. He did realize that poverty leads to degradation and demoralization He worked, heart and soul, throughout his life to wipe the tears of those who suffered from pangs of hunger in the shortest possible time. ".......for them liberty, God and all such words are merely letters put together without the slightest meaning. They jar upon them".[26] He, therefore, thought of growth and development in terms of the millions. When we talk of development the focus has to be not on machines or institutions but on people and all-round development of human personality. "The new generations of the world need not only economic solutions, they need ideas to improve them, hopes to encourage them, and first steps to implement them. They need a belief in man, in human dignity, in basic human rights, a belief in the values of justice, freedom, peace, mutual respect, in love and generosity, in reason rather than force".[27] Maurice Strong held "It will take a moral and spiritual revolution which goes far enough to alter our life styles and penetrate our political and industrial system".[28]

Changing life style means a fundamental change in our ways of living and also a change in collective life and thought. Similar sentiments were expressed by E.F. Schumacher in "Small is Beautiful". Eminent economists have been talking of Gross National Happiness. In his introduction to the Report of the Independent Commission on International Development Issues, Dr. Willy Brandt has emphasized that ideologies of growth in the North have had too little concern for the quality of growth and that there is need for industrialized countries not to stick to a guiding philosophy which is predominantly mate-rialistic and based on a belief in the automatic growth of the gross national product and of what they regard as living standards. It is only when this basic attitude is changed that one can think of a new world order.

E. The Change Agent

(i) The Individual

Gandhiji's concept of growth and development of the individual was not one of an isolated individual, cut off from society, but an integral part of the social system trying to uplift himself and in this process uplift the society — the small community, the nation and the world community. He expre-ssed this ideal when he reacted to the suggestion that he should retire from active socio-political work and devote himself to spiritual pursuits. His characteristic reply was that his Kashi or Himalayas are where injustices are to be fought and tears to be wiped out.

On another occasion Gandhiji had remarked: "My life is my message". We should, therefore, assess the various facets of Gandhiji's life to have an idea about his ideals for upliftment of individuals as an integral part of the society and as an instrument of change.

A new socio-economic order based on justice and fair-play can be ushered in within a short period and with lesser tensions and strains if efforts are made to change the social system and the individual simultaneously. Thus, while Gandhi ji made efforts to change the socio-economic and political system radically, he also laid equal, rather greater emphasis on radical changes in aspirations, motivations and value patterns for individuals in the society. Gandhiji laid down eleven vows for inmates of his Ashram. These summarized his idea for the upliftment of the individual and the society. These vows are:

1. Non-violence;
2. Truth;
3. Non-stealing;
4. Brahmacharya (control of senses);
5. Non-possession;
6. Bread Labour;
7. Fearlessness;
8. Equal respect for all religions;
9. Swadeshi; and
10. Removal of untouchability.

The observation of these vows will lead to the upliftment of individuals and communities.

Truth and Non-violence are basic principles for the understanding of Gandhiji's ideals. These are two sides of the same coin. One cannot be non-violent unless he sticks to truth and discards falsehood. These words have wide connotations and do not refer to some metaphysical concepts. Exploitation, unfair practices, misuse of authority etc. are all manifestations of untruth and cannot be preserved, defended and retained, except by methods which are not in social interests. So also non-activity and surrender to and compromise with what is untruth as explained above is violence in terms of Gandhiji. On the other hand non-violence means active opposition to social, political and economic injustices, i.e., 'Satyagraha' in Gandhian language.

But to be a 'Satyagrahi', that is to be devoted and dedi-cated to truth and to be crusader for the right cause one must observe the other vows mentioned above. All these vows prefer to the technique whereby the individuals will rise above their narrow, petty and personal interests and work for social good.

Thus, practice of Brahmacharya, non-palate, non-stealing and non-possession, in their broader sense refer to control of one's baser instincts and desires which can be satisfied only at the expense of others. One cannot be an enlightened individual if his energies are used in the satisfaction of desires, which lead to conflicts and tensions for other individuals. The State tries to regulate individual behaviour through fiscal and monetary measures. Gandhiji wanted that instead of external control these restraints should start from within the individual. External action undermines individuality and freedom; internal restraints on the other hand uplift the individual.

The ideal of bread labour (in modern terminology dignity of labour), is a comprehensive concept. In the first place it means that a minimum amount of physical labour shall be undertaken by all able-bodied persons for the good of the society; and secondly it implies that distinctions of high and low in respect of payments for various vocations and professions will be obliterated. It need not be confused with dead equality but equitable and fair distribution of the national resources. It will also lead to a more cohesive and integrated society.

The quality of fearlessness, in reality, means one's capacity to resist unfairness, inequalities and abuse of authority. It should not be equated with obstinacy and recourse to anti-social activities. In fact the quality of fearlessness can be acquired only by those who lead a contented life and avoid use of unfair means for the satisfaction of their wants and who have identified themselves with the society.

Swadeshi and respect for all religions have special significance for our country. But in their larger connotation Swadeshi means an effort to bring about economic improvement in small communities and thereby their social cultural regeneration. The need for equal respect for all religions means cultural affinity with mankind. The significance of removal of untouchability for upliftment of the individual and society in the context of India is beyond question. Removal of untouchability means the capacity of the individual to rise above the feeling of caste, race, region and of high and low. It also means not only avoidance of exploitation of those who are in lower social stream but offering them active assistance to acquire their rightful place in society.

But one should realize the inter-dependence of these vows. An individual cannot adhere to truth if he does not practice non-violence; which in its turn cannot be practised if the individual is acquisitive, i.e., does not follow the principle of non-stealing and non-possession which in modern parlance means control of consumption and control of wealth in the hands of individuals. And one cannot practice them if he is slave of baser instincts and desires, i.e., he does not observe Brahmacharya.

The relevance of these ideals in a world on the brink of holocaust because of race in sophistication and perfection of arms for mass destruction which threaten the whole humanity; a world facing the problems of ecological imbalances, exhaustion of resource, of over centralization stands justified.

Nobel Laureate Albert Schweizer observes: "But civilization can only revive when there shall come into being a number of individuals with a new tone of mind independent of the one prevalent in the crowd and in opposition to it, a tone of mind which will gradually influence over the collective one, and in the end determine its character. It is only an ethical movement which can rescue us from the slough of barbarism, and the ethical comes into existence only in individuals".[29]

Gandhiji said, ".......begin with the first convert. If there is one such, you can add zeros to the one and first zero will account for ten and every addition will account for ten times the previous number. If, however, the beginner is a zero, in other words, no one makes the beginning; multiplicity of zeros will also produce zero value".[30]

(ii) Structural Change

As has been mentioned earlier, Gandhiji wanted a new social order and, therefore, his views on consumption, planning, technology, and decentralization etc. have been discussed at some length in the earlier paragraphs. Gandhiji advocated these changes because he was of the view that if one wants to have a peaceful order the social order should be one where exploitation, inequality, centralization of power and authority may not be possible. "I have privilege and monopoly. Whatever cannot be shared with the masses is taboo to me"[31] said Gandhiji. On the other hand power and authority should vest in the common man who will be guided by ethical and moral considerations. Masses will be organised to resist attempts to acquire authority, power and riches and will offer non-violent resistance (Satyagraha) against such attempts. Gandhiji's definition of Swarajya (freedom) was not the acquisition of the authority by few but capacity of the masses to resist authority when abused. However, in a non-violent order occasion for such misuse of authority will generally not arise and in the rarest of cases when such an occasion does arise the wrong doer will change as he faces non-violent resistance (Satyagraha) from the people. In 1946 when a question was posed about the place of Satyagraha in making the rich realize their duty towards the poor, he replied, "The same as against the foreign power. Satyagraha is a law of universal application. Beginning with the family its use can be extended to every circle".[32]

On another occasion he remarked: "I have always held that social justice even unto the least and the lowliest is impossible of attainment by force........At times non-cooperation becomes as much a duty as cooperation. No one is bound to cooperate in one's undoing or slavery".[33]

In such a social order both production and consumption at least where basic wants are concerned, will become localized and the temptation to speed up production, indefinitely and at any price will disappear. To quote Gandhiji, "My idea of village Swarajya is that it is complete republic independent of its neighbours for its own vital wants, and yet inter-dependent for many others in which dependence is a necessity.......Non-violence with its technique Satyagraha and non-cooperation will be the sanction of village community".[34]

In a small booklet, 'Constructive Programme' written as a guide for co-workers he clarified his position, "Khadi mentality means decentralisation of the production and distribution of necessaries of life.......Heavy industries will necessarily be centralised and nationalized. But they will occupy the least part of the vast national activity in the villages".[35]

He did not approve of concentration of power in the hands of the State. His idea was "Our capacity for Swaraj depends upon our capacity for solving without reference to, or intervention of, the Government, all the varied and complex problems that must arise in the affairs of one of the biggest and the most ancient nations like ours".[36]

F. Methodology

(i) Non-violent Action or Satyagraha

Unadulterated non-violent and the technique of Satyagraha was the technique of Gandhi to change the present world order. He observed, "I would advise the adoption of non-violence to the utmost extent possible and that will be India's great contribution to the peace of the world and the establishment of a new world order".[37]

Gandhiji was so confident of the possibility of changing the present order, which he quite often termed as Satanic, that he once remarked, "The existing structure of economic society will not last for twenty four hours if any weapon of Satyagraha can be gripped by the people".[38]

These are not mere expression of sentiments and values of Mahatma (Saint) as we in India called him; but a practical proposition. Gandhiji used to call himself as a 'practical idealist' and had demonstrated in his life-time the efficiency of the non-violent technique of socio-economic changes.

In South Africa with unlettered coolies, indentured labourers who had become slave labour, as his soldiers he demonstrated to the world that non-violence has capacity to test the might of the mightiest power. Thereafter when he came to India he tried this technique for the redress of economic, social and political problems with commendable success and organised several Satyagrahas. The experience of Bardoli Satyagraha when the Government unleashed severe repression is noteworthy. When every leader and worker was in prison the women of Bardoli came to the forefront. Some 380 women challenged the might of the British Government and took the pledge of independence. 'Not one of the women stood up, not one retreated and not one cried out, although more than half of them had their saries drenched in blood. But they would not budge. The Police had to drag them into waiting lorries and take them away to prison:.[39] The Government with all its might, resources and in spite of a frightful reign of terror failed to crush the no-tax campaign and had to yield to practically all the demands of the Satyagrahis.

Gandhiji's Salt Satyagraha needs special mention, as a result of which the whole nation was infused with new courage and hope like a flash. On 12th March 1930 Gandhiji set out for his historic Dandi March. The whole nation watched and when Gandhiji broke the law the whole nation rose. Pt. Nehru wrote "It seemed as though a spring had been suddenly released." Everywhere people began to make salt. They collected "pots and pans and ultimately succeeded in producing some unwho-lesome stuff, which we waved in triumph, and often auctioned for fancy prices". "The main thing", Pt. Nehru continued, "was to commit a breach of the 'obnoxious salt law'. As we saw the abounding enthusiasm of the people and the way salt-making was spreading like a prairie fire, we felt a little ashamed for having questioned the efficacy of this method when it was first proposed by Gandhiji. And we marvelled at the amazing knack of the man to impress the multitude and make it act in an organised way."

The rapidity with which non-violent techniques succeeded is amply demonstrated by sheer personal deeds of Gandhiji during the period of communal disturbances that took place in the country during 1945 and 1947. On the eve of independence the country faced communal carnage. But Gandhiji was able to stop this communal carnage from engulfing the whole sub-continent. At Calcutta he fasted and the result was peace. The same results followed his last fast at Delhi. What the military failed to achieve was realized by Gandhiji. Lord Mountbatten described him as 'one man force'.

One essential condition for success of non-violent methods is a faith that non-violence can be organised on a mass-scale effectively. "Non-violence, however, is not a cloistered virtue confined to the hermit and the cave-dweller. Being soul force, it is capable of being practised equally by all, children, young men and women, and grown-up people, by individuals as well as groups. Even the masses can practise non-violence, Gandhiji who claimed to be a practical idealist demonstrated that given proper guidance "it is possible to run a Satyagraha campaign with people who have no faith in non-violence as a creed provided they sincerely and implicitly follow the rules as discipline and work under the leadership of unadulterated non-violence".[40]

The leader of non-violent action must also have confidence and faith in the efficacy of non-violent technique. It is true that non-violence works in a subtle, non-dramatic but sure manner. "In violence there is nothing invisible. Non-violence, on the other hand, is three-fourth invisible, and so the effect is in the inverse ratio to its invisibility. Thus, non-violence when it becomes active, travels with extraordinary velocity, and then it becomes a miracle".[41] On another occasion Gandhiji explained: "Passive resistance is a misnomer for non-violent resistance. It is direct, ceaseless, but three-fourths invisible and only one-fourth visible.......In its invisibility it appears ineffective but it is really intensely active and most effective in ultimate result........ Non-violence is an intensely active force when properly understood and used. A violent man's activity is most visible while it lasts. But it is always transitory".[42]

The success of non-violent technique largely depends upon the leadership. The leaders have to 'make revolutionary changes in their own lives, Gandhiji prescribed a number of vows for his Ashram inmates. Thus those who wanted to be true Satyargahis were to subject themselves to strict discipline. "The discipline involves the control and sublimation of divisive appetites and, emotions, particularly those of sex, acquisitiveness, pugnacity, fear and hatred. The discipline is, in the words of Mr. Andrews, 'a singular blending of different inward acts of conscience which issue in outward acts of observance........."[43]

Even though Gandhiji felt that every one has within him the divine spark and the potentiality to acquire this discipline, such discipline is essential only for the leaders who seek to evolve truth by their own effort. It may be pertinent to remember that Gandhiji did not permit the use of 'fasts' by anyone except his own self. The followers of the leaders, are only expected to accept the advise like disciplined militia of the non-violent army. When the question was posed before Gandhiji that can masses practise non-violence, when we know that they are all prone to anger, hate, illwill and fight for the most trival things, his reply was, "They are, and yet I think, they can practice non-violence for the common good. Do you think the thousands of women that collected contraband salt had ill-will against anyone? They knew that the Congress or Gandhi had asked them to do certain things, and they did those things in faith and hope. To my mind, the most perfect demonstration of non-violence was in Champaran. Did the thousands of ryots who rose up in revolt against the agrarian evils harboured the least ill-will against the Government or the planters? Their belief in non-violence was unintelligent, even as the belief in the earth being round is unintelligent. But their belief in their leader was genuine and that was enough. With those who lead it is another matter. Their belief has to be intelligent, and they have to live up to all implications of the belief.......".[44]

But such belief and faith in the leadership will not come simply by the example of personal lives of the individual leaders. These vows will train the leaders to be non-violent in thought, words and deeds. But they must identify themselves with the common man, the down-trodden who must be able to give vent to their aspirations in a non-violent manner. The problems that they face, the hardships which is their lot and the exploitation and injustices that they face, must be constantly attacked by the leader. He must evolve a strategy of action in which those who are affected can participate. Through this mass action the situation must be changed for a better socio-economic order. The leader must feel one with the masses. It was for this reason that Gandhiji insisted upon his constructive programme. Through the successful implementation of various items of constructive programme Gandhiji wanted to identify the leadership with the masses, create conditions for the coming up of new leaders and revive the confidence of the masses in their capacity to solve their problems without recourse to violence or help from an external authority. At the same time he felt that foundation of a really non-violent socio-economic order can be laid through such actions. To Gandhiji, "Constructive work, therefore, is for a non-violent army what drilling etc. is for an army designed for bloody warfare. Individual civil disobedience among an unprepared people and by leaders not known to or trusted by them is of no avail, and mass civil disobedience is an impossibility......."[45] On another occasion he remarked: "unaccompanied by the spirit of service, courting imprisonment and inviting beating and lathi charges, becomes a species of violence..."[46] "Civil disobedience, without the backing of the constructive programme, is criminal and waste of effort".[47] In 1942 he wrote: "He who has no belief in the constructive programme has no concrete feeling for the starved millions. He who is devoid of that feeling cannot fight non-violently".[48]

If one analyses various items of constructive programme, he is bound to be impressed by the fact that — nearly all these items can be worked only with the cooperation of the masses. The initiative will pass on to them and thus the foundation of a truly non-violent socio-economic order will be laid. Let us not remain under any misconception that Gandhiji was for 'status quo'. On the contrary he was ceaselessly working through his non-violent technique, to bring about revolutionary changes in the shortest period of time.

We must also not forget that what Gandhiji did was an experiment in the use of non-violence. Never before in history this method was tried to solve problems of society. Gandhiji was trying to evolve new methodology. His Ashrams were laboratories in the use of Ahimsa of the brave. He might not have succeeded fully. "Had he been to select the crusaders and to train them for their respective roles in the Satyagraha operation, the movements might have been ever more dramatic, even so, the degree of success with which they met is specially striking when one considers that they worked on an ad hoc basis, and that they dealt with a mass populace which had no prior understanding of the techniques involved and very few of whom had any consistent discipline in the application of these techniques".[49]

We who are to carry forward the task that he had left behind must take up the work in right earnest. "You cannot take up non-violence in the same way as you take to throwing stones. It is insane to ask a nation or group to answer an invasion with non-violence if that nation or group does not have leaders who believe in non-violence. There must be the cultivation of the basic attitudes of non-violence before the question becomes meaningful......."[50]

Satyagraha may be the only means available to an oppressed people in this age of highly technical means of oppression. The chances of success are certainly as great as are the chances of violent revolutions under the modern police-State system. Gandhiji's experiments have not yet been completed.

To quote Gandhiji, "Ahimsa is one of the world's great principles which no power on earth can wipe out. Thousands like myself may die to vindicate the ideal but Ahimsa will never die. And the gospel of Ahimsa can be spread only through believers dying for the cause........".[51] "Let those who believe in non-violence as the only method of achieving real freedom, keep the lamp of non-violence burning bright in the midst of the present unpenetrable gloom. The truth of the few will count; the untruth of millions will vanish like chaff before a whiff of wind........."[52]

(ii) Trusteeship

Fortified by the efficacy of non-violent techniques of social change, Gandhiji propounded his doctrine of Trusteeship, voluntary abdication of riches and power and sharing the same for common good. As mentioned earlier, Gandhiji was not enamoured of state action. State can conscript property, it cannot conscript talent. It can only inhibit use of talent. It cannot solve the problem of recurring inequalities. It is only through voluntary sharing that these problems can, not only be solved but foundations laid for a new social order. We are faced with a dilemma. Left alone people become unequal. If we try to make them equal they cease to be free. Gandhiji's Trustee-ship formula provides the way out of this dilemma".[53]

Under the doctrine of trusteeship there is no room for serving the personal interest either of the owners or of the workers alone or even of an enterprise as a whole at the cost of the rest of society.

The following principles can be enunciated:

Before we can think of bringing under Trusteeship an enterprise we have to consider whether it is socially useful or harmful (e.g., armament factories, breweries and distilleries are an evil for all time).

Secondly, the principle of Trusteeship applies not only to the owning class but to everybody even to those who have special talents, e.g., doctors, artists, etc.

In the third place Trusteeship cannot come into existence through legislation alone. Legislation may help remove some obstacles in the way of enforcement of this concept. Trusteeship by legislation, when nobody is practising it, would be like putting the cart before the horse.

And finally voluntary transformation of the social order is the essence of Trusteeship.

Let there be no skepticism on this score. To the critics who argued that no capitalist ever behaved as a trustee Gandhi ji's reply was: "It is highly probable that my advice will not be accepted and my dream will not be realized. But who can guarantee that the socialists dream will be realized".[54]

Gandhiji was repeatedly questioned whether history at any time records such a change in human nature. His answer was, "Such changes have certainly taken place in individuals. One may not be able to point to them in a whole society. But this only means that up till now there has never been an experiment on a large scale in non-violence......Ahimsa (non-violence) is definitely an attribute of society. To convince people of this truth is at once my effort and experiment".[55]

He, therefore, asserted, "My theory of Trusteeship is no make-shift, certainly no camouflage. I am confident it will survive all other theories. That the possessors of wealth have not acted up to the theory does not prove its falsity; it proves the weakness of wealth. No other theory is compatiable with non-violence. In the non-violent method the wrong doer compa-sses his own end, if he does not undo the wrong. For, either through non-violent non-cooperation he is made to see his error, or he finds himself completely isolated".[56]

Sanction behind Trusteeship is mass action (made possible by decentralized economic order and a technology under human control). "Exploitation of the poor can be extinguished not by affecting the destruction of a few millionaires but by removing the ignorance of the poor and teaching them to non-cooperate with their exploiters. That will convert the exploiters also".[57]

It may be argued that most men and women are not fit to act upto this ideal. They are too selfish, irresponsible and unresponsive. "If that be so, and if these qualities are too deeply rooted for anything to be done about them, all I can say is that the outlook for humanity is poor indeed".[58] Albert Camus, the great French novelist and humanist wrote: "Over the expense of five continents throughout the coming years an endless struggle is going to be pursued between violence and friendly persuasion, a struggle in which, granted, the former has a thousand times more chances of success than the latter. But I have also held that, if he who bases his hope in human nature is a fool, he who gives up in the face of circumstances is a coward".[59]

G. Concluding Observations

We have discussed at some length ideas of Gandhiji and examined their relevance for the present world situation. To summarize Gandhiji's technique as manifested in his life is an exemplary struggle of mass truth against degradation. Non-violence as practised by Gandhiji had three basic elements: (i) Creation of a human society involving non-violent methods of resisting exploitation, (ii) education of oppressed to take positive and constructive steps to resist exploitation and development of good and harmonious relationship between oppressed and oppressor once the struggle was over, and (iii) ushering in of a non-exploitative decentralized economic and political institutions.

These are no utopian concepts. We have to practise these. "Never before in history has so much responsibility been inheri-ted by a group of human beings. Wherein in previous times the lives of individual nations and culture were at stake, today the stake is destiny of all humanity".[60] This is the time when all the goodness in man must be called forth to subjugate the bad; when our survival depends upon the victory of wisdom and knowledge over stupidity and dogma. "We must divorce ourselves from unreasoned slogans and dogmas, from the sooth- sayer, from the person whose selfish interest compels him to draw false conclusions, from the man who fears truth and knowledge, from the man who prefers indoctrination to education".[61]

Each one of us must make his own humble contribution for the creation of a peaceful world order. Why hate and aggression would often have the better of love and cooperation is because enough thought, effort and courage have not gone into the building up of the forces of love and altruism. It goes without saying that peace technology lags far behind war technology. The same author observes: "Our 'age of anxiety' is in great part a result of trying to do today's job with yesterday's tools, with yesterday's concepts".

Gandhiji advised that individuals and nations must tread on this line. "I have been taught from my childhood and tested the truth by experience that the primary virtues of mankind are possible of cultivation by the meanest of the human species. It is this undoubted universal possibility that distinguishes the human from the rest of God's creation. If even one great nation were unconditionally to perform the supreme act of renunciation many of us would see in our life-time visible peace established on earth".[62]

"Our doubts are traitors,
And make us loose the good
Which we oft might attain,
By fearing to attempt".

—Longfellow

On another occasion answering a correspondent Gandhi ji replied:

"Whether such plain living is possible for an isolated nation, however large geographically and numerically in the face of a world armed to the teeth and in the midst of pomp and circumstance, is a question open to the doubt of a sceptic. The answer is straight and simple. If plain life is worth living, then the attempt is worth making even if only an individual or a group makes the effort".[63]

It is significant to mention that one of the songs dear to Gandhiji was:

Walk alone,
If they answer not thy call, walk alone,
If they are afraid and cower mutely facing the wall,
O thou of evil lack,
Open thy mind and speak out alone,
If they turn away and desert
You when crossing the wilderness,
O thou of evil luck,
Trample the thorns under thy tread,
And along the blood-lined track travel alone,
If they do not hold up the light,
When the night is troubled with storm,
O thou of evil luck
With the thunder flame of pain ignite thine own heart,

And let it burn alone.

— Gurudeo Ravindra Nath Tagore

Let the spirit of Gandhiji guide us to perform our duty towards humanity. Sarojani Naidu, India's Nightingale, whom Gandhiji affectionately addressed as Ammijan (mother) while paying tributes to him on his martyrdom invoked his spirit in the following words:

"May the soul of my master, my leader, my father rest, not in peace, not in peace. Donot rest. Keep us to our pledge. Give us the strength to fulfill our promise, your heirs, your descendants, your students, guardians of your dreams".

References

1. Gurudev Tagore, page xiv of Economic Thought of Mahatma Gandhi.
2. Economic Thought of Mahatma Gandhi, p. 257.
3. *Ibid.*, p. 477.
4. Pyare Lal: Last Phase, Vol. II, p. 9.
5. *Ibid.*, p. 544.
6. B. Russel: Impact of Science on Society, p. 27.
7. Economic Thought of Mahatma Gandhi, p. 81.
8. *Ibid.*, p. 623.
9. Introduction to a Programme for Survival: Ralph Smith, p. 12.
10. Economic Thought of Mahatma Gandhi, p. 461.
11. *Ibid.*, p. 612.
12. *Ibid.*, p. 529.
13. Geoffrey Lean: Rich World-Poor World, p. 319.
14. Economic Thought of Mahatma Gandhi, pp. 488-89.
15. *Ibid.*, p. 496.
16. *Ibid.*, p. 477.
17. Wilhelmsen: Introduction to Junegar's Failure of Technology, p. vi.
18. Economic Thought of Mahatma Gandhi, p. 475.
19. *Ibid.*, p. 323.
20. *Ibid.*, p. 212.
21. *Ibid.*, p. 319.
22. *Ibid.*, p. 623.
23. *Ibid.*, pp. 86-87.
24. *Ibid.*, pp. 529-30.
25. Rich World-Poor World, p. 321.

26. Economic Thought of Mahatma Gandhi, p. 59.
27. Willy Brandt in 'A Programme for Survival' by Ralph Smith — Introduction, p. 12.
28. Rich World Poor World, p. 324.
29. Decay and Restoration of Civilization, p. 68.
30. Economic Thought of Mahatma Gandhi, p. 632.
31. *Ibid.*, p. 494.
32. *Ibid.*, p. 620.
33. *Ibid.*, p. 601.
34. *Ibid.*, p. 323.
35. *Ibid.*, p. 212.
36. *Ibid.*, p. 277.
37. Harijan, 21.6.1942.
38. G. Ramchandran: Truth and Non-violence — UNESCO Symposium on Gandhi, p. 173.
39. *Ibid.*, p. 100.
40. Pyare Lal: Quoted by Bondurant Joan, V. In Conquest of Violence, pp. 103-104.
41. Non-violence in Peace and War, Vol. I, p. 130.
42. Harijan: March 20, 1937.
43. Dhawan G. : Political Philosophy of Mahatma Gandhi, pp. 101-02.
44. Harijan, March 25, 1939.
45. Young India: January 9, 1930.
46. Harijan: March 25, 1939.
47. Dhawan, G.: Political Philosophy of Mahatma Gandhi, p. 191.
48. *Ibid.*, p. 191.
49. Bondurant, Joan, V: Conquest of Violence, p. 41.
50. Arne Naess: UNESCO Symposium on Gandhi, p. 123.
51. Harijan: May 19, 1946.
52. Quoted by Gopi Nath Dhawan in Political Philosophy of Mahatma Gandhi, p. 345.
53. Pyare Lal: Gandhian Thought — Contemporary Society, p. 23.
54. Economic Thought of Mahatma Gandhi, p. 589.
55. *Ibid.*, p. 609.
56. *Ibid.*, p. 201.
57. *Ibid.*, p. 605.
58. G.D.H. Cole: The Case for Industrial Partnership, p. 117.
59. Quoted by A.J. Musts in Gandhi: His Relevance for Our Times, p. 23.

60. Harris Brown: The Challenge of Man's Future, p. 266.
61. *Ibid.*
62. Economic Thought of Mahatma Gandhi, p. 509.
63. *Ibid.*, p. 517.

18

Industrial Civilisation

Gandhiji had worked for the political freedom of India. His message was, however, deeper and was meant for the whole of humanity. He was striving for creating a society based on equality – economic, religious and social. This he considered to be an impossibility in a society based upon materialism. He therefore, worked for economic simplicity and did not subscribe to the view that multiplicity of wants is in any way desirable. It is only when material wants are limited that an environment can be created which will free the individual from external influences and enable him to discover his true purpose — the mission of human life. This may be described for the common man as the task of losing one's ego or self in the service of others.

He attempted to set right the wrong values that the present industrial civilisation has developed. Modern industrial structure has been erected on the disruption of the society and community. Old values have been lost and they have not been replaced by newer ones which may guide human life. In fact the society has ceased to exist. Writing about conditions in America, Erich Fromn remarked: "The American citizen today is concerned almost exclusively with private problems. By "concerned" I mean enough interested in a problem to lose one's sleep sometimes not merely just to talk about it. He loses his sleep about health, money and family problems. He does not lose his sleep about problems of society, because he has cut himself off from the experience of social concern, from the relatedness to others as a part of his life. He is a private individual with only private interests separated from a general interest in the whole and has projected his relatedness to government, to the specialist".[1] The individual has, however, not gained from this weakening of the community life. The motives that a man has in the modern society are predomi-nantly monetary or economic. "The basis on which good repute in any highly organised industrial community ultimately rests is pecuniary strength; and the means of showing pecuniary strength".[2] "The economy of acquisition", remarks Lewis Mumford, "which had hitherto been practised by rare and fabulous creatures like Midas and Croesus, became once more the everyday mode; it tended to replace the direct 'economy of needs' and to substitute money values for life values".[3]

This motive leads to the multiplication of wants on the one hand and considering labour as painful on the other. An individual to be considered advanced must not only have all varieties of material wants that he is able to satisfy but he must also be able to demonstrate that he is not involved in direct productive labour. This has created a situation in which the individual finds himself lost. He is fighting a losing battle. "In the nature of the case the desire for wealth can scarcely be satisfied in any individual instance and evidently a satiation of the average or general desire for wealth is out of the question. However, widely or equally or 'fairly' it may be distributed, no general increase of the community's wealth can make any approach to satiating this need, the ground of which is the desire of every one to excel every one else in the accumulation of goods......since the struggle is substantially a race for reputa-bility on the basis of an invidious comparison, no approach to a definitive attainment is possible".[4] Because "the standard of expenditure which commonly guides our efforts is not the average, ordinary expenditure already achieved, it is an ideal of consumption that lies just beyond our reach, or to attain which requires some strain".[5] If all the wants can be satisfied at any stage, economic functioning and the present economic setup shall receive a rude shock. It implies that our wants should always remain ahead of our income, that is, there should always remain permanent dissatisfaction for the individual. "Indeed, means have become ends. Material production was once supposed to be a means for a more dignified, happier life and the aim was clearly the fuller, more dignified and more human life. Today production and consumption have become ends in themselves. Nobody asks any longer, why or what for? We are happy discovering how we can produce more. In fact our economic system is based on ever increasing consumption and production. But why we want to produce more, why we want this, that, and the other......is a question which is not asked".[6]

Our consumption also is an end in itself. One might say that modern man's concept of heaven is a tremendous departmental store with many new things every day and with enough money to buy everything he pleases. We are the eternal sucklings, drinking in cigarettes and lectures and movies and television. Many people speak of love as one talks of milk. "The child did not get enough of love, it did not get enough affection". You drink it in. That is exactly the picture described in the Brave New World by Huxley. "Why postpone a satisfaction until tomorrow when you can have it today"?[7]

"The expansion of the machine during the past two centuries was accompanied by the dogma of increasing wants. Industry was directed not merely to the multiplication of goods and to an increase in their variety; it was directed towards the multiplication of the desire for goods. We passed from an economy of need to an economy of acquisition".[8]

This setup also means a desire on the part of all to avoid direct productive work. The more distant you are from work, the more leisure you have, the more civilized you are. Labour is considered painful and work is not considered a source of satisfaction. This has been made possible because of progressive use of mechanisation and technological advancements and an extreme division of work into as many small parts as possible.

"But in that process of the disintegration of the whole man which released the forces of a new economic era, work fell from its high place of honour as a creative social centre and came to be equated with pain. Since men do not usually form societies round pain centres, cultural formations came to grow up around anything but the old honourable ideal of that work which brings men their daily bread. Today go into any town and you will find the society for this and that and the association of whatnots, all contributing something to the civilization of the age. But not one in a thousand are formed round the centre of daily work. We have too long ceased to associate industrial work with civilization. And, in so far as it fails to represent the spontaneous creative urge of a group-life dedicated to a worth- while purpose; it carries the mark of a certain artificiality.......the character of so much modern factory work which does amount to so much spiritual pain". [And"9] And, "it is partly a despair of finding a solution to this latter problem and partly the persistence of this insidious identification of work and pain apparent in monotonous and discordant drumming of the work 'incentive' that has tempted many to flee to the comforting idea of the Leisured State. The ideal associated with it may not be wholly wrong, but as substitute for an honourable and dignified solution of the social problem of the modern daily work, it is sheer escapism".[10]

"The normal satisfaction of work, the pleasure of physical activity, the opportunity of self-expression and the development of personality through work, the self-esteem and self-respect derived from useful work well done, and the social esteem won by recognition from others of the importance of one's work, are none of them properly realizable under industrial conditions. Moreover, the conditions of industrial work have disintegrated the unity of the satisfaction of the craftsman. When a worker is employed by another he is at once to some extent separated from the personal contact with the consumer of his product; and the more the division of labour is developed the further is he separated from the person whom his labour ultimately serves. This separation hinders the operation of the motive of service to others and thus reduces its strength, and at the same time the division of labour reduces the satisfaction to be obtained from work itself. Thus the satisfactions of work become divorced from each other, so that in the pursuit of personal gain the satisfaction of having given good service is no longer obtained, and the pursuit of good service no longer brings the satisfaction of the craftsmen, of social prestige or of personal gain. The motive of personal gain thus tends to become the dominating motive of the worker, for there remains little or nothing in work to make it worthwhile except the money that can be got out of it".[11]

This has resulted in monetisation of the various aspects of life. This monetisation has been of extreme type and is an essential element of a growing industrial economy. It also makes an individual increasingly helpless and his life insecure. "As long as men had the greater part of their living in real income produced by themselves, the uncertainties of money wage could be tolerated. The minimum requirement of food, shelter and care in times of sickness and old age, in infancy and childhood, in the emergency of death and misfortune, could be and were provided. The procurement of a real income was and had to be either a family or a community effort. Either the community or the family acted as the natural social security agency for the fatherless, the aged, and the weak. The greater the dependence upon a real income, the larger was the role of the family and community. The heavier the dependence on a money wage, the fuller became the individualization, equality and isolation of each member of the family and each member of the group.

"When the time arrived in our urbanized industrial society when a money wage came to represent the sole income for the mass of individuals it carried with it not only complete inde-pendence and isolation, but also complete helplessness against the vicissitudes and needs that each individual faces at some time in life. The money as the only source of life destroyed both the home and the parish. The insecurity suddenly became universalized because money wage is precarious and unstable and also because the children, the helpless widow, the sick, and the old, not to speak of the unemployed cannot and do not earn a money wage. All men and women begin as infants and an increasing population are now ending their lives aged and helpless, beyond the competence to earn a money wage".[12]

Such a society is likely to diminish the status and importance of the individual even further. "A society in which all men have a money wage as their only source is a society of very great complexity and full of hazards to the working of the economy itself. It is also a society in which all men become subject to the threat of insecurity for which as individuals they have no remedy......."[13] These insecurities have to be provided for and some agency has to step in, which is likely to become increasingly more and more powerful. "One thing is clear, a complete dependence upon money wage income for all, or even for the vast majority of men, can only end in tyranny by the State that provides the needed security, for to provide the security it will not only tax the substance of the community savings, but also interfere in the operation of our industrial society to lessen the unemployment and friction that complexity makes possible and perhaps inevitable. To save man from the insecurity, the State will in time, as the increasing dependence of the individual force it to assume greater control over prod- uction, and over the members of the community itself, so as to regulate and make efficient the 'welfare' that it will have to provide".[14]

The welfare state has no option but to go on limiting individual choices and liberties. "They, too, are caught in the consequent complexities of our society, over which they have no control and which they meddle like blind mice gnawing at the rope that will spring the trap".[15]

The state will have to provide security against various risks and "in the process it will destroy the liberties of our time and make them subservient to an all absorbing Leviathan. The feeling of independence the welfare state would ultimately destroy with the best intent in the world and in the name of freedom".[16]

"Today we see about us on all sides a steady drift towards increased human organisation. Governments are becoming more centralised and universal. In practically all areas of endeavour within industrial society — in our system of production, in the fields of labour, capital, commerce, agriculture, science, education and art — we see the emergence of new levels of organisation designed to coordinate, integrate, bind and regulate men's action.

The justifications for this increasing degree of organisation to which man must accommodate himself are expressed in terms such as 'stability', 'security', and 'efficiency'. The end result of this rapid transition might well be the emergence of a universal, stable, efficient, industrial society within which, although all persons have complete personal security, their actions are completely controlled. Should that time arrive society will have become static devoid of movement fixed and permanent. History will have stopped".[17]

"In a modern industrial society the road towards totalitarianism is unidirectional........Today our science and technology have placed in the hands of rulers of nations weapons and tools of control, persuasion, and coercion of unprecedented power. We have reached the point where once totalitarian power is seized in highly industrial society successful revolt becomes practically impossible. Totalitarian power, once it is gained, can be perpetuated almost indefinitely in the absence of outside forces, and can lead to progressively more rapid robotization of the individual".[18]

The industrial order today does not provide conditions, which offer individual freedom and ability to avoid the conditions, which impose these rigid organisation and totalitarian controls. "Indeed, when we examine all of the foreseeable difficulties which threaten the survival of industrial civilisation it is difficult to see how the achievement of stability and the maintenance of individual liberty can be made compatible".[19]

All these value patterns have come in the wake of mecha-nisation and increasing technical development. It is being argued that the evils that have emanated from the present age are not inherent in the machine. These have been human faults and can be set right. "All the evils of the age cannot be blamed on the bad will of men who misuse machines; some of them are intrinsic to the very nature of the machine itself".[20] "During the stages of economic science when the economists limited the physical sciences the individual was treated in economic theory like atoms, molecules, steam engines, horse-power, and the like controlled by external forces and not self-controlled".[21] Men became interchangeable, equal, unrelated and subject to manipulation. They ceased to be human. Morality and ethics disappear because they have no place among atoms, and the only force that keeps state and society from splintering is the selfish but equal economic motivation".[22]

This has created a situation when man feels lost; a non-entity. "We live at a time when man believes himself fabulously capable of creation, but he does not know what to create. Lord of all things, he is not lord of himself. He feels lost amidst his own abundance. With more means at his disposal, more knowledge, more technique than ever, it turns out that the world today goes the same way as the worst worlds that have been; it simply drifts".[23] "Is there not a direct connection between the increase of knowledge concerning mechanically exact processes and the fact that modern man, in a strange manner, loses his individuality, loses his balance his grip upon life, feels increasingly endangered and susceptible to attack in the security that is his due".[24] Further, "there is no doubt that the efforts of the technician have intensified the spiritual vacuum, that feeling of emptiness, to the same degree that he has constricted the scope of human life. And so the horror vacui; the horror of the void, is part of the technician's world; in many forms this horror enters into human consciousness; as a feeling of depression, of boredom, of futility, lack of purpose, nervousness and mechanical restlessness".[25] "A technology bent on easing the tragedy of life would be good indeed. But there is no real ease. On the contrary, life is invaded as by an automation. Nature withers. The springs of piety corrupt. Man is left to shuffle along the pavements of modern city surrounded by, and formed in the likeness of a dream world of puppets, of flickering shadows created by minds bent on reducing the human subsistence to a burlesque of the machine".[26]

Our economy has been rightly described as "that whole system of appetites and values with its deifications of the life of snatching to hoard and hoarding to snatch, which now, is the hour of its triumph, while the plaudits of the crowd still ring in the ears of the gladiators and the laurels are still unfaded on their brows, seems sometime to leave a taste as of ashes on the lips of civilization which has brought to the conquest of the material environment resources unknown in earlier ages, but which has not learnt to master itself".[27] Wilhelmsen remarks, "Unless we act, the tombstone of mankind will be read under the snows of other years only by dumb eyes, those of a twisted remnant pausing amidst the dead creatures of what we once called the western world".[28] Mr. Juenger observes that "Everywhere it is threatened by decay, given over to decay and decay follows upon its heels all the more insistently and closely, the faster it marches on towards new triumphs".[29]

"People were so preoccupied with their daily cares and the pursuit of material welfare that they never gave thought to the dangers threatening humanity. It is an oppressive, breath-taking age in which we live filled with haste, insecurity and discord".[30] "Ours is pretty such a civilization without purpose except that there is general agreement that the good life should be made available to all members of the community. But the problem of what is the good life receives little attention".[31] "Today, by the fact that everything seems possible to us, we have a feeling that the worst of all is possible, retrogression, barbarism; decadence".[32]

The remedy lies in fully emphasizing the non-economic aspects of life. "If the nineteenth century is the culmination of three centuries of the scientific revolution, the twentieth century, beginning with two world wars is preeminently the century of an ethical revolution to correct world massacres resulting from the triumphs of science".[33] "For the scientific revolution consisted in dropping both the divine will and the human will from the restraint of ethical investigation and reducing not only physical nature but also human nature to a blind war of atoms, molecules, protons, electrons, statistics quanta and a bloody struggle for existence and survival".[34] "The major error of the last century has been the assumption that a total society can be organised upon an economic motive".[35] "If the dignity of human nature to be respected, each man must shoulder the main responsibility for the working out his own salvation, an omnibus purpose which, since man has body as well as soul, must include economic wellbeing. Money which, however, is but the means, is, therefore, a real and right motive for work, but it is only one among many; only a part of much larger purpose. It is when the other factors of this wider purpose are obscured or deliberately disregarded that money incentives rise to the first place and dominate the whole conduct of man's activities. But this is unnatural, almost pathological, state of mind, and it makes no difference whether the incentive is connected with a wage-packet or a profit. As a prime motive — as a total purpose it is deplorable; and to hold it up as the necessary basis of all economic activity is to do unpardonable violence to the dignity of human life".[36] "Economic incentive has its right place, and in so far as it provides a common medium for the correlation of various forms of human initiative, it fulfills a most useful purpose. But its over emphasis.......which has led to an absurd prestige being attached to economic measurements of human worth, is largely to be accounted for by an economic organisation which has failed to emphasise other sources of satisfaction, and which has blinded so many to the ultimate purpose of work.......".[37] "Man has to belong to something real, purposeful, useful, creative; he must belong to his job and to his industry, or it must belong to him. There is no way of permanently separating the two. What gnaws at the psychological and moral roots of the contemporary world is that most urban people, workers belong to nothing real, nothing greater than their own impersonal pecuniary interests. To escape from this profound tragedy of our industrial society is the great issue of our time, for a world in which neither the owner nor the workers is morally identified with his source of income has no principle of continuity. No institution can survive a moral vacuum".[38]

"Human life by its very nature has to be dedicated to something, an enterprise glorious or humble, a destiny illustrious or trivial. We are faced with a condition, strange but inexorable, involved in our very existence. On the one hand, to live is some-thing, which each one does himself and for himself. On the other hand, if that life of mine which only concerns myself, is not directed by me towards something, it will be disjointed, lacking in form. In these years we are witnessing the gigantic spectacle of innumerable human lives wandering about lost in their own labyrinths, through not having anything to which to give themselves. All imperatives, all commands are in a state of suspension. The situation might be an ideal one, since every existence is left entirely free to do just as it pleases — to look after itself.......But the result has been contrary to what might have been expected. Given over to itself, every life has been left empty, with nothing to do. And it is to be filled with something. It invents frivolities for itself, gives itself to false occupations which impose nothing intimate and sincere......... Life is lost at finding itself all alone..... Really to live is to be directed towards something, to progress towards a goal. The goal is not my mission, not my life, it is something to which I put my life and which consequently is outside it, beyond it."

It means that we must believe in the curtailment of wants. "I suggest, it will be necessary to start by defining certain 'limits'. Material things are of real importance — for a person, a family or a nation — only 'up to a point'. So we can distinguish three economic conditions; misery, sufficiency and surfeit. Of these, two are bad — for a person, family or a nation — and only one, sufficiency is good. Economic progress is good only to the point of sufficiency, beyond that it is evil, destructive, uneconomic. These distinctions will be the most important of all for the type of economics I am thinking of".[39]

"The test to which all expenditure must be brought in an attempt to decide that point is the question whether it serves directly to enhance human life on the whole — whether it furthers the life process taken impersonally......The question is, therefore, not whether, under the existing circumstances, a given expenditure conduces to the particular consumer's gratification or peace of mind; but whether, aside from acquired tastes and from the canons of usage and conventional decency, its result is a net gain in comfort or in the fullness of life".[40]

This will mean giving up technology to a very large-extent. "The control of technology means a severe limitation of its hitherto unchecked growth, a limitation demanding almost savage asceticism on the part of an age drunk, not merely with the synthetic emotions and pleasures manufactured hourly by the entertainment factories, but with dreams of power and of the conquest of the outer space".[41] "Perhaps the greater danger of liberties, craftsmanship, peace of mind and fraternity is....... The nature of large scale industry itself; if so, the real adjustment we have not yet learned how to make properly is to an environment of industrialisation and technology. At any rate, this has been the cry of many sensitive social critics, from Godwin to Lewis Mumford".[42] "If man cannot once again make freedom, security and work synonymous he will destroy the machine. Our industrial civilisation will not survive state planning, socialist control, communist bureaucracy or fascist moral perversion, for they all postulate this disparity between labour and freedom".[43] "And if the basic needs of the labour are to be diagnosed......they will all be found to revolve round the need for an industrial organisation in which the worker belongs, belongs to the instrument of production, belongs to purpose, to its results; with the necessary corollary that his place of work belongs to him, and that the whole work value of the finished product is recognized as his property. In short social and economic integration. Until this is achieved, the ugly word exploitation will continue to have substance".[44]

The new industrial unit has to be entirely different. "The final test must always concern the development of the civilisation of the age. For the greatest failure of all is when industrial organisation fails to be a creative social institution. What shall it profit a man if he gains the whole world and loses his own soul".

"So the new industrial unit must answer a number of tests which stretch away and beyond the limited circle of economic results. Does it grow naturally out of the experience of tradition? Is it built round a full recognition of its essential structure without short-cuts, elimination and substitution? Does it serve the public with goods and services it requires? Is it providing a harmonious society round the function of daily work? Does it offer the individual the maximum opportunity to develop his natural gifts, not making use merely of the strongest but satisfying the hunger of the weak to be useful and to live full, interesting and purposeful lives.......?[45] "If there is any meaning that can be derived from the persistent grouping of men about their tools or within their industry, it is that work must fill a social and moral as well as economic role. The vacuum created between the job and the man has proceeded intolerably, and it cannot be filled by higher wages, shorter hours, better conditions of labour, music in the shops, or baby clinics. Man has to belong to something real, purposeful, useful, creative; he must belong to his job and to his industry, or it must belong to him. There is no way of permanently separating the two".[46]

"The machine has divorced man from the world of nature to which he belongs, and in the process he has lost in large measure the power of contemplation with which he has endowed. A pre-requisite for the preservation of the cannons of humanism is a re-establishment of organic roots with one natural environment and related to it, the evolution of ways of life, which encourage contemplation and the search for truth and knowledge. The flower and vegetable garden, green grass, the fireplace the primeval forest with its wonderous assemblage of living things, the uninhabited hill top where one can silently look at the stars and wonder — all of these and many others are necessary for the fulfilment of man's pressing needs for food and living space. But they are as necessary to the preservation of humanism as food is necessary to the preservation of human life."

The world is passing through very difficult and critical time. "Never before in history has so much responsibility been inherited by a group of human beings. Wherein previous times the lives of individual nations and culture were at stake, today the stake is the destiny of all humanity."[47] This is the time of grave decisions when all the goodness in man must be called forth to subjugate the bad; when our survival depends upon the victory of wisdom and knowledge over stupidity and dogma. "We must divorce ourselves from unreasoned slogans and dogma, from the soothsayer, from the person whose selfish interest compels him to draw false conclusions, from the man who fears truth and knowledge, from the man who prefers indoctrination to education..........We must learn not to fear change, for of one thing we can be certain — no matter what happens in the world of next few decades, change will be the major characteristic......"[48] And here the values that will count are those that are considered useless and those which are unknown today. "The unknown values are those of what in the last analysis, will prove to be the critical resources — those within the mind and the spirit of man himself, the 'human resources'. To what extent can man subjugate selfishness to generosity, ignorance to wisdom and hate to love? To what extent will he be able to realize in time that if he continues to follow the present path he will soon be confronted by disaster."[49]

The I.L.O. President had also these fears in mind when he quoted Bertand de Jouvenal: "Justice is a quality not of social arrangements but of the human will.......What we should be concerned with is that the whole ceaseless process of change should be increasingly permeated by the quality of justice in our individual wills. Every immediate field of chance open to us, in either our private or public capacity, offers us opportunity for the exercise of justice. Whenever, we miss this opportunity we feed the sum of social injustice a sum, which is comfortable but untrue to regard as the product of some single institution or mode of arrangement."

"These words, I suggest, bring us back to the proposition that man in society is a moral agent.......Unless the quality of justice permeates social leadership and individual behave with social responsibility, I believe the aims for which this organisa-tion (I.L.O.) works cannot be realized and its achievements will not endure. And this is where our efforts for social progress join with the larger task of ensuring permanent and lasting peace. During the last 39 years, we, in the I.L.O. have had recurrent cause to question whether civilization has achieved any real and lasting growth in the moral statute of man. Scientific and technical advance seems, at times, to march with an insensitive disposition to destroy dignity, which is the very essence and seat of freedom. Without the respect for the innate worth of personality and of the individual there can be no civilisation. Whatever the I.L.O. may achieve to this end will, I believe, be counted its noblest work."

Mahatma Gandhi had been working throughout his life towards the attainment of these ideals. He had realized that "the problem of (industrial) discontent is inherent in, and arises from, the structure of society; from its religious and ethical forms and the attitude to property and work which these inculcate and which are given expression in its laws. In fact it is true to say that in the last analysis the problem of (Industrial) discontent is rooted in fundamentals of our way of living which are so much a part of ourselves that we seldom stop to question them. Consequently we may fail to realize that these fundamentals are neither universal nor immutable, and that, in other times and places and in other forms of society, they may be quite different."[50]

Gandhiji had realized that if economic motive predominates as social aim, social life will be dominated by violence and universal corruption as we see in modern times. People in search of possession will be inevitably driven to military conquests or economic advancement at any cost as the Highest Good and end in producing warmongers and tycoons. If indulgence is the predominant aim of the life, it will lead to a social system based on pleasure. People will be addicted to the joy of the flesh and luxurious living. Moral decay and social disintegration would follow. In either case moral vacuum will follow and people would have little chance to pursue the path of the Highest

Good. Hence we should create a society where economic motives are kept in check. But "the exclusive empha-sis on pleasures and possessions........makes the very idea of a society led by man devoted to high ideals and ouster poverty absurd. A life of truth, dedication and self-mastery, appears to us as a painful struggle, a sacrifice of values, while the universal distress and frustration that modern life entails is ignored." "Economics means a certain ordering of life according to the philosophy inherent and implicit in economics. The science of economics does not stand on its own feet; it is derived from a way of the meaning and purpose of life — whether economist himself knows this or not."[51]

"Those who are intoxicated by modern civilisation are not likely to write against it"[52] remarked Gandhiji. "This booklet (Hind Swaraj) is a severe condemnation of 'modern civilization'. It was written in 1903. My conviction is deeper today than ever. I feel that if India will discard 'modern civilization' she can only gain by doing so."[53] "The fact is that this industrial civilization is a disease because it is all evil. Let us not be deceived by catchwords and phrases.......Our concern is, there-fore, to destroy industrialism at any cost."[54] Yet at another occasion he remarked, "What is industrialism but a control of majority by a small minority. There is industrialism but a control of majority by a small minority. There is nothing attractive about it nor is there anything inevitable in it,"[55] and "Industrialism is, I am afraid, going to be a curse for mankind".[56]

He was of the view that we should believe in the deliberate curtailment of wants. "If by abundance you mean every one having plenty to eat and drink and to clothe himself with, enough to keep his mind trained and educated, I should be satisfied. But I should not like to pack more stuff to my belly than I can digest and more things than I can ever usefully use. But neither do I want poverty, penury, misery, dirt and dust in India."[57] To the question of an interviewer that "The fact is, the material resources of the West have advanced out of proportion to its moral resources, and something need be done to bring them in a level with each other," Gandhiji replied: "That is precisely what the charkha is intended to do."[58] In 1938 while discussing the possibility of peace he had occasion to remark: "This again seems impossible without great nations ceasing to believe in soul-destroying competition and to multiply wants and thereby increasing their material possessions."[59] He clarified his views further, "I cannot only imagine but am working for a civilization in which possession of car will be considered no merit and railways will find no place. It would not be for me as unhappy even if the world once more became as large as it used to be at one time.......it is not an attempt to go back to the so-called ignorant, dark ages. But it is an attempt to see beauty in voluntary simplicity, poverty and slowness.......the modern rage for variety, for flying through the air, for multiplicity of wants, etc. have no fascination for me. They deaden the inner being in us."[60] "High thinking is inconsistent with complicated material life based on high speed imposed on us by Mammon worship. All the graces of life are possible only when we learn the art of living nobly."[61] To the question whether such plain living is possible for an isolated nation, he replied: "The answer is straight and simple. If plain life is worth living, then the attempt is worth making even if an individual or a group makes the effort."[62] "As I was picturing life based on non-violence, I saw that it must be reduced to the simplest terms consistent with high thinking."[63] "A certain degree of physical harmony and comfort is necessary, but above a certain level it becomes a hindrance instead of help. Therefore, the ideal of creating an unlimited number of wants and satisfying them seems to be delusion and snare. The satisfaction of one's physical needs, even the intellectual needs of one's narrow self, must meet at a certain point a dead stop, before it degenerates into physical and intellectual voluptuousness. A man must arrange his physical and cultural circumstances so that they do not hinder him in his service of humanity on which all his energies should be concentrated."[64] "Our civilisation, our culture, our Swaraj depend not upon multiplying our wants — self-indulgence, but upon restricting our wants—self-denial."[65] He had occasion to remark quite early: "I should not have laboured my point as I have done, if I did not believe that, in so far as we have made the modern materialistic craze our goal, so far are we going downhill in the path of progress. I hold that economic progress in the sense I have put it is antagonistic to real progress. Hence the ancient ideal has been the limitation of activities promoting wealth. This does not put an end to all material ambition. We should still have, as we have always had, in our midst people who make the pursuit of wealth their aim in life. But we have always recognized that it is a fall from the ideal......That you cannot serve God and Mammon is an economic truth of the highest value. We have to make our choice. Western nations are today groaning under the heel of the monster god or materialism. Their moral growth has become stunted. They measure their progress in £.s.d. American wealth has become the standard. She is the envy of other nations. I have heard many of our countrymen say that we will gain American wealth but avoid its methods. I venture to suggest that such an attempt, if it were made, is foredoomed to failure. We cannot be 'wise, temperate and furious' in a moment...It is not possible to conceive gods inhabiting a land which is made hideous by the smoke and the dim of mill chimneys and factories and whose roadways are traversed by rushing engines, dragging numerous cars crowded with men who know not for the most part what they are after, who are often absent-minded, and whose tempers do not improve by being uncomfortably packed like sardines in boxes and finding themselves. In the midst of utter strangers, who would oust them if they could and whom they would, in their turn oust similarly. I refer to these things because they are held to be symbolical of material progress. But they add not an atom to our happiness."[66]

He despised modern industrialisation and wanted eco-nomic regeneration of India in decentralised pattern. "To change to industrialism is to court disaster. The present distress is undoubtedly insufferable. Pauperism must go. But industrialism is no remedy."[67] "The revival of the village is possible only when it is no more exploited. Industrialisation on a mass-scale will necessarily lead to the passive or active exploitation of the villages as the problem of competition and marketing comes in."[68] "My views on national planning differ from the prevailing ones. I do not want it along industrial lines. I want to prevent our villages from catching the infection of industrialisation."[69] "I do not believe that industrialisation is necessary in any case for any country. It is much less so for India. Indeed I believe that independent India can discharge her duty towards a groaning world by adopting a simple but ennobled life by developing her thousands of cottages and living at peace with the world."[70]

He was skeptical about machinery and technological advancement. "Machinery is the chief symbol of modern civilization. It represents a great sin……Machinery is like a snake-hole which may contain from one to a hundred snakes…….. I cannot recall a single good point in connection with machinery. Books can be written to demonstrate its evils."[71] These are very extreme views and may lead one to believe that Gandhiji was opposed to all types of machinery. This is not so. "To say that is to caricature my views. I am not against machinery as such, but I am totally opposed to it when it masters us."[72] He was practical enough to realize that machinery cannot be discarded whole-sale. "Still less I am trying to destroy all machinery and mills. It requires a higher simplicity and renunciation than the people today are prepared for."[71] He, therefore, explained that "I am aiming not at eradication of all machinery but limitation."[74] Explaining further he observed, "My machinery must be of the most elementary type which I can put in the homes of the millions. Under my system again it is labour, which is the current coin, not metal. Any person who can use his labour has that coin, has wealth."[75] And he said that he will "welcome every improvement in the cottage machine but I know that it is criminal to displace the hand labour by the introduction of power driven spindles unless one is at the same time ready to give millions of farmers some other occupation in their homes."[76] It may be argued that to what extent this process of improvement of the cottage machinery be taken. The reply of Mahatma Gandhi was "just where they cease to help the individual and encroach upon his individuality. The machine should not be allowed to cripple the limbs of man."[77] He was opposed to machinery because it leads to evil and exploitation. "What I object to, is the craze for machinery, not machinery as such. The craze is for what they call labour-saving machinery. Men go on 'saving labour' till they are without work and thrown on the open streets to die of starvation. I want to save time and labour, not for a fraction of mankind, but for all. I want the concentration of wealth not in the hands of a few to ride on the backs of millions. The impetus behind it all is not the philanthropy to save labour but greed. It is against this cons-titution of things that I am fighting with all my might."[78]

To the argument that machinery will save time and provide leisure he argued that "if the craze for the machinery method continues, it is highly likely that a time will come when we shall be so incapacitated and weak that we shall begin to curse ourselves for having forgotten the use of the living machines given to us by God. Millions cannot keep themselves fit by games and athletics. And why they should exchange the useful, productive, hardy occupations for the useless, unproductive and expensive games and exercises? They are all right today for a change and recreation. They will jar upon us when they become a necessary occupation in order that we may have the appetite for eating the food in the production of which we had no hand or part."[79]

"Leisure and free activity are not accessible to every body and they are conditions in no way connected with machine. A man who is relieved of work is not capable of leisure; a man who gains time does not thereby gain the capacity to spend this time in free activity; for leisure is not a mere doing nothing, a state that can be defined negatively. Leisure to be fruitful, presupposes a spiritual and mental life from which it draws its meaning and its worth. An *otium sine dignitate* (leisure without dignity) is hollow, empty loafing. Nor is leisure, as many seem to think, a mere intermission in work, a limited time, no, by definition it is unlimited and indivisible, and from it originates all meaningful work. Leisure is the prerequisite of every free thought, every free activity.......many when they have gained time kill it.........Thus even if the machine did relieve man of work, this would be no guarantee that man would profit by the time gained and use it intelligently. The unemployed worker who does not have this capacity goes to pieces; because he does not know what do with the empty time that befalls him...... No connection whatsoever exists between the reduction of work and leisure and free activity; as little in fact, as an increase in the speed of locomotion implies a rise in the mortality, or the invention of telegraphy an increase in the clear thinking."[80] The same author remarks at another place: "It (technology) has brought about a situation where man no longer has time, where he is destitute of time, where he is hungry for time".[81]

Gandhiji, therefore, did not desire that hours of work should be unnecessarily reduced. These are likely to create several new problems. "Any one who knows the present day situation realizes what would happen to the United States if we had a general 20 hours week today. We would have thousands more psychiatrists to take care of the nervous breakdowns which would occur if people had that much more free time on their hands without knowing what to do with it."[82] He remarked that he "should never be satisfied until all men had plenty of productive work, say eight hours a day, because I know that millions will not employ themselves in work for the sake of it. If they did not need to work for their bread they would lack the incentive."[83] This he suggested not only because absence of productive work will hurt the self-respect but "especially because it strikes at the root of the fundamental law of our being, viz., that we must work for our bread, that we eat our bread by the sweat of our brow".[84] Yet on another occasion he observed: "Leisure is good and necessary upto a point only. God created man to eat his bread in the sweat of his brow, and I dread the prospect of our being able to produce all that we want, including our food stuffs, out of a conjurer's hat."[85]

As a practical idealist Gandhiji had realized that the society may not be able to adopt simplicity to the extent he would like. Therefore, as a concession to human weakness he will permit use of machinery sparingly. "My condemnation of rail road etc., whilst true where it stands, has little or no, bearing in present movement which disregards none of the institutions mentioned by the writer. In the present movement I am neither attacking rail roads nor hospitals......."[86] "The heavy machinery for work of public utility which can not be undertaken by human labour has its inevitable place, but all that would be owned by the State and used entirely for the benefit of the people. I can have no consideration for machinery, which is meant either to enrich the few at the expense of many, or without cause to displace the useful labour of many".[87] He had observed quite early that wherever there are such industries they shall be working under ideal conditions. "But I am socialist enough to say that such factories should be nationalized, or state-controlled. They ought only to be working under the most attractive and ideal conditions, not for profit, but for the benefit of humanity, love taking the place of greed as motive. It is an alteration in the conditions of labour that I want. This mad rush for wealth must cease, and the labour must be assured, not only of a living wage, but a daily task that is not mere drudgery".[88]

But while permitting the use of machinery under such exceptional circumstances he was quite clear and unequivocal about production of the necessities of life like food, cloth etc. through cottage and small scale industries. "Mass production, then, at least where the vital necessities are concerned, will disappear........When production and consumption both become localized, the temptation to speed up production indefinitely and at any price, disappears. All the endless difficulties and problems that our present day economic system presents, too, would then come to an end."[89] The importation of dried milk for village children may be good enough from a humanitarian point of view, but it would be monstrous inroad on the economic freedom of the village".[90] He, therefore, advised that the revival of village is possible only when it is no more exploited. Industrialisation on a mass-scale will necessarily lead to passive or active exploitation of the villagers as the problem of competition and marketing comes in. Therefore, we have to concentrate on the village being self-contained and manufacturing mainly for use. Provided this character of village industry is maintained there would be no objection to villagers using even the modern machinery and tools that they can make and can afford to use. Only they should not be used as a means of exploitation of others. "If I can convert the country to my point of view, the social order of the future will be based predominantly on the Charkha and all it implies. It will include everything that promotes the well-being of the villagers. It will not exclude the industries mentioned by my correspondents so long as they do not smother the villages and village life. I do visualize electricity, ship-building, iron-works, machine-making and like existing side by side with village handicrafts, but the order of dependence will be reversed. Hitherto the industrialisation has been so planned as to destroy the villages and village crafts. In the state of future it will subserve the villages and their crafts. I do not share the socialist belief that centralisation of the necessaries of life will conduce to the common welfare when the centralised industries are planned and owned by the State".[91] He had held this view since long. "I hold that the machinery method is harmful when the same thing can be done easily by millions of hands not otherwise occupied.......These villages can not retain the freedom they have enjoyed from time immemorial, if they do not control the production of prime necessaries of life".[92] It was only when there was extreme decentralisation in respect of such needs that a correct social order can be brought about. "Exploitation brings in its train the craving for markets.........This craving must be destroyed, and it can be done only by every cottage being able to satisfy its vital necessities, and thus making the nation self-contained".[93]

The message of charkha has to be viewed in this light. "........the message of the spinning wheel is much wider than its circumference. Its message is one of simplicity, service of mankind, living so as not to hurt others, creating an indissoluble bond between the rich and the poor, capital and labour, the prince and the peasant. The large message is naturally for all.......it is not an attempt to spiritualise the machinery—because that seems to me an impossible task—but to introduce, if it is at all possible, a human or humane spirit among the men behind the machinery......The movement of the spinning wheel is an organised attempt to displace machinery from that state of exclusiveness and exploitation and to place it in its proper state".[94]

It is only when machine is placed in its proper place that we can think of a society based on non-violence. To a questioner who feared that 'mechanisation might get hold of India' Gandhiji replied: "Then there is no escape from violence. I saw it as long as 1908, and ever since I have shaped all my activities in terms of non-violence. Complete mechanisation is impossible in India without its resulting in violence in some shape or other."[95]

It is only when there is decentralisation of the production of basic needs of people and a limited reliance on centralised industry that all other postulates of Gandhian economic order can function. Then alone we can build up an order where "The Brahmans will be very few. Fewer still will be the soldier class who will not be the hirelings or the unrestrained rulers of today, but the real protectors of the nation laying down their lives for its service. The fewest will be Shudras for in a well ordered society a minimum numerous will be the Vaishyas — the agriculturists, the traders, the artisans etc. This scheme may sound utopian. I, however, prefer to live in this utopia of my imagination to trying to live upto the unbridled licence of a society that I see tottering to its disruption".[96]

It is only in such a society that the different vows of non-stealing, non[possession, Swadeshi and the doctrine of bread labour shall become the social values in place of the modern ones. And only under these circumstances can we lay the foundation of a setup where "there must be always enough occupation......for all who are willing to work"[97] and concentration of riches in a few people and unemployment amongst millions and robotization of the individual shall not be possible. He had to remark ".......quick traveling, motor cars, the cinema, radio, electric light, and a thousand and one thrills provided by what Stuart Chase has called 'the toys of civilisation' are what the city bred intellectual, who today guides our social destinies wants. The handicrafts, on the other hand, depend for their success on a different system of economics. If a rural-minded society provided these, no power on earth would be able to compete with handicrafts. But then such a society shall have to be content with the simple joys and satisfactions which the countryside provides and not dream of utopia in which all the villages would be equipped with the latest 'modern convenience'. The so-called economical character of the factory production as compared to handicrafts production is not an inherent quality, but only a conferred attribute depending on the standard of values which society has adopted or considers desirable to adopt".[98]

"Our only alternative to the danger of robotism is humanistic communitarianism. The problem is not primarily the legal problem of property ownership, nor that of sharing profits; it is that of sharing work, sharing experiences. Changes in ownership must be made to the extent necessary to create a community of work, and to prevent the profit motive from directing production into socially harmful directions. Income must be equalized to the extent of giving everybody the material basis for dignified life and thus preventing economic differences from creating fundamentally different experiences of life among various social classes. Man must be reinstituted in his supreme place in society — never a means, never a thing to be used by others or by himself. Man's use by man must end, and economy must become the servant for the development of man. Capital must serve labour, things must serve life. Instead of the exploiting and hoarding orientation dominant in the ninteenth century, and the receptive and marketing orientation dominant today, the productive orientation must be the end that all social arrangements serve. Freedom in work situation is not freedom from work (in order to have leisure), it is not freedom from crude exploitation, it is the freedom to spend one's energy in a meaningful, productive way by being an active, responsible, unalienated participant in that total work situation."[99]

Another author had to remark that "Framing a human relations policy in the fullest and widest meaning of the term means in the last analysis, respecting the individual man as a member of the economic system. Just as labour is not a commodity, a human being is not a tool or a machine, his dignity has got to be safeguarded and provision made for his fundamental needs. These are imperative human considerations that cannot be disregarded with impunity. The undertaking has a dual existence. It is not only an economic profit making unit in which the workers are an element in production costs, it is also a social unit, which in addition to its responsibilities towards the community, has a liability towards the worker it employs, and it must accordingly offer them every possibility.... For the full expression of their personalities." "An undertaking is intended to be servant of humanity and should never make humanity is slave."[100]

It may be argued as to how shall it be possible to bring about such changes. There have been several instances when individuals have tried to apply a brake. "Nevertheless, while economic associations have for the most part, become entirely utilitarian, the ideal of using the industrial unit as an organ for the enrichment of the spiritual sphere has never entirely died down. The factory school of Owen and his successors, the sports ground, the factory social, the attempt to create complete industrial communities, and today, the employment of works chaplains, are all pale reminders that the place of man's work should be creative social centre. But it is uphill work — generally depending upon the vision of some outstanding personality."[101] Mahatma Gandhi was such an outstanding personality who did not look upon the existing structure with a dwarfed vision. "Gandhi, like Christ, lit beacons on distant hills, towards which posterity must grope its way in darkness."[102] To quote Gurudev, "He stopped at the thousands of huts of the thousands of dispossessed, dressed like one of their own. He spoke to them in their own language; here was only living truth at last and not only quotations from book……In direct contact with truth, the crushed forces of the soul rise again……."

It may then be argued that what Gandhiji wrote and suggested is not economics but ethics and spirituality. "……… Western civilization, with its exaggerated economism, was exclusively preoccupied with the technical domination of the forces of nature. And while it was thus engaged with the problems of economic exploitation and the creation of wealth man and his problems were entirely forgotten."[103] "Science or knowledge is one. It has been divided into several sections, not because they are mutually unconnected or independent frag-ments, but simply because man's faculties are limited, his capacity is finite, his ability or opportunity is, under the most favourable conditions, inadequate. But because man has made, for his own convenience, these divisions or compartments, their essential unity and integrity, their mutual affinity and dependence, cannot be gainsaid."[104] Gandhiji said, "I must confess I do not draw a sharp or say distinction between economics and ethics. Economics that hurts the moral well-being of an individual or a nation are immoral and therefore sinful,"[105] and "That economics is untrue which ignores or disregards moral values. The extension of law of non-violence in the domain of economics means nothing less than the introduction of moral values as a factor to be considered in regulating international commerce."[106]

"It is amply clear that, if men will it, a world community can be created in which human beings can live comfortably and in peace with each other. But it is equally clear that the achievement of this condition will require the application of intelligence, imagination, courage, unselfish help, planning and prodigious effort. And it is equally clear that the time for the decision is the present......Man is rapidly creating a situation from which he will have increasing difficulties extricating himself."[107] This society can be based only on a decentralised economy. "Society based on non-violence can only consist of groups settled in villages in which voluntary cooperation is the condition of dignified and peaceful existence. A society which anticipates and provides for meeting violence with violence will either lead a precarious life or create big cities and magazines for defence purposes."[108] It is only on the foundations of a decentralised economic pattern that a truly democratic society can be built. "India is trying to evolve true democracy, i.e. without violence. Our weapons are those of Satyagraha expressed through charkha, the village industries, primary education through handicrafts......prohibition and non-violent organisation of labour......."

To us, who are intoxicated by the present materialistic civilisation, this may sound either utopian or reactionary, Gandhiji thought otherwise. "In short the reactionary turn", he remarked, "if at all it was, meant a return to commonsense, meant restoration of what appears to commonsense to be a natural order as distinguished from the present unnatural order, in a work not everything overturned or everything petrified but everything restored to its proper place." It is only by scrupulously following the advice of Mahatma Gandhi that the ideal of Gurudev can become the creed of all men, our civilization and our freedom can survive:

"Where the mind is without fear and the head is held high;

Where knowledge is free;

Where the world has not been broken up into fragments by narrow domestic walls;

Where words come out from the depth of truth;

Where tireless striving stretches the arms towards perfection;

Where the clear stream of reason has not lost its way into the dreary desert sand of dead habit;

Where the mind is led forward by Thee into every widening thought and action;

Into that heaven of freedom, my Father, let my country awake."

References

1. Labour in a Free Society, p. 3.
2. Veblen: The Theory of Leisure Class, p. 83.
3. Lewis Mumford, Techniques and Civilisation, p. 23.
4. Veblen: The Theory of Leisure Class, p. 23.
5. *Ibid.*, pp. 102-104.
6. Erich Fromm, Labour in a Free Society, p. 4.
7. *Ibid.*
8. Lewis Mumford: quoted in Harris Brown, the Challenge of Man's Future, p. 187.
9. Somervell: Industrial Peace of Our Times, p. 191.
10. *Ibid.*, p. 192.
11. A.E.C. Hare, First Principles of Industrial Relations, p. 59.
12. Tannebeun, The Philosophy of Labour, pp. 146-148.
13. *Ibid.*, p. 148.
14. *Ibid.*, p. 149.
15. *Ibid.*, p. 150.
16. *Ibid.*, p. 151.
17. Harris Brown: The Philosophy of Labour, pp. 254-55.
18. *Ibid.*, p. 255.
19. *Ibid.*, p. 255.
20. Wilhelmsen, in Introduction to Juenger's Failure of Technology, p. vi.
21. Commons: Economics of Collective Action, p. 154.
22. Tannebaun: The Philosophy of Labour, p. 52.
23. Gasset Y. Ortega: Revolt of the Masses, pp. 31-32.

24. Juenger: Failure of Technology, p. 106.
25. *Ibid.*, p. 131.
26. Wilhelmsen in Introduction to Failure of Technology, p. x.
27. R.H. Tawney, quoted in Paul Sultan: Labour Economics, p. 12 (footnote).
28. Wilhelmsen, Introduction to Failure of Technology, p. xiii
29. Juenger: Failure of Technology, p. 24.
30. Adenaur Dr., Statesman, 21 Dec. 1961.
31. Silchter: Freedom in Work Situation, p. 6.
32. Gasset Y. Ortega: The Revolt of the Masses, p. 32.
33. Commons: Economics of Collective Action, p. 166.
34. Tannebaun: The Philosophy of Labour, p. 168.
35. Somervell: Industrial Peace of Our Times, p. 77.
36. *Ibid.*, p. 77.
37. *Ibid.*, p. 77.
38. Gasset Ortega Y: The Revolt of the Masses, pp. 103-04.
39. F.F. Schumacher, quoted in J.P. Narain, Reconstruction of Indian Polity, p. 87.
40. Veblen: The Theory of Leisure Class, pp. 97-101.
41. Wilhelmsen: Introduction to Juenger's Failure of Technology, p. vi.
42. H.B. Mayo: quoted in Reconstruction of Indian Polity.
43. Tannebaun: The Philosophy of Labour, p. 11.
44. Somervell: Industrial Peace of our times, p. 84.
45. *Ibid.*, p. 86.
46. Tannebaun: The Philosophy of Labour, p. 105.
47. Harris Brown: The Challenge of Man's Future, p. 266.
48. *Ibid.*, p. 266.
49. *Ibid.*, p. 266.
50. A.E.C. Hare: First Principles of Industrial Relations, pp. 3-4.
51. E.H. Schumacher, quoted in Reconstruction of India Polity.
52. Hind Swaraj, p. 12.
53. *Ibid.*, Introduction.
54. Young India, 1926, p. 348.
55. *Ibid.* 1925, p. 273
56. *Ibid.* 1931, p. 355.
57. Harijan, 1938, p. 1.
58. Young India, 1927, p. 276.
59. Harijan, 1938, p. 153.
60. *Ibid.* 1939, p. 303.
61. *Ibid.* 1946, p. 285.

62. *Ibid.*
63. *Ibid.* 1940, p. 410.
64. *Ibid.* 1936, p. 226.
65. Young India, 1921.
66. December, 1916.
67. Young India, 1926, p. 349.
68. Harijan, 1936, p. 226.
69. *Ibid.* 1949, p. 293.
70. *Ibid.* 1946, p. 285.
71. Hind Swaraj, p. 56.
72. Harijan, 1937, p. 18.
73. Hind Swaraj, p. xi.
74. Young India, 1924.
75. Harijan, 1934, p. 301.
76. Young India, 1925, p. 377.
77. *Ibid.* 1924, p. 386.
78. *Ibid.* 1924, p. 378.
79. *Ibid.* 1931, p. 161.
80. Jung: Failure of Technology, pp. 5-6.
81. *Ibid.*, p. 44.
82. Erich Fromm: in Labour in a Free Society, pp. 3-4.
83. Harijan, 1935, p. 340.
84. *Ibid.*
85. *Ibid.* 1936, p. 114.
86. Young India, 1925, p. 321.
87. Harijan, 135, p. 146.
88. Young India, 1924, p. 378.
89. Harijan, 1934, p. 301.
90. *Ibid.* 1936, p. 43.
91. *Ibid.* 1940, p. 428.
92. Young India, 1931, p. 161.
93. *Ibid.* 1927, p. 276.
94. *Ibid.* p. 321.
95. Harijan, 1935, p. 399.
96. Young India, 1927, p. 384.
97. *Ibid.* 1925, p. 56.
98. Harijan, 1940, p. 202.
99. Erich Fromm in Labour in Free Society, pp. 15-16.

100. International Labour Review.
101. Somervell: Industrial Peace of Our Times, pp. 191-92.
102. Lord Altrincham, A.B. Patrika, December 23, 1961.
103. J. Huxley, quoted in Geography of Hunger by Da Costa, p. 18.
104. K.T. shah: Ancient Foundation of Economics in India, p. 13.
105. Young India, 1921, p. 531.
106. *Ibid.* 1924, p. 421.
107. Harris Brown: Challenge to Man's Future, p. 265.
108. Harijan, 1940, p. 410.

19

Defending Human Rights: Gandhiji's Method

Let me begin by repeating the old saying: "The road to hell is paved with good intentions". This is what has happened with the oft-repeated desire to safeguard and further Human Rights. With everybody getting conscious about safeguarding Human Rights, resolutions being passed and Human Rights days being observed, sections and articles for the provision of Human Rights in constitutions of different countries, this problem baffles and continues to be a challenge for those who are making efforts for a peaceful social order.

It is true that the setting up of UN, the Universal Decla-ration of Human Rights and the observance of 10th December as Human Rights day every year and subsequent development in this regard have made everyone conscious of the rights that people should enjoy. But, as mentioned earlier, these rights are being violated. Except for those who have political support or those who belong to elitist groups these declarations are expressions of pious sentiments and the masses remain largely untouched.

Our approach to the question of Human Rights should not simply be setting up institutions whom people or various organisations devoted to the preservation of these Rights can approach or appeal to or of codifying these Rights and making them elaborate or explicit. The approach should be to create a socio-economic environment where violation of these Rights will not be possible. In those rare cases where such violations take place individuals and small groups need be strong enough to preserve and protect these.

Gandhiji while fighting for India's independence, laid foundation of a methodology, which should be given, serious thought by all advocates of Human Rights. He had an universal appeal. He remarked in 1921: "Through the deliverance of India.........I seek to deliver the so-called weaker races of the earth from the crushing heels of Western exploitation......India's coming to her own will mean every nation doing likewise".

In human history we can recall several examples and a number of persons who fought against injustice and worked to bring solace and comfort to suffering humanity. The name of Mahatma Gandhi will naturally find a place of pride in such a list. High tributes have been paid by eminent persons from all walks of life to Gandhiji. "Gandhi, like Christ, lit beacons on distant hills, towards which posterity must grope its way in darkness" observed Lord Altrincham. Gurudev Tagore observed: "He stopped at the thousands of huts of the thousands of dispossessed, dressed like one of their own. He spoke to them in their own language; here was only living truth at last and not only quotations from books. In direct contact with truth, the crushed forces of the soul rise again........."

Seldom has a man's death evoked such widespread grief, sorrow and sense of personal loss among all classes and people as Gandhiji's. The United Nations flag was flown at half-mast. A remarkable feature of the world reaction to Gandhiji's death was the sense of bereavement it brought to people who had never met or even seen him. Typical of the reaction of the common man was the one expressed by a French citizen, " never saw Gandhi........I do not know his language. I never set foot in his country and yet I feel the same sorrow as if I had lost someone near and dear". The whole world has been plunged into mourning by the death of this extraordinary man........ Pope John Paul II during his recent visit to India paid tribute to Gandhiji by describing him as 'hero of humanity'.

Why does Gandhiji evoke such fine sentiments even among those who had never seen him or read about his life and deeds? All through his life, it may appear to many, he was fighting for his countrymen. He began his public career in South Africa fighting against the humiliation to which Indians were subjected. He organised mass movements, Satyagrahas, in South Africa against racial discrimination and challenged the might of one of the mightiest government. In our own country he lead a number of mass movements and challenged the British power. He fought against age-old social evil of untouchability and came in conflict with orthodox religious leaders. He worked for emancipation of backward classes and women. He worked all through his life to bring the two powerful religious groups of Hindus and Mussalmans and even made the supreme sacrifice. When there was all-round darkness, when violence was at its height, when government machinery had completely broken down to maintain even a semblance of civilized living, when even the military force proved ineffective Gandhiji's method and techniques proved effective. Lord Mountbatton described Gandhiji as "one man force". He tracked down the whole area of Noakhali on bare feet which quite often bled and became numb, with Tagore's inspiring song as his every day prayer.......

Walk alone
If they answer not thy call, walk alone,
If they are afraid and cower mutely facing the wall
O Thou of evil luck
Open thy mind and speak out alone.
If they turn away and desert you
when crossing the wilderness,
O Thou of evil luck,
trample the thorns under thy tread
and along the blood-line track travel alone.
If they do not hold up the light
when the night is troubled with storm
O Thou of evil luck
with the thunder-flame of pain ignite thine own heart
and let it burn alone.

At the age of 78 he learnt Bengali and practised to cross the bamboo bridges single-handed to fulfill his mission of 'do and die' and uphold the right of individuals and communities to lead dignified lives. Gandhiji earned his top most place as a champion of Human Rights because of his sheer personal efforts, courage and conviction. When prople were of the view that he should withdraw from the political scene, his comment to them was that "the Himalayas of my penance are where there is misery to be alleviated, oppression to be relieved...."[2] When even his closest associates had parted company he struck to his ground and ploughed his lonely furrow. Sarojini Naidu blessed his efforts in the following words:

"Beloved Pilgrim,

You are, I learn setting out once more on your chosen Via Dolorese in Bihar. The way of sorrow for you may indeed be the way of hope and solace for many millions of suffering human hearts. Blessed be your pilgrimage......"[3]

Gandhiji remarked: "May be, mine will prove to be a cry in wilderness. But I cannot want to go down as an unprotesting witness of what is taking place around me in the country today". It was undoubtedly the sacrifice of Gandhiji that saved the country from the evil consequence of violence and communal hatred in 1947.

Gandhiji's claim as crusader for Human Rights was his emphasis on non-violence as a method of social change and his repeated warning that violence only leads to greater violence. "Violence is bound sooner or later to exhaust itself but peace cannot issue out of such exhaustion. I am uttering God's truth when I say that unless there is return to sanity, violent people will be swept off the face of the earth.......Those who have their hands dyed deep in blood cannot build a non-violent order for the world".[4]

His definition of violence was wide enough to include exploitation of man by man, and groups and nations of one another "I am positive", asserted Gandhiji, "if they are so arrogant as to think that they can have lasting peace while the exploitation of the coloured and the so-called backward races goes on, they are living in a fool's paradise".[5] These words of wisdom hold good for socio-economic conditions prevailing inside individual nations as well.

He tried to prevent exploitation even of the weakest and the unorganized. This could be possible only when the move-ment of social change is based upon non-violent techniques, "Liberty won non-violently will belong to the least. That is why I swear by non-violence. Only when the least can say "I have got my liberty have I got mine".[6] He wanted Swaraj in which the fruits of freedom would be shared equally by all. But unless the weakest were able to contribute in the winning and defending of it with an equal share with physically the strongest this could not happen. "That can be under Ahimsa only. I would, therefore, stand for Ahimsa as the only means of obtaining India's freedom even if I were alone".[7]

Pope John Paul II began his tour of India as a 'Pilgrim of peace'. He knelt before the Samadhi of Mahatma Gandhi and observed that he considered it appropriate that his pilgrimage 'should begin here' expressing his conviction in Gandhian methodology of non-violence in the following words: "I wish to express to the people of India and of the world my profound conviction that the peace and justice of which contemporary society has such great need will only be achieved along the path which is at the core of his (Mahatma Gandhi's teaching: the supremacy of the spirit and Satyagraha, the 'truth force' which conquers without violence by the dynamism intrinsic to just action" (Times of India 3.2.86). He continued: "Mahatma Gandhi taught that if all men and women, whatever the difference between them cling to the truth with respect for the unique dignity of every human being, a new world order — a civilization of love — can be achieved. And today we hear him still pleading with the world; "Conquer hate by love, untruth by truth, violence by suffering".

But Gandhiji's claim to be the champion of Human Rights is to be examined in the background of powerful governments based on brute force with powerful instruments of violence at their command. "In our days the State has come to be a formidable machine which works in marvellous fashion of wonderful efficiency by reason of the quantity and precision of its means. Once it is set up in the midst of society it is enough to touch a button for its enormous levers to start working and exercise their overwhelming power on any portion whatever of the social framework".[8] ....In days gone by men could revolt against despotism. People could rise against their governments and with simple weapons, sticks, knives and the like defeat the military forces of the central authorities. But today our science and technology have placed in the hands of rulers of nations, weapons and tools of control, persuasion and coercion of unprecedented power. The road towards totalitarianism is unidirectional.

In such a situation Gandhi stands like a watch-tower reminding all of us that in a fight for Human Rights the target should be the increasing power of the State and this tendency towards centralisation. He warned "I look upon an increase of the power of the State with the greatest fear, because although while apparently doing good by minimizing exploitation, it does the greatest harm to mankind by destroying individuality...."[9] His opinion was that "the State represents violence, in a concentrated and organised form.....it can never by weaned from violence to which it owes its very existence".[10] Therefore, he said, real Swaraj will come not by acquisition of authority by the few but when the masses learn to oppose authority when abused.

And towards the acquisition by the masses of this right to oppose authority, he evolved his weapon of Satyagraha — non-violent action which could be undertaken by individuals, small groups and even large nations. In these days of organised violence, unorganized violence has no chance to even register a protest. Gandhiji demonstrated in his own lifetime what a potent weapon non-violent mass, and under certain circumstances, individual action can be. In South Africa, where he began his experiments, with unlettered coolies, indentured labourers who had become slave labour as his soldiers he demonstrated to the world that non-violence has capacity to test the might of the mightiest power and that a small unlettered, poverty-striken minority could defy the might of great States armed to the teeth. Similar were the experiences in India. At Bardoli where a Satyagraha was organised the British government unleashed severe repression. When all the authentic leadership was absent some 380 women challenged the might of the British Government and took the pledge. "Not one of the women stood up, not one retreated and not one cried out, although more than half of them had their sarees drenched in blood......"[11] The Government with all its mighty resources and in spite of a frightful reign of terror had to yield to practically all the demands of the Satyagrahis.

Gandhiji demonstrated in his own life what a single individual truly non-violent can do to fight against injustice and social evil. He fasted against the communal award and the gates of temples all over the country were thrown open for the Harijans. He decided to walk bare-footed and there was a campaign to keep the roads on which he was to walk clean. He fasted against the tide of communal violence and there was peace.

It is no use advancing the argument that Gandhiji's was an exceptional case. He argued that these techniques can be successfully tried even by less perfect persons who accepted his methods as a matter of policy. "I could not have done otherwise". He remarked, "If I was to introduce it, (non-violence into politics)...if I had started with men who accepted non-violence as a creed, I might have ended with myself. Imperfect as I am, I started with imperfect men and women and sailed on an unchartered ocean."[12] And again, "I go so far as to say that if ahimsa cannot be practised by the millions, I have no use for it myself".[13] Sri Pyarelal, Gandhiji's personal secretary and his biographer has expressed Gandhi's view on practice of non-violence by ordinary persons in the following words.

".....If one aspires to harness the power of Satyagraha or soul force one must seek it, like a prospector of fissionable material in infinitesimals. He was no impossible Mahatma, he maintained; his life was made up of a number of small things which were by themselves commonplace and which even an ordinary individual could practise. Therefore, what he had achieved everybody else could, and the practice of mass non-violence, the only effective answer to the challenge of unbridled brute force, was a present possibility".[14]

We may be tempted to dismiss these ideas as Utopian. It may be argued that most men and women are not fit to act up to this ideal. They are so selfish, unresponsible and irresponsible. "If that be so, and if these qualities are too deep rooted for anything to be done about them, all I can say is that the outlook for humanity is poor indeed".[15] Albert Camus, the French novelist and humanist expressed the view: "Over the expanse of five continents throughout the coming years an endless struggle is going on to be pursued between violence and friendly persuasion, a struggle in which, granted the former has a thousand times more the chances of success than the later. But I have also held that it is he who bases his hope on human nature is a fool, he who gives up in the face of circumstances is a coward".[16+]

To make his technique workable under different circum-stances be evolved a two-fold strategy. The one was of training individuals in the art of non-violent resistance through strict discipline. The inmates of his Ashram had to undertake several vows like that of Non-violence, Truth, Non-stealing, Non-possession or poverty, Bread labour, Swadeshi, fearlessness, etc. He wanted to train a few to be non-violent in thought, words and deed so that they can take up cudgels against denial of Human Rights and inspire the common man to follow their lead. He held the view that "it is possible to run a Satyagraha campaign with people who have no faith in non-violence as a creed provided they sincerely and implicitly follow the rules as a discipline and work under the leadership of unadulterated non-violence".[17] The role of leadership is important. The leaders should not only have confidence and faith in the efficacy of non-violent techniques but should make radical changes in their own personal lives and should identify themselves with the common men—their aspirations and evolve a methodology of fighting the exploitation, hardships and injustices to which they are subjected to through their active cooperation and involvement. This is how he made martyrs of ordinary men of clay.

While advocating the use of non-violent means for protection of Human Rights, the efficacy of which he demonstrated in various walks of life during his life time, Gandhiji laid emphasis on a radical restructuring of the socio-economic system. Thus he advocated control of consumption as against unbridled consumerism that is prevalent today. He laid emphasis that technology should be severely contained and put under restraint. If there are too many clever machines we will have too many stupid people. Technology beyond human control has resulted in concentrations of power, violence, irresponsibility and utter hopelessness, and helplessness, aggression and exploitation. Gandhiji wanted to give new direction to technological developments. To quote him: "The movement of the spinning wheel is an organised attempt to displace machinery from that state of exclusiveness and place it in its proper place".[18]

He advocated decentralisation. His concept of decentralisation is radically different from 'decentralisation and delegation' as is being talked about these days. Under modern concept power and authority remains with centralised authority and decentralisation under this concept permits, if at all, insignificant freedom to the people. Decentralisation as conceived by Gandhiji has the basic philosophy of giving strength to small groups to be able to resist exploitation, injustice and unfairness.

His strategy was to strive for socio-economic order, which will lead to the upholding of Human Rights through initiative that will rest with the masses. This he tried to attain through various items of his constructive programme. The items that he adopted for India are only illustrative. Under different circumstances these could be different. But the basic idea underlying these items was that a strategy need be evolved which will permit effective participation of those whose problems the leadership wants to solve. He repeatedly laid emphasis on this aspect of strategy. "Civil disobedience, without the backing of the constructive programme is criminal and waste of effort".

As Gandhiji saw it, the problem not only in India but all over the world was that people allowed themselves to be led by catch-words and slogans. In the prevailing confusion about "isms" they quarrelled over shadows and let the substance slip through their fingers. He tried to demonstrate in troubled Noakhali that after all it was the daily things of life that mattered most and that if the masses could solve them to their satisfaction and become masters of their destiny by dint of their own industry, intelligence, power of contribution and mutual cooperation, irrespective of any 'ism', its effect would be felt not merely in Noakhali but over the whole of India, and might even point the way to the future peace of the world.

Through the successful implementation of various items of constructive programme he was working for ushering in a socio-economic order, which will be devoid of injustices and exploitation. "India is trying to evolve true democracy i.e. without violence. Our weapons are those of Satyagraha expressed through charkha, the village industries, primary education through handicrafts, removal of untouchability, communal harmony, prohibition and non-violent organisation of labour.... This is permanent part of the non-violent effort. From this effort is created the capacity to offer non-violent resistance..... The experiment has in it promise of a brilliant future......."[19]

Gandhiji's greatest contribution in the struggle for fight for Human Rights is the inspiration, guidance and technique of resistance based on mass participation that he provided to men in all countries. He has become symbol of Human Rights, a valiant fighter against oppression, exploitation and injustice. During his life time we heard of Gandhijis of different parts of the country. One such person was Frontier Gandhi. After his death we heard of Gandhis in different countries. He has inspired a number of individuals like Martin Luther King, A.T. Ariyaratne, popularly known as little Gandhi of Sri Lanka, Rev. Scott, and a host of others. Martin Luther King observed "Gandhi was the only morally and practically sound method open to oppressed people in their struggle for freedom". This is a significant contribution. Eternal vigilance is the price of liberty and Gandhiji has been able to inspire a host of individuals who will keep on fighting for Human Rights and freedom. For freedom, we know, is a thing which we have to conquer afresh for ourselves everyday, and we are losing freedom because after each victory we think we can now settle down and enjoy it without further struggle. The battle of freedom is never done and the field never quiet.

Mr. B.R. Nanda, Gandhiji's biographer remarked, "Gandhi instigated, if he did not initiate, three major revolution of our times —the revolution against racism, the revolutions against violence". I will add a few more to this list— revolution against unbridled consumerism, revolution against technology that is beyond human control and revolution to provide human moti-vations in our dealings with fellow men.

Gandhiji had been the greatest warrior for Human Rights. To quote Sarojini Naidu, "Far greater than all warriors who led armies to battle was this little man, the bravest, the most tried friend of all". Let us pray with her...... "....May the soul of my master, my leader, my father rest not in peace, not in peace. Do no rest. Keep us to our pledge. Give us the strength to fulfill our promise, your heirs, your descendants, your students, guardians of your dreams......"

References

1. Pyarelal: The Last Phase, vol. II, p. 786.
2. *Ibid.*, p. 24
3. *Ibid.*, p. 86
4. *Ibid.*, Vol. I, p. 118.
5. *Ibid.*
6. *Ibid.*, Vol. I, p. 119.
7. *Ibid.*, p. 332.
8. Gassett Ortega: Revolt of the Masses, p. 87.
9. Mathurs: Economic Thought of Mmahatma Gandhi, p. 579.
10. *Ibid.*, p. 578.

11. G. Ram Chandran: Truth and Non-violence – UNESCO Symposium, p. 100.
12. Pyarelal: The Last Phase, Vol. I, p. 67.
13. *Ibid.*, Vol. I, p. 149.
14. *Ibid.*, Vol. I, p. 426.
15. C.D.H. Cole: The Case for Industrial Partnership, p. 117.
16. Quoted: A.J. Muste, Gandhi-His Relevance for Our Times, p. 23.
17. Pyarelal: Quoted by Bondurant Joan V in Conquest of Violence, pp. 103-104.
18. Mathurs: Economic Thought of Mahatma Gandhi, p. 477.
19. *Ibid.*, p. 603.

20

New Values for Growth

In our times when every one thinks in terms of material comforts and welfare, it may sound paradoxical to write about non-economic aspects of growth and development. But the world is at a point where it is imperative to think about the dangers to which mankind is exposed because of the dominance of what are termed as purely economic interests, motivations and welfare. It is no exaggeration to state that even the existing economic structure cannot sustain itself if we lose sight of non-economic values that the society need cherish. Bertrand Russel had warned us against these dangers. "I do not know what horrors may be in store for us, but no one can doubt that, unless something very radical is done, scientific man is a doomed species. In the world in which we are living, there is an active and dominant will towards death which has, so far, at every crisis got the better of sanity. If we are to survive, this state of affairs must not continue".[1] Albert Schweitzer remarked: "It is clear now to everyone that the suicide of civilization is in progress. What yet remains of it is no longer safe. It is still standing, indeed because it was not exposed to the destructive pressure which overwhelmed the rest, but like the rest, is built upon rubble, and the next landside will very likely carry it away".[2]

Humanity faces these dangers because the present economic system is based upon a wrong appreciation of fundamental human instincts and emphasises wrong values. Thus one of the basic assumptions of modern economic structure is ever increasing wants and naturally ever increasing effort and organisation to satisfy these insatiable wants. Economists regard this characteristic as a factor of economic growth and development. In fact, people are judged not with the qualities of men that they possess but with material affluence they command. "The expansion of machine during the past two centuries was accompanied by the dogma of increasing wants. Industry was directed not merely to the multiplication of goods and to an increase in their variety; it was directed towards the multiplication for the desire for goods. We passed from an economy of need to an economy of acquisition".[2] The economy of acquisition has become the everyday mode. This was the wish of king Midas. Every one knows what grief fell on king Midas. The same is happening to the society at present. The modern man's definition of heaven today is most likely to be a big departmental store with new things every day and with enough of money to buy everything he pleases. Our system of production keeps on producing all sorts of wants and things to satisfy these wants. Production and consumption have become ends in themselves. But why do we want to produce more, why we want this, that and the other is a question which is never asked.

In a society where reputability depends upon the variety of goods a man possesses and consumes there shall remain a constant competition to possess something more than others with whom one is in the habit of comparing himself. "In the nature of the case the desire for wealth can scarcely be satiated in any individual instance and evidently a satiation of the average or general desire for wealth is out of question. However, widely or equally or 'fairly' it may be distributed, no general increase of the community's wealth can make any approach to satiating this need, the ground of which is the desire for every one to excel every one else in the accumulation of goods— since the struggle is substantially a race for reputiability on the basis of an invidious comparison, no approach to a definitive attainment is possible".[4]

This mad pursuit of material affluence has given a system of production which is dominated by machine culture and which has given rise to factory civilization. Production is becoming more and more round about, mechanized and centralised. This, in turn leads to misuse of natural resources, fast exhaustion of irreplaceable sources of power and efforts to discover newer sources of energy and power. Coal as a source of power was replaced by steam, later electricity which in turn is being substituted by atomic energy. Our energy is directed towards discovering newer and newer sources of energy as the old sources die out. "Since even the smallest mechanical process consumes more energy than it produces; how could the sum of all these processes consume create abundance? There can be no talk of riches produced by technology. What really happens is rather a steady, forever growing consumption.' It is a ruthless destruction, the like of which the earth has never before seen. A more and more destruction of resources is the characteristic of our technology. Only by this destruction can it exist and spread".[5] This is the reason that in the long run the characteristic of the industrial society is one of exhaustion of natural resources and ultimate impoverishment of the human race. "This poverty cannot be overcome by technological efforts; it is inherent in technology itself, it has marched in step with the industrial age and it will be so to the end".[6]

Exhaustion of resources has also resulted in the progressive nationalization of organisation, the comprehensive administration and management of man by a bureaucracy of experts especially trained for the task. "And as poverty spreads, the pressure of the organisation upon man increases, for it becomes more urgent to squeeze from him the last drop. This mercilessness is characteristic of all moments of human distress. Beleaguered towns, blockaded countries, ships whose food and water are running low have shown like conditions".[7] Industrial organisations increasingly require an enormous personnel, a personnel which is wholly unproductive, yet increasing in number all the faster. "If today inventors are called upon and exhorted to give new proofs of their genius, to forge ahead, to deliver more quickly, the purpose is to increase the pillage of earth through a rationalization of the methods of plunder".[8]

Increasing organisation and its perfection have opened new fields of exploitation. The expert, even in socialist societies, acquires increasing power to command others. This is the inevitable result of greater degree of organisation that scientific technique brings about. It is apt to be irresponsible and behind the scene power. "This tyranny of the officials is one of the worst results of increasing organisation, and one against which it is of the utmost importance to find safeguards if a scientific society is not to be intolerable to all but an insolent aristocracy of Jacks-in-office".[9]

In such a socio-economic setup an individual feels lost and isolated. With media of mass persuasion, rather hypnotism, we have been able to persuade the large masses that their welfare can best be decided by those in authority. For two or three generations number of individuals have been living as workers, not as human beings. The feeling of helplessness and insecurity have increased with every change in the technology. Constant and rapid change has accelerated this feeling. "The efforts of the technician have intensified the spiritual vacuum, that feeling of emptiness, to the same degree that has constricted the scope of human life. And so the horror vacui, the horror of the void, is part of the technicians' world; in many forms this horror enters into human consciousness as a feeling of depression, of boredom, of futility, lack of purpose, nervousness and mechanical restlessness".[10]

This approach has made every individual extremely self-centred and selfish. He is unmindful of the problems of others and does not pause even for a moment to think of the conesquences of his actions on other members of the community. Describing the attitude of an average American in society a sociologist of repute remarked: "The American citizen today is concerned almost exclusively with private problems. By 'concerned' I mean enough interested in a problem to lose one's sleep sometimes not merely just to talk about it. He losses his sleep about health, money and family problems. He does not lose his sleep about problems, of the society because he has cut himself off from the experience of social concern, from relatedness to other as part of his life. He is a private individual with only private interest".[11]

"Society within the nation and without it is breaking down in groups that show ever increasing hostility to each other, irrational hates are taking the place of cooperation. This, historically, has been the precursor of downfall for many valiant civilisations. There is no reason to suppose that our own fate will be otherwise, if we do not at once state explicitly the problem and struggle to develop a better elite than we can at present show in public, private or academic life. Social life resembles biological in at least one aspect, when normal process ceases, pathological growth begins. It is a short step from friendship or tolerance to distrust and hatred when the normal social relationships disintegrate".[12]

It is thus clear that such self-centredness and lack of concern for the society of which one is a part and parcel cannot sustain the society. This may cause serious dislocation and therefore some external agency has to come into existence to curb these values, which motivate large number of individuals. Collectively we think in terms of 'welfare', 'equality, 'equity', 'fairness' etc. But such movements get little or no momentum of their own because of the inherent contradiction in individual values and traits and collective or group norms and standards. Since the individual is not trained to look to the good of others some omnipotent external agency, i.e., the government and the state has to bring about collective good. Gasset refers to this tendency as "the greatest danger threatening European civilization.........this is born of civilisation itself. More than that, it constitutes one of its glories".[13] He continues "In our days the state has become a formidable machine which works in marvellous fashion, wonderful efficiency by reason of the quality and precision of its means. Once it is set up in the midst of society, it is enough to touch a button for its enormous levers to start working and exercise their overwhelming power on any portion, whatever of social framework.[14] State intervention is one of the gravest danger that today threaten civilisation. In fact a time has arrived when it appears that society will have to live for the state, man for governmental machine. Gandhiji remarked: "I look upon an increase of the power of the State with the greatest fear; because although apparently doing good by minimising exploitation, it does the greatest harm to mankind by destroying individuality which lies at the root of all progress".[15] For him the state represented organised and concentrated violence.

These tendencies that threaten civilisation today have made serious minded thinkers to be skeptical about the present society. We need to heed the warning of Lord Russel that 'we are perhaps living in the last age of man, and if so, it is to science that he will owe his extinction".[16]

Gandhiji therefore, advocated that we must deliberately put a stop to this desire to keep on increasing our wants adinfinitum. He emphasised, "Our civilisation, our culture, our Swaraj depends not upon multiplying our wants—self-indulgence but upon restricting our wants, self-denial".[17] Gandhiji quoted from the Holy Bible to drive home his point—'How hardly shall they that have riches enter into the kingdom of God.......It is easier for a camel to go through the eye of a needle than for a rich man to enter the kingdom of God'. Man's happiness really lies in contentment. He who is discontented, however much he possesses, becomes a slave to his desires. That every one in this world should be able to maintain as high a standard as possible with the least output of labour is fantastic. Luxurious living is an impossible proposition for any society as a whole. And when there is no limit to luxury where shall we stop? Therefore, we must think in terms of regulating our wants. "A certain degree of physical harmony and comfort is necessary, but above a certain level it becomes a hindrance instead of help. Therefore the ideal of creating an unlimited number of wants and satisfaction of one's physical needs, even the intellectual needs of one's narrow self, must meet at a certain point a dead stop, before it degenerates into physical and intellectual voluptuousness. A man must arrange his physical and cultural circumstances so that they do not hinder him in his service of humanity on which all his energies should be concentrated". Nay, we need go a step further and identify ourselves with all forms of life, not only human life, but even with inanimate objects.

This may mean a complete change in our system of production and reducing it to simpler forms. It may mean abandoning technology and all that it represents to a large extent. "The idolatory of the machine is abomination" remarked Lord Russel. "The machine as an object of adoration is the modern form of Satan, and its worship is modern diabolism".[18] Another sociologist remarked: "The control of technology means a severe limitation of its hitherto unchecked growth a limitation demanding an almost savage asceticism on the part of an age drunk not merely with synthetic emotions and plea-sures manufactured hourly by entertainment factories, but with dreams of power and of conquest of outer space".[19]

It was for these reasons that Gandhiji wanted India to adopt a system of economic development, which will shun industrialism and develop its cottage and village. His belief was that "Independent India can discharge her duty towards a groaning world by adopting a simple but ennobled life, by developing her thousands of cottage and living at peace with the world."[20] His message of spinning wheel has to be viewed in this light ".......the message of spinning wheel is much wider than its circumference. Its message is one of simplicity, service of mankind, living as not to hurt others........The larger message is naturally for all".[21] Similar sentiments were expressed by Lord Russel when he remarked—"The root of the matter is very simple that I am almost ashamed to mention it, for fear of the derisive smile with which wise cynics will greet my words. The thing I mean—please forgive me for mentioning it—is love, Christian love or compassion. If you feel this, you have a motive for existence, a guide in action, a reason for courage, an imperative necessity for intellectual honesty. If you feel this, you have all that anybody should need in the way of religion. Although you may not find happiness, you will never know the despair of those whose life is aimless and void of purpose, for there is always something that you can do to diminish awful sum of human misery".[22]

Gandhiji trained leaders in his Ashram to accept these values. The vows that the members of his Ashram were to adopt were non-possession, voluntary poverty, non-violence, i.e., love, compassion and reverence for all living beings nay even towards nature. This is quite contrary to accepted and current values. "As a matter of fact, the most utterly inhuman thoughts have been current among us......in all the ugly clearness of language and with the authority of logical principles. There has been created a social mentality which discourages humanity in individuals......The stand-off-ishness and want of sympathy which are shown so clearly in every way to strangers are no longer felt as being really rudeness, but pass for the behaviour of the man of the world. Our society has also ceased to allow to all men, as such, a human value and a human dignity, many sections of the human race have become merely raw material and property in human form".[23]

We may dismiss these values by dismissing them as religious or ethical ideas. Gandhiji felt otherwise. He said, "I must confess that I do not draw a sharp or any distinction between economics and ethics. Economics that hurts the moral well-being of an individual or a nation are immoral and therefore sinful".[24] Albert Schweitzer also agrees with the view that "ethical progress is, then, that which is truly of the essence of civilization.....We shall not succeed in re-establishing our civilization of the superficial concept of civilization which now holds us in thrall, and give ourselves up again to the ethical view".[25] To quote Gandhiji once again "Economics to be worth anything, must also be capable of being reduced to terms of religion and spirituality".[26]

A world community can be created in which human beings can live comfortably and in peace with each other. Today destiny of humanity is at stake. We need new training so that man can subjugate selfishness to generosity, ignorance to wisdom and hate to love. "Civilization can only revive when there shall come into being in a number of individuals a new tone of mind independent of the one prevalent among the crowd and in opposition to it, a tone of mind which will gradually influence over the collective one, and in the end determine its character. It is only an ethical movement which can rescue us from the slough of barbarism".[27]

We need individuals who can swim against the current. No society can be progressive without a leaven of rebels. Let us hope a large number of dedicated souls will rise and be inspired by the song of Gurudev Tagore—

Walk alone,
If they answer not to thy call, walk alone,
If they are afraid and cower mutely facing the wall,
O thou of evil luck,
Open thy mind and speak out alone.
If they turn away and desert you
when crossing the wilderness,
O thou of evil luck,
Trample the thorns under thy tread,
And along the blood-lined track travel alone.
If they do not hold up the light

When the night is troubled with storm,
O thou of evil luck,
With the thunder-flame of pain ignite
thine own heart
And let it burn alone.

References

1. Has Man a Future, pp. 36-37.
2. Decay and Restoration of Civilisation, p. 16.
3. Lewis Mumford: quoted in Harris Brown, 'The Challenge of Man's Future, p. 187.
4. Veblen: The Theory of Leisure Class, p. 32.
5. Juenger, F.G.: The Failure of Technology, p. 80.
6. *Ibid.*, p. 13.
7. *Ibid.*, p. 17.
8. *Ibid.*, p. 83.
9. Russel B.: The Impact of Science on Society, p. 72.
10. Juenger F.G.: Failure of Technology, p. 131.
11. Erich Fromm: Freedom in Work Situation, pp. 6-7.
12. Mayo: Social Problems of an Industrial Civilization, p. 119.
13. Ortega y. Gasset: The Revolt of the Masses, p. 85.
14. *Ibid.*, p. 87.
15. Mathurs: Economic Thought of Mahatma Gandhi, p. 579.
16. Russel B: Impact of Science on Society, p. 127.
17. Mathurs: Economic Thought of Mahatma Gandhi. P. 527.
18. Russel B. : The Impact of Science on Society, p. 106.
19. Juenger F.G. : Failure of Technology, p. (vi).
20. Mathurs, Economic Thought of Mahatma Gandhi.
21. *Ibid.*
22. Russel, B. : Impact of Science on Society, p. 149.
23. A. Schweitzer: Decay and Restoration of Civilization, p. 32.
24. Mathurs: Economic Thought of Mahatma Gandhi, p. 528.
25. Decay and Restoration of Civilization, p. 6.
26. Mathurs: Economic Thought of Mahatma Gandhi, p. 86.
27. Decay and Restoration of Civilization, p. 68.

21

Gandhiji's Concept of Trusteeship

Gandhian Economic Equality

G.D.H. Cole defined his concept of a socialist economic order in the following words: "What I have in mind is an economic order in which there will be no more than relatively modest differences of income, but these differences will be fairly generally accepted as legitimate and just because they either correspond to the need for monetary incentives to good work or are regarded as fair rewards for more exacting or responsible kinds of work.'[1] Mahatma Gandhi observed: 'My ideal is equal distribution but so far as I can seek it is not to be realized. I, therefore, work for equitable distribution.'[2] In the context of India's economic requirements in terms of her masses he elaborated his ideas: "By all means let moneyed people have tasteful ornamentation, whether in dress or office surroundings; but I do plead for an observance, as between themselves and their starving brethren, of a due sense of proportion such as is always observed in well-ordered society. India's minimum is a *langoti* requiring less than 1/6 of a square yard. Let our fashion have some correspondence to this minimum".[3] On another occasion he remarked: "I do not envisage a dead artificial level among the people. There will be a variety amongst them as among the leaves of a tree".[4] His scheme of constructive programme, he remarked, "will, however, be a structure on sand if it is not built on the solid foundation of economic equality. Economic equality must never be supposed to mean possession of an equal amount of worldly goods by every one......It also means that the cruel inequality that obtains today will be removed by purely non-violent means".[5]

Gandhiji realized that in the garb of an equitable distribution, efforts might be made to justify the existing pattern of income distribution. He was against this approach and remarked, "Let no one try to justify the glaring differences between the classes and the masses, the prince and the pauper, by saying that the former need more. That will be idle sophistry and a travesty of my argument".[6] He realized that peace will not reign if inequalities persist. His advice was that "A non-violent system of government is clearly an impossibility so long as the wide gulf between the rich and hungry millions persists........A violent and bloody revolution is a certainty one day unless there is voluntary abdication of riches and the power that riches gives......"[7] Similar sentiments were expressed by Wootten when she observed that "it is not only that gross economic inequalities are incompatible with respect for individual human dignity, political democracy itself degenerates into a sham in a privilege-ridden environment".[8] Like Gandhiji, Marx was also opposed to privilege and authority. The cause of the have-nots was the basic sentiment running through his ideas. He too intensely felt for the well-being of the poor and the oppressed.

The paradoxical situation is that while we regard equality as the ideal we have created a socio-economic system, which has resulted in increasing inequalities and the conferment of greater and greater power in the hands of the few. Cole had foreseen this. He said, ".......under conditions of large-scale operation, central bureaucracies have a strong tendency to gather more and more power into their hands, and to choose yes-men to occupy key subordinate posts".[9] Scientific and technological developments that have taken place during the last century have accentuated these tendencies. "By supplying the ruling oligarchy with more effective instruments of coercion and persuasion, applied science has contributed directly to the centralisation of power in the hands of the few. But it has also made important indirect contributions to the same end. It has done it in two ways; first by introducing over ever large areas of the industrial and agricultural economy the methods of large-scale mass production and mass distribution; second, by creating, through its very progressiveness, an economic and social insecurity which drives all those concerned, owners and managers, no less than workers, to seek the assistance of the national state".[10] Russel observes, "This tyranny of officials is one of the worst results of increasing organisation, and one against which it is of the utmost importance to find safeguard, if a scientific society is not to be intolerable to all but an insolent aristocracy of Jacks-in-office".[11]

Centralist and Decentralist Solutions

The question that is to be answered is how can such a society, which has an inherent tendency towards centralisation, concentration of power and the resultant exploitation, become one which is just, fair and equalitarian. A solution has been sought by two schools of thought—the centralists and the decentralists. The centralists believe that inequalities are inherent in the existing systems of society. Motivation factors lead to individual aggression and the desire to possess more of material goods and powers. The real solution, therefore, is to concentrate greater power in the hands of the state, so that it can keep in proper check these individual traits in order to make them subserve the common good. They feel that reforming the individual is out of the question. The centralist thinking can be sub-divided into two broad types: the leftists and the supporters of the welfare state.

Those who advocate socialism suggest that these inequalities and class distinctions can be abolished through organised and concerted action on the part of those who are being oppressed and exploited. The proletariat needs organisation and revolutionary fervour to overthrow the economic system that promotes the concentration of wealth. This will necessitate capturing state power, which, under capitalistic order, is the handmaid of the bourgeois. Class conflict is inherent in this order. Yet in spite of, or rather through class conflict, the socio-economic system is destined to march towards its goal of a classless society. The oppressed and the exploited have only to capture state power and utilize this power to speed up this change. The wise, therefore, should help the destined, the inevitable, to happen speedily and offer their cooperation towards this transformation. Accentuating of class differences and worsening of the plight of the masses are therefore to be welcomed and positively encouraged. With passage of time political power will ultimately pass into the hands of the proletariat and there will be no privileged class of people in the state. When this stage is reached human society would become class- less, and ripe for peace, equality and freedom from war and violence. Thereafter, there will be no classes and class conflicts no private property in the means of production and no profiteering or exploitation. In the absence of exploitation non-violence will become a natural way of individual and group behaviour. Very soon the state will wither away leading to 'enlightened anarchy' wherein the maxim 'from each according to his capacity and to each according to his need' will be the order of the day. Since the course of events is predetermined—i.e., the march of human progress points to the direction of a classless society—the means are subsidiary. Hence recourse to violence is not ruled out; rather, violent means are welcome because these are likely to speed up the transformation of a class-ridden society into a classless society. Ends justify the means.

However, the ultimate goal of the communists is a non-violent socio-economic order—an enlightened individual who acts in the interests of the society, who owns nothing and who is willing to perish for the common good.

All this has resemblances with the Gandhian concept of trusteeship. Gandhiji however, did not subscribe to the view that ends justify the means. To him ends and means were convertible. He felt that good and desirable ends could not be attained through wrong means. Violence and hatred will breed violence. The communist way implies worsening condition of the masses before any good could be brought about. Only after a complete overhaul of the society class distinctions would be obliterated. However, in this strategy the individual has no role to play. He has to be passive; he must abandon, if need be, all canons of civilized behaviour, even though temporarily, in the fervent hope that his behaviour is helping the cause of the revolution.

Gandhiji's Solution

Gandhiji felt that such a classless society is just a mirage. "A true classless society is possible only when there is almost no permanent division of functions, and all people take part in almost every act necessary for life. But in a complicated society, such as we live in, it does not seem possible, even with a decentralised economy, to have a state of classlessness. What can be achieved as best as possible is class harmony".[12] "If you want capital to be extinct or you want to abolish moneyed men or the capitalist, you will never succeed".[13] For him there was 'nothing like an inevitability of class conflict' because he was confident that he could bring about class harmony through his method of non-violent mass action. He emphasised "I do not see the necessity of class conflict. If I thought it inevitable I should not hesitate to preach it and teach it".[14] It does not mean that Gandhiji did not believe in the existence of class struggle. He did not believe in the necessity of fermenting it and keeping it up.

Another objection to the Gandhian approach is that such an approach undermines the position of the common man, makes him weak, and creates an environment wherein the individual can be exploited. While recognizing the need of trade unions and labour organisations he once remarked, "I can tell you from experience that your every union can become one of the causes of your bondage if you do not comply with other conditions which I shall mention to you."[15] These conditions were that "each one of you should consider himself to be a trustee of the rest of his fellow labourers and not be self-seeking" and "use your union as much for internal reformation as for defence against assaults from without".[16] He had a feeling that unless these conditions were satisfied, labour could become 'more tyrannical than capital'.

The welfare social scientists also feel that there is no inevitability about class conflict. Inequities can be reduced and the aspirations of the common man fulfilled through progressive action in various fields. Provision for educational facilities assurance of minimum incomes and comprehensive social security measures, progressive taxation like income tax, control of expenditure through measures like expenditure tax and allocation of scarce resources, and speedy state action will ensure the removal of the evils associated with the existing system and provide for fuller, better and more contented individual and social life. They, like the communists, believe in increasing the power of the state so that individual urges, which keep the system working, are held in check. If the citizens' methods of earning, spending and savings do not lead to the cherished ideal of a stable, every growing and economically viable society, the state must step in and through its policy of public spending and investment ensure the even working of the economic system. Government and those who guide state policies, should acquire greater and greater powers to meet the situation that modern technology is creating.

Such an all-powerful state will decide everything for its citizens. It will decide what industries should develop and at what rate. It will allocate labour and other resources amongst different industries. It will determine money incomes that individuals should earn.

In the words of Huxley, "Socialism by autocracy or oligarchy is not socialism, or anything like it. It is just benevolent despotism; and there is nothing in the record of history to justify us in the belief that any benevolent despotism will for long retain its benevolence".[17] Gandhiji remarked, "The state represents violence in a concentrated and organised form. The individual has a soul, but as the state is a soulless machine, it can never be weaned from violence to which it owes its very existence. Hence, I prefer the doctrine of trusteeship".[18] Again, "I look upon an increase of the power of the state with the greatest fear because although while apparently doing good by minimizing exploitation, it does the greatest harm to mankind by destroying individuality which lies at the root of all progress".[19] Gandhiji had realized that the use of force and violent methods would have the masses largely untouched. A process of change in which the masses are not actively participating will not mean any improvement in their status. He had faith that his technique of non-violent non-cooperation confers upon every individual considerable power to resist injustice. "I have always held that social justice, even unto the least and the lowliest is impossible of attainment by force. I have further believed that it is possible by proper training of the lowliest by non-violent means to secure redress of the wrongs suffered by them. That means non-violent non-cooperation......Freedom received through the efforts of others, however benevolent, cannot be retained when such effort is withdrawn.......But the lowliest can feel its glow as soon as they learn the art of attaining it through non-violent non-cooperation".[20]

Gandhiji did not believe in inherited riches. He observed "What belongs to me is the right to an honourable livelihood no better than enjoyed by millions of others. The rest of my wealth belongs to the community and must be used for the welfare of the community".[21] He opposed unconscionable dividends and advocated that profits of big concern must bear due relationship to the wages of the workers. He held the hope that "a time must come, and the sooner the better, when there would be a respectable proportion between dividends, wages and prices".[22] Gandhiji thought that individuals would be willing to bring about this change voluntarily. He did not want to deprive the talented ones of the opportunity to earn more. His wish was that these persons would take out of the common pool whatever was fair and reasonable. Fair and reasonable return will not be determined in isolation by those who are in command of the economic forces but will have to bear some definite relationship with minimum incomes. No plan makes sense unless it includes restrictions on movements upwards as well as downwards; a desirable income policy will imply maximum incomes in relation to minimum incomes. He repeatedly pointed out that no one had a right to live more comfortably than ordinary workers and peasants. But this does not imply that those who have greater ability and better talents should waste them. "People with talents will have more, and they will utilize their talents for this purpose. If they utilize their talents kindly, they will be performing the work of the State. Such people exist as trustees, on no other terms. I would allow a man of intellect to earn more. I would not cramp his talent. But the bulk of his greater earnings must be used for the good of the State".[23] He explained that "the rich man would be left in possession of his wealth, of which he would use what he reasonably required for his personal needs and he would act as a trustee for the remainder to be used for the society".[24]

What will happen if these individuals do not voluntarily surrender their privileges? Gandhiji considered it to be criminal that some should possess so much of wealth. "In this, in all countries of the world, possession of inordinate wealth by individuals should be held as a crime against humanity. Therefore, the maximum limit of taxation of riches beyond a certain margin can never be reached........Why should there not be death duties? ....the inheritance should rightly belong to the nation".[25] Yet on another occasion he observed, "I would be very happy indeed if people concerned behaved as trustees, but if they fail, I believe we shall have to deprive them of their possessions through state with the minimum exercise of violence". But he believed that the smooth working of the society depended upon non-monetary motivations and incentive, which he explained as a sense of trusteeship. Only when it was inevitable did he advocate a minimum of state power and action. "What I would personally prefer would be not a centralisation of power in the hands of the State, but an extension of the sense of trusteeship, as in my opinion the violence of private ownership is less injurious than the violence of the State. However, if it is unavoidable, I would support, a minimum of state ownership."[26]

The real sanction, however, behind the theory of trustee-ship is mass action against those who refuse to behave with a sense of social responsibility. "Exploitation of the poor can be extinguished not by effecting the destruction of a few millionaires, but by removing the ignorance of the poor and teaching them to non-cooperate with their exploiters. That will convert the exploited also".[27] Gandhiji held the view that if masses are organised on trully non-violent lines the socio-economic environment could be so designed that exploitation would be abolished. Still there may be a few who may refuse to act as trustees. For such Gandhiji's prescription was non-violent non-cooperation and civil disobedience. "If however, in spite of the utmost effort, the rich do not become guardians of the poor in the true sense of the term—what is to be done? In trying to find the solutions to this riddle I have lighted on non-violent non-cooperation and civil disobedience as the right and infallible means. The rich cannot accumulate wealth without the cooperation of the poor in society.......If this knowledge were to penetrate to and spread amongst the poor, they would become strong and would learn how to free themselves by means of non-violence from the crushing inequalities."[28] He did not want that independence should in any way weaken the capacity of the masses to organise mass non-violent action against injustices, 'Swaraj', he affirmed, "will come not by acquisition of authority by a few but the acquisition by all of a capacity to resist authority when it is abused."

R.H. Tawney holds the view that democratic societies will survive only when two conditions are satisfied. The one is a "resolute elimination of all forms of special privileges' and the second is 'the conversion of economic power, now often an irresponsible tyrant, into the servant of society, working within clearly defined limits and accountable for its action"......"If democracy fails, it will fail not through any fortuitous combi-nation of unfriendly circumstances, but from the insincerity of some of its professed defenders and the timidity of the remainder. If it stands, it will stand, not because it has hitherto stood, but because ordinary men and women were determined that it should, and throw themselves with energy into broadening its foundations".[29]

Such non-violent mass action cannot be had for mere asking. Conscious efforts have to be made to organise and awaken the masses.

Conclusion

It can be argued that the scheme of trusteeship is unlikely to work. The sceptic can point out that even Gandhiji was not able to bring about this conversion. No capitalist ever behaved as a trustee. To the critics Gandhiji's reply was, "It is highly probable that my advice will not be accepted and my dream will not be realized. But who can guarantee that the socialist's dream will be realized."[30] He concluded, 'Trusteeship, as ! conceive it, has yet to prove its worth. It is an attempt to secure the best use of property for the people by competent hands".[31] He was repeatedly questioned whether history at any time records such a change in human nature. His reply was, "Such changes have certainly taken place in individuals. One may not be able to point to them in a whole society. But this only means that uptill now there has never been an experiment on a large scale in non-violence........Ahimsa (non-violence) is definitely an attribute of society. To convince people of this truth is at once my effort and experiment".[32] He, therefore, asserted, "My theory of trusteeship is no make-shift, certainly no camouflage. I am confident it will survive all other theories......That the possessors of wealth have not acted upto the theory does not prove its falsity; it proves the weakness of wealth. No other theory is compatible with non-violence. In the non-violent method the wrong-doer compasses his own end, if he does not undo the wrong. For, either through non-violent non-cooperation he is made to see his error, or he finds himself completely isolated".[33]

We may dismiss these ideas at our peril. It will be argued that most men and women are not fit to act up to this ideal. They are too selfish, irresponsible and unresponsive, "If that be so, and if these qualities are too deeply rooted for any-thing to be done about them, all I can say is that the outlook for humanity is poor indeed".[34] Alkbert Camus, the great French novelist and humanist wrote: "Over the expanse of five continents throughout the coming years an endless struggle is going to be pursued between violence and friendly persuasion, a struggle in which, granted, the former has a thousand times more the chances of success than the latter. But I have also held that, if he who bases his hope on human nature is a fool, he who gives up in the face of circumstances is a coward".[35]

References

1. Cole, G.D.H.: The Case for Industrial Partnership, p. 99.
2. Mathur and Mathur (Ed, Economic Thought of Mahatma Gandhi, p. 83.
3. *Ibid.*, p. 85.
4. *Ibid.*, p. 320.
5. *Ibid.*, p. 608.
6. *Ibid.*
7. *Ibid.*, p. 611.
8. Wootten, Barbara: Social Foundations of a Wage Policy, p. 176.
9. Cole, G.D.H. : The Case for Industrial Partnership, p. 74.
10. Huxley, Aldous: Science, Liberty and Peace, p. 12.
11. Russel, B.: The Impact of Science on Society, p. 72.
12. Mashruwala, K.G.: Gandhi and Marxs, p. 67.
13. Economic Thought of Mmmahatma Gandhi, p. 559.
14. *Ibid.*, p. 315.
15. *Ibid.*, p. 372.
16. *Ibid.*
17. Huxley, op. cit.
18. Economic Thought of Mahatma Gandhi, p. 78.
19. *Ibid.*, p. 579.
20. *Ibid.*, p. 601.
21. *Ibid.*, p. 594.
22. *Ibid.*, p. 367.
23. *Ibid.*, p. 608.
24. *Ibid.*, p. 609.
25. *Ibid.*, p. 556.
26. *Ibid.*, p. 579.
27. *Ibid.*, p. 605.

28. *Ibid.*, p. 610.
29. R.H. Tawney: quoted in Barbara Wootten's Social Foundation of Wage Policy.
30. Economic Thought of Mahatma Gandhi, p. 589.
31. *Ibid.*
32. *Ibid.*, p. 609.
33. *Ibid.*, p. 201.
34. Cole, G.D.H., op.cit., p. 117.
35. Quoted by A.J. Muste in Gandhi: His Relevance for Our Time, p. 23.

22

Technology From a Gandhian Angle

Several attempts have been made to study the conesquences of automation—the technological developments—on the economic and social life of a nation. That automation is causing a lot of worry to the people is being revealed by the fact that in the latter half of 1965 a public opinion poll in Detroit showed that, after the danger from Soviet Russia, it was automation that was causing people most concern. The world automation, the American Federal Secretary of Labour observed, engendered a whole host of fears in the minds of the workers—fear of change, fear of technology itself, fear of displacement, fear of unemployment, fear of machines, fear of science in general. It is therefore, very opportune that a study of the likely effects of those technological changes should be undertaken. In the absence of reliable statistics, no one can be able to substantiate the conclusion to which we may arrive at. The experience in the field of automation has not been wide enough as to enable formulation of correct opinion. Automation is in its infancy though it is making rapid strides as is revealed by the invention of automatic production devices in different industries. In U.S.A., as compared to other countries of the world, automation has made considerable progress. Therefore, one has to rely on the experience of U.S.A. Here too, the results have to be qualified because this experience cannot be relied upon, as the American economy is at present an economy, which cannot be termed as normal.

Automation has been defined as "a technique of industrial production combined with a method of processing data introduced since the Second World War, with the aid of the most advanced techniques and devices—but with certain economic limitations—this method of production attempts to perform by machinery all the functions hitherto performed by human beings. The machines are controlled by machines".[1]

The supporters of this new technological development hold the view that automation is a natural concomitant of changes in the technique of production introduced by the Industrial Revolution and that it is not going to have any remarkable adverse economic and social consequences because of shortage of skilled staff, need of high capital investment and the gradual introduction of automation in different industries. It is believed that adjustment will be brought about without causing too much dislocation. In the transitionary period some suffering is bound to be there which they advocate should be cheerfully borne. The protagonists have relied on American experience.

It may, however, be suggested that American experience should be taken cautiously. New technology may create grave economic and social consequences "as a result of technical unemployment increased danger of slumps, decreased elasticity of productive capacity (which might perhaps be corrected only at the expense of complete freedom of consumers' choice), increased danger to output owing to strikes" etc. Mr. Pollock has taken pains to focus attention on the possibility of automation becoming a 'serious danger to the stability of both the economic and social structure'. The arguments of the optimists have been carefully examined and the author opines that automation will tend to promote technological unemployment in the United States in the near future, even though in 1955 the redundant workers (as a result of automation) did find new jobs. "But that does not mean that their successors in later years will always be equally fortunate. If there were a slowing down or a cessation of the continued expansion of the economy it is indeed doubtful if even the combined efforts of Government industry and organised labour could stem the flood of technological unemployment unless all three agreed to make planned and fundamental changes in the entire structure of American economy".[2] Similarly, economic stability may be shaken if the demand for ever increasing production is not forthcoming. "There could be a vast competitive race to speed up production of more and more in automatic factories; to create bigger and better purely technical solutions of production problems; to condition men to want more and more of the goods that were being poured off the production lines—such an approach would not create a feeling of plenty, but a feeling of dissatisfaction". It is therefore, obvious that the increased use of automatic machinery presents a serious threat to the stability of the economy. It is no use arguing that some suffering is bound to be in the transitionary period and that all such technological developments strengthen the economy which has the power of providing continually increasing opportunities of employment in spite of rapid progress of mechanisation. All this may be quite true in the long run. But this does not enable one to feel that all those who are likely to be displaced because of automation will be easily absorbed. What will happen during the transitional stages? Such an approach "cannot reveal the sum total of avoidable human sufferings, of avoidable loss of productive capacity, and of the productive capacity which was technically possible but never came to function".

It is true that we are drawing attention to phenomenon, which are often significant only 'in the short run'. But the 'short run' may last for many years and the phenomenon may have serious repercussions upon all aspects of public and private life.

It is the social consequences of such technological changes that have to be carefully studied. Automation has already created the problem of changes that should be affected in educational facilities and the problem of how men will use the abundant leisure, which a good many people think (perhaps wrongly) will very soon be enjoyed by workers as a consequence of the spread of automation. These technological developments might create 'leisured masses'. Such a situation has certain inherent dangers. "Technology has mastered the art of saving time, but not the art of spending it". This problem is likely to become more serious as automation spreads. The United States of America is facing this problem. Dr. Donald D. Greares holds the view that "many Americans are resting their every night into mental illness". He has suggested that people should be taught the art of 'leisuremanship'—doing something while doing nothing. Dr. Greares has pointed out that "idleness causes trouble—mental trouble. We are getting patients now who are bored, restless and depressed and apathetic because they do not know how to rest".[3] And therefore, he has suggested that the art of 'leisuremanship' should be taught and people should be encouraged to undertake any activity which will help in self-expression and relaxation.

Similarly, the spread of automation will have the effect of conferring very great advantages upon big business in a highly competitive world. Consequently the trend towards the growth of large concerns will receive a powerful stimulus from automation. "It seems clear too, that automation will be an important factor in rapidly strengthening the position of the big concerns as against the medium sized and smaller business" and "encourage concentration of economic power and financial control over the production, distribution of goods and services."[4]

The structure of the labour class will also undergo remarkable change. Undoubtedly, in the new technological age "the engineers and technicians will exercise a dominating influence not only at every stage of production on the shop floor but also on the management side of industry". What will be the effect of such developments on the maintenance of healthy industrial relations? People having authority generally become intolerant of other people's views. This attitude is dangerous for the maintenance of healthy industrial relations. The political influence of the engineering class may create grave social problems. "The small number of engineers with the ultimate control of these automatic factories could......hold society up to ransom, the ransom being control of man's consumption and habits in the interests of the machines. The automatic factory, then, will provide an open sesame to Huxley's 'Brave New World'. It will lead to the creation of a class of people who may be termed as 'working class aristocrats".[5] It will be very difficult to provide incentive to the workers and maintain their interest in the production process. Measurement of efficiency will become a difficult task, as it will be hardly possible to devise any measures, which may estimate contribution of individuals. This may result in a decline in the interest of the workers. Workers may also lose interest in jobs in automatic factories because they will have absolutely nothing to do for hours except looking for a light or hearing a sound to denote that something has gone wrong with the machinery. Under these circumstances efficiency and interest can be maintained only if every individual is intelligent and understanding enough to identify completely with the plant. All the employees, from the most senior to the most junior, need be united in the conviction that they belong to a special and superior caste of workers. The lot of workers engaged in dull routine work may be undermined even further. Undoubtedly "the fate of the underdog in the social structure of the automatic age is one of the most serious problems that will one day have to be faced".

The whole economic and social structure will become too much dependent on the top executive of automatic concerns. Because of the high degree of interdependence, the decisions of these executives will intimately affect the lives of millions of people. "So it is probable that any major decisions taken by the heads of the 200 largest American companies would powerfully affect the lives of three quarters of wage earners and salary earners in the country".

Above all, it is likely to usher in a group of senior executives who have nearly all the main characteristics of a ruling group. "Those who belong to this class think alike on fundamental questions. They have the pride and exclusive feelings of a ruling class whose members have to solve similar problems and overcome similar difficulties. They are linked by the knowledge that they hold great power in their hands and that, both from an intellectual and a material point of view, they are the superiors of the vast mass of population. This new social class controls (directly or indirectly) all the mass media of influencing public opinion.......The resulting attitude of mind to both material and spiritual matters coincide with the authoritarian tendencies in all phases of management".......Such a class structure would be a very insecure foundation for a free society. The great power of the minority coupled with the ignorance and weakness of the majority might well lead to the establishment of an authoritarian in place of a democratic form of government".[6] Hence Mr. Pollock rightly asserts that 'the social consequences of automation cannot be ignored because a group of individuals might make money from it......The too rapid introduction of automation might bring with it social catastrophe that only a totalitarian government would be strong enough to handle".

It is, however, being suggested that if automation could be introduced only in a planned and sensible way, it may enable man to master economic process in a way that has not happened in the past. Dangers in an unregulated use of automation are there. But it has been suggested that there need be no despair or gloom over these new technological developments. "Human freedom is not necessarily doomed. If only automation is deliberately used to promote the welfare of the human race it could help to banish poverty relatively quickly from the face of the earth. And this could be done on a scale that has hitherto been regarded as a mere Utopian dream". Therefore, "What must be done is to take a long-term view and to plan for the future with the aid of new machines and new techniques. And the object of economic planning must be to integrate automation with a free and democratic society. Success in such planning would mean that the second industrial revolution could help to establish a social system based upon reason".[7]

However, it will not be wrong to quote Norbert Wiener at some length to demonstrate that such a situation might not be brought about at all. He writes: "Those of us who have contributed to the new science of cybernetics thus stand in a moral position which is, to say—that least, not very comfortable. We have contributed to the initiation of a new science, which, as I have said, embraces technical possibilities for good and for evil. We can only hand it over into the world that exists about us, and this is the world of Belson and Hiroshima. We do not even have the choice of suppressing these new technical developments. They belong to the age........There are those who hope that the good of a better understanding of men and society which is offered by this new field of work may anticipate and outweigh the incidental contribution we are making to the concentration of power (which is always concentrated by its very conditions of existence in the hands of the most unscrupulous). I write in 1947 and I am compelled to say that it is a very slight hope".[8]

In view of what has been amply demonstrated it may be a fond hope that under the new technological development it will be possible to build up a truly free and democratic state where the individual will be the corner-stone of the socio-economic setup. It appears that we are building up a society which we do not know ourselves and in which the individual will be the helpless victim of his own creation. These vast technological developments unmistakably demonstrate the urgent need for thinking afresh of the fundamental guiding principles on which the whole social superstructure is to be built up.

The need for clear and careful thinking is imperative in our country where we are on the threshold of vast economic development and where we have ushered in an era of planned economic development. The goal to be attained and the means to be adopted for the attainment of these goals should be such that we do not lend this country in a situation where we may hold on the matter for the spirit. It will not be out of place to mention the views of Gandhiji in this connection. People in the West have been struggling with the idea that modern technology in itself does not lead to these social evils and that it is possible to build up an era in which justice and equality will become the order of the day. Gandhiji, on the other hand, felt that this mechanisation is bound to be harmful to the free development of individuals. "Industrialism is, I am afraid, going to be a curse for mankind",[9] he observed. It was realized by Gandhiji that if India follows the Western method and technology the vast masses can never feel the glow of freedom and prosperity, and particularly when the vast masses are being subjected to awful poverty, introducing mechanisation will dehumanize them even further. And, therefore, he kept on emphasizing that future economic reorganization must not be built upon the exploitation of the masses and of villages. And exploitation is himsa (violence) pure and simple. He emphasised "In modern times it is beneath human dignity to lose one's individuality and become a mere cog in the machine. I want every individual to become a full-blooded and fully developed member of the society. The villages must become self-sufficient I see no other solution if one has to work in terms of Ahimsa (non-violence)".[10] Yet on another occasion he remarked that if India becomes industrialised "we shall need a Nadir Shah to find out other worlds to exploit, that we shall have to pit ourselves against the naval and military power of Britain, Japan and America, of Russia and Italy".[11] And therefore, he was afraid of the modern, Western type of industrialisation. He did not believe that "industrialisation is necessary in any case for any country. It is much less for India. Indeed, I believe that Independent India can only discharge her duty towards a groaning world by adopting a simple but ennobled life by developing her thousands of cottages and living at peace with the world".[12] He had an early realisation that technology in the sense of large-scale mechanisation cannot be dissociated with the attendant evils which are bound to follow in the wake of increasing mechanisation. "I have heard many of our countrymen say that we will gain American wealth but avoid its methods. I venture to suggest that such an attempt, if it were made, is foredoomed to failure. We cannot be 'wise, temperate and furious' in a moment".[13]

Let it not be concluded that Gandhiji was advocating compulsory poverty. He was opposed to the low economic standards of living to which vast masses were condemned. He held the view that poverty itself is demoralising and a poor, starving individual cannot attain high moral status. He was against pauperism. "No one has ever suggested that grinding poverty can lead to anything else than moral degradation". His move to revive hand-spinning and other village industries was a careful and well thought out plan to root-out mass poverty, unemployment and all its evil concomitants. He however, realized that economic uplift should be brought about in a way that it does not burden and crush the multitudes.

He was not against machinery as such. For him even the spinning wheel was a delicate piece of machinery meant for the common good and not for the exclusive profit of a few. "I am not fighting machinery as such", he observed, "but the madness of thinking that machinery saves labour. Men 'save labour' until thousands of them are without work and die of hunger on the streets. I want to secure employment and livelihood not only to a part of the human race, but for all. I will not have the enrichment of a few at the expense of the community. At present, the machinery is helping a small minority to live on the exploitation of the masses. The motive force of this minority is not humanity and love of their kind but greed and avarice. This state of things I am attacking with all my might".[14] Increasing mechanisation and production in a round-about manner always leads to concentration of power and wealth. In such a social and economic setup the masses are exploited for the benefit of the few. Whatever cannot be shared by the masses is a taboo. Gandhiji hates privilege and monopoly; whatever cannot be shared with masses was taboo to him. That such a development is inevitable has been unmistakably demonstrated in the West. Hence he wrote: "What I object to is the craze for machinery, not machinery as such. The craze is what they call labour-saving machinery. Men go on 'saving labour' till thousands are without work and thrown on the open streets to die of starvation. I want to save time and labour, not for a fraction of mankind, but for all. I want the concentration of wealth, not in the hands of a few, but in the hands of all. Today machinery helps a few to ride on the backs of millions. The impetus behind it all is not the philanthropy to save labour, but greed".[15]

He was in favour of simple machines that will help in the productive efficiency of the individual worker, that will enable a man to produce more and at the same time lighten his task. He was aiming "not at eradication of all machinery, but limitation". He even advocated electrification of the villages and the villagers plying their crafts with the help of power. He was in favour of retention—even propagation of "any machinery which does not deprive masses of men of the opportunity to labour, but which helps the individual and adds to his efficiency and which a man can handle at will without being its slave".[16] He had no consideration for machinery "which is meant either to enrich the few at the expense of the many, or without cause to displace the useful labour of many". His machinery was to be of the most elementary type which could be put in the homes of millions". While advocating the cause of village industries for the economic revival of the village he said, "Dead machinery must not be pitted against the millions of living machines represented by the villagers scattered in the seven hundred thousand villages in India. Machinery to be well used has to help and ease human effort. The present use of machinery tends more and more to concentrate wealth in the hands of a few in total disregard of millions of men and women whose bread is snatched by it out of their mouths".[17]

Gandhiji, therefore, advocated the revival of rural and cottage industries. He wanted that the basis of India's economic structure should be these villages producing mainly for use. He was opposed to industrialisation of the Western pattern wherein the villager is likely to be exploited. "The revival of the village is possible only when it is no more exploited. Industrialisation on a mass scale will necessarily lead to passive or active exploitation of the villagers as the problems of competition and marketing comes in. Therefore, we have to concentrate on the village being self-contained, manufacturing mainly for use. Provided this character of the village industry is being maintained, there would be no objection to villages using even modern machines and tools that they can make and can afford to use. Only they should not be used as a means of exploiting others".[18]

Gandhiji, likewise, did not believe that mass production—the gift of modern technology—would be of real and everlasting benefit for the masses. Once a question we put to Gandhiji whether he believed that mass production would raise the standard of living of the people. "I do not believe in it at all" replied Gandhiji. "There is a tremendous fallacy behind this reasoning. Without simultaneous distribution on an equally mass-scale the production can result only in a great world tragedy".[19] He even said that "the manner for mass production is responsible for the world crisis. Granting for the moment that the machinery may supply all the needs of humanity, still it would concentrate production in particular areas, so that you would have to go in a round-about way to regulate distribution; whereas, if there is production and distribution both in the respective areas where things are required, it is automatically regulated, and there is less chance for fraud none for speculation".[20] Production essentially for the market is the base of economic evils resulting in periodic economic crisis because there ceases to be any positive and direct correlation between real consumers demand and production. Hence Gandhiji held the view that both consumption and production should be localized. "When production and consumption both become localized, the temptation to speed up production indefinitely at any price disappears. All the endless difficulties and problems that our present-day economic system presents, too, would then come to an end". The evil cannot be remedied by suggesting that distribution should become more equitable. Gandhiji's view, however, was that "the evil is inherent in the system. Distribution can be equalized when production is localised; in other words when distribution is simultaneous with production".

Gandhiji is not alone in holding this view. The view that a round-about system of production is responsible for recurring booms and depression is held by others also. "That the period of production is often unalterably determined for a long time in the future, once the time consuming processes have been started, it is of great significance for the theory of business cycle. The inherent difficulties of the cycle cannot well be explained without reference to those rigidities which are due to the fact that time consuming processes cannot be easily interrupted and that the factors of production cannot be shifted at will from earlier to later stages of production or vice versa. One time consuming processes have got in underway there is a strong presumption that they will have to be continued and that they are therefore, not very sensitive to adverse price changes. If the business cycle theory has to explain why the adjustment of the economic system to irregular changes does not come about smoothly and continuously then it is obvious that technological rigidities which determine the length of the period of production are of great importance".[21]

That technological developments are likely to lead to unemployment was also very clearly visualized by Gandhiji. To him the machinery method was harmful when the same thing could be done easily by millions of hands not otherwise occupied. The argument that unemployment as a result of technological developments is frictional and therefore temporary did not appeal to him. In his view "concentration of production at infinitum can only lead to unemployment. You may say that workers thrown out of work by the introduction of improved machinery will find occupations in other jobs. But in an organised country, where there are only fixed and limited avenues of employment, where the worker has become highly skilled in the use of one particular kind of machinery, this is hardly possible".[22] That even in a highly industrialised and technologically advanced country like U.S.A. full employment has not been possible except under abnormal circumstances of war, is ample proof of the fact that it is mere wishful thinking that technological developments have taken us anywhere near the cherished goal of full employment. "A permanent margin of unemployment among industrial workers is a feature of economic systems called into existence by the industrial revolution in Western countries. Palliatives as unemployment insurance, allowance of relief funds, etc., do not touch the fundamental cause of unemployment".[23]

It may be argued that the State will step in and intervene to usher in a 'welfare state' and that under such an order every one will be free and happy. Even while supporting the view that public utility industries, wherever they have to be centralised and run on a large scale, should be nationalized and run under ideal conditions, Gandhiji was suspicious of an ever-increasing power of the State. "I look upon an increase of the power of the State with the greatest fear, because although while apparently doing good by minimizing exploitation, it does the great harm to mankind by destroying individuality which lies at the root of all progress. We know of so many cases where men have adopted trusteeship, but none where the State has really lived for the poor".[24] Real freedom, according to him, consisted in making individuals powerful enough to withstand the whole might of the world. "Real Swaraj will come not by the acquisition of authority by a few but by the acquisition of the capacity by all to resist authority when abused. In other words, Swaraj is to be attained by educating the masses to a sense of their capacity to regulate and control authority".[25]

Ever-increasing material wants is another aspect of a highly mechanized and technologically advanced economy. "Our modern civilisation under conditions of industrial progress is continually manufacturing new and previously unwanted sources of pleasure so that the old luxuries become new necessities alike for those who can afford and those who cannot".[26] The view that the multiplication of our wants is conducive to human well-being did not find any favour with Gandhiji. He was of the opinion that "in so far we have made the modern materialistic craze our goal, so far we are going downhill in the path of progress. I hold that economic progress in the sense I have put it is antagonistic to real progress........That you cannot serve God and Mammon is an economic truth of the highest value". For Gandhiji the ideal to be kept before us was to be voluntary reduction of wants consistent with moral progress. "Civilisation, in the real sense of the term, consists not in the multiplication, but in the deliberate and voluntary reduction of wants. This alone promotes real happiness and contentment, and increases the capacity for service.

Modern civilisation with its ever-increasing wants and technological advancement has drifted mankind to a position from where we do not know how to get out. "Despite the immense hopes which humanity has placed on modern civilisation, such a civilisation has failed in developing men of sufficient intelligence and sagacity to guide it along the dangerous road on which it is stumbling. Human beings have not grown so rapidly as the institutions sprung from their brain. It is chiefly the intellectual and moral deficiencies of the political leaders and their ignorance which endanger modern nations".[27] "Modern civilization finds itself in a difficult position because it does not suit us. It has been erected without any knowledge of our real natures. It was born from the whims, discoveries, from the appetites of men, their illusions, their theories and their desires. Although constructed by our efforts, it is not adjusted to our size and shape". A situation has been created in which each one of us finds himself powerless and at the mercy of forces, which we cannot control. "The enormous advances gained by the sciences of inanimate matter over those of living things is one of the greatest catastrophes ever suffered by humanity. The environment born of our intelligence and invention is adjusted neither to our stature nor to our shape. We are unhappy. We degenerate morally or mentally. The groups and nations in which industrial civilisation has attained its highest development are precisely those which are becoming weaker and whose return to barbarism is the most rapid. But they do not realize it. They are without protection against the hostile surroundings that science has built about them. In truth, our civilization has created conditions of existence, which, for reasons obscure, render life itself impossible. We are the victims of backwardness of the sciences of life over those of matter".[28]

It was against degeneration and degradation that Gandhi ji was fighting with all his might. "The movement of the spinning wheel is an organised attempt to displace machinery from that state of exclusiveness and exploitation and to place it in its proper state. Under my scheme, therefore, men in charge of machinery will think not of themselves or even of the nation to which they belong but of the whole human race".[29] That the individual cannot progress and come to his own so long as the 'machinery method' continues was also clearly recognized. "It then dawned on me that to suppress and exploit the millions the machine was the device par excellence: it had no place in man's economy if, as social units, all men were to be equal. It is my belief that the machine has not added to man's stature and it won't serve the world but disrupt it, unless it is put in its proper place".[30] It must be clearly recognized that "as an ideal we should strive for a form of society, an association of free men in which the free development of each is the condition of the free development of all. In a society in which a few individuals are very wealthy the poor will not lead free and happy lives. Real progress will not be possible if we neglect the man for whom we profess and plan". In the words of Gandhiji, "Khadi represents and represented a way of life based on non-violence..........Through Khadi we were struggling to establish the supremacy of man in the place of supremacy of power-driven machinery over him. Through Khadi we were striving for equality of all men and women in the place of gross inequality to be witnessed today. We were striving to attain subservience of capital under labour in the place of the insolvent triumph of capital over labour".[31]

That even in the land of Gandhiji his opinions and views are at a discount is a painful fact. The material advancement of the West has dazzled our vision. We have become oblivious of the evils that may creep in our blind imitation of the West. These ideas of Gandhiji must give us food for thought for many decades to come.

References

1. Pollock: Economic and Social Consequences of Automation.
2. *Ibid.*
3. Times of India, March 9, 1958.
4. Pollock: Economic & Social Consequences of Automation.
5. *Ibid.*
6. *Ibid.*
7. *Ibid.*
8. Quoted by Pollock in Economic & Social Consequences of Automation.
9. Young India, 1931, p. 351.
10. Harijan, 1939, p. 438.
11. *Ibid.*, 1935, p. 329.
12. *Ibid.*, 1946, p. 285.
13. Speeches and Writings of Mahatma Gandhi.
14. Vincent Sheean: Lead Kindly Light, p. 171.
15. *Ibid.*
16. Harijan, 1935, p. 146.
17. *Ibid.*, p. 244.
18. *Ibid.*, 1937, p. 226.
19. *Ibid.*, 1934, p. 301.
20. *Ibid*
21. Halm: Monetary Theory.
22. Harijan, 1934, p. 301.
23. Jathar and Beri: Indian Economics.
24. Modern Review, 1935.
25. Young India, 1925, pp. 40-41.
26. Josiah Wedgewood: Economics of Inheritance.
27. Alexis Garrel: Man, the Unknown.
28. *Ibid*
29. Young India, 1935, p. 321.
30. Harijan, 1946, p. 281.
31. *Ibid.*, 1947, p. 470.

23

Classless Society — Gandhian Approach

The modern economic system has become highly complex and this tendency is increasing with alarming rapidity. Every country is trying to imitate the West in its desire for industrialisation. Apart from the several problems that the modern economic system has created, the most outstanding one is the division of the whole society into different classes, which feel that they can profit only at the expense of the other classes. They always try to take advantage of the weak bargaining position of the other class. This leads to violent outbursts in the shape of strikes and lockouts. The economic war measures cause a lot of hardship to the people. There are not only economic evils but also social and even psychological evil effects of these manifestations. In every country efforts are being made to find out a solution to these economic mal-adjustments. Thinking people have devoted their whole lives for finding a solution. But it appears that we are as yet very far off from our cherished goal of a classless society. It is very doubtful, and no one can say with any amount of confidence, that these measures have proved successful. The society stands divided in two broad classes - the haves and the have-nots; the exploiters and the exploited. There may be years of comparative economic peace and all may appear to be smooth. But these are only lulls before the storms and are always followed by increased industrial and economic strife, mutual misunderstandings, etc. It appears that there is a permanent class conflict and that the whole structure needs some radical reform.

Like every other thinking man, Gandhiji also gave considerable thought to this problem of class conflict. He was alive to the necessity of bringing about some radical changes in the present economic structure. But his methods were peculiarly his own and those which were never tried in any other country before. Briefly speaking, it may be said that he did not believe in the permanence of class conflict; but on the other hand he believed that all progress is essentially based on healthy cooperation between different sectors of the society. Without this healthy cooperation no progress is possible whatsoever. Similarly, he had firm belief that the changeover can be brought about by non-violent and peaceful methods.

After all, why do we want to change the present order of society? Why should not the present order be continued for some more years? In brief, the answer may be that the present order does not meet our demand. It has led to the exploitation of people and classes by others who are, for the time being more powerful. This exploitation of a group of people by another, of individuals by a group is highly undesirable and should be removed; or we may conveniently assert that the modern economic structure is to be changed for certain non-economic (or we may say certain ethical) considerations also and should be replaced by an order of society where there is no room for exploitation (or at least, it is considerably minimized) of one group by another and where individual personality can develop fully. Therefore, we may safely conclude that for certain ethical and non-economic considerations also the social and economic structure has to be changed. This was what Gandhiji said and preached throughout his life. He did not believe in compartmentalization of life. He regarded life as a whole where every sort of consideration is to be given due importance. Gandhiji is not alone in this approach. Even Western thinkers had to concede that if socialism ever comes it will be because of ethical and non-economic considerations.

What do we mean by a classless society? Really a classless society will be one where there are no classes whatsoever or, in other words, where there is perfect mobility between different classes, where people can conveniently change from one vocation to another. It will mean that a perfect classless society will be possible only when an individual has opportunities and competence to follow each and every vocation. Gandhiji did realize that, except in a highly primitive society, such a classless state is not possible. Classes in the sense of functional groups have existed in the past and shall continue to exist in the future also. And, therefore, what we should aspire is not a classless society but a social and economic structure where there is perfect class harmony. "The existence of classes in the sense of functional division is a permanent feature of any but the most primitive society and, in a complicated society such as we live in, it does not seem possible even with a decentralised economy to have a state of classlessness. What can be achieved as best as possible is class harmony".[1]

And here lies the difference between Gandhiji and others. Gandhiji did not believe in the permanence of class conflict. He did not believe that no progress is possible without this class conflict. Is it not that whatever progress we have made in the various spheres is at too heavy a price that we had to pay in the past. Every section of the people is essential for the progress of the society. They make contributions in their own way and according to their own capacities. That such a society is possible appears very doubtful. We have been so much obsessed by the present economic order and our outlook has been so much vitiated that we cannot contemplate even for a moment that such a society where there will be perfect class harmony is possible. And this can be realized only to the extent men and women become good, truthful, loving, simple and self-contained, respecters of life and anxious to serve and make happy the people over whom they exercise authority. In a society of such men where will be all-round prosperity, peace and harmony, and absence (or minimum) of conflicts and disputes. It presumes that men are moved with a sense of duty and not by motives of profit or pleasure and that they shall not utilize their superior powers for personal benefits and that they will take no more rewards for their services than what is consistent with a real classless society where everyone gives to the best of his capacity and takes no more than just what is necessary for his own maintenance consistent with the means of the society.

In such a social order there shall be perfect equality between man and man and at least there shall not be wide disparities between the incomes of different sectors. "The real implication of equal distribution", said Gandhiji, "is that each man shall have the wherewithal to supply all his natural wants and no more".[2] It does not mean that everyone will literally get the same amount. It also does not mean that people should be reduced to the smallest number of material wants and that nobody should have anything above certain minimum. The idea that Gandhiji favoured poverty is a fiction. He simply wanted certain selected idealists to serve the people through self-sacrifice. Is it Utopian to think that the existence of such people is possible? Have not such a class of people always lived in every society? He wrote, "No one has ever suggested that grinding poverty can lead to anything else than much degeneration". He was against extremes of pauperism and wealth. His whole emphasis was that luxuries of the few should come only after necessities of each and everyone have been fully satisfied. First things must come first. Everyone who is prepared to put in a minimum of honest labour must be guaranteed a comparable standard of living. "I hold, wrote Gandhiji, "that whoever devotes eight hours daily to any socially useful productive work is entitled to get a living. My ideal of socialism is that everyone should get the same wage. A lawyer, a physician, a teacher, a labourer, a sweeper — all should get equal wages".[3] With glaring inequalities class harmony cannot be brought about. The first requisite for such a social order is equality of incomes.

But how can such an order be brought about? Gandhiji was quite clear in his mind that it will be well-nigh impossible to attain this ideal by western standards of material comforts. An order based on competition and complicated price economy, an order where the ideal before everyone is personal progress at all costs cannot bring about such a radical change. He believed that modern industrialisation, coupled with rise of complicated city life, has done positive harm to mankind. The rising number of mental and nervous disorders, declining intelligence of the townfolk is a clear proof that the modern industrial order has failed. "The groups and nations in which industrial civilisation has attained its highest development are becoming weaker and whose return to barbarism is the most rapid. But they do not realize it. They are without protection against the hostile surroundings that science has built about them. In truth our civilisation has created conditions of existence, which for reasons still obscure render life itself impossible. The anxieties and the woes of the inhabitants of the modern society arise from their political, economic and social institutions but above all from their own weakness. We are the victims of the backwardness of the science of life over those of matters".[4] Such a change can be brought about only if we lead a simple life and use simple methods of production. Gandhiji believed that "higher thinking is inconsistent with complicated material life based on high speed imposed on us by Mammon worship. All the graces of life are possible only when we learn the art of living nobly". Simplicity of life and the economic and the political order are more conductive to the growth of a classless society rather than an order based on excessive centralisation, mechanisation and production on a gigantic scale. It may be argued that these are all non-economic and only ethical considerations. Gandhiji drew no distinction between economics and ethics. "An economics", he wrote in Harijan, "that inculcates Mammon worship, that enables the strong to amass wealth at the expense of the weak, is a false and dismal science. It spells death. True economics stands for social justice".

Decentralisation of the economic system follows automatically from what has been said above. Gandhiji was an ardent advocate of economic decentralisation. Not only this, he wanted that production should be mainly for use and not so much for the market. At least in respect of essentials of life there was to be self-sufficiency of regions and in respect of these the trade was to be severely restricted. "We have to concentrate on the village being self-contained manufacturing mainly for use" was his advice. This local self-sufficiency in essential commodities will mean that money shall be dethroned from the important position that it occupies today. Whatever trade will be there, and let it be clearly understood that Gandhi ji was not against trade and commerce, shall be in respect of surplus production and exchange on the basis of barter.

Decentralisation of the economic system naturally means that the scope of modern complicated machinery shall be needed; those that will lighten the burden of all and not permit few to exploit others. Gandhiji was not opposed to the use of all machinery. According to him machines could be used but should be discarded "just where they cease to help the individual and encroach upon his individuality. The machine should not be allowed to cripple the limbs of men". Machines generally lead to mass production and the consequent evils. Gandhiji wanted that production should be mainly for use. "Provided this character (self-sufficiency and production mainly for use) of the village industries is maintained", he wrote in Harijan of Aug. 29, 1936, "there would be no objection to villagers using even the modern machines and tools that they can make and afford to use. Only they should not be used as a means of exploiting others".

Some centralised sector of the economy shall have to be there. This was conceded by Gandhiji also. He was not opposed to all centralised production. He remarked, "At the same time I believe that some key industries are necessary but they will occupy the least part of the vast national activity which will mainly be in the villages". The centralised system was not to remain predominating. It was to supplement and not to compete with small-scale industries. Their place was to be minimum possible. In their limited scope they are not to be the private property of any individual or groups of individuals. They are to belong to the society as a whole. "Hence without having to enumerate key industries I would have State ownership, where a large number of people have to work together. The ownership of the products of their labour, whether skilled or unskilled, will vest in them through the State" and that these should be run under ideal conditions and not for profits or money-making.

We may also refer, in brief, that if such an order can be brought about, there shall be no such distinct economic groups as we have at present. There shall be no such classes of labourers and of capitalists, as production shall be mainly carried on through small-scale and cottage industries. There shall be only limited centrally producing units. In all such cases the workers are to be organised in unions and the labourers should be regarded as equal partners in the industrial venture. Work should be done under ideal conditions. Every worker shall be entitled to a living wage, restricted hours of work and other comforts. "It is vital for the well-being of the workers that workmen should be regarded as equals with share-holders and that they have therefore to possess an accurate knowledge of the transactions of the mills". These organisations must be run on non-violent lines and should work not only for the good of their members but the society as a whole.

The use of strike as a labour weapon shall be obviated. There shall be no need for workers to go on strike for the fulfilment of their legitimate demands. There shall be no grounds for friction and consequent strikes or lockouts. The trade unions shall refer the points of discord to arbitration and abide by the decisions arrived at. "The principle of arbitration is essential to Gandhiji's philosophy. It eliminates violence and the compulsion, which may be present even in peaceful strikes and struggles. It teaches people tolerance and conciliation". Gandhiji fasted in Ahmedabad for the establishment of this idea. Even modern labour leaders are agreed that voluntary arbitration is the best solution of industrial disputes. He was also against exploitation of labourers and labour organisations for political purposes so long as the labourers themselves have not reached the stage of political consciousness, which we desire for them. There is no objection, and it is our duty, to educate the working classes in politics and to make them take interest in Congress work, though we may not use their organisation as pawns" (Young India, 23.11.1922).

Thus Gandhiji was striving to build up an economic order which will provide for simple life and the chief characteristics of which shall be truthfulness, non-violence equality of status and of opportunities, equal distribution of wealth and of necessaries and comforts of life, minimum state control, decentralisation and non-mechanisation. In such an order the possibilities of anyone amassing huge personal property or wealth is reduced considerably. And for those who are able to do so has the other remedy, which he described as the principle of trusteeship.

Gandhiji's views on private property were highly radical. He did not believe that private property is essential for human development or progress.

He was in favour of abolition of all private property. But he also realized, at the same time, that the abolition of all private property is a remote ideal and is not likely to be attained in the fore-seeable future. He, therefore, provided that all personal property should be held in trust, i.e., the holder should realize and feel that his personal property and qualities have been given to him not for personal profits, but that he is to benefit the society by his special gift or talents. He wanted to make people realize that social obligations are more valuable and that they should get precedence over personal gains and profits. And if a large number of people accept this principle of trusteeship, the wide disparities in the income and standard of living of different classes will go automatically and a suitable atmosphere shall be prepared for the establishment of a classless economic order.

It may be asked as to what should be the basis of the remuneration of the trustee; and how can this scheme of trusteeship be enforced? Should the trustee have a right to appoint his successors, etc.?

As regards the remuneration to which a trustee is entitled, enough has been said when the principle of equality was discussed. According to that principle no one, even though he may be a trustee, is entitled to anything more than his essential requirements. But since such a scheme does not appear to be practicable, Gandhiji wanted that there should be an equitable remuneration. Thus, a trustee could earn more than his neighbours. But his income was not to exceed by more than a certain amount, say ten times the lowest income. "In a state built on the basis of non-violence the commission of the trustee will be regulated".

But a trustee has no right to pass on his property to his heirs. The question of inheritance of the trust property should solely depend on the competence of the heirs. The trustee may be given the right to suggest some names to be successors, but that the final choice should not rest with him. The choice of the successors should rest both with the original trustee and the state. "Choice should be given to the original owner who became the first trustee, but the choice must be finalized by the state. Such arrangement puts a check on the state as well as the individual" (Harijan, 2.2.47), Gandhiji had also expressed his opinion that "a trustee has no heir but the public".

As regards the enforcement of the trusteeship scheme, Gandhiji held that public opinion should be expected to bring about the desired results. In a decentralised economy where production is mostly for use public opinion will become powerful enough to force the trustee to play the fair game. Gandhiji believed that any extra possession is possible only with the cooperation of others, which may be forthcoming either because of helplessness or ignorance. But if people become conscious of their strength and if they are organised on non-violent lines no trustee can afford to act against the public will. If they do try to go against the popular will it should be too powerful to be resisted. Through his scheme of trusteeship Gandhiji wanted to convert the existing moneyed people in a non-violent way. He was against use of force or any other violent methods. "Exploitation of the poor can be extinguished not by affecting destruction of a few millionaires, but by removing the ignorance of the poor and teaching them to non-cooperate with their exploiters. That will convert the exploiters also" (Harijan, July 28, 1940). And, again, he explained, "But as I can conceive of such a state only based on non-violence. I would not dispossess moneyed men by force but would invite their cooperation in the process of conversion to state ownership". This scheme of trusteeship was regarded by him to be in the self-interest of the moneyed and the propertied class people. In the Constructive Programme he wrote, "Economic equality is the master key to non-violent independence. Working for economic equality means abolishing the eternal conflict between capital and labour. It means the leveling down of the few rich in whose hand is concentrated the bulk of the nation's wealth on the one hand and, leveling up of the semi-starved naked millions on the other. A non-violent system of government is clearly impossibility, so long as the wide gulf between the rich and the hungry millions persists. The contrast between the palaces of New Delhi and the miserable hovels of the poor labouring class nearby cannot last one day in a free India in which the poor shall enjoy the same power as the richest in land. A violent and bloody revolution is a certainty one day unless there is voluntary abdication of riches and the power that riches give and sharing them for the common good. I adhere to my doctrine of trusteeship in spite of the ridicule that has been poured upon it. It is true that it is difficult to reach. So is non-violence difficult to attain" (Constructive Programme, Item No. 13). Later on, Gandhiji had also become in favour of legislation to bring about equality. He was in favour of highly progressive taxation and said, "Why should there be no death duties?" He went a stage further when he said that "a trustee has no heir but the public". This was how Gandhiji wanted to bring about lasting socialism through non-violence.

We may have our doubts as regards the possibility of attainment of economic equality through the scheme of trusteeship and through a change of heart or by non-violent methods. We may feel like using any means for the attainment of our ideal. The ideal is clear and we may be tempted to use violent means — class struggle, bloody revolution, etc. For us ends may justify the use of any means whatsoever. But Gandhiji's emphasis on pure non-violent and truthful means was exclusive. He was not prepared to compromise on this issue; for him ends and means were convertible terms. He believed that good ends cannot be attained through improper means because in this process the ends themselves get vitiated and changed. So many wars have been fought to end wars, but we are still far far away from the cherished goal of no war. "The strength to be given to the people has to be non-violent if the dispossessed are in their turn not to become as bad as the present possessors" (K.G. Masruwala). Gandhiji did not also believe in bringing about sudden and drastic changes or reforms in the society. Any such enforcement would deliver men from one set of evils only to plunge them into another. Human nature is essentially conservative and reformers should refrain from introducing sudden and drastic changes. It is only after an atmosphere has been created and the general mass of people are prepared for a change that the same should be introduced.

Thus, we see that the two most important desirables of a Gandhian society are non-violent society and Satyagraha to attain it. Satyagraha is the vindication of truth not by inflicting suffering on the opponent but on one's self. It requires considerable amount of self-control. This was one reason why Gandhiji laid considerable emphasis on the simplification of wants. Multiplication of wants and all that the modern economic system stands for is based on exploitation, i.e., on violence in one shape or the other. One who is a party to exploitation or violence cannot forcefully ask others to give up exploitation. Gandhiji was therefore opposed to unnecessary multiplication of wants. Moreover, Satyagraha requires strong self-discipline in its followers. In a society where multiplication of wants is the ideal, where people aspire to live in luxury and have all sorts of wants, it will be very difficult (if not impossible) for them to renounce these material luxuries, stand for the truth, and resist things which are otherwise unjustifiable. Public conscience under such an order is dead. Again, simplification of wants comes after deliberate self-control. Practice of non-violence and Satyagraha also requires deliberate control over one's instincts. Hence, for all these reasons also Gandhiji was opposed to this mad rush after multiplication of wants and for wealth.

The ultimate ideal, however, was the fullest possible development of the individual and his personality. A class-ridden society does not permit an individual to develop and grow and, therefore, it is to be replaced by a classless society. In the modern over-centralised social order we find that an individual is lost. We profess and swear by the common man; but we find that everywhere man appears to be lost in his surroundings.

"Man should be measure of all. On the contrary he is a stranger in the whorl that he has created. He has been incapable of organising this world for himself because he did not possess a practical knowledge of his own nature. Thus the enormous advance gained by the science of inanimate matter over those of living things is one of the greatest catastrophes ever suffered by humanity. The environment born of our inventions and intelligence is adjusted neither to our stature nor to our shape. We degenerate morally and mentally" (Man, the Unknown). Gandhiji wanted that the individual should be the corner-stone of our society — not passive obedience to authority but intelligent cooperation should be the guiding principle. Such development of human personality is clearly impossibility in the modern top-centralised structure. "What shall it avail a man if he gains the whole world and loses his soul?", remarked Gandhiji. "In modern times", he continued, "it is beneath human dignity to lose one's individuality and become a mere cog in the machine. I want every individual to become full-blooded, fully developed member of human society". "The welfare of the individual himself must be regarded as the most important purpose of all; and if the sacrifice of one's material good was demanded for any idealistic end it must be voluntary. He (Gandhiji) did not subscribe to the theory that for the good of the many that of the few, and for the good that might accrue to the future generations, that of the present generation might be sacrificed by men possessed of power" (K.G. Masruwala). Gandhiji's emphasis on the individual was not absolute. He did realize that an individual has certain social obligations. But he did not want that discipline should be enforced from outside by any outside authority. It is demoralising. "I value individual freedom", he wrote, "but you must not forget that man is essentially a social being. He has risen to his present status by learning to adjust his individualism to the requirements of social progress. Unrestricted individualism is the law of the beast, of the jungle. We must learn to strike a mean between the individual freedom and social restraint".

There is need for deep thinking over Gandhiji's prescriptions. If we are to carry out most of Gandhiji's economic prescriptions — decentralisation of the economic system, development of cottage and small-scale industry, production by simple methods and technique, use of simple and easy-to-handle machines, voluntary curtailment and limitation of one's material wants, his theory of trusteeship, etc., — we can bring about within a reasonably short period an economy depending upon a full employed, self-governing village enjoying maximum self-sufficiency and minimum mechanisation; where industries are shared by a few capitalists, municipal, state and federal governments, strong trade unions and cooperatives and one generation capitalists whose wealth, since they cannot bequeath it, will revert to the society.

References

1. K.G. Mashruwala — Gandhi and Marx, p. 72.
2. Harijan, 25.9.1940.
3. *Ibid*
4. Alexis Carrel : Man, The Unknown, p. 38.

24

Gandhian Approach to Property Relations and Class Conflict

Gandhiji's attitude towards property is best represented by the simple fact that on his unfortunate death his countrymen inherited, in terms of material goods, the three monkeys; his meager personal possessions. He symbolized non-possession. As a votary of non-violence he considered property in the hands of individuals as a hindrance for their adopting a non-violent way of living. He equated property with theft and robbery. "The rich, moneyed man who made his riches by exploitation or other questionable means was no less guilty of robbery than the thief who picked a pocket or broke into a house and committed theft......... all amassing or hoarding of wealth, above and beyond one's legitimate requirement was theft. There would be no occasion for thefts and therefore, no thieves, if there was wise regulation of riches and absolute social justice prevailed.[1] Gandhiji held the firm opinion that capital "accumulation by private persons was impossible except through violent means".[2]

As early as 1916 while addressing Y.M.C.A. at Madras on 16 February, Gandhiji propounded his views on property. "I suggest that we are thieves in a way. If I take anything that I do not need for my immediate use, and keep it, I thieve it from somebody else".[3]

Inequality, as is reflected in the present day socio-economic order was a taboo to Gandhiji. "A non-violent system of Government is clearly an impossibility so long as the wide gulf between the rich and the hungry million persists........ A violent and bloody revolution of riches and the power that riches give and sharing them for the common good".[4] Inequalities are to a large extent due to accumulation of wealth by individuals and groups of individuals. Gandhiji had realized that in times to come such inequalities will not be tolerated. If a non-violent and peaceful method of dispossessing the rich of their wealth and the privileges associated with these riches is not discovered the society will witness a violent upsurge.

Gandhiji once remarked: "In this (India) of all countries in the world, possession of inordinate wealth by individuals should be held as a crime against humanity. Therefore, the maximum limit of taxation of riches beyond a certain margin can never be reached.........Why should there not be death duties..........For the inheritance should rightly belong to the nation.........."[5]

He did not believe in inherited riches. "The well-to-do should educate and bring up their children so that they may learn to be indepenldent".[6]

In this connection it may be pointed out that Gandhiji recognized the right of the society to curb the right to property in most unambiguous terms. Addressing the Round Table Conference he remarked, — "I want to state, with all the emphasis I can command, that I could not even endorse the formula that the rights of all Indian born subjects themselves could even be guaranteed or equal........for years to come India would be engaged in passing legislation in order to raise the downtrodden, the fallen, from the more into which they have been sunk by the capitalists, by the landlords, by the so-called higher classes".[7] He continued that if national interests so desire these classes "will be dispossessed without any compensation, because, if you want........to pay compensation it (State) will have to rob Peter to pay Paul, and that would be impossible."[8]

Gandhiji was against the institution of private property. In 1928, replying to questions of students about Bolshevism he remarked, "All that I know is that it aims at the abolition of the institution of private property. This is only an application of the ethical idea of non-possession in the realm of economics and if the people adopted this ideal of their own accord or could be made to accept it by means of peaceful persuasion there would be nothing like it".[9] Explaining his views to an Egyptian interviewer in 1937 he emphasised once again that he was against the institution of private property. He observed: "If communism came without violence it would be welcome. For then no property would be held by anybody except on behalf of the people and for the people".[10] Elucidating his point on another occasion he emphasised that the right to property is not at all sacred. ".......I must know that all that wealth does not belong to me, what belongs to me is the right to an honourable livelihood, no better than that enjoyed by millions of others. The rest of my wealth belongs to the community and must be used for the welfare of the community."[11] He equated property and concentration of riches in a few people and unemployment amongst millions as a social crime or disease which needs to be remedied.

It is significant to point out that Gandhiji visualized that those leaders who want to change the socio-economic order should not have any private property. The inmates of Ashrams, his laboratories where he was building and training new leaders, were to accept certain principles. Non-possession or voluntary poverty, non-stealing were some of the vows that were emphasised. Non-possession means non-dependence on material things. In economic terms it implies total abolition of private property in all kinds of belongings — whether material possessions, personal talents, and even earnings beyond ones immediate needs.

He demonstrated in his personal life the revolutionary potentiality of a man who is not attached to property and baser instincts that lead to accumulation of property. As a matter of fact he insisted that one of the qualifications of franchise should be manual labour for the service of the society. In 1924 he observed "the qualification for the franchise should be neither property nor position but manual work......."[12] These views were reiterated again in 1947 when in reply to a question he answered— "All adults above a certain age, male or female, who would contribute some body labour to the state would be entitled to vote."[13]

Concept of 'bread labour' was to ensure that nobody escapes socially desirable physical labour. It will be helpful in ushering a better socio-economic order. Statements quoted above only indicate that he did not attach importance to property or wealth as a symbol for conferring benefits upon members of the society.

Gandhiji was opposed not only to accumulation of property by individuals, but was also against the use of talent by those who possessed these to amass wealth or power for themselves. That was the reason he put greater stress on varana of his definition which was a method to limit our material ambition in order to set free the talents and energy of those who are above average for social service and upliftment of the poverty striken. To the doubt that this effort to sublimate material ambition is possible only under ideal conditions and that every one hankers after paying professions, Gandhiji replied 'Highway robbery is not open to every one......There cannot be millions of millionaires".[14]

This proposition does not preclude acquisition of new skills and avenues by those who have talent. "But we need not, ought not, to seek new avenues for gaining wealth......One may do anything he likes so long as he does it for love or service"[15], was his advice.

It will be no exaggeration to state that while he disapproved accumulation of wealth by individuals and condemned it as theft or robbery, he did not also approve the accumulation of wealth even by the society beyond a certain limit. Property or wealth is required to enable the owner — be it the individual or the society — to increase material standards of living of the owner. Gandhiji held the view that any effort to raise material standards of living ad-infinitum is bound to lead to an exploitative society. "Civilization in the real sense of the term, consists not in the multiplication, but the deliberate and voluntary reduction of wants. This alone promotes real happiness and contentment and increases the capacity for service".[16] He left no occasion to emphasize that there is nothing sacred about present approach to material prosperity at the cost of social and moral values. For Gandhiji "economics to be worth anything must be capable of being reduced to terms of religion or spirituality."[17]

It was for this reason that he advocated a much simpler style of life and extreme decentralization of the economic system. The modern rage for variety, for flying through the air, for multiplicity of wants etc., had no fascination for him. He was opposed to industrialization, as the term is popularly understood. "I believe that an independent India can only discharge her duty towards a groaning world by adopting a simple but ennobled life, by developing her thousands of cottages and living at peace with the world."[18]

Gandhiji had realized that an economic system that gives rise to competitive consumption patterns must necessarily give rise to exploitation and an effort to acquire property and wealth by the few at its ugliness in developing economics like ours. "It was because this process of multiplication of wants out of proportion to our surroundings was discovered to be going on with increasing velocity that Non-cooperation was conceived. And thus conceived it was not Non-Cooperation with persons, but an attitude which was responsible for the system which had seized us in its serpentine coil and which was reducing us to dust. The system has raised the standard of living among us, its creatures, wholly unwarranted by the general condition of the country. And since India did not live upon exploitation of other people, the expansion of middle class......meant an extinction of lower strata."[20]

Prof. Gunner Myrdal too has forbidden about this incessant rise in standards of living. He warns "………we shall invite catastrophic developments, unless we are prepared now to introduce and enforce various restraints on and deflections of, production and consumption and indeed our ways of life".[21] Prof. Myrdal had only the catastrophe of depletion of natural resources, pollution and problems of a similar nature in mind. Besides these, Gandhiji, also had in mind the other catastrophe of social upheavals and bloody revolutions which may tear the society to pieces, without in any way bringing about fundamental changes in the socio-economic set up.

Gandhiji, as a practical person had also realized that such austerity is difficult of attainment and that, unless a different value pattern becomes acceptable, people will like to hold property. As has been mentioned earlier, in respect of right of property Gandhiji had more radical views than the communists "He would like to dispossess every person of all kinds of belonging. If he tolerates the institution of private property, it is not because he loves it, or holds it to be necessary for the progress of humanity, but because he has as yet to discover a truthful and non-violent method of abolishing that institution…….all socialists believe that possessions are absolutely essential, to make mankind happy. Gandhiji does not accept that position in theory. But as a practical proposi-tion, he feels that mankind is not going to give up possessions, within a time, which can be estimated. The only thing, therefore, to be considered is in what capacity persons having actual control over and possession of property should be deemed to have it or in what spirit they should be suffered to possess it…….[21]

In order to solve this riddle Gandhiji propounded his thesis of Trusteeship. Trusteeship means, in a nutshell, socialisation of the benefits that one derives of wealth and talents. The bulk of the income of the wealthy and the talented is to be utilized to promote social good. In the words of Gandhiji "It is an attempt to secure the best use of property for the people by competent hands"[22] To a question whether these classes have any justification to live more comfortably than the ordinary worker and peasant who does the work which provides their wealth Gandhiji replied categorically 'No justification'. He then explained "My idea of society is that while we are born equal, meaning that we have a right to equal opportunity all have not the same capacity. It is in the nature of things impossible……. People with talents will have more and they will utilize their talents for this purpose. If they utilize their talents kindly, they will be performing the work of the State. Such people exist as trustees, on no other terms. I would allow a man of intellect to earn more. I would not cramp his talent. But the bulk of his greater earning must be used for the good of the State."[23]

It need to be emphasised that Gandhiji did not justify inequalities or a few roaring in wealth while the masses are subject to abject poverty. He had forewarned the privileged that 'a bloody revolution is a certainty' unless they change their ways. He did not rule out slightly higher incomes for those who possess property or talents or both. He quoted with approval Marx — "To each according to his need", he did not approve the inequalities that prevail on the plea of the need of those who somehow attained standards of living that were out of all proportion to conditions of poverty of the country. "Let no one try to justify the glaring differences between the classes and the masses........ by saying that the former need more. That will be idle sophistry and a travesty of my argument."[24] He did not rule out some enjoying slightly higher standards of living but this must bear some relationship with the living standards of the masses. "I plead for the necessary courage to set aside fashion, which can only be sustained at the expense of our starving neighbours.......I do plead for an observance, as between themselves (the rich) and their starving brotheren, a due sense of proportion such as is always observed in a well ordered society".[25] First things come first and even a reasonable rise in the standards of living of the few must come after the essential needs of the poor are satisfied.

He therefore, advocated severe regulation of higher incomes. The trustee is entitled to reasonable income. The test of reasonableness will be relationship between minimum and maximum incomes and the approval of enlightened public opinion "India's minimum is a langoti requiring less than 1/6 of a square yard. Let our fashions have correspondence to this minimum."[26]

The pertinent question is how to enforce this concept of Trusteeship which is, as we have defined earlier, to socialize the benefits because of ownership of property and talent. The word 'Trusteeship' was used by Gandhiji to denote possibility of conversion of propertied and the talented to behave in best interests of the society and not be motivated solely by considerations of the narrow self. As a believer in non-violence and having implicit faith in the capacity of the human soul to rise to dizzy heights he held the belief that people can be persuaded to behave as Trustee. He wanted a peaceful conversion of mill owners, so that mill owners and their employees would all come under social control voluntarily. When doubts were raised about the practicality of this approach Gandhiji remarked — "Such changes have certainly taken place in individuals. One may not perhaps be able to point to them in a whole society. But this only means that uptil now there has never been an experiment on a large scale in non-violence..... Ahimsa is definitely an attribute of society. To conceive people of this truth is at once my effort and my experiment".[27] He wanted to give, so to say, a last chance to the privileged to move with the times and give up their privileges and share them with the masses.

If, however, they refuse to do so Gandhiji advised the masses to organise, resist and offer non-violent non-cooperation "My means are no cooperation. No person can amass wealth without the cooperation, willing or forced, of the people concerned". Replying to the points once raised by Dr. Lohia, Gandhiji observed that 'agitation against every form of injustice is the breath of political life'. But he did realize that unless this agitation is conducted on non-violent lines the masses will continue to suffer as one plunderer gives place to another. "I have always held that social justice, even unto the least and the lowliest is impossible of attainment by force. I have further believed that it is possible by proper training of the lowliest by non-violent means to secure redress of the wrongs suffered by them. That means non-violent cooperation. At times non-cooperation becomes as much a duty as cooperation. No one is bound to cooperate in one's own undoing or slavery. Freedom received through the efforts of others, however benevolent, cannot be retained when such effort is withdrawn. In other words such freedom is not real. But the lowliest can feel its glow as soon as they learn the art of attaining it through non-violent non-cooperation."[28] On another occasion he remarked "Exploitation of the poor can be extinguished not by effecting the destruction of a few millionaires, but by removing the ignorance of the poor and teaching them to non-cooperate with their exploiters. This will convert the exploiter also."[29] To a question in March 1946 — what is the place of satyagraha in making the rich realize their duty towards the poor ?, his reply was "The same as against the foreign power. Satyagraha is a law of universal application."[30]

Gandhiji was not favourably inclined towards use of state power to curb property rights. This was because, on the one hand, he was confident that through peaceful non-cooperation the desired result will follow, and on the other hand he looked with suspicion on increasing power of the state. "The state represents violence, in a concentrated and organised form. The individual has a soul, but as the state is a soulless machine, it can never be weaned from violence to which it owes its existence. Hence, I prefer the doctrine of trusteeship".[31] He continued "I look upon an increase in the power of the state with greatest fear, because although while apparently doing good by minimizing exploitation, it does the greatest harm to mankind by destroying individuality, which lies at the root of all progress. We know of so many cases where men have adopted trusteeship but none where the state has really lived for the poor".[32]

Gandhiji advocated use of non-violent power of the people for removal of the evils that are associated with the present system of production. One of the reasons was that governments can easily crush violent revolt. They cannot overcome non-violent movements by military force. Gandhiji, all through his long public life remained preoccupied with a relentless war against evil. His contribution has been devising a new moral strategy to regulate group life in its political, social economic, national and international aspects.

Gandhiji was not sceptic about the success of non-violent action in future. "I can only say that my own experience in organising non-violent action for half a century fills me with hope for the future".[33]

Gandhiji's emphasis on non-violent non-cooperation was also because of possibility of quick action without waiting for the capturing of state power by those who profess to curb exploitation and prevent concentration of wealth and property. State action in the absence of popular mass-based organisation may quite often become ineffective. It was for this reason that Gandhiji laid emphasis on a constructive programme which included the charkha and the allied industries, which if successful, would practically abolish all inequalities both economic and social.

Even, with his suspicions of the state he gave his consent to a minimum use of state power to enforce the concept of trusteeship on delinquent capitalists and the privileged. In his scheme of things the number of such delinquents will keep on progressively decreasing because of decentralised economic system of production and the resultant increase in the power of mass-based organisation. It is only when the economic system is decentralised that public opinion really becomes effective. It was for this reason that Gandhiji was opposed to industrialisation. "What is industrialism but control of the majority by a small minority? There is nothing attractive about it nor is there anything inevitable in it".[34] Gandhiji held the belief that industrialisation will lead to inequalities and exploitation. In his terminology these were species of violence. To a suggestion in 1935 that after India wins freedom mechanisation might get hold of India his answer was "Then there is no escape from violence......coming mechanisation is impossible in India without its resulting in violence in some shape or other".[35]

Restructuring of our economy on the basis of revival of villages will enable decentralisation of the economic system. It will help reduce accumulation of wealth and strengthen the society to enforce the concept of trusteeship. Under this system production and consumption will get localized, at least in respect of basic necessities of life. Such autonomous self-sufficient units can easily apply sanctions against the few centralised industrial units – whether owned by private industrialists or the state.

The few centralised units will work under most attractive and ideal conditions, and not for profit but for the benefits of humanity. "I (Gandhiji) can have no consideration for machinery which is meant either to enrich the few at the expense of many or without cause to displace the useful labour of many".[36]

Gandhiji described economic constitution under Swaraj of his concept as:

"According to me the economic constitution of India and for that matter, that of the world should be such that no one under it should suffer for want of food and clothing. In other words everybody should be able to get sufficient work to enable him to make the two ends meet. And this ideal can be universally realized only if the means of production of elementary necessaries of life remain in the control of masses ....they should not be made a vehicle of traffic for exploitation of others......It is this evil that khadi movement is calculated to remedy."[37] He felt that only under such an economic system those in authority will remain wedded to public good.

Shri Pyarelal, Gandhiji's Secretary has described that Gandhiji's Trusteeship concept provides the way out of the dilemma in which we find ourselves. Left alone people become unequal. If we try to make them equal they cease to be free.

"Gandhiji's trusteeship formula is not a device to accomodate the owning class, with its shady past and shadier current practices, in the framework of the existing order, but a means of putting an end to the order by transforming the basis of ownership. The owning class dare not shut their eyes to the plain writing on the wall. This is their last, perhaps, their only chance."[38]

In Gandhiji's scheme there was no place for class struggle as we understand it i.e. a struggle based on violence. As has been mentioned in earlier paragraphs Gandhiji was dead set against a socio-economic order that is based on exploitation. He had realized that recourse to violence for far reaching socio-economic changes will leave the masses in whose name the struggle is supposed to be waged largely untouched. "I gladly conclude", he remarked, "that you can easily fight the Government with arms.......The result will be no Swaraj, but one plunderer giving place to his superior and between the two a greater grinding of the masses."[39] He did not, therefore, see the necessity of class conflict. He was bold enough to proclaim that if "I thought it inevitable I should not hesitate to preach it and teach it."[40]

All through his public life Gandhiji was fighting against injustice. When we had freedom it was suggested to him to withdraw from public life as the goal of India becoming inde-pendent was to be realized. His characteristic reply was "people ask me to retire to Kashi or to Himalayas. I laugh and tell them that the Himalayas of my penance are where there is misery to be alleviated, oppression to be relieved."[41]

It is wrong to suggest that Gandhiji did not believe in the existence of classes and consequently class struggle in terms of the exploited class trying to prevent their exploitation. What he did not advocate was the idea that a non-exploitative society cannot be ushered in except through recourse to violence. Replying to a letter Gandhiji observed, "The correspondent is wrong in suggesting that I do not believe in the existence of class struggle. What I do not believe in is the necessity of fomenting and keeping it up......The problem therefore is not to set class against class but to educate labour to a sense of its dignity. Moneyed men after all form a microscopic minority in the world. They will act on the square immediately labour realizes its power and acts on the square".[42]

It may be suggested that the capitalists will not behave as trustee. During his life time Gandhiji was not able to point out a single person who came up to his definition — not even Jamnalal Bajaj. Gandhiji's answer as given by him in 1937 was — "It is highly probable that my advice will not be accepted and my dream will not be realized. But who can guarantee that the socialists' dream will be realized? .....I am engaged in solving the same problem that faces scientific socialists. It is true, however, that my approach is always and only through unadulterated non-violence."[43] Gandhiji had the desire to end capitalism almost, if not quite, as much as the most advanced socialist or even communist. "But our methods differ our languages differ. My theory of trusteeship is no makeshift, certainly no camouflage.......No other theory is compatiable with non-violence."[44]

It may be argued that to think of peaceful resolution of class conflicts is utopian. People, and particularly those enjoying affluence are too selfish, irresponsible and unresponsive "If that is so, and if these qualities are too deeply rooted for anything to be done about them, all I can say is that the outlook for humanity is poor indeed."[45] Albert Camus observes "Over the expanse of five continents throughout the coming years an endless struggle is going to be pursued between violence and friendly persuasion, a struggle in which, granted the former has a thousand times more the success than the latter. But I have also held that, if he who bases his hope on human nature is a fool, he who gives up in the face of circumstances a coward."[46]

References

1. J.S. Mathur (Ed.), Economic Thought of Mahatma Gandhi, p. 626.
2. *Ibid.*, p. 628.
3. *Ibid.*, p. 520.
4. *Ibid.*, p. 610-11.
5. *Ibid.*, p. 444.
6. *Ibid.*, p. 617.
7. *Ibid.*, p. 36-37.
8. *Ibid.*, p. 439.
9. *Ibid.*, p. 550.
10. *Ibid.*, p. 587.
11. *Ibid.*, p. 594.
12. *Ibid.*, p. 533.
13. *Ibid.*, p. 630.
14. *Ibid.*, p. 544.
15. *Ibid.*, p. 545.
16. *Ibid.*, p. 612.
17. *Ibid.*, p. 427.
18. *Ibid.*, p. 517.
19. *Ibid.*, p. 480.
20. Gunnar Myrdal, Against the Stream – Critical Essays in Economics, p. 201.
21. K.G. Mashruwala, Gandhi and Marx, p. 28.
22. J.S. Mathur (Ed.), Economic Thought of Mahatma Gandhi, p. 589.
23. *Ibid.*, p. 564.
24. *Ibid.*, p. 619.
25. *Ibid.*, p. 85.
26. *Ibid.*, p. 85.
27. *Ibid.*, p. 609.
28. *Ibid.*, p. 601.
29. *Ibid.*. p. 605.

30. *Ibid.*, p. 620.
31. *Ibid.*, p. 578.
32. *Ibid.*, p. 579.
33. *Ibid.*, p. 628.G.N. Dhawan quoted, Political Philosophy of Mahatma Gandhi, p. 344.
34. J.S. Mathur (Ed.), Economic Thought of Mahatma Gandhi, p. 476.
35. *Ibid.*, p. 495-96.
36. *Ibid.*, p. 497.
37. *Ibid.*
38. J.S. Mathur, Gandhian Thought and Contemporary Society, p. 30.
39. J.S. Mathur, Economic Thought of Mahatma Gandhi, p. 41.
40. *Ibid.*, p. 315.
41. Pyare Lal, The Last Phase, Vol. II.
42. J.S. Mathur (Ed.), Economic Thought of Mahatma Gandhi, p. 395.
43. *Ibid.*, p. 598.
44. *Ibid.*, p. 201.
45. G.D.H. Gole, The Case for Industrial Partnership, p. 117.
46. A.J. Muste, Gandhi – His Relevance For Our Times, p. 23.

25

A New Life Style: Ideas of Mahatma Gandhi

1. Introduction

The salient features of a new world economic order should be emergence of a society which eschews violence and exploitation, encourages cooperation amongst individuals, groups and nations, brings about greater equality and enables socio-economic changes through the initiative of the people not only through non-violent means but also with adequate rapidity. If this does not happen "people and sometimes whole nations come to lose their confidence in peaceful change through demo-cratic and non-violent means and so become desperate and opt to resort to force."[1]

I am putting forth the views of Mahatma Gandhi, the opposite of non-violence and peace. I do so for the following reasons:

While it is true that Gandhiji was trying to solve the problems that beset India, his nationalism did not exclude internationalism. In fact he was not prepared to free India through violent means. He was making experiments in India but he was trying to evolve a method and technique, which will apply to all people and all countries. "India is trying to evolve true democracy, i.e., without violence. Our weapons are those of satyagraha expressed through Charkha, the village industries, primary education through handicrafts prohibition and non-violent organisation of labour."[2]

In the second place India represents a less developed country where the conditions of the masses are woeful. Most of the countries of the world today have similar problems of growth, development and reduction of poverty. What holds good for India will hold good for the vast majority of world's population.

It may be argued that the problems of a country which has a vast population are entirely different. Yet, let is be remembered that rising population is a problem that the world as a whole is facing. In the face of increasing world population prescriptions that hold good for a country like India today will hold good for other countries and a short time lag.

The problem of poverty — and it is a relative term — has not been solved in any country. There are the haves and have-nots — the affluents and the poor in every society. Conditions in India are acute and a solution that can be successfully applied in this land of ours can succeed to a greater degree in societies where the problem of poverty is not so acute.

I have quoted Mahatma Gandhi extensively because I hold the view that he had significant contributions to make towards a new international economic order. It must, however, be remembered that he addressed himself to Indian audiences which have an altogether different social and cultural background and whose standards of austerity and whose capacity to sacrifice were demonstrated during the struggle for independence under the guidance of the greater leader. He was able to inspire the lowliest and the humblest who rose to great heights. Mahatma Gandhi did not look upon the existing structure with a dwarfed vision. "Gandhi, like Christ, lit beacons on distant hills towards which posterity must grope its way in darkness".[3]

It may also be clarified that we should not try to interpret Gandhiji's message in literal terms. He used a predominantly religious terminology because of cultural background of Indian people. His use of the term Religion or God does not imply any sectarian or dogmatic approach. He used this term as interchangeable with social and human good. "People ask me to retire to Kashi or to the Himalayas. I laugh and tell them that the Himalayas of my penance are where there is misery to be alleviated, oppression to be relieved."[4]

Similarly, the use of the term Charkha, spinning wheel, implies a machine that does not cripple human personality but permits its all-round development, and enables the evolution of a new socio-economic system through the initiative of the common man and enables him to build an organisation on non-violent lines. Such an organisation will be able to challenge the evils of present system. Gandhiji asserted that "the existing structure of economic society in India will not last for twenty hours if my weapon of Satyagraha can be gripped by the people."[5] Shri Pyarelal, Gandhiji's biographer and his personal secretary explains Gandhiji's technique of satyagraha as follows:

"If one aspires to harness the power of satyagraha or soul force, one must seek it, like a prospector of fissionable material in infinitesimals. He was no impossible Mahatma, he maintained. His life was made of a number of small things which were by themselves commonplace and which even an ordinary individual could practise. Therefore, what he had achieved everybody else could and the practice of mass non-violence, the only effective answer to the challenge of unbridled brute force was a present possibility."[6]

To have international peace the economy of the participating units must be free from exploitation of the poor by the rich, of the masses by the classes, of the village by the town and of the weaker or so called underdeveloped races by the stronger and more advanced ones. In a large measure international tensions are because of socio-economic tension within the nations. "Peace is unattainable by part performance of conditions, even as a chemical combination is impossible without complete fulfilment of the conditions of attainment thereof. If the recognized leaders of mankind who have control over engines of destruction were wholly to renounce their use with full knowledge of its implications permanent peace can be obtained. This is clearly impossible without the great powers of earth renouncing their imperialistic design. This again seems impossible without great nations ceasing to believe in self-destroying competition and to multiply wants and thereby increase their material possessions".[7]

2. Inherent dangers of the present economic order

The present economic order has not only resulted in the exploitation of man, groups and nations by one another but has bred open violence in our relationships. The long drawn Vietnam War, the Arab-Israel conflicts are but only few of the aggravated symptoms of the deep malaise. Large scale manufacture of armaments and increasingly sophisticated instruments of mass destruction have opened flood-gates of the mankind reverting to dark old ages. Lord Russel warned us, "I do not know what horrors may be in store for us, but no one can doubt that, unless something very radical is done, scientific man is a doomed species. In the world in which we are living, there is an active and dominant will towards death which has, so far, at every crisis got the better of sanity. If we are to survive, this state of affairs must not continue".[8] Albert Schweitzer remarked, "It is clear now to everyone that the suicide of civilization is in progress. What yet remains of it is no longer safe. It is still standing, indeed because it was not exposed to the destructive pressure which overwhelmed the rest, but like the rest is built upon rubble; and the next land-slide will very likely carry it away".[9] Lord Russel cautions that "we are perhaps living in the last age of man, and if so, it is to science that he will owe his extinction".[10]

Gandhiji in his introduction to a new edition of his book Hind Swaraj or Indian Home Rule wrote, "The booklet is a severe condemnation of 'modern civilisation'. It was written in 1908. My conviction is deeper today than ever. I feel that if India will discard 'modern civilisation', she can only gain by doing so". Prof. Gunnar Myrdal too has only recently observed, "But let me again finally touch upon the anxiety natural scientists and technologists — and indeed, all of us — now feel about the advances in natural sciences and the uncontrolled technological application of new knowledge leading to disaster. This problem has become acute in regard to the pollution of air, water and soil and the depletion of natural resources following industrial progress and, of course, to the even more threatening armaments race, which develops by the automatism of the competitive application of new discoveries and inventions in the field of weaponry".[11]

"..........the whole world and every individual country on 'this spaceship earth' is in a most perilous situation; facing dangers greater than at any earlier period in mankind's history".[12]

3. Need for stressing the ethical aspect of economic activities

The one major consideration should be that we must not lose sight of ethical aspects while considering the new economic model. Gandhiji advised, "Economics to be worth anything must be capable of being reduced to terms of religion and spirituality".[13]

Yet on another occasion he remarked, "I do not draw a sharp or any distinction between economics and ethics. Economics that hurts the moral well-being of an individual or a nation are immoral and therefore sinful".[14] He emphasised this point when he emphasised "that economics is untrue which ignores or disregards moral values. The extension of the law of non-violence in the domain of economics means nothing less than the introduction of moral values as a factor to be considered in regulating international commerce".[15]

Gandhiji is not alone in laying emphasis on an overall and integrated science of economics laying due emphasis on several values which are at present regarded as not relevant for economic consideration. Prof. Gunnar Myrdal observes, "I believe we are going to see rapid development of economic science in the institutional direction and that much that is now held as most sophisticated theory will in the hindsight be seen to have been a temporary aberration into superficiality and irrelevance".[16] He further comments — "I believe that the border- lines between disciplines should be transgressed. Research should be focused on areas of specific problems, not confined to the separate disciplines as they have become established for the purposes of teaching and specialization in research,"[17] and quotes John Dewey — "Anything that obscures the fundamental moral nature of the social problem is harmful".[18] To quote Gandhi once again "whereas religion to be worth anything must also be capable of being reduced to terms of economics, economics to be worth anything must also be capable of being reduced to terms of religion or spirituality. In this scheme of religion cum economics there is no room for exploitation there is no room in true economics for the owning of slaves whether they are human beings, cattle or machinery. There is no room for slavery in economics".[19] He wanted to curb severely that which we understand as economic motive today. "Now it is this 'human element' on which the entire economics of Khadi rests, and human selfishness, Adam Smith's "pure economic motive" constitutes the 'disturbing factor' that has got to be overcome".[20]

Gandhiji trained leaders to accept these values. Of the several vows that members of his Ashram were to adopt were non-possession, voluntary poverty, non-violence i.e., love, compassion and reverence for all living things — nay even towards nature. This is quite contrary to current values. "As a matter of fact, the most utterly inhuman thoughts have been current among us......... in all the ugly clearness of language and with the authority of logical principles. There has been created a social mentality in individuals which discourages humanity in individuals — our society has also ceased to allow to all men, as such, a human value and human dignity, many sections of the race have become merely raw material and property in human form".[21]

It was because of the inherent deficiencies in measuring progress by GNP that scholars have started thinking in terms of GNP (utility) and Prof. Tinbergen has given the idea of Gross National Happiness. It is true that this idea cannot be quantified. It is a clear indication of the unhappiness of eminent economists about ignoring moral and ethical considerations in economic choices and alternatives.

4. Regulations of Wants and Consumption

Regulation of wants and consumption of individuals and groups should be another important consideration. Gandhiji had realized that a lot of tension and misuse of resources is taking place because of a feeling that multiplication of wants and efforts to satisfy them is civilisation and culture. He remarked, "I do not believe that multiplication of wants and machinery contrived to supply them is taking the world a single step nearer its goal Comrade Sakletwale swears by modern rush. I whole-heartedly detest this mad desire to destroy distance and time, to increase appetites and go to the ends of the earth in search of their satisfaction. If modern civilisation stands for all this, and I have understood it to do so, I call it satanic......"[22] and observed that "everything in this world should be able to maintain as high a standard of life as possible with the least output of labour is just as fantastic as to expect a camel to pass through the eye of a needle".[23]

He believed, "civilisation, in the real sense of the term consists not in the multiplication but in the deliberate and voluntary reduction of wants. This alone promotes real happiness and contentment, and increases the capacity to service".[24] While advocating the spinning wheel he observed, — "It is a standing rebuke against the modern mad rush for adding material comfort upon comfort and making life so complicated as to make one doubly unfit for knowing oneself and one's God".[25]

He visualized his whole movement as an effort to change this process.

"It is because this process of multiplication of wants out of proportion to our surroundings was discovered to be going on with increasing velocity that Non-Cooperation was conceived. And thus conceived it was not Non-cooperation with persons, but with an attitude that was responsible for the system which has seized us in its serpentine coil and which was reducing us to dust".[26]

We must not carry the misconception that Gandhiji pleaded for poverty. He was one individual who fought against poverty and tried to improve the standard of living of crores of downtrodden, poverty-stricken people in the shortest possible period. "When all about me are dying for want of food, the only occupation permissible to me is to feed the hungry.......To a people famishing and idle, the only acceptable form in which God can dare appear is work and promise of food as wages".[27] He continued, "I have found it impossible to sooth the suffering patients with a song of Kabir. They cannot be given it. They must earn it. And they can earn only by the sweat of their brow".[28] During his talk with Lancashire mill operators he referred to the poverty of his countrymen and opened his heart "I dare not take them the message of God. I may as well place before the dog over there the message of God as before those hungry millions who have no luster in their eyes and whose only God is their bread, I can take before them a message of God by taking the message of sacred work before them. It is good enough to talk of God whilst we are sitting here after a nice breakfast and looking forward to a nice luncheon, but how am I to talk of God to the millions who have to go without two meals a day. To them God can appear only as bread and butter".[29]

Gandhiji while opposed to poverty did not believe that ad- infinitum multiplication of wants is in any way conducive to proper growth and development. "A certain degree of physical harmony and comfort is necessary, but above a certain level it becomes a hindrance instead of help. Therefore, the ideal of creating an unlimited number of wants and satisfying them seem to be a delusion and snare. The satisfaction of ones physical needs, even the intellectual needs of one's narrow self, must meet a certain point a dead stop, before it degenerates into physical and mental voluptuousness. A man must arrange physical and cultural circumstances to that they do not hinder him in his service of humanity on which all his energies should be concentrated".[30]

In the circumstances in which we find ourselves Gandhiji's advice was "Such a society is necessarily cultural in which every man and woman knows what he or she wants, and, what is more, knows that no one should want anything that others cannot have with equal labour". His advice to the rich was "I plea for the necessary courage to set aside fashion, which can only be sustained at the expense of our starving neighbours. By all means let moneyed people have wasteful ornamentation, whether in dress or in office surroundings, but I do plead for an observance, as between them and their starving brethren, of a due sense of proportion such as is always observed in well-ordered society. India's minimum is a langoti requiring 1/6 of a square yard. Let our fashions have some correspondence to this minimum, let not those who would raise the minimum, and multiply India's wants in order to wake her up to action, think that they would achieve the end by first multiplying their own wants at the expense of the poor......"[31] Gandhiji said his is "an attempt to see beauty in voluntary simplicity, poverty and slowness. The modern rage for variety, for flying through the air, for multiplicity of wants etc., have no fascination for me. They deaden the inner being in us".[32] We cannot now neglect these views of Gandhiji any more. Prof. Gunnar Myrdal too has observed, "And, as has been demonstrated in a broad way, the reservations about the uncertainty of all forecasts I have piled up merely imply that the future, when uncontrolled growth comes up against serious limit, is somewhat indeterminate, but usually within the range of only one or at most a few generations. In any case, with the unprecedentedly rapid and still accelerating growth of the world's population, which we must now take as fairly certain to continue for many decades we shall invite catastrophic developments, unless we are prepared now to enforce various restraints on, and deflections of, production and consumption and, indeed, our ways of life".[33] He continues "one broad inference is that any hope that the living levels in under-developed countries would ever even approach those in developed countries would presuppose radical increase in their use of irreplaceable resources. Particularly with the new growing awareness of their threatening depletion, this would, in turn, necessitate acceptance of a substantial lowering of living levels in developed countries".[34] He disapproves expensive, conspicuous public consumption such as moon flights and too heavy military expenditure, and quotes Mansholt when he says that if our purpose is to reach a "non-polluting system of production and the creation of recycled economy one must foresee considerable reductions in the consumption of material goods per inhabitant to be compensated by the extension of less tangible goods".[35]

It may be pertinent to point out that voluntary poverty was one of the vows in Gandhiji's Ashram where he was trying to build up leadership for the future.

5. Inequalities

Gandhiji had realized that in our desire to have rapid industrial and material progress through large-scale mechanisation and industrialisation we will be fanning economic and resultant social and political inequalities. State machinery will be used for the good and benefit of the well-to-do class. Prof. Gunnar Myrdal's studies have only confirmed Gandhiji's suspicion. "In particular, we have kept away from interesting ourselves in the need in underdeveloped countries for radical egalitarian reforms, which I have found necessary for rapid and steady development by raising productivity".[36]

"Egalitarian reforms are not felt to be in the short-term interests of the upper strata which mostly have the power in these countries, whatever their system of government. As in colonial times it is also almost inevitable that both governments and business in developed countries have, through all their relations, come to support these strata, which have not been enthusiastic about egalitarian reforms, but have stood against them or distorted them to favour the none-so-poor".[37]

Gandhiji had foreseen these developments and wanted to strengthen the masses to prevent these developments. "Exploitation of the poor can be extinguished not by effecting the destruction of a few millionaires, but by removing the ignorance of the poor and teaching them to non-cooperate with their exploiters".[38] He therefore advocated that both science and technology should be reduced to the terms of the masses. Tools and processes of production must be within the capacity and comprehension of the common man. These should be commensurate with the level of his understanding. He advocated improvement in the cottage machine and was in favour of machinery that will increase the productivity of the individual, cottage worker. Thus he wanted to develop the non-violent power of the masses who are subjected to all forms of exploitation in the name of science, peace and prosperity.

On the other side he warned the privileged classes to give up power and privilege and use them for the benefit of those whom they had exploited thus far "A non-violent system of government is clearly an impossibility so long as the wide gulf between the rich and the hungry millions persists. A violent and bloody revolution is a certainty one day unless there is voluntary abdication of riches and the power that riches give and sharing them for common good".[39]

He advocated the doctrine of trusteeship — voluntary abdication of riches and power and sharing the same for common good. He was not enamoured of state action not only because 'the State represents violence, in a concentrated and organised form' but also because state can conscript property only, it cannot conscript talent. It can only inhibit use of talent. State action cannot solve the problem of recurring inequalities. It is only through voluntary sharing that these problems can, not only be solved, but foundations laid for new social order. This device is not to uphold the status quo but to give the owning class a last chance to read the writing on the wall. If they refuse to listen to the appeal of reason they can be dispossessed by the weapon of Satyagraha and non-violent non-cooperation.

6. The Machine Civilization

The future economic order should abandon or at least severely control the speed of machine culture which is based upon the principle of exploitation. We are even exploiting the future generations. Pollution and depletion of non-renewable sources is ample testimony of this exploitation. Gandhiji while advocating the use of spinning wheel under Indian conditions observed, "No doubt the authors of the movement do think that so far as human understanding can go, there seems to be no hope of finding a better substitute than the spinning wheel. Indeed their conviction is that as soon as the existing exploitation of the so-called weaker nations of the earth by the strong nations of the West ceases, as it is bound some day to cease, the whole world will have to return to spinning wheel. Whether, however, that event comes to pass or not, unless India becomes an exploiting nation and discovers new nations to exploit, or unless an independent India develops brute strength enough to compel the nations of the West to buy the goods that she may dump on their soil as India is virtually compelled today to receive goods dumped down her soil, India must, if she is to get rid herself of economic distress manufacture the articles of necessity in her own fields".[40] In 1928 he pictured the menace of an industrialised India to the world "God forbid that India should ever take to industrialisation after the members of the West. The economic exploitation of a single tiny island kingdom (England) is today keeping the world in chains. If an entire nation of 30 millions took to similar economic exploitation, it would strip the world bare like locusts".[41] He therefore, believed that "Independent India can only discharge her duty towards a groaning world by adopting a simple but ennobled life by developing her thousands of cottages and living in peace with the world. High thinking is inconsistent with complicated material life based on high speed imposed by Mammon worship. All the graces of life are possible only when we learn the art of living nobly".[42] Replying to the opponents of his movement of economic decentralisation he wrote, "The critics say that water, air, soil and electricity should be fully utilized as they are being utilized in the go ahead West. They say that control over these hidden powers of nature enables every American to have 33 slaves". Repeat the process in India and I dare say that it will thirty time enslave every inhabitant of this land, instead of giving every one thirty three slaves. Mechanisation is good when the hands are too few for the work intended to be accomplised. It is an evil when there are more hands than required for the work, as is the case in India".[43]

The whole philosophy of growth and development is to exploit nature for narrow selfish ends of material comforts. This race has to be abandoned and a severe restraint put on technological changes. "The control of technology means a severe limitation demanding almost savage asceticism on the part of an age drunk, not merely with the synthetic emotions and pleasures manufactured hourly by entertainment factories, but with dreams of power and of the conquest of outer space".[44]

We must accept that man, like all other living things, is a part of one great biological scheme. Nation and civilizations in the past have vanished for lack of such realisation. Marvels of modern technology and our deep concern with our narrow self have deadened all considerations of a social nature. "There is only one solution. Man must recognize the necessity of cooperating with nature. He must temper his demands and use and conserve the natural living resources of the earth in a manner that alone can provide for the continuation of his civili-zation. The final answer is to be found only through compre-hension of the enduring processes of nature. The time for defiance is at an end".[45]

7. The future set-up

If international peace is to be maintained, the new inter-national economic order has to be radically different from the existing one.

"You cannot build non-violence on a factory civilisation, but it can be built on self-contained villages. Even if Hitler was so minded he could not devastate seven hundred thousand non-violent villages: he would himself become non-violent in the process. Rural economy, as I have conceived it, eschews exploitation altogether, and exploitation is the essence of violence. You have therefore to be rural minded before you can be non-violent, and to be rural minded you, have to have faith in the spinning wheel".[46]

It will mean control of consumption and discovering newer methods of motivating people. "As I was picturing life based on non-violence I saw that it must be reduced to simplest terms consistent with high thinking. Society based on non-violence can only consist of groups settled in villages in which voluntary cooperation is the condition of dignified and peaceful existence. A society which anticipates and provides for meeting violence with violence will either lead a precarious life or create big cities and magazines for defence purposes".[47]

"In this structure composed of innumerable villages, there will be ever widening, never ascending circles. Life will not be a pyramid with the apex sustained by the bottom. But it will be an oceanic circle whose centre will be the individual always ready to perish for the village, the latter ready to perish for the circle of villages till at last the whole becomes one life, composed of individuals never aggressive in their arrogance but ever humble, sharing the majesty of the oceanic circle of which they are integral units".[48]

It is in this background that we have to understand the message and efforts of Gandhiji. "The message of the spinning wheel is much wider than its circumference. Its message is one of simplicity, service of mankind, living so as not to hurt others, creating indissoluble bond between the rich and the poor, capital and labour, prince and the peasant. The large message is naturally for all........it is not an attempt to spiritualise the machinery because that seems to be an impossible task but to introduce, if it is at all possible, a human or human spirit among the men behind the machinery.......The movement of the spinning wheel is an organised attempt to displace machinery from the state of exclusiveness and exploitation and to place it in its proper state".[49]

To us who are intoxicated by what we have jin our ignorance defined as 'modern' 'growth' and prosperity all this may sound reactionary and going back to dark old ages. But Gandhiji had different approach.

"In short the reactionary turn, if at al, it was meant a return to common sense, meant a restoration of what appears to common sense to be a natural order as distinguished from the present unnatural order in a word not everything overturned or everything petrified but everything resorted to its proper place".[60] A world community can be created in which human beings can live comfortably and in peace with each other.

We need new training so that man can subjugate selfishness to generosity, ignorance to wisdom and hate to love. We all feel hopeful that the youth now growing up in developed countries will have other ideals than those now motivating our policies. Gandhiji's advice was "Let those who believe in non-violence as the only method of achieving real freedom, keep the lamp of non-violence burning bright in the midst of the present unpenetrable gloom. The truth of the few will count: the untruth of millions will vanish like chaff before a whiff of wind".[51]

We cannot wait as if we have ample time at our disposal to solve the manifold problems that human society is facing. Gandhiji's advice was, "We must refuse to wait for generations to furnish us with a patent solution of a problem which is ever growing in seriousness. Nature knows no mercy in dealing stern justice. If we do not wake up before long, we shall be wiped out of existence".[52] "It is never late to retrace our steps and start afresh from the point where we took the wrong turnings. One day dawns from the moment we are awake".[53] "Satan's snares are most suitably laid and they are the most tempting when the dividing line between right and wrong is so thin as to be imperceptible. But the line is there all the same, rigid and inflexible. Any crossing of it may mean certain death".[54]

It is only by restructuring the world economic system that we can attain the ideal described by Gurudev Tagore, our great poet:

Where the mind is without fear and the head is held high;
Where knowledge is free;

Where the world has not been broken into fragments by narrow domestic walls;

Where words come out from the depth of truth;

Where tireless striving stretches the arms towards perfection;

Where the clear stream of reason has not lost its way into the dreary desert sand of dead habit;

Where the mind is led forward by Thee into ever widening thought and action.

Into that heaven of freedom, my Father, let my country awake.

References

1. Gunnar Myrdal: Against the Stream – Critical Essays on Economics, p. 288.
2. J. S. Mathur (Ed.): Economic Thought of Mahatma Gandhi.
3. Lord Altrincham: A.B. Patrika, Dec. 23, 1961.
4. Pyare Lal: Last Phase, Vol. II, p. 211.
5. G. Ram Chandran: Truth and Non-violence, UNESCO Symposium 'quote' p, 173.
6. Pyare Lal: Last Phase, Vol. I, p. 426.
7. J.S. Mathur (Ed.): Economic Thought of Mahatma Gandhi
8. Has Man A Future, pp. 36-37.
9. Decay and Restoration of Civilisation, p. 16.
10. Impact of Science on Society, p. 127.
11. Against the Stream, op.cit., p. 156.
12. *Ibid.*, p. 281.
13. J.S. Mathur : Economic Thought of Mahatma Gandhi, p. 421.
14. *Ibid.*, p. 530.
15. *Ibid.*, p. 533.
16. Gunnar Myrdal: Against The Stream, p. 11.
17. *Ibid.*, p. 16.
18. *Ibid.*, p. 134
19. J.S. Mathur (Ed.): Economic Thought of Mahatma Gandhi, pp. 86-87.
20. *Ibid.*, p. 148.
21. Albert Schweitzer: Decay and Restoration of Civilization, p. 32.
22. J.S. Mathur (Ed.): Economic Thought of Mahatma Gandhi, p. 81.
23. *Ibid.*, p. 616.
24. *Ibid.*, p. 612.
25. *Ibid.*, p. 25.

26. *Ibid.*, p. 480.
27. *Ibid.*, pp. 528-29, 531.
28. *Ibid.*, p. 143.
29. *Ibid.*, p. 383.
30. *Ibid.*, p. 85.
31. *Ibid.*, p. 512.
32. Gunnar Myrdal: Against the Stream – Critical Essay on Economics, p. 201.
33. *Ibid.*, p. 216.
34. *Ibid.*, p. 284.
35. *Ibid.*, p. 226.
36. *Ibid.*, p. 12.
37. *Ibid.*, p. 214.
38. J.S. Mathur (Ed.): Economic Thought of Mahatma Gandhi, p. 605.
39. *Ibid.*, p. 510-511.
40. *Ibid.*, p. 127.
41. *Ibid.*, p. 486.
42. *Ibid.*, p. 577.
43. *Ibid.*, p. 297.
44. Withelwisen: Failure of Technology (Introduction), p. vi.
45. Fairfield Osborn: Our Plundered Planet, p. 201.
46. J.S. Mathur (Ed.): Economic Thought of Mahatma Gandhi, p. 319.
47. *Ibid.*, p. 596.
48. *Ibid.*, p. 623.
49. *Ibid.*, p. 447.
50. *Ibid.*, p. 535.
51. G.N. Dhawan: Political Philosophy of Mahatma Gandhi, p. 345.
52. J.S. Mathur (Ed.): Economic Thought of Mahatma Gandhi, p. 24.
53. Pyare Lal: Gandhian Thought and Contemporary Society, p. 15.
54. J.S. Mathur (Ed.): Economic Thought of Mahatma Gandhi, p. 29.

26

Gandhiji on Growth and Development — Some Issues

Gandhiji talked of growth and development, and a new social and economic order and the role of people, organisations, governments much before the development decade. During his life time he made efforts, under severe limitations of a subject country, and gave us a glimpse of Swarajya of his concept.

Development growth for Gandhiji was with a purpose, with some objective. This purpose was an overall development of the individual and his full personality, of society and nations with a view to usher in a new national and international order based on mutual goodwill and trust, peaceful settlement of differences and absence of exploitation in whatever shape or form. Exploitation was for him violence.

In view of this integrated approach Gandhiji never bothered about growth models. The economic development model with its emphasis on an industrial order, pure and simple reliance on mechanisation (increasingly becoming sophisticated and automated) materialism and a consumption oriented society had no appeal for Gandhiji. This model enslaves man to machine, dwarfs his personality, concentrates wealth and leadership, results in competition, exploitation and scramble for world resources, tensions and war.

The distribution model while accepting the basic premises of the economic development model tries to ensure distributive justice by trying to reach the lowest man through fiscal measures. Controlled growth model on the other hand is based upon central planning.

Gandhiji's approach to growth and development was a happy mixture of all these three approaches. His emphasis was mainly upon arousing consciousness among the masses so that exploitation is made impossible. This necessitates laying down a strict priority scale — first things first according to Gandhiji — to attack the problem of mass poverty and to find a solution to poverty in the shortest possible period. This also entailed evolving a strategy that will pass on initiative to the common people. He advocated simple solutions to complex problems. Gandhiji did not advocate charity. Constructive programme as practised by Gandhiji was to lay the foundation of an ideal village — progressive, happy, self-sufficient, and non-exploitative, providing full employment to the labour force. The unemployed develop a psychology of alienation and in Gandhiji's approach to growth and development the problem of unemployment and under-employment received top priority.

Gandhiji, therefore, suggested a different educational system for development laying emphasis on dignity of labour. In this model there will be real and effective decentralisation of economic, political and social power ensuring economic and social equality and simultaneously ecological balance. Power will be in the hands of ordinary people. Man should be the maker of the system and he should not be subservient to the system.

Several scholars hold the view that Gandhiji was not an economist. This is true that he was not an economist in the traditional sense of the term. He had a pragmatic approach to economic problems and he did not subordinate his judgment to western ideas and economists. This is however a fact that, placed as he was in the context of his fight for India's freedom, his role as an organisor and crusader for human rights was outstanding. He was not static in his thinking but constantly growing and evolving. He was alive to the use and disuse of the eastern civilisation and talked in the context of the problems that the human race is facing.

In different countries of the world there is greater realisation of the contribution that Gandhiji made in the evolution of a new culture. The Intermediate Technology Group in London, setting up of departments of Gandhian Studies in educational institutions in West Germany and translation of Gandhiji's work in Moscow are pointers to the fact that Gandhiji's approach towards growth and development for the creation of a world without fear, exploitation and one based on non-violence are subjects worth study and understanding.

What makes us talk about Gandhiji today and more particularly in our country? Why did we not think of Gandhiji's ideas just after independence? An attempt is being made to answer in the background of the experience of India — an experience which holds good for developing countries of the world. This approach has and is likely to influence developed countries if we think in terms of a new international order.

We can attempt a few answers to the question that we had raised at the outset — "What makes us talk about Gandhiji now?

One of the reasons for this interest is the non-fulfilment of the expectation that we had from conventional ideas concerning growth and development. Anticipated results did not follow. The dominant idea in this line of approach was that growth and development is a linear process and these nations which are at the bottom can rise to any limits. Development is equated with growth and growth depends upon modernization. Growth and modernization was equal to industrialisation. Fruits of growth will percolate and trickle down to the underprivileged and distributive justice will be brought about through fiscal and monetary measures.

This experiment did not succeed and has given rise to several contradictions — poverty and affluence exist side by side. In fact poverty of the common men has worsened. Rising industrialisation is accompanied by increasing industrial unrest and unemployment. Rising exports have not benefited the masses. New economic relationships are making individuals, small groups (villages), regions (states) and the nations increasingly dependent on external sources, bodies and agencies. Initiative and decision-making process is getting centralised and concentrated in fewer hands. Our experiment with growth and planning has led us to disillusionment. We have to unlearn the past in terms of something which promises a brighter future. This probably accounts for our interest in Gandhiji's ideas so that we can discover a new approach.

In this process of discovery we should have a fresh look at poverty. External manifestation of poverty — hunger, disease, misery — are due to structural deficiencies. Certain structural designs give more power to the top few who think and plan in terms of their abstract notions of poverty and backwardness which in their turn does not help solve this problem. These structural relationships are causative, relative factors in the non-solution of the problem of poverty. These structural and relational factors were more important in Gandhiji's thinking, and he advocated fundamental structural changes. These were not given sufficient importance in our plan to fight poverty. In the absence of these structural changes increased resources have been misused and are likely to be misused in future giving rise to social and economic inequalities, worsening of the social and economic conditions of the less privileged leading to individual, group and social tensions which may even lead to disintegration and give rise to fissiparous tendencies.

Gandhiji, when he talked of poverty, identified poverty with people. Who are the poor? The poor are people. We generally talk only in terms of aggregates as if people did not matter. This approach has given rise to artificial pockets of affluence. International economic justice should imply a focus on the poor. Gandhiji is an indigenous soundboard. The I.L.O. has given the concept of basic needs approach to tackle the problem of poverty more particularly in developing countries.

The problem of poverty has an economic as well as spiritual connotation. To the poor it is frustrating economically and spiritually. But the reverse side of the coin — affluence and inequality are equally dehumanizing. It is a spiritual phenomenon. Those who are rich are dehumanized too. They are insensitive to poverty. They are more worried about affluence and security for themselves. Relative inequality leads to spiritual poverty of the rich and the poor.

Social divisions are very alien to Gandhiji's concepts. The people are not to be driven but are to be activated. Gandhiji was not in favour of reliance and dependence on Government. Welfarism is a danger as it saps the energy of the people. Redistribution through government agency (the Indian experience of distributive justice through monetary and fiscal measures has not been very happy) will encourage dependence of people and may even encourage irresponsible competitive demands. The concept of self-reliance has to be judged in this broader perspective.

Gandhiji's warning against blind imitation of western technology has assumed greater significance now. Technology has to be accepted in a responsible manner. Mere transfer of technology will not solve problems of developing countries. This may even counter social and justice requirements. The technology that we import requires scarce resources and does not use those resources that are abundant in the country.

Gandhiji had repeatedly pointed out and emphasised that technology is not a neutral force, it is not value free. It does not define efficiency in social welfare terms. Modern technology represents a system. Multinational corporations negotiate with national governments — millionaires talking to millionaire. Each represents a value system. This sort of technology goes counter to our basic requirements. We need an altogether different type of technology.

At this juncture we must plan for a shift in our direction. We must identify road blocks on our way and reject them. Our experiment with mixed economy has been a failure. We must think in terms of a new synthesis.

In evolving a new synthesis conflicts will come on the surface. Gandhiji was basically militant, a revolutionary. He did not avoid conflicts. In fact he brought conflicts in the open. Gandhiji did realize the class nature of the existing society and was planning and working for a new social and economic order where class distinctions will be obliterated. He not only advocated that the prime needs of the poor should be satisfied first before the comforts of the few but also suggested that only permissible maximum incomes in terms of social needs and good for the upper classes be admissible. His slogan was 'unto the last' — Antodaya.

There are, however, several constraints in our way. Ever since Gandhiji wrote Hind Swaraj or Indian Home Rule and made experiments during his life time towards the achievement of his concept of growth and development considerable changes have taken place in the socio-politico-economic and cultural milieu. In the post-independence period forces which hinder thinking in terms of Gandhiji's 'Daridra Narayan' have got an upper hand. We do not, at this juncture, have freedom to start from a clean slate. We come up against several vested interests.

The large scale sector itself is a big constraint. It has entrenched itself. The interests of the capitalists and the organised labour class is a factor that hinders correct perspective.

The growing Defence Sector is another factor to be reckoned with. Increasing defence expenditure, of which we are a helpless witness, is not only a question of misdirection of resources but also helps the dominance of large sector. It imposes capital intensive and sophisticated technology on defence production, which affects technology, in other sectors, as well. One may under these circumstances, think of controlled economic dualism—but it will be a different political system.

Yet another constraint has been a change in value. Urban culture and ethos at present seem to dominate. Assisted by the modern means of mass communication they have invaded rural areas. Whatever is being tried for our villages is being termed as village or rural development—irrespective of the fact that whether or not these steps lead to a lasting solution of the rural areas. Only during recent years difference between agricultural development and rural or village development has been realized.

Similarly, the need to draw a distinction between urbanisation of rural areas and rural development must be made explicit and clear. All these years we have made efforts to urbanise rural areas. 'This kind of planning has an irresistible fascination for the town bred intellectuals. It enables privilege to be equated with patriotism and progress with urban values and the sophisticated way of life in which they have grown up and which in consequence have grown upon them. The rural masses will have ample opportunities to jack themselves upto the urban level of culture and civilisation by providing voluntary labour. In brief it means political and social domination of the town and power and much-coveted perquisities for the elite who constitute the ruling class".[1] Are we prepared to change these values?

Another constraint is the leadership that has emerged after independence. Those who acquired power did not hear Gandhiji's ideas. Those who were in opposition too had no clear perspective of Gandhiji's ideas and methodology. Each shade of leadership cried hoarse in the name of Gandhi but betrayed him in policies, action and life style. An approach to growth and development as consequences thereof has subjected us to a lot of international pressures. Only a courageous, ideologically committed and dedicated leadership which can own past mistakes, abandon those policies and follow new radical policies can lead our country to a new era of growth and development.

Gandhiji's ideas are integrated, wholistic. They give an insight of a non-violent peaceful exploitationless socio-economic system; commitment towards an ideal and goal. Even if we do not work for his concept of socio-economic order acceptance of even fragmented parts may bring some good to our country.

Reference

1. Pyare Lal, The Last Phase, Vol. II, 644.

27

Gandhiji's Challenge

Humanity stands at cross-road today. Several scholars and statesmen are worried about the catastrophy that humanity faces if we do not act with restraint and reason. One of the scholars remarked, "Today, by the fact that everything seems possible; retrogression, barbarism, decadence". This is just an example of the despondency that has struck the thinking people all over the world. Developments in the international sphere have compelled people to have a new look at the social, economic and political problems that stare us in the face today. Ecological imbalances, exhaustion of non-renewable resources, proliferation, nuclear power, the division of the world and nations in groups and blocs; the problem of exploitation of nations by another is a serious threat to stability and prosperity. There are reasons to doubt and question the concept of growth and development as is widely prevalent today.

The problems of developing countries like ours with mass poverty and unemployment, the demoralization that poverty leads to and the inadequacy of the accepted techniques of growth and development to solve these problems have compelled people to think in terms of a new approach to these problems. Gandhiji had visualized these problems and in his own way, suggested solutions to the problems that this country is facing so that the process of growth and development enables even the lowliest and humblest to feel the glow, to get deeply involved in the process of growth for sectional and group interests. Some people think that in independent India of today Gandhiji's concrete scheme of production of wealth through decentralized industries had no validity or meaning. This will be true only if the conditions under which Gandhiji formulated his scheme had undergone radical change. This is not so. Even after nearly 60 years of independence and 10 five-year plans we remain where we were in terms of teeming millions. In the social sphere also there is no perceptible change. The masses remain largely untouched by our schemes of development and have lost whatever strength they had acquired during the struggle for independence. We look for the solution of our problems in external factors and forces and have been incapacitated to take initiative even in respect of minor matters. Under these circumstances people and sometimes whole nations come to loose their confidence in peaceful change through democratic and non-violent means and so become desperate and opt to resort to force.

In the western world one comes across a number of movements associated with the problems of peace. These efforts have proved ineffective largely because they do not try to tackle the problem of emergence of non-exploitative society within national boundaries. Gandhiji had realized that in order to be a peaceful nation in the international sphere, we have to be a non-exploitative society inside national borders.

The participants at a seminar discussed several issues concerning peaceful rapid changes of the existing socio-economic order and held the view that such changes are possible through peaceful methods.

The salient features of a new socio-economic order should be emergence of society which eschews violence and exploitation, encourages cooperation among individuals, groups and nations, brings about greater equality among the people not only through non-violent means but also with adequate rapidity. In contrast what one notices is a split personality of individuals, groups and nations. On the one hand man cannot live without man and on the other hand he fears the other man. One wants love and truth for oneself; but gives hatred to others. Before Gandhiji made his experiments some sort of vested interest had developed in respect of qualities like truth and non-violence and they were considered the exclusive preserve of the saints. As a consequence while science was progressing, humanity was lagging behind. Love, compassion and kindness were not the concern of the scientist. Gandhiji demonstrated that there is need for radical change in our attitude and the environment.

If we examine the concept of non-violence as advocated by Gandhiji we will realize that his was a prescription not of the weak but of the strong. He proved in his life-time that even the unorganized and the weak can perform miracles if they got trained in the art of non-violent techniques of change.

Non-violence does not mean, passivity or inaction; but a dynamic living force. His non-violence was an instrument in the struggle for justice and freedom. It is a permanent revolution and therefore it is dynamic.

Gandhiji's technique as manifested in his life is an exemplary struggle of mass truth against degradation. Non-violence as practised by Gandhiji had three basic elements: (i) creation of a human society involving non-violent methods of resisting exploitation, (ii) education of oppressed to take positive and constructive steps to resist exploitation and development of good and harmonious relationship between oppressed and oppressor once the struggle was over; (iii) ushering in of a non-exploitative decentralised economic and political institution. According to Gandhiji non-violence is a rule of action, it is the duty. His non-violence is not merely a philosophical principle, it is the rule of life. Many regard it as an abstract idea but it is a simple yet relentless imperative. Non-violence as preached and practised by Gandhiji is not a single virtue or a single quality of life but congeries of qualities or virtues like compassion, selflessness, self-renunciation, to the extent of reducing oneself to zero and fearlessness and therefore to Gandhiji quality matters rather than numbers. He advocated the practice of non-violence in every walk of life – individual, institutional, political, social and economic. He believed that Ahimsa is a weapon of matchless potency even though the results may not be clearly visible. Non-violence works in a silent, subtle, unseen way and leavens the whole society. Non-violence, the greatest force at the disposal of mankind, like charity, must begin at home and those who advocate the use of these weapons must work to ensure a just, social order within. Non-violence is a must for democracy and can make the parliamentary system really effective.

There is a wrong notion amongst people and they seem to favour violent techniques in the false belief that thereby rapid changes can be brought about, but "we need not be afraid that the method of non-violence is a slow long-drawn difficult process. It is swiftest, the world has seen, for it is surest".

Several instances of non-violent techniques bringing about rapid socio-economic and consequential institutional change having been brought about can be sighted from Indian experience, and the campaigns organised by Gandhiji. He gave a death blow to the system of untouchability —an age-old practice—through his non-violence. His non-violent struggle against the Rowlett Bill and his Salt Satyagraha are other examples of the success of this technique. The rapidity with which non-violent techniques succeeded during the communal disturbances was proved by him during 1946-1947. Lord Mountbatten described him as 'one man force'. Gandhiji himself held the opinion that "the existing structure of economic society will not last for 24 hours if my weapon of Satyagraha can be gripped by the people".

It must, however, be realized that the success of non-violence depends largely upon the quality of leadership. It was for this reason that Gandhiji laid down a very strict code of discipline at his Ashrams, which were his training schools in the art of non-violent technique. He believed that it may be difficult for the masses to be disciplined and trained in the theory and art of non-violent action. The masses, however, can be made effective soldiers of a non-violent army by leaders thoroughly trained in the art of non-violent techniques who can set personal example before the followers; who have identified themselves with the masses through various items of constructive programmes that were suggested by him. That the masses can use these techniques successfully, was very clearly demonstrated during several campaigns organised under his direct leadership as also during campaigns organized by others with his blessings. What Gandhiji said and did were experiments in the use of non-violence. Had he been alive during the post-independent era he might have carried these experiments further. Humanity must steadily march towards the attainment of a socio economic society based on justice and fair play through non-violence.

We need also mention that a violent change need not be a success, and even rapid. Several examples can be quoted of either the complete failure of these violent efforts or their snail's- pace progress, right from the French Revolution to the present day problems of Vietnam, Korea and Arab-Israel conflict as also of our relationship with Pakistan. A violent revolution creates a violent structure in which after having killed one's enemy it is always easy to kill one's friends for holding opposite views and wrong positions. Therefore, the revolution must be based on non-violence. A non-violent revolution does not simply seek the liberation of a class or a nation or a race, but it seeks the liberation of mankind. Violence liberates one group and imprisons another, destroys one authoritarian structure but creates another.

Gandhiji believed that a parliamentary system and democratic functioning of institutions is not possible without practice of non-violence. He described the Parliament a "Sterile woman and prostitute". This he did because he felt that centralised institution as such can not permit effective participation of the masses. The humblest and the weak cannot feel close to other sections of the society. The rule of law should mean that the weakest member will have his rights upheld against the most powerful. The proponents of non-violence feel that it is only through non-violence that equality before the law can be established.

Gandhiji subscribed to the views that fundamental far- reaching changes can be brought about in an institution and the society through non-violence, campaigns and mass action. Gandhiji wanted to change the present economic and political system, educational and religious institutions to develop a sense of altruism amongst individuals so that the present moto of individual success and security par excellence at social cost may be reduced. Gandhiji demonstrated through his experiments that the practice of truth and non-violence is possible not only by saints but also by ordinary individuals, groups, communities and nations to solve the multifarious problems that arise in everyday life. Gandhiji's technique of truth and non-violence is self-acting and does not depend for its propagation on a material medium. This technique has its own rules which are definite, precise and are capable of being objectified. The change brought by Satyagraha transfers power to the masses and make them better organized to resist evil and oppression.

Eminent scholars are now advocating increasing relevance on Gandhian techniques. Professor Toynbee observes: "In this hurricane of annihiliating material power mankind will not be able to save itself from self-destruction unless we, all of us manage to practise non-violence in our relations with our fellow men". He charged us, our countrymen with the responsibility of spreading his ideas and observed, "You have incurred a rather formidable obligation both to Gandhiji and history....."

28

Minimum Wage Legislation

Legislation to fix minimum wages for workers both on the farm and in the factory is gaining momentum. It was recognized much earlier in the industrial field. Recently, and more so after the great depression, attention is being paid to the worker on the farm and field so much so that new minimum wage legislation in one form or the other both for agricultural and industrial worker is to be found in nearly all the economically advanced countries of the world or those which are gaining independence. In India too we have passed a Minimum Wages Act in 1948.

But before we in India go any further, let us think, examine and analyse the implications of any such legislation in all its perspectives and our capacity to enforce the same. Minimum wage legislation to cover both the industrial and agricultural workers will imply an overall price policy—a policy in which we fix reasonable economic prices both for agricultural and industrial products. Are we in a position to do it? Do we have the necessary statistics and data to enforce any such measure? It is quite evident that agricultural wages everywhere are nearly half of those of the industrial wage earners except in certain exceptional agriculturally advanced countries. Can we be able to raise agricultural wages by such an extent without disturbing the economic equilibrium and giving it a rude shock? And above all we have the problem of the petty farmer and landholder. In India we have a large number of such a landholding class and any such scheme should see to it that in our attempt to raise the standard of agricultural labourers we do not depress that of the farmer who has his back already to the wall. And therefore, any such legislation will have to give due allowance to factors like productivity of individual worker, the share of industry or agriculture in the size of the national income, regional differences, type of work undertaken (whether seasonal or otherwise), conditions of service like holidays with pay, regularity of employment, payments in kind and periodicity, time, place and medium of wage payments, etc.

But even starting on the assumption that sooner or later we will be able to surmount these problems, a question springs up: After all what is the necessity of any minimum wage legislation for all categories of workers? We are told that the necessity arises because of utter exploitation of the masses and the way of life to which they have been condemned because of their abject poverty. Minimum wage legislation everywhere has the lofty ideal of preventing payment of unduly low wages as if payment of low wages will be tolerated by the society and that it is quite right for any class of entrepreneurs to do whatever they like only if they guarantee a wage, which may not be termed as unduly low. Does it not then appear true that all such sorts of legislation are a move on the part of the interested parties to maintain the status quo and continue their reckless exploitation under a fashionable garb and an honourable form? We do not aim to prevent exploitation and inequitable distribu-tion. We simply aim to guarantee a minimum standard of life to those who have been condemned to a standard which cannot be justified by any human standards. It is unjustifiable to lay down a minimum without any reference to a maximum. The State everywhere recognizes that the masses have become conscious and alive to the harm done to them by a class; they cannot keep the mouths of those shut who toil to the last drop of their blood. The masses cannot be exploited as recklessly as before. The agony of years when frustrated and disappointed young men see that they cannot face the future with confidence may lead to all such legislations. The State everywhere is concerned to prevent suffering from driving men to the point where they can contemplate of revolution without hesitation. All such types of legislation keep peace within the framework of profit-making systems, because continuity of production is impossible without peace, and continuity of production is necessary if profits are to be made. We should not confuse the term profit with simply monetary gains but associate it with all types of extra-monetary gains, otherwise fixation of minimum without a reasonable maximum has no meaning. It is another device to perpetuate the exploitation of the common man. What one fails to understand is that with all our talk of democracy and power of the common man we are still legislating to guarantee a minimum living standard to the vast masses and not an equitable standard for all where there will be no wide disparities between any standard and that of my neighbour. Any solid foundation of a world peace order cannot be built on a foundation which does not recognize the essential validity of this argument unless peace is to be kept only for a short time and by the use of force.

Another argument that is advanced for minimum wage legislation is the well-known phrases, which one finds in the preamble of I.L.O. Charter, namely, 'equal pay for work of equal value' and this is a society based on money economy where values are associated with particular commodities on the demand and supply formula irrespective of human considerations. My work may be very valuable for the society today but the moment the businessman likes he may force me to starve by giving no value to my work. Equal pay for equal work should have long become a dead letter for us. We should go much ahead and plan for a society where our motto is 'equitable work and equitable pay' if we want to make our lives and those of others happy and prosperous.

And, again, all such sorts of legislation are based on the concept that the society essentially comprises two classes—the employers and the employees, the haves and the have-nots, with their interests conflicting and contradictory, where one can gain only at the expense of the other. Because minimum wage legislation does not seek anywhere an equitable distribution, it seeks to provide certain advantages to workers. But can we plan our future on the understanding that society will continue to be divided in classes and that the emergence of a classless society is an impossibility in which everyone is a worker and contributes according to his capacity for the social good, in which the interests of each are bound with everyone else and where the individual works for the society and the society for the good and well-being of even the humblest and lowliest of its individual?

But, then, if our end in view is not 'to prevent the payment of unduly low wages' and 'equal pay for work of equal value' but the bringing in of a classless society and equitable distribution, minimum wage legislation as a transitory step is highly commendable as thereby we contemplate to achieve our end by peaceful and evolutionary methods. Any sudden change is not desirable as it gives rise to many complex problems in which we hold means more important than ends. If we want to deprive the rich class gradually of all their illegitimate and unjustifiable privileges, such a legislation has much in its favour. But, then, each one of us should be perfectly clear about the end in view which should forever enlighten our path.

We should however, be clear that the problem is not simply of providing a decent and equitable standard to everyone here and now; but it is one of guaranteeing the same for future. And therefore, the enforcing of any such measures should not depend much on outside influence and regulation but on the people as a whole. The community as a whole should be held responsible to guarantee a decent standard to everyone without wide disparities. And therefore, the necessity of decentralizing production naturally springs up where production will be done not for money, profit or wide markets but for a particular decentralised locality, thus correlating consumption, production and distribution. If our aim is to ensure a decent standard to everyone and a right to work, the proper course is to link local production with local consumption where the emphasis shifts from production for markets and profits to production for use for human well-being. Price fluctuation should not be permitted to make paupers of people in spite of their best and sincere efforts. What is needed today is the development of a sense of responsibility towards our fellow beings, a social consciousness and a code of conduct in which every producer who tries to thrive by exploiting others stands self-condemned and an economic system in which the public is powerful enough to enforce its decision on the producers by sheer non-cooperation in the form of refusal to purchase and consume the goods of the producer concerned. It may be thought that such an economic arrangement will retard production and material prosperity, but is it not a price worth paying for a happy contented and, above all, a free humanity?

29

Trade Unionism—A Gandhian View

In the words of Dr. Rajendra Prasad, "the work which he (Mahatma Gandhi) had taken in hands was not only the achievement of political freedom but establishment of social order based on truth and non-violence". It was clearly realized that any change in the existing social order may lead to a conflict between different sections and classes in our own country unless people realize the inevitability of the change and are guided in their actions by certain social considerations. It means that our ideas about property must undergo a radical change. "The development of capitalism brought the new habits of abstraction and calculation into the lives of city people; only the country folk, still existing in their more primitive local basis were partly immune. Capitalism turned people from tangibles to intangibles; its symbol, as Sombart observes, is the account book: 'its life-value lies in its profit and loss account'. The 'economy of acquisition', which had hitherto been practised by rare and fabulous creatures like Midas and Croceus, became once more the everyday mode; it tended to replace the direct 'economy of needs' and to substitute money-values for life-values. The whole process of business took on more and more an abstract form: it was concerned with non-commodities, imaginary futures, hypothetical gain".[1]

The root cause of class conflict lies in this possessive or acquisitive instinct. As long as the emphasis is on possession, multiplication of wants, higher and still higher standards of living this acquisitive spirit will last. "If egalitarianism is to endure it has to be based not on the possession of the maximum of material goods, whether by few or by all but on voluntary, enlightened renunciation—denying oneself what cannot be shared by others or can be enjoyed only at the expense of others". In the words of Gandhiji: "Under the new outlook multiplicity of material wants will not be the aim of life; the aim will be rather their restriction consistently with comfort. We shall cease to think of getting what we can but we shall decline to receive what all cannot get".[2]

It should not, however, be concluded that Gandhiji was advocating poverty. "No one has ever suggested that grinding pauperism can lead to anything else than moral degradation. Every human being has a right to live and therefore, to find the wherewithal to feed himself and where necessary to clothe and house himself". But he was against this mad craze for increasing material wants. He opined that "insofar as we have made the modern materialistic craze our goal, so far we are going downhill the path of progress. I hold that economic progress in the sense I have put it, is antagonistic to real progress......That you cannot serve God and Mammon is an economic truth of the highest value".

Thus Gandhian concept of social order will try to simplify the material life of the people. Everyone must have enough of material goods to satisfy his primary needs and live comfortably. "If by abundance you mean everyone having plenty to eat and drink and to clothe himself with, enough to keep his mind trained and educated, I should be satisfied. But I could not like to pack more stuff in my belly than I can digest and more things that I can ever usefully use. But neither do I want poverty, penury, misery, dirt and dust in India".[3] We must not think that he wanted everyone to move out in loin cloth and live shabbily. He was emphatic that he did not advocate any such idea. He suggested that "it will not necessarily be a return to the old absolute simplicity. But it will have to be a reorganization in which village life will predominate and in which brute and material force will be subordinated to the spiritual force".

Thus it was advocated by Gandhiji that a non-violent social and economic order is an impossibility with a modern materialistic approach. Our life should be simplified and we should give up the notion that multiplication of material wants beyond a reasonable limit is an indication of progress.

In order to satisfy these necessary wants of the people he advocated decentralisation of the production process, i.e., development of cottage and small scale industries which can be run in the villages by the people themselves. He held the view that "to change to industrialism is to court disaster. The present distress is undoubtedly insufferable. Pauperism must go. But industrialism is no remedy". He held the view that centralisation of production, at least in respect of prime necessaries of life, will be harmful for the development of a non-violent society. His contention was that nationalization or socialization is no remedy. "The elimination of exploitation (exploitation is violence according to Gandhian concept) by abolition of private ownership of production and distribution does not reach the root of the trouble. The factory's ineradicable attributes will still remain to plague mankind. Socialisation or functionalisation of the factory will never produce the utopia for which many idealists are working. Socialisation must fail as a remedy because it does not treat the real disease, which the factory system has inflicted upon mankind. Socialisation must fail because it contains no balm for efficiency-scourged mankind for the efficiency that is the quintessence of factory civilisation is the real disease which the factory has inflicted upon mankind.......comfort would have to be sacrificed at the altar of the great God efficiency under socialism precisely as it has to be under capitalism, because the factory system ceases to be economic unless it is efficient, unless it is efficient enough to absorb the institutional burden which is its inescapable concomitant".[4] In the words of Mahatma Gandhi "the machinery method is harmful when the same thing can be done easily by millions of hands otherwise occupied". He held the view that "these villages cannot retain the freedom they have enjoyed from time immemorial, if they do not control the production of prime necessaries of life".

All the same there are bound to be a few centralised industries. These will be complementary to small-scale and cottage industries. Their overall importance in the economy will be negligible. "The heavy machinery for work of public utility which cannot be undertaken by human labour has its inevitable place, but all that would be owned by the State and used entirely for the benefit of people. I can have no conside-ration for machinery which is meant either to enrich the few at the expenses of many or without cause to displace the useful labour of many".[5] But at the same time he believed that "some key industries are necessary......Hence without having to enumerate key industries, I would have state ownership, where a large number of people have to work together. The ownership of the products of their labour, whether skilled or unskilled, will vest in them through the State". Those who will be working in these factories will not be exploited. On the other hand they too are not likely to profit at the expense of others. "They (nationalized factories) ought only to be working under the most attractive and ideal conditions, not for profit, but for the benefit of humanity, love taking the place of greed as motive".[6]

It may then be observed that an economic order of a Gandhian concept will be based on decentralised system of production. Production will be for use and not for the market. Trade will be confined to surplus production and for the benefit of all. There will be local self-sufficiency in respect of prime necessaries of life. A few centralised basic and key industries are bound to be there but these shall be nationalized and shall work for the common good. Those who will be employed there shall work under ideal conditions.

This is the ideal, the ultimate goal. Efforts are to be made to reach the cherished goal speedily. But the means that are to be employed for this transformation are to be non-violent means. It is only gradually that private profit centred industries can be replaced by nationalized ones. Similarly, decentralisation of the production process gradually will also take time. Hence the need for the organisation of labour on proper lines so that it may play an effective and important role in the transitionary period of bringing about an economic order based on justice, equity and fair play and where exploitation is severely curtailed if not abolished altogether.

The first essential requisite for labour to prevent exploitation non-violently is organisation of labour on right lines. In his opinion, "labour can always vindicate itself if labour is sufficiently united and self-sacrificing........If labour would only understand and recognize that capital is perfectly helpless without labour, labour will immediately come to its own".[7] On another occasion he wrote, "The labourer has but to realize that labour is also capital. As soon as labourers are properly educated and organised and they realize their strength, no amount of capital can subdue them. Organised and enlightened labour can dictate its own terms".[8] Organisation of labour is essential and does not depend upon the labour policies of employers however good and enlightened these may be. A large number of workers' grievances cannot be attended to. Labour policy will be subordinated to the good of the company. The workers' grievances point to the necessity of a strong labour union, "for however much the company may do by way of welfare work, it would do so only from its point of view".

But then, organisation of labour must be done on proper lines, i.e., by non-violent means. Organised labour must work for the removal of evils of present day industrial labour—as improvement in working and service conditions, a living wage, reduction in hours of work, etc. But, at the same time, organised labour should not try to misuse its power, and adopt a capitalist mentality of advancing its selfish interests. If labour does so it is likely to lose in its battle to bring about justice and fair-play. "The whole reason why labour so often fails is that instead of sterilizing capital, as I have suggested, labour (I am speaking as a labourer myself) wants to seize that capital and become capitalist itself in the worst sense of the term. And the capitalist therefore who is properly entrenched and organised, finding among the labourers also candidates for the same office, makes use of a portion of these to suppress labourers. If we really were not under this hypnotic spell, everyone of us, men and women, would recognize this rock-bottom truth without the slightest difficulty".[9] "In the struggle between capital and labour, it may generally be said that more often than not the capitalists are in the wrong box. But when labour comes fully to realize its strength, I know it can become tyrannic than capital".

Therefore, Gandhiji constantly kept on warning that labour should be organised on right lines. The obligations and responsibilities of labour must be equally emphasised. They should never misuse the strength that organisation will give them. He, therefore, emphasised that "all that is required is the proper education of the peasantry and labour. They need to be informed that if they are properly organised they have more wealth and resources through their labour than the capitalists through their money. Only capitalists have control over the money market, labour has not over its labour market, although if labour had been well served by its chosen leaders it would have become conscious of the irresistible power that comes from proper instruction in non-violence. Instead, labour in many cases is being taught to rely on coercive methods to compel compliance with its demand. This kind of training that labour generally receives today leaves it in ignorance, and relies upon violence as the ultimate sanction".[10] Further, he observed: "Labour was a great leveler of all distinctions.. If they realized that truth, he would like them to go a step further. Labour, because it chose to remain unintelligent, either became subservient or insolently believed in damaging capitalists...... As such he wished to tell them that violence would never save them. They would be killing the goose that laid the golden egg".

His advice, therefore, was that trade unions should look after internal reforms and toning up the morale of the workers and guiding them on proper lines. Trade unions should not become an end in themselves. They should simply remain means for the attainment of certain conditions under which workers' personality may develop fully on non-violent lines. For this purpose he remarked: "combination among yourselves (workers) in the forms of unions is undoubtedly the first. But I can tell you from experience that your every union can become one of the causes of your bondage if you do not comply with other conditions which I shall presently mention to you".[11] These conditions were elaborated in some detail. The workers should consider themselves to be the trustees for the welfare of the rest of their fellow labourers. They should use the unions "as much for internal reformation as for defence against assaults from without and remember that while it is quite proper to insist upon your rights and privileges it is imperative that you should recognize the obligation that every right carries with it". He also advised the workers to establish a living bond between the unfortunate millions and labourers so that labour unions may well weigh the effect of their actions on the teeming millions.

In order to enable labour to be properly organised his insistence on non-violence was exclusive, as without it "they would have internecine strife, and would never be ready to develop the strength that is needed to enable them to realize the power that they possess".[12] "It would be suicidal if the labourers rely upon their numbers of brute-force, i.e., violence. By so doing they will do harm to industries in the country".[13] "Workmen would be committing suicide and India would have to suffer indescribable misery if working men were to vent their anger by criminal disobedience of law of the land".

Thus he emphasized that labour should be more particular about its duties and then alone unions can speak with strength. Internal democracy inside the union should be perfect and they should be motivated by the best interests of the society. If labour could be organised on these lines he was sure that labourers will always win. "If all the labourers in any part of the world combined together, they could not be tempted by higher wages or helplessly allow themselves to be attracted for, say, a pittance. A true and non-violent combination of labour would act like a magnet attracting to it all the needed capital. Capitalists would then exist only as trustees. When that happy day dawned, there would be no difference between capital and labour".[14]

It should not be thought that Gandhiji did not advocate that labourers have certain rights. They should get all the ordinary amenities of life that a rich man enjoys, and to him Swarajya was not Purna Swarajya until these amenities were guaranteed to them under it. Not only that, his criteria for judging the conditions of labour as being satisfactory or not was most radical. The only test is: "How long, if at all, would we ourselves exchange places with them".

That the workers have an inherent right to go on a strike for getting redress of their grievances has been recognized. But this right to strike should be used most sparingly and cautiously. They should not go on strike without a real grievance. The strikers must fix an unalterable minimum demand and declare the same before embarking upon their strike. But who is to judge the justifiability of a strike or lockout? Since interested men cannot impartially judge the merits of their case, "there must be an arbitration accepted by the parties or a judicial adjudication".[15] Gandhiji had been advocating the principle of voluntary arbitration right from the beginning. "I know that strikes are an inherent right of the working men for the purpose of securing justice", he observed in 1920, "but they must be considered a crime immediately the capitalists accept the principle of arbitration". To the employers also his advice was similar. "The strongest combination of employers must accept the principle of arbitration if capital and labour are to live in peace".[16]

If, however, the workers are forced to go on a strike it must be a battle on non-violent lines. The workers must understand the cause for which they are fighting, believe in its righteousness and be prepared to put up with any hardship that such a strike must cause. They should remain non-violent throughout, never molest those who differ from them and are black-legs. They should be persuaded to make common cause with the strikers but never intimidated. This strength to withhold labour and suffer will come only when the workers individually believe in the justice of their claims. Strikes should not be declared without the consent of trade unions. While on a strike Gandhiji advised trade unions to prevent demoralization among the rank and file. This demoralization is bound to set in if the leaders fail to present the correct picture of hardship that the workers shall have to shoulder and if workers do not fully realize the gravity of the step that they are likely to take. This demoralization will inevitably set in if the striking workers do not have resources to fall back upon. "The essence of the experiment consists in training its members to a supplementary occupation in addition to their principal occupation in the mills so that in the event of a lockout, strike or loss of employment otherwise, they would always have something to fall back upon, instead of being faced with the prospects of starvation". He continued, "The working class will never feel secure or develop a sense of self-assurance and strength unless its members are armed with an unfailing subsidiary means of subsistence to serve as a second string to their bow in a crisis. I hold that a working knowledge of a variety of occupations is to the working class what metal is to the capitalist".[17] He also realized that an average worker does not get the requisite training and time and inclination in the modern factory to look after his interest. In order to broaden his outlook and develop his self-

to the making of which they contribute so much labour. And then there will be no question of mills charging exorbitant prices, just to swell the shareholders' dividends irrespective of the interests of the working men or the consumer. A time must come, and the sooner the better, when there would be a respectable proportion between dividend, wages and prices".[24]

The task of assigning a proper role to trade unions and making them effective instruments to bring about a just economic order should not remain a one-way traffic. That adjustment can be easily and speedily brought about if the employers also think beyond their personal profits, are willing to treat workers on an equal footing and try to look after their interests. He, therefore, reminded the employers that "unless they voluntarily recognized the due status of labour and treated it as they treated themselves, time was not far distant when labour would dictate its own terms".[25] His advice was that the rich should hold all their riches as a trust to be used solely in the interest of those who sweat for them and to whose industry and labour they owe all their position and prosperity. He advised the capitalists to adopt the right and honourable course of being just and fair to their workers. The way of suppressing labour demands through organised goondaism was wrong and destructive. The other way, right and honourable, consists in considering every strike on its merits and giving labour its due—not what capital considers as due but what labour itself would so consider and enlightened public opinion acclaim as just. The profits of big concerns must bear relation to the wages of workers. The capitalists have no right to continue their business if they can thrive only at the expense of the workers' property. There need be no conflict between them under such circumstances. "I do not think", observed Gandhiji "there need be any clash between capital and labour. Each is dependent on the other. What is essential today is that the capitalist should not lord over the labour. In my opinion the mill hands are as much the proprietors of their mills as the shareholders and when the millowners realize that the mill hands are as much mill owners as they, there will be no quarrel between them".[26]

Thus if labourers are properly organised, Gandhiji was hopeful that labour unions can channelise capital on proper lines. He did not consider that capital is necessarily an enemy of labour. Coordination of the two is perfectly possible. "He wanted marriage between capital and labour. They could work wonders in cooperation. But that could happen only when labour was intelligent enough to cooperate with itself and then offer cooperation with capital on terms of honourable equality. "A true and non-violent combination of labour would act like a magnet attracting to it all the needed capital.

Capitalists would then exist only as trustees. When that happy day dawned, there would be no difference between capital and labour".

He however realized that if trade unions are not guided on proper lines, they may combine with employers and may be tempted to further their selfish interests at the expense of the consumer. He, therefore, repeatedly emphasised the need of proper non-violent approach and considering everything unworthy which is gained at the expense of others. Labour should realize that "effective non-violent approach is needed for all times and not simply for formation of unions". "But after that realisation has come, and they have come to their own, non-violence does not become superfluous. If they were to bid good-bye to it, they would be as bad as capitalists and turn exploiters themselves. The realisation of their strength combined with adherence to non-violence would enable them to cooperate with capital and turn it to proper use........In fact, capital and labour will be mutual trustees, and both will be trustees of consumers. The trusteeship theory is not unilateral and does not in the least imply superiority of the trustee. It is a perfectly mutual affair, and each believes that his own interest is best safeguarded by safeguarding the interests of the other. There is no species called gods in the universe, but all who have the power of production and will work for the community using that powers are gods—labourers no less than the capitalists".[27]

We may be tempted to dismiss away these views of Mahatma Gandhiji as dreams of an idealist, an utopia. But what is this talk about humanizing industry and efforts to bring about an improvement of human relations in industrial undertakings? The modern labour experts want that the common bond between the worker and the undertaking should be strengthened by encouraging workers to take interest in it. We cannot confine workers' interest to superficial things for all times to come. Sooner or later workers will like to have a dominating voice in the more vital policies of the undertaking, viz., price policy, production policy, etc. It is very doubtful whether employers who are guided by profit motives will tolerate this interference. A change in attitude of the employers is imperative. Gandhiji's trusteeship scheme is a distinct contribution. He had realized that a pure service motive is difficult to be practised. His trusteeship idea, therefore, assigns an important place to private gain, of course indirectly and passively. He wanted to establish a definite relationship between maximum and minimum income. Thus an important safeguard against vagaries of private profit is that no one can be allowed to profit himself exclusively. All should advance. This also places important limitation on individual accumulation of wealth and power and is based upon the realisation of mutuality of interests, equal importance of different factors of production.

"Framing a human relations policy in the fullest and widest meaning of the term means in the last analysis respecting the individual man as a member of the economic system. Just as labour is not a commodity, a human being is not a tool or a machine; his dignity has to be safeguarded and provision made for his fundamental needs. These are imperative human considerations that cannot be disregarded with impunity. The undertaking has a dual existence. It is not only an economic profit-making unit in which the workers are an element in production costs, it is also a social unit which, in addition to its responsibility towards the community, has a liability towards the workers it employs, and it must accordingly offer them every possibility compatible with sound financial management for the full expression of their personalities. "An undertaking is intended to be the servant of humanity and should never make humanity its slave".

References

1. Lewis Mumford, Techniques and Civilization, p. 23.
2. Young India, dated 3.9.25, p. 304.
3. Harijan, dated 12.2.38, p. 2.
4. Quoted by Mahadeo Desai from "This Ugly Civilization" by Borsodi in Harijan, dated August 29, 1936, p. 228.
5. Harijan, dated 22.6.1945, p. 146.
6. Young India, dated 13.11.1924, pp. 377-378.
7. Young India, dated 4.1.1932, p. 17.
8. Harijan, dated 1.3.1935, p. 23.
9. Young India, dated 14.1.1932, p. 17.
10. Harijan, dated 29.7.1939, p. 216.
11. Mahatma, by D.G. Tendulkar, Vol. II, p. 391.
12. Harijan, dated 25.6.1938, p. 131.
13. Young India, dated 11.2.1920, p. 7.
14. Harijan, dated 7.9.1947, pp. 309-311.
15. *Ibid.*, 11.8.1946, p. 256.
16. Young India, dated 19.9.1929, p. 308.
17. Harijan, dated 3.7.1937, p. 161.
18. *Ibid.*, 3.7.1937, p. 161.
19. *Ibid.*, 21.4.1946, p. 96.

20. *Ibid.*, 11.8.1946, p. 256.
21. Constructive Programme, 1941 edition, p. 20.
22. Young India, dated 16.2.1921, p. 52.
23. Harijan, dated 11.8.1946, p. 256.
24. Young India, dated 11.8.1921, p. 250.
25. Harijan, dated 13.6.1936, p. 141.
26. Young India, dated 4.8.1927, p. 248.
27. Harijan, dated 25.6.1938, p. 161.

30

Gandhi Disowned

The nation celebrates Gandhiji's birth anniversary and his day of martyrdom every year. Rich tributes are paid to the Father of Nation. Let us pause and think for ourselves as to how sincere are our tributes to this apostle of non-violence about whom Albert Einstein remarked:

Generations to come, it may be scare believe that such a one as this ever in flesh and blood walked upon this earth.

The ten year old son of Pearl Buck, the Nobel Laureate said with tears in his eyes, "I wish no one had ever learned how to make guns".[1] Pearl Buck described the death of Gandhiji as another crucification. She continued, "none of us had even seen Gandhi. But we all knew him. The children were as familiar with his face as though he lived in the house with us".[2]

A remarkable feature of world reaction in Gandhiji's death was the sense of personal loss and bereavement that it meant for people who had never met or seen him.

"I never saw Gandhi, I do not know his language, I never set foot in his country and yet I feel the same sorrow as if I had lost some one near and dear. The whole world has been plunged into mourning by the death of this extraordinary man".[3] General Douglas Mac Arthur described Gandhiji as one of those prophets "who lived far ahead of the time" and said "In the evolution of civilization, if it is to survive all men can not fail eventually to adopt his belief that the process of mass application of force to resolve contentious issue is fundamentally not only wrong but contains within itself the germs of self destruction."[4] Another significant tribute was by Mrs. Mary Bethuna, the Negro leader, "A great warm light has been extinguished. His spirit reached far the stars and sought to win a world without gun or bayonet or blood. As we mothers of the earth stand in awesome fear of the roar of jet planes, the crash of atom bombs and the unknown fear of germ warfare, we must turn our eyes in hope to the east where the sun of the Mahatma blazes."[5]

The United Nations' flag was flown at half-mast. The Security Council interrupted its proceedings to pay homage to the Mahatma. Philip Noel Baker referred to him as the friend of the poorest, the lowliest and lost.

In our country every one was eloquent in his tributes to Gandhiji. Pt. Nehru observed, "for the light that shone in the country was no ordinary light. The light was that illuminated this country for these many years will illumine this country for many more years and a thousand years later that light will be seen in this country and the world will see and it will give solace to innumerable hearts......." On another occasion Pt. Nehru said, "where he sat became a temple and where he trod was hallowed ground".[6] Acharya J.B. Kriplani exclaimed, "the country has been orphaned".[7] Sarojini Naidu expressed her tributes as, "......Far greater than all warriors who led armies to the battle was this little man the bravest, the most tried friend of all.[8] She invoked his spirit in the following words.

"May the soul of my master, my leader, my father rest is not in peace. My father do not rest. Keep us to our pledge. Give us the strength to fulfil our promise, your heirs, your descendants, your students, guardians of our dreams, fulfilling of India's destiny".[9]

These were outbursts of emotions on the death of Gandhiji, which was sudden, and under such circumstances that these tributes were natural and spontaneous. He alone kept the torch of hope and sanity alight. He was the main figure not only on the Indian scene but also of the world for nearly half century.

Let us examine for a shortwhile whether we have been true to the memory of the great leader. Rev. Stanley Jones, A Christian Missionary remarked: "Just as the spirit of Jesus shines all the more against the background of the treachery of Judas, so the spirit of Mahatma Gandhi shines all the more against the background of the betrayal of his spirit, often by those who named his name."

Dr. Rajendra Prasad, India's first President, who was a close associate of Gandhiji observed: "what I see going in all ground in the country sometimes disappoints me. Jesus Christ once said to a disciple of his "before the cock crowstwice, thou will deny me thrice". It strikes me that we are doing the same thing to Gandhiji. It would seem that we who call ourselves his devotees are discarding all his values one by one after his death. It is doubtful whether we shall ever act on them again.[10] He continued :

"I see that a gloom has come over the various items of Gandhiji's programme. It seems that we are giving them up one by one[11].......but fact remains that the Government neither the Central Government nor the Government of any State, is following the programme chalked out by Gandhiji. We have not been able to implement fully even one item of his programme.[12]

Former Prime Minister Mr. Narasimha Rao remarked that nothing much was being done in the country to keep alive the memory of Mahatma Gandhi, the Father of the Nation. He regretted "the amount of research in Mahatma Gandhi being carried out in other countries is mind-boggling but not even a fraction of it is being done in this country. He further observed that the whole world was observing the 125th birth anniversary of Mahatma Gandhi but nothing was being done in India. He said, "what we did to Buddhism, we may do to Gandhism."

Gandhi was disowned by his own followers. On June 25, 1946 Gandhiji's note was read out at the meeting of the Congress Working Committee which was not to the liking of the members. When he decided to leave with the permission of the members Maulana Azad wanted to know as to the wish of the members of the working committee. "What do you desire?" he asked. "Every body was silent and Bapu returned to his residence. Thereafter the Working Committee met again at noon and sent a reply to the Cabinet Mission. The members of the Working Committee met the Cabinet Mission. On their return nobody told Bapu a word about what had happened at the meeting."[13]

Gandhiji realized that the parting of ways has taken place. Gandhiji felt ill at ease and in the first week of April, 1947 he wrote, "I have been here for four days but I have not met the Sardar for more than a few minutes. Sometimes I feel that perhaps I am the only one here in the whole company with spare time on hand."[14] His advise was not sought because it was not easy to change over after one gets used to the ways of power. The resolution for the partition of Panjab was passed without even informing Gandhiji of his.

Gandhiji had started realizing that the leadership has no use for his values. In third week of July, 1946 Gandhiji wrote to Asif Ali that he felt that he was back member. He wrote "it is no secret that Congress had willingly said goodbye to non-violence when it accepted power. The plain fact of the matter is that I am not the current coin that I had fancied, I once was. Mine is a voice in wilderness."[15] He noticed Indian volunteers at the Inter-Asian Relations Conference and sadly remarked:

"Did you notice that while the delegates from other countries were befittingly dressed in simple style, reflecting the respective culture of their countries. Our own visitors and lady volunteers on duty, attired in silk and wearing lipstick and rouge in the western style, presented a very incongruous picture? I feel humiliated. How my heart would have danced with joy if they were seen there in the Congress women volunteers simple khadi uniform."[16]

The strain on Gandhiji was too much. Dr. B.C. Roy advised him rest. His reaction was, "when there is raging fire all around I have no desire to prolong my life by taking rest."[17] When Dr. Roy suggested that people need your services more than ever Gandhiji reacted: "What's the good – neither the people nor those in power have any use of me....I am today alone in my thoughts."[18] He had realized that in India that was shaping there was no place for him yet he clunged to the hope that one day not only India but also the world will listen to his voice.

Gandhiji was opposed to partition. Maulana Azad, after witnessing the holocaust observed, "it was a big mistake on our part not to have listened Bapu at that time."[19] Pt. Nehru also expressed similar views.

Gandhiji had foreseen the sinister design of the British Government to balkanize India. Prime Minister Atlee on the one hand announced that no minority will hold back the progress of majority. But their representatives in India Mountbatten did the opposite. He knew full well that Jinnah will not survive a few months and therefore advanced the date from 1948 to 1947 so that the object of dividing the country is achieved. If the British Government could arrest and detain Mahatma Gandhi, apostle of non-violence and peace, what prevented them to do likewise with Jinnah and others who were a stumbling block. How could they do so to their pampered ones.

Gandhiji had even suggested that if partition is inevitable, let it take place after the British yoke is removed.

But Nehru, Patel and other Congress leaders having come to power, out of sheer desperation accepted a truncated India like alms in begger's bowl. This happened to Jinnah as well. It need be mentioned that Gandhiji old in age yet young in spirits was prepared to launch another battle to preserve the unity of the country (as told by Accharya Kripalani to the author) but his followers young in age but very old in spirits and courage did not respond to Gandhiji's courage and wisdom.

As partition became a settled fact, much against his advice and wish he felt that his life work seemed to be over. He yet tried to make a last effort to prevent partition under British intervention. If it has to take place, it may take place after British withdrawal. He observed: ".....today I find myself all alone. Even the Sardar and Jawahar Lal think that my reading of the situation is wrong and peace is sure to return if partition is agreed upon..... They wonder if I have not deteriorated with age....."[20] Gandhiji described himself as a spent bullet,[21] a back member[22] Pyare Lal observed that one sentence that was constantly on his lips was "Do not you see I am mounted on my funeral pyre"[23] and sometimes when he wanted particularly to bring home a peremptory warning, "You should know it is a corpse that is telling you this."[24] The realization was fast growing in him that "the ways of power are inseparable from the exercise of power and that his erstwhile colleagues have no use for him." "...... If India has no further use of Ahimsa, can she have any for me. I would not be in the least surprised if in spite of all homage that the national leaders pay to me, they were one day to say, we had enough of this old man why does he not leave us alone."[25]

How prophetic were these words. Pt. Nehru, whom Gandhiji had declared his heir in 1942 and later reiterated in 1945 in his letter to Firoz Khan Noon. Gradually disowned all that Gandhiji stood for.

While delivering Dr. Kohli Memorial Lecture on 1st April 20^1 Dr. R.K. Raghvan, Director CBI mentions a few facts about Gandhiji's fast unto death in November 1947. At the time of partition India had to pay Rs. 52 crores to Pakistan. The Government of India decided to revoke their promise. Gandhiji's fast was against not adhering to an ethical commitment. A committee headed by Pt. Nehru met Gandhiji to persuade him to end his fast in public interest. Members argued with Gandhiji for nearly four hours and Gandhiji's observation was, ".....I am going to pray to my God to speed up my end so that I can escape from this country which makes its foundation on a glaringly unethical basement by the naked breach of promise....." As the fast continued and Gandhiji's condition deteriorated the Cabinet decided to revoke its earlier decision. However, Gandhiji insisted on immediate transfer of money because according to Dr. Raghvan..... in Gandhiji's words "once you solemnly promised to pay that amount and later you unilaterally revoked that promise...... I have no confidence that after my death you would not again revoke it".

In 1955 Nehru is reported to have called Gandhiji, "An awful old hypocrite" in a remark (at the end of 1955) to the visiting Canadian Foreign Minister (later Prime Minister). Lester Pearson, a remark which according to

Pearson memoirs (Vol. II) shocked the Canadian statesman (S.C. Gangal, Hindustan Times, Sept. 3, 1990).

Gandhiji had enthroned Nehru by declaring him as his heir and he in his turn dethroned all that Gandhiji stood for. And thus, we today talk of India of Nehru's dream of Indira Gandhi's dream. So much so that Panchayati Raj, a dream of Gandhiji is now Rajiv Gandhi's dream.

We have become counterfeit, spurious, coins and imitators of western culture and civilization. We have not been able to solve our major problems of hunger, poverty, health and employment and tried to keep public enthralled by demonstration of sophisticated military equipment on Republic Days and giving wide publicity to our desire and capacity for export of these goods.

It is reported that when Gandhi was returning from Lahore via Delhi, on his way to Patna to proceed to Noakhali via Calcutta, nobody tried to persuade him to stay in Delhi. They all realized that the way he felt about partition and 15th August celebrations he would be out of place in the midst of officials rejoicing at the capital on the Independence day.[26]

Even after Gandhiji's death so sudden and shocking, his heirs did not respect his wishes. The idea of embalming his body had to be given up because of strong protest of Shri Pyare Lal – Gandhiji's personal secretary and Shri Deodas, Gandhiji's son. Gandhiji was totally opposed to the idea of parading dead or people exploiting death for political purpose. "If anybody tried to take out my body in a procession after I died, I would certainly tell them if my corpse could speak to spare me and cremate me where I have died."[27]

But our leadership did just the opposite. His mortal remains were paraded not only through the city of Delhi but the ashes were deposited in all important rivers. Pots of ashes were sent to all provincial capitals, which shared these with lesser urban centres. Everywhere the ashes were for public display. Ashes were sent to some countries – Burma, Tibet, Ceylon and Malaya. The idea of immersion of ashes in all major rivers of the world was dropped because of opposition.

What an irony that the body of the Mahatma, the apostle of non-violence was carried in a military weapon carrier. The body could as well as carried in a bullock cart instead of machine driven carrier, the engine of which was kept silent.

The Government of India declared 30th January as Martyr's Day the day Gandhiji was shot. The day is also being observed to pay tributes to the unknown soldiers the legacy of British days. It is surprising that the

Government of India could not declare any other day except 30th January to pay homage to the symbol of military power. What a tribute to the messiah of non-violence?

Gandhiji's Samadhi has become place to take foreign dignitaries who visit India and make them lay wreaths and pay floral tributes. Whenever such a visit is planned, the security arrangements are perfect. Roads are blocked and traffic stopped. It appears that this country has nothing except Gandhiji's Samadhi to inspire foreign dignitaries. We have copied the western nations slavishly.

Sometimes one feels that his Samadhi has become a place for political dramas. The place was once washed by Ganges water by a set of political leaders to remove impurities because of visit of another set of political leaders. The Janata Dal took oath at Rajghat Samadhi under the leadership of Jai Prakash Narain and Acharya Kripalani, Rajiv Gandhi began his yatra from Rajghgat, Sri Chandra Shekher, after being sworn as Prime Minister also visited Rajghat Samadhi.

India's culture, tradition does not provide for celebration of days of death/martyrdoms. We celebrate birth-days – Ram Naumi, Janamashtami. We do not even know the days of 'MAHAPRAYAN' of either Ram or Krishna.

Since those who assumed leadership at the time of Independence had nothing else to put before the people of India and the world that was distinctly Indian they took political advantage of Gandhi's martyrdom.

It can be argued that atmosphere on the eve of Indepen-dence was full of violence, it required a sacrifice of the highest order. Gandhiji once remarked...... the situation calls for sacrifice on the part of top rankers. Hitherto, with a couple of exception, the members of rank-and file have been the victim of the holocaust...... that is not enough.[28] It was Gandhi's sacrifice that saved the country from a worse holocaust that would have followed because of the acceptance of partition.

Instance can be quoted to demonstrate that in the game of political power Gandhiji was being side-tracked. As early as 1941 the Congress Working Committee relieved Gandhiji (On his own request) of his command as the members did not agree with his interpretation of opposition to war.

Pt. Nehru presented to the Constituent Assembly the flag of free India which was different from the one under the banner of which the battle of freedom was fought and won. The argument was that in order to give the flag an artistic touch the need for these changes was required. Gandhiji's reaction to such a move was: 'The improved condition of the flag has value only if it answers the significance attached to the original. If it does not, it is valueless in my estimation."[29] When it was pointed to him that the new flag represents values that are different from the previous ones, his reaction was, "I would refuse to salute the flag that bears the foregoing interpretation, however artistic it may appear."[30] He reiterated his stand when he observed, "I say that if the flag of the Indian Union will not contain the emblem of the Charkha, I will refuse to salute that flag."[31] Pt. Nehru and others tried to convince him that the sign of the wheel or chakra symbolizes the charkha also.[32]

On August 15, 1947 when there were festivities all over the land, Gandhiji did not participate in these rejoicing. When he was approached for a message, he replied that "he had run dry".[33] When told again that it will not be good if he did not give any message, Gandhiji replied, "There is no message at all. If it is bad, let it be so."[34]

Gandhiji had started realizing that his views are not acceptable to the leadership commenting on the neglect of charkha. He remarked, "But this seems to be receding into the background. The same thing can be said of many other things, of which I used to draw a tempting picture. I can no longer dare to do so."[35] He continued, "There was a time when India listened to him. Today, he was a back member. He was told he had no place in the new order, where they wanted machines, navy and air force, and what not".[36]

"In India as I see it shaping today there is no place for me. There is communal frenzy and they are talking of military power and industrialization. India might become a first class military power and highly industrialized country. But where is the place for village industries or Khadi symbols of non-violence in such India".[37]

Similar statements of being sidetracked by his own followers were expressed by him when on October 2, 1947 messages of congratulations were sent to him. He observed: "Where did the congratulations come in? would it not be more appropriate to say condolences."[38] He had lost will to live for 125 years and invoked the aid of the all-embracing power to take me away from this 'vale of tears'.[39]

When Acharya J.B. Kripalani resigned from Presidentship of the Congress because he had neither been consulted by the government nor had been taken into their confidence. Gandhiji favoured the name of Acharya Narendra Dev to be Congress president. However, at the request of Patel and Nehru Dr. Rajendra Prasad agreed to accept the Presidentship inviting the comments, "I don't like it"[40] from Gandhiji.

On the assumption of power by the Congress leaders, Gandhiji advised that all in power should lead simple and truthful lives. As an illustration, Gandhiji emphasized that (1) an Indian Governor should in his own person and his surroundings be teetotaller, (2) he and his surroundings should represent hand- spinning as a visible token of identification with the dumb millions of India, a token of the necessity of bread labour and organised non-violence what a contradiction today, (3) he must dwell in a cottage accessible to all.....for him no expensive furniture, foreign or indigenous, plain living and high thinking must be his motto.....[41] Among those who come to power by means – fair or foul, there is severe competition for artificial and luxurious life style. This has not only distanced the leadership, from the people but also resulted in criminalization of politics of India.

Those who come to power take every advantage and go for medical treatment to U.S.A. In this connection it is recorded that when a devoted co-worker asked for Gandhiji's approval to proceed to U.S.A. for treatment of his deafness, Gandhiji disapproved of his scheme. Today every political leader takes pride in getting treatment abroad.

Gandhi had realized that those in power are not likely to listen to him. He remarked, "May be mine will prove to be cry in wilderness. But I cannot remain silent, as I don't want to go down as an un-protesting witness of what is taking place around me in the country today."[42] When a member of his party asked sometime after Independence, "What would you take up next now that India is free." He replied, "To reform the politics of the country and purify it". It is worth remembering that in 1930 he had written, "I know that if I survive the struggle for freedom, I might have to give non-violent battles to my own countrymen which may be as stubborn as that in which I am now engaged."[43]

What significance we attach to Gandhiji will be illustrated by several facts. On 30th January 1992 Gandhiji's martyrdom and the news connected therewith was announced at the third place and a poorly presented programme was telecast at 11.00 p.m. the time of adult movies by Doordarshan. In-between commercial advertisements were relayed. On 30th January 1993 the news got a second place. Indian Express, a national Daily mentions in its 1st June 1994 issue that for the first time, the Father of the Nation, Mahatma Gandhi will feature in an advertisement campaign. The Lakhani Shoes advertisement shows a man bending down and touching Mahatma Gandhiji's feet. The caption at the top states, India, the land where feet are respected. "Below the photograph runs another caption Lakhani the shoes that respect your feet". "The Government of India did not even react to this sort of advertisement and insult to the memory of the Father of the Nation. In 1995 at the Republic Day celebration when Nelson Mandela was the chief guest, Bapu's life size replica in white was made to peep through spectacles and observe the military might of the government and listen to the commentary of their deadly striking capacity. What a tribute to Gandhiji, symbol of non-violence and peace. Riturik Ghatak referred to Gandhiji as "the son of a pig". Acharya Kripalani wanted this reference to be banned. Nothing happened. He was given a Republic Day award (Gandhi Marg, April-June 1998, p. 90).

The original route of Dandi March had long since disappeared with the ascent of the highway (Thomas Weber, p. 162). Similarly formerly spacious bungalow that housed Gandhiji during Dandi March has been demolished. A factory now graces the spot (ibid, p. 306). The government did not preserve the symbol of historic national struggle.

Similarly, the clause that "no duties on salt shall be levied by the union" was eventually deleted. Pt. Nehru, however did not favour this clause because it could come in the way of national good of the future" (Thomas Weber, pp. 200-01) – An outrage on the history of the freedom movement after Mahatma Gandhiji's death was done.

In one of his letters to Pt. Nehru, Gandhiji expressed his regret over the British extravagance, which the country could ill afford. His advice was that the Viceroy should be allowed to go to an unpretentious building unwilling and wrote to Gandhiji about "difficulty in finding a suitable accommodation and making arrangements for change over when we are so busy."[44] No change has been since then made because those who count considered that the President of the largest democracy should represent the grandeur of the vast country. Some even felt that the standard maintained was considered "inadequate" by foreign dignitaries.

Wine flows freely and has become a symbol of prosperity and modernization. It will bring revenue to the Government. Its injurious effect on the health and moral of the people are of no consequence. What an expression of gratefulness by those who repeat Gandhiji's name ad-infinitum.

It is interesting to note that country's first floating hotel at the cost of Rs. 6.65 crores will be ready for commercial operation by March 1995. There is competition in luxurious living and conspicuous consumption – what a contrast with Gandhiji's Daridra-Narayan.

There were awards to honour the memory of Pt. Nehru, Smt. Indira Gandhi, Dr. B.R. Ambedkar, Shri Rajiv Gandhi. Until a few years back there was no award for Mahatma Gandhi which was constituted only recently. By Prime Minister Narasimha Rao.

The United Nations has resolved to hold 2nd October, Gandhiji's birthday as non-violence day. Congress leaders who have disowned Gandhiji in every walk of life are scratching their backs. Ever since Gandhiji's martyrdom in 1948 these leaders were silent. In fact those in power, whenever they celebrate any event of Gandhiji's life (Dandi March) there is some ulterior motive.

It is reported that Shri J.C. Kumarappa, the eminent disciple of Gandhi once wept and remarked "instead of burying Gandhi into our heart we are burying him deep into the earth" (Gandhi Marg, July-Sept 1992, p. 323).

Bernard Shaw's remark is also worth mentioning. He is reported to have observed that when destiny could not find how to punish great men for their greatness then destiny gave them disciples. How true with reference to Gandhiji.

References

1. Pearl Buck, quoted P.D. Tandon, Humanities Homage to Gandhi, p. 89.
2. *Ibid.*, pp. 89-90
3. *Lion Blum, quoted in Pyare Lal* – The Last Phase, Vol. II, p. 786.
4. *Ibid.*, pp. 786.
5. *Ibid.*, pp. 787.
6. P.D. Tandon, Humanities Homage to Gandhi, p. 17.
7. *Ibid.*, p. 34.
8. *Ibid.*, p. 27.
9. *Ibid.*, p. 31.
10. Dr. Rajendra Prasad, Legacy of Gandhiji, p. 79.
11. *Ibid.*, p. 69.
12. *Ibid.*, p. 79.
13. Pyare Lal – The Last Phase, Vol. I, p. 259.
14. *Ibid.*, Vol. II, p. 34.
15. *Ibid.*, Vol. II, p. 652.
16. *Ibid.*, Vol. I, p. 211.
17. *Ibid.*, Vol. I, p. 309.
18. *Ibid.*, Vol. I, p. 332.
19. *Ibid.*, Vol. II, p. 256.
20. *Ibid.*, Vol. I, p. 211.
21. *Ibid.*, Vol. II, p. 309.

22. *Ibid.*, Vol. II, p. 332.
23. *Ibid.*, Vol. II, p. 685.
24. *Ibid.*
25. *Ibid.*, Vol. II, p. 86.
26. *Ibid.*, Vol. II, p. 360.
27. *Ibid.*, Vol. II, p. 417.
28. *Ibid.*, Vol. I, p. 407.
29. Tendulkar, Vol. VIII, p. 66.
30. *Ibid.*, Vol. VIII, p. 67.
31. *Ibid.*, Vol. VIII, p. 81.
32. *Ibid.*, Vol. VIII, p. 81.
33. *Ibid.*, Vol. VIII, p. 95.
34. *Ibid.*, Vol. VIII, pp. 95-96.
35. *Ibid.*, Vol. VIII, p. 105.
36. *Ibid.*, Vol. VIII, p. 105.
37. Quoted by L.M. Bhola. Gandhi Marg, Oct-Dec. 1991, p. 327.
38. Tendulkar, the Mahatma,Vvol. VIII, p. 172.
39. *Ibid.*, Vol. VIII, p. 176.
40. *Ibid.*, Vol. VIII, p. 233.
41. *Ibid.*, Vol. VIII, pp. 99-100.
42. Pyare Lal – Last Phase Vol. II, p. 123.
43. *Ibid.*, p. 748.
44. *Ibid.*, p. 641.

Bibliography

1. *Mathur* - Economic Thought of Mahatma Gandhi.
2. *Mathur* - Ailing World and Gandhian Alternatives.
3. *Mathur* - Peace Non-violence and Social Change.
4. *Veblen* - Theory of Leisure Class.
5. *Erich Fromm* - Labor in Free Society.
6. *A. E. C Hare* - The First Principles of Industrial Relations.
7. *Harris Brown* - The Challenge of Man's Future.
8. *Juenger*- Failure of Technology.
9. *Gasset Y. Ortega* - The Revolt of the Masses.
10. *J. P. Narain* - Reconstruction of Indian Polity.
11. *M. K. Gandhi* - Hind Swaraj.
12. *M. K. Gandhi* - The Story of My Experiment with Truth.
13. *M. K. Gandhi* - Harizan.
14. *M. K. Gandhi* - Young India.
15. *Pyare Lal*- Last Phase Vol. 1 & 2.
16. *Tendulkar*- The Mahatma (8 Vols.)
17. *Tribute* (W. C. E. D. Report).
18. *Rajendra Prasad* - Legacy of Gandhi.
19. *Caldicott Helin* - Missile Envy.
20. *B. Russel*- Impact of Science on Society.
21. *B. Russel*- Has Man a Future.
22. *Fritjof Caprta*- The Turning Point.
23. *Gunnar Myrdal*- Against the Scream (Critical Essays on Economics).
24. *Geoffrey Olean* - Rich World: Poor World.
25. *Al Gore* - Earth in Balance.
26. *N. Bilpudiwala* - Social Order and Servodaya.

28. *Barbare Wooten* - Social Foundations of Wage Policy.
29. *Fairfield Osborn* - Our Plundered Planet.
30. *Albert Schweitzer* - Decay and Restoration of Society.
31. *Masanobu FukuoluJ* - One Straw Revolution.
32. *G. N. Dhawan* - Political Philosophy of Mahatma Gandhi.
33. Truth and Non-violence UNESCO Symposium.
34. *A. L Muste* - Gandhi His Relevance for Our Times.
35. *P. D. Tandon* - Humanities Homage to Gandhi.
36. *Joan V Bondurant* - Conquest of Violence.
37. *Aldous Huxley* - Science Liberty & Peace.
38. *K. G. Mashruwala* - Gandhi and Marks.
39. *Pollock* - Economic & Social Consequences of Automation.
40. *A.lexis Garrel*- Man The Unknown.
41. *M. K. Gandhi* - Constructive Programme.
42. *L B. Kriplani* - Gandhian Outlooks and Techniques.
43. *Richard B. Gregg* - Economics ofK.haddar.
44. *N. K. Bose* - Selections from Gandhi.
45. J.C. Kumarppa :Why Village Industries.
46. J.C. Kumarppa :Economy of Permenance.
47. B. Kumarappa : Villagism, Capitalism Socialism.

Index